VIETNAM WAR ERA

Other titles in the Perspectives in American Social History series

African Americans in the Nineteenth Century: People and Perspectives

American Revolution: People and Perspectives

Baby Boom: People and Perspectives

British Colonial America: People and Perspectives

Civil Rights Movement: People and Perspectives

Civil War: People and Perspectives

Cold War and McCarthy Era: People and Perspectives

Early Republic: People and Perspectives

Great Depression: People and Perspectives

Industrial Revolution: People and Perspectives

Jacksonian and Antebellum Age: People and Perspectives

Jazz Age: People and Perspectives

Making of the American West: People and Perspectives

Reconstruction: People and Perspectives

Women's Rights in the Age of Suffrage: People and Perspectives

PERSPECTIVES IN
AMERICAN SOCIAL HISTORY

Vietnam War Era

People and Perspectives

Mitchell K. Hall, Editor
Peter C. Mancall, Series Editor

A B C ❧ C L I O

Santa Barbara, California · Denver, Colorado · Oxford, England

Library of Congress Cataloging-in-Publication Data
Vietnam War era : people and perspectives / Mitchell K. Hall, editor.
    p. cm. — (Perspectives in American social history series)
   Includes bibliographical references and index.
   ISBN 978-1-59884-129-9 (hard copy : alk. paper) — ISBN 978-1-59884-130-5 (ebook)   1. Vietnam War, 1961–1975—United States.   2. Vietnam War, 1961–1975—Social aspects—United States.   3. Vietnam War, 1961–1975—Influence.   4. United States—Social conditions—1960–1980.
I. Hall, Mitchell K.
   DS558.V565 2009
   959.704'3373—dc22
                          2009008717

13 12 11 10 09   1 2 3 4 5

ABC-CLIO, LLC
130 Cremona Drive, P.O. Box 1911
Santa Barbara, California 93116-1911

This book is also available on the World Wide Web as an e-book.
Visit www.abc-clio.com for details.

This book is printed on acid-free paper. ∞

Manufactured in the United States of America

Contents

Series Introduction, vii
Introduction, xi
About the Editor and Contributors, xxi
Chronology, xxv

1 Divisions within the Containment Generation: U.S. Policy Makers and the Vietnam War, 1
   Joseph A. Fry

2 "The Needs Are Enormous, the Time Short": American Advisers and the Invention of South Vietnam, 1954–1960, 23
   James M. Carter

3 Vietnam Military Personnel, 41
   Carol Reardon

4 Antiwar Activists, 61
   Rhodri Jeffreys-Jones

5 The Silent Majority, 79
   Kenneth J. Heineman

6 Religious Communities and the Vietnam War, 97
   Jill K. Gill

7 Women and the Vietnam War, 117

Natasha Zaretsky

8 Wartime Journalists, 131

Clarence R. Wyatt

9 African Americans and the Vietnam War, 149

James E. Westheider

10 "Labor's Falling Dominoes": The AFL-CIO and the Vietnam War Era, 167

Edmund F. Wehrle

11 Students and Political Activism, 185

Caroline Hoefferle

Primary Documents, 203
Reference, 219
Bibliography, 229
Index, 249

Series Introduction

Social history is, simply put, the study of past societies. More specifically, social historians attempt to describe societies in their totality, and hence often eschew analysis of politics and ideas. Though many social historians argue that it is impossible to understand how societies functioned without some consideration of the ways politics works on a daily basis or what ideas could be found circulating at any given time, they tend to pay little attention to the formal arenas of electoral politics or intellectual currents. In the United States, social historians have been engaged in describing components of the population that had earlier often escaped formal analysis, notably women, members of ethnic or cultural minorities, or those who had fewer economic opportunities than the elite.

Social history became a vibrant discipline in the United States after it had already gained enormous influence in Western Europe. In France, social history in its modern form emerged with the rising prominence of a group of scholars associated with the journal *Annales Economie, Societé, Civilisation* (or *Annales ESC* as it is known). In its pages and in a series of books from historians affiliated with the École des Hautes Études en Sciences Sociale in Paris, brilliant historians such as Marc Bloch, Jacques Le Goff, and Emmanuel Le Roy Ladurie described seemingly every aspect of French society. Among the masterpieces of this historical reconstruction was Fernand Braudel's monumental study, *The Mediterranean and the Mediterranean World in the Age of Philip II*, published first in Paris in 1946 and in a revised edition in English in 1972. In this work Braudel argued that the only way to understand a place in its totality was to describe its environment, its social and economic structures, and its political systems. In Britain the emphasis of social historians has been less on questions of environment, per se, than in a description of human communities in all their complexities. For example, social historians there have taken advantage of that nation's remarkable local archives to reconstruct the history of the family and details of its rural past. Works such as Peter Laslett's *The World We Have Lost*, first printed in 1966, and the multiauthored *Agrarian History of England and Wales*, which began to appear in print in 1967, revealed that painstaking work could reveal the lives and habits of individuals who never previously attracted the interest of biographers, demographers, or most historians.

Social history in the United States gained a large following in the second half of the 20th century, especially during the 1960s and 1970s. Its development sprang from political, technical, and intellectual impulses deeply embedded in the culture of the modern university. The politics of civil rights and social reform fueled the passions of historians who strove to tell the stories of the underclass. They benefited as historians adopted statistical analysis, which allowed scholars to trace where individuals lived, how often they moved, what kinds of jobs they took, and whether their economic status declined, stagnated, or improved over time. As history departments expanded, many who emerged from graduate schools focused their attention on groups previously ignored or marginalized. Women's history became a central concern among American historians, as did the history of African Americans, Native Americans, Latinos, and others. These historians pushed historical study in the United States further away from the study of formal politics and intellectual trends. Though few Americanists could achieve the technical brilliance of some social historians in Europe, collectively they have been engaged in a vast act of description, with the goal of describing seemingly every facet of life from 1492 to the present.

The 16 volumes in this series together represent the continuing efforts of historians to describe American society. Most of the volumes focus on chronological areas, from the broad sweep of the colonial era to the more narrowly defined collections of essays on the eras of the Cold War, the baby boom, and America in the age of the Vietnam War. The series also includes entire volumes on the epochs that defined the nation, the American Revolution and the Civil War, as well as volumes dedicated to the process of westward expansion, women's rights, and African American history.

This social history series derives its strength from the talented editors of individual volumes. Each editor is an expert in his or her own field who selected and organized the contents of his or her volume. Editors solicited other experienced historians to write individual essays. Every volume contains first-rate analysis complemented by lively anecdotes designed to reveal the complex contours of specific historical moments. The many illustrations to be found in these volumes testify too to the recognition that any society can be understood not only by the texts its participants produce but also by the images they craft. Primary source documents in each volume will allow interested readers to pursue some specific topics in greater depth, and each volume contains a chronology to provide guidance to the flow of events over time. These tools—anecdotes, images, texts, and timelines—allow readers to gauge the inner workings of America in particular periods and yet also to glimpse connections between eras.

The articles in these volumes testify to the abundant strengths of historical scholarship in the United States in the early years of the 21st century. Despite the occasional academic contest that flares into public notice, or the self-serving cant of politicians who want to manipulate the nation's past for partisan ends—for example, in debates over the Second Amendment to the U.S. Constitution and what it means about potential limits to the rights of gun ownership—the articles here all reveal the vast increase in knowledge of the American past that has taken place over the previous half century.

Social historians do not dominate history faculties in American colleges and universities, but no one could deny them a seat at the intellectual table. Without their efforts, intellectual, cultural, and political historians would be hard pressed to understand why certain ideas circulated when they did, why some religious movements prospered or foundered, how developments in fields such as medicine and engineering reflected larger concerns, and what shaped the world we inhabit.

Fernand Braudel and his colleagues envisioned entire laboratories of historians in which scholars working together would be able to produce *histoire totale:* total history. Historians today seek more humble goals for our collective enterprise. But as the richly textured essays in these volumes reveal, scholarly collaboration has in fact brought us much closer to that dream. These volumes do not and cannot include every aspect of American history. However, every page reveals something interesting or valuable about how American society functioned. Together, these books suggest the crucial necessity of stepping back to view the grand complexities of the past rather than pursuing narrower prospects and lesser goals.

Peter C. Mancall

Series Editor

Introduction

No event in the past half-century of American history has commanded a more prominent place in the public consciousness than the Vietnam War. The first baby boomers turned draft age just as America's military escalation demanded its first commitment of combat troops, and the war became that generation's defining issue. Ultimately, America's Vietnam experience touched nearly every aspect of life. It affected the economy, influenced college enrollments and careers, challenged citizens to reassess their values, and played a key role in the downfall of two presidential administrations. A person's view on Vietnam helped define his or her political and cultural views for a lifetime, setting the stage for the "culture wars" that have been part of American society for decades.

Interest in this era has persisted beyond the Vietnam generation. College courses on the war continue to draw large numbers of students, who are often intrigued by the war's impact on their own family histories. Vietnam appears regularly in motion pictures and books and remains a favorite reference point in foreign policy debates. National political candidates such as Bill Clinton, Dan Quayle, George W. Bush, and John Kerry had to field difficult questions about their wartime attitudes and experiences.

Analysis of the war has played out at various levels. Historical scholarship has passed through different phases, but a consensus has existed since the early 1980s. George Herring stated this position clearly and concisely in his highly regarded *America's Longest War,* concluding that "I do not believe that the war could have been won in any meaningful sense or at a moral or material price Americans would—or should—have been willing to pay" (Herring 2002, xiv). Despite the dominance of this view, challenges continue from both within and outside academe.

The typical American is probably more familiar with popular arguments, regularly exposed in cultural and political discussions and spread widely through such films as *The Deer Hunter* (1978), *Rambo: First Blood Part II* (1985), and *Platoon* (1986). This public analysis has reached no comparable consensus. One strongly held view among many conservatives is the belief that the U.S. military could have won the war had it not been "stabbed in the back" by some group of Americans at home, with the media, the antiwar movement, or the government the most popular targets of blame.

Scholars have overwhelmingly refuted these charges, but they nevertheless persist. A basic understanding of the war and the issues involved can help interested citizens avoid superficial or misleading interpretations.

The Vietnam War era is commonly identified as 1965–1975, the years from the first introduction of U.S. combat troops into Vietnam to the communist capture of Saigon. The origins of the conflict actually grew out of World War II. Wartime cooperation between the United States and Vietnamese nationalists broke down as the Cold War emerged. Ho Chi Minh led a communist-dominated front—the Vietminh—that hoped to expel French colonial rulers from their country and achieve independence. Efforts to negotiate a peaceful settlement of their differences failed, leading to the outbreak of the First Indochina War in 1946, which also encompassed neighboring Laos and Cambodia. The French effectively portrayed the struggle as a fight against communism rather than as a colonial war, and the United States threw its financial support behind France. The fighting proved inconclusive, and after years of warfare France suffered a major defeat at Dien Bien Phu in May 1954. Within weeks France joined other nations in signing the Geneva Accords, which provided for a cease-fire and a temporary division of Vietnam at the 17th parallel, governed in the north by the Vietminh and in the south by former emperor Bao Dai. Planned national elections in 1956 would reunify the country under a single government. American president Dwight D. Eisenhower refused to sign the accords and, although he informally agreed to their conditions, his administration covertly planned to block further communist expansion in the region by building a separate pro-American South Vietnam.

After Geneva, the United States replaced French power in Indochina and worked to make permanent the temporary division between North and South Vietnam. When the anticommunist Ngo Dinh Diem won a corrupt 1955 election as president of the Republic of Vietnam (South Vietnam), the United States supported his decision to avoid national unifying elections, fearing democracy would bring Ho Chi Minh to power. Diem overcame armed sectarian rivals and, with American aid, worked to destroy Vietminh remnants in the south. Despite some initial success, Diem established a tightly controlled and repressive government that grew increasingly unpopular with communists and noncommunists alike. America increased its support for Diem, even as he resisted advice to implement social reform. Diem's successful repression blunted communist efforts to unify the country politically and pushed southerners to armed insurgency by 1957. In 1960, this resistance created the National Liberation Front (NLF), a broadly based but communist-dominated united front supported by the northern government in Hanoi. To tap Cold War fears, both Diem and the United States portrayed the conflict as an invasion of South Vietnam by the communist Democratic Republic of Vietnam (North Vietnam). The growing war then set the United States, South Vietnam, and their allies against North Vietnam, the NLF, and their allies.

The administration of President John Kennedy increased U.S. aid to the Saigon government and sent thousands of military advisers to train its armed forces. NLF influence grew, despite American intervention, and threatened Diem's control by 1963. Massive social upheaval that year convinced the United States to withdraw its support for Diem. A military coup overthrew and assassinated Diem in November 1963, but the situation continued to deteriorate.

The Gulf of Tonkin incident in 1964 marked a significant American escalation in the war. North Vietnamese torpedo boats attacked the U.S. ship *Maddox* in the Gulf of Tonkin on August 2. During a late-night storm two days later, the *Maddox* and a second ship reported being under attack, though later evidence indicates that this second incident probably did not occur. This action led President Lyndon Johnson to retaliate with air attacks on North Vietnam. Congress quickly passed the Gulf of Tonkin Resolution, which gave Johnson formal authority to use military force. Johnson delayed escalation for several months, but initiated Operation Rolling Thunder, a sustained aerial bombing campaign over North Vietnam, in the spring of 1965. Shortly thereafter the United States began a gradual buildup of ground forces. This infusion of American power caused the communists to adopt a protracted war strategy to produce a stalemate that would wear down the Americans over time.

To meet the demands of escalation, President Johnson relied on higher military draft calls, which shifted resources away from domestic needs. This contributed to growing public opposition and ultimately damaged the economy. Disenchantment with the war produced the largest antiwar movement in the nation's history. Demonstrations ranging from small local protests to national mass rallies challenged government policy and authority. An estimated 4 million antiwar activists called for the war's end but disagreed on the best way to achieve that goal. A major turning point came at the end of January 1968, when North Vietnamese and NLF forces launched the Tet Offensive, a coordinated military attack against most of the major cities in South Vietnam. The communists hoped to weaken the Saigon government and win bargaining concessions from the United States, but the offensive generally failed as a military operation. Politically, however, the Tet Offensive proved the resilience of the communists, undermined the optimism and credibility of the Johnson administration, and further eroded public support for the war. President Johnson dropped out of the presidential race and initiated peace talks with the North Vietnamese in Paris that May.

Richard Nixon won the presidency in 1968 partly because of his implied secret plan to end the war. His initial hope of achieving a military victory evaporated within a few months, however, and he crafted a policy borrowed from President Johnson. Vietnamization, as he called it, gradually withdrew U.S. combat forces from Vietnam but escalated the air war and increased activity by the South Vietnamese Army. Nixon anticipated that Vietnamization would weaken antiwar efforts and that détente with the Soviet Union and China might pressure North Vietnam into making concessions. Despite these changes, the war dragged on. Under the Nixon administration, the United States secretly bombed neutral Cambodia in 1969, conducted a joint ground incursion into Cambodia the following year, and provided support for South Vietnam's invasion of Laos in 1971. Nixon's actions energized the antiwar movement, which conducted its largest demonstrations of the entire war in 1969 and 1970. Publication of the Pentagon Papers, exposure of the

My Lai Massacre, and the shootings at Kent State University further eroded public confidence in the government. Furthermore, by 1972 the shrinking U.S. military force in Vietnam experienced serious morale problems. With the United States having failed to end the communist threat, and with North Vietnam unable to overthrow the Saigon regime during its Easter Offensive, both sides were finally ready to compromise. Henry Kissinger and Le Duc Tho met secretly in Paris and reached a tentative peace agreement in October 1972. When South Vietnamese president Nguyen Van Thieu objected to conditions he believed would threaten his government, however, President Nixon ordered Kissinger to reopen negotiations. North Vietnamese officials felt betrayed and the talks broke down. Nixon renewed aerial attacks on North Vietnam, known as the Christmas Bombings, to persuade the North Vietnamese to resume negotiations.

The combatants finally signed the Paris Peace Accords on January 27, 1973, which contained essentially the same conditions reached the previous October. North Vietnam agreed to return U.S. prisoners of war and the United States would withdraw its remaining military forces, both within 60 days. President Thieu's government retained power, but North Vietnamese troops remained in the south. President Nixon acquired Thieu's assent by indicating that the United States would sign regardless of his participation, but Nixon covertly promised that he would not abandon South Vietnam. The war between North and South Vietnam continued after the Americans left. Saigon finally fell to the communists on April 30, 1975, unifying Vietnam under communist rule.

This brief historical background provides a necessary diplomatic and political context for a closer look at the war. This volume's esteemed collection of authors presents a social history, revealing the war's impact on individuals and various groups within American society. What they provide individually and collectively illuminates our understanding of this important subject.

Joseph Fry writes of the decisions American political leaders made that affected the nation's direction in Vietnam. Highlighted are five members of the containment generation who were influenced by the events of World War II and the early Cold War. President Lyndon Johnson and Secretary of State Dean Rusk were ardent anticommunists and firm believers in American exceptionalism and the power of technology. Despite personal misgivings, they believed intervention in Vietnam was necessary to maintain U.S. credibility, to avoid damaging political attacks from the right, and to prevent initiation of the domino theory. Johnson especially believed losing in Vietnam would doom his domestic reforms. Undersecretary of State George Ball and Senators J. William Fulbright and Al Gore Sr. shared the president's anticommunism stance, but dissented from his Vietnam policies. Ball challenged Johnson privately in his role as an executive adviser, while the senators used public platforms for their criticisms. Each questioned the administration's assumption that the war represented foreign aggression, seeing instead Vietnamese national resistance to foreign domination. They further argued Vietnam's lack of strategic importance and the limitations of American power. Their personalities—as well as political and strategic concerns—

shaped the responses of these men and many other government decision makers.

James Carter targets the critical role played by advisers in American efforts at nation building in South Vietnam. People such as Wesley Fishel and the agency for which he worked, the Michigan State University Vietnam Advisory Group, were responsible for helping to create a democratic state and to promote economic development. Throughout most of the Eisenhower years, they established, organized, or trained police and administrative systems, built roads and other infrastructure, and devised methods of modernizing agriculture and stimulating industry. By 1961, however, these same advisers recognized the failure of their endeavors. The regime of President Ngo Dinh Diem resisted many of their economic reforms, preferring government-owned enterprises to American-style capitalism and creating a centralized and repressive police state. With a narrow base of support, Diem led a government plagued by waste, mismanagement, and corruption, a "dictatorship that is neither benevolent nor efficient" (Child 1961, 14). In spite of this evaluation, higher-level U.S. officials remained optimistic, at least publicly, even as their emphasis became more heavily oriented toward military support.

Carol Reardon covers the American military experience, ranging expertly from overall strategy and collective statistics to interesting insights from individual soldiers. Early U.S. military advisers developed concerns about the quality of South Vietnamese armed forces. When Saigon appeared to be losing the war, President Johnson sent in U.S. forces. American military commanders generally relied on technology, overwhelming air superiority, and a conventional search-and-destroy strategy on the ground. At the personal level we are reminded in poignant detail that there is no single "soldiers' story." What individuals encountered in Vietnam depended on when they were there, where they were stationed, and what jobs they performed. The first of nearly 3 million American soldiers landed in 1965. Most who served were working-class draftees or draft-motivated volunteers with a high school education. Only one in five was assigned to front-line combat units. They had to contend with difficult climate and terrain, an elusive enemy, and an unfamiliar culture. At their best they performed effectively and courageously. Vietnam also took its toll. Frustrated by enemies and allies alike and, especially after the 1968 Tet Offensive, uncertain of the nation's commitment, the military suffered declining morale. Some soldiers lapsed into drug use, insubordination, and worse. Their return to a conflicted nation required significant readjustment, and they received only a delayed recognition of their contributions.

Rhodri Jeffreys-Jones captures the breadth of antiwar sentiment as he details some of the movement's many constituencies. An antiwar movement grew along with U.S. military escalation in Vietnam and eventually mobilized college students, religious groups, women's organizations, business leaders, African Americans, military veterans, and others. They acted from a variety of motives. Some believed the war violated national or religious principles or opposed backing a corrupt regime. Others reacted to government deceit, feared the draft, or hoped to avoid a damaged economy. Although most antiwar actions occurred at the local level, mass demonstrations coordinated by broad coalitions gave it the most visibility. The movement's diverse constituencies fell into three primary categories. Liberals preferred education, electoral politics, and legal demonstrations. Pacifists sometimes added nonviolent resistance, and radicals occasionally endorsed violence. Activists divided over the best solution, arguing either for an immediate U.S. withdrawal from Vietnam or a negotiated settlement. Although support for the war declined, the movement's inclusion of political leftists and cultural rebels, plus misleading propaganda by government leaders, made it unpopular among a public uncomfortable with its views and actions. In the long run the antiwar movement did not directly end the war, but it created conditions that limited government options and made ending the war possible.

Ken Heineman examines the Silent Majority, which he interprets as growing largely out of a civil war within the Democratic Party. The Vietnam War dissolved that party's tenuous New Deal coalition along class and ethnicity lines. George Wallace attracted Democratic conservatives in the 1968 election, which the Republicans effectively exploited in the ensuing years. Playing to cultural conservatives, President Richard Nixon popularized this term in November 1969 during a major televised address regarding his Vietnam policy, which became known as the "Silent Majority Speech." Nixon faced constant public discontent over the war and various other social and political issues, including the extensive Moratorium antiwar demonstrations in mid-October. The president explained his new policy of gradually withdrawing U.S. military forces from Vietnam, which he called "Vietnamization." Nixon also chastised protesters as defeatists who could "humiliate" the United States and appealed to "the great silent majority of my fellow Americans" to support his negotiations to achieve a favorable peace settlement (Hall 2008, 108–109). When public opinion polls revealed a positive reaction to the speech, the term became widely accepted as a description of those who did not publicly advocate for their political viewpoints but quietly accepted the president's wartime policies. Later in the war, elements of this support group became more active and provided the base constituency for the conservative side of the culture wars that wracked American society for the next 40 years.

Jill Gill reveals not only the differences between America's major faith traditions but also the sometimes fierce contests within those religions. She identifies four primary ideological positions within the religious community regarding Vietnam. The first two groups condoned the war. Crusaders viewed communism as evil and equated antiwar dissent with godlessness. Nationalists, the largest of these categories, were also strongly anticommunist but were less militant and more inclined to weigh the cultural factors involved. Dissenters were anticommunists who came primarily from mainline denominations but opposed the war based on its historical and political context. Pacifists rejected all war. In tracing these groups through the war's different phases, we learn how America's major religious bodies used a variety of tactics and proposed different solutions as they jockeyed for political and moral influence. Tensions emerged within denominations as well, especially over the roles played by affiliated nongovernmental organizations engaged in providing wartime relief. At the same time, presidential administrations appealed to various religious leaders for an endorsement of their policies. Although these efforts sometimes succeeded, a number of ecumenical organizations emerged to dissent from those policies. As Gill makes clear, however, the Vietnam War was always about more than the war for America's religious communities.

Natasha Zaretsky's essay on women is wonderfully representative of the diverse war-related experiences within American society. She deals specifically with those who served in Vietnam, others who protested the war, and family members of American prisoners of war. Estimates of the number of women who served in Southeast Asia vary, but perhaps 11,000 were on active military duty and about 55,000 American women lived or worked there during the war years. Most military women worked in the dangerous and disturbing occupation of nursing or in a related medical field, but many others worked in Vietnam as civilians for the military, the government, and nongovernmental organizations. Female war protesters initially emphasized maternalism—their unique role as mothers—as motivating their concern, but the growing women's movement produced a more militant position of women as independent political activists. Family members of U.S. prisoners of war were conflicted about the war, but ultimately they pressed the government to speak about prisoners publicly and resisted efforts to make it a domestic political issue. Whether serving enthusiastically in the military or working diligently in antiwar organizations, women often faced harassment and discrimination. Although many felt invisible at the time, their contributions were enormous.

Clarence Wyatt notes that print and television journalists attracted a significant degree of controversy. Their harshest critics claim press coverage was biased and distorted, which caused a decline in public support for the war and undermined American goals. Wyatt explains how changing economic conditions and increased government secrecy of the Cold War affected the news business, which became more cautious at the top levels. By the 1960s, both military and civilian officials tried to manage the news by limiting access and information. In response, some of the earliest reporters assigned to cover Vietnam built relationships with military advisers in the field, sharing their risks and frustrations. News stories often reflected their shared views. At the same time, American and Vietnamese officials tried to suppress negative reports. Under the Johnson administration, officials shifted to a policy of "maximum candor," which ironically offered the government more control in shaping the news as the press grew more reliant on centralized sources. This created what Wyatt identifies as a "largely complementary relationship," which runs counter to the common assumption of the press and government as adversaries. At a time when mistrust of the government was widespread, the press offered a generally reliable option to official pronouncements. Most scholarship rejects the notion of a politically biased media that significantly influenced the war's outcome.

James Westheider uses the personal stories of several veterans to reveal the racial implications of America's war in Indochina. Blacks often viewed the armed forces as more egalitarian than the larger society, and many saw military service as an opportunity to prove they deserved equal access to the benefits of American life. To a significant extent, however, they did not find full equality. African Americans faced higher draft rates than whites and encountered biased placement exams, barriers to promotion, and a discriminatory military justice system. In the first years of fighting, African Americans made up a disproportionate percentage of U.S. combat soldiers and deaths, a situation that the military corrected by the end of the war. Wartime service often fostered growing racial pride, which sometimes clashed with attitudes held by some whites. By the late 1960s, racial tensions within the armed forces mirrored those in civilian society, which contributed to the military's declining morale. These experiences led many blacks to wonder whether fighting for democracy might be more appropriate back in the United States rather than in South Vietnam. Nevertheless, many performed heroically, and, like future Chairman of the Joint Chiefs of Staff Colin Powell, laid the groundwork for successful military careers. The words and actions of African Americans in this era helped stimulate necessary reforms.

Edmund Wehrle analyzes part of the Silent Majority constituency in his coverage of organized labor. Workers benefitted from the war through additional jobs and higher wages, and much of the AFL-CIO (American Federation of Labor and Congress of Industrial Organizations) membership was hawkish on the war for economic and political reasons. American unions solidly backed Lyndon Johnson's foreign policy and sought to develop independent trade unions in South Vietnam as a means of contesting communism. By 1968, this unified front was crumbling. Walter Reuther was the most visible example of labor's growing antiwar sentiment, while inflation and charges of racial discrimination weakened workers' traditional ties to the Democratic Party. A significant percentage of labor, divided from liberals over social and cultural issues, supported independent George Wallace for president in 1968 and Republican Richard Nixon in 1972. Symbolic of this shift was the hardhat. During an antiwar demonstration on May 8, 1970, only days after Ohio national guardsmen had killed four students at Kent State University, almost 200 hardhat-wearing construction workers attacked student protesters near Wall Street in New York City, injuring nearly 70 people. President Nixon publicly sided with the workers, and the following week thousands of hardhats demonstrated to support Nixon's war policies. Wehrle identifies the war as a critical factor in organized labor's decline.

Caroline Hoefferle finds extensive political activity among college students. Before the 1960s, McCarthyism stifled political dissent and universities often constrained students by regulating their social behavior through in loco parentis rules. During the 1960s, however, the campus population increased dramatically as the first baby boomers reached college age, and by mid-decade their sheer numbers made students a significant new constituency. African American students initiated nonviolent sit-ins across the South to erode racial discrimination and established the interracial Student Nonviolent Coordinating Committee. Students for a Democratic Society pursued a broad leftist agenda but gained attention and recruits from their opposition to the Vietnam War and the military draft. Conservatives organized Young Americans for Freedom, and generally advocated a free market economy, victory over communism, and limited federal power. Even more than these national and global issues, students worked—sometimes across ideological lines—for greater liberty on campus by attacking in loco parentis and demanding a role in university governance. Government repression and social resistance helped radicalize a minority of student activists, some of whom plunged into violent revolutionary fantasies. The triumph of Berkeley's Free Speech Movement and the tragedy at Kent State represent the highs and the lows of the student movement, which ultimately claimed real but limited achievements.

What each of these essays has in common is the recognition that the Vietnam War bitterly divided the United States more than at any time since the Civil War. The extraordinary diversity of viewpoints that existed during the war, which are reflected in these pages, makes it impossible to identify a Vietnam experience that fits everyone. Instead we have millions of unique experiences. In both the essays and corresponding documents, we can find confidence and indecisiveness, anger and hope, courage and fear.

In retrospect, Vietnam turned out to be less significant to American national security than many believed at the time, and the consequences of defeat were not as extensive as some had imagined. At the same time, communist victory in Vietnam marked a new phase in the struggle for economic and social stability rather than the attainment of those goals. If one phrase encapsulates Vietnam's determination to prevail against remarkable odds, it would be Ho Chi Minh's 1946 warning directed at the French prime minister. It could as easily have been addressed to the Americans. "If we must fight, we will fight," he promised. "You will kill ten of our men, and we will kill one of yours. Yet, in the end, it is you who will tire" (Hall 2008, 86).

Mitchell K. Hall
Professor of History
Central Michigan University

References and Further Reading

Child, Frank. "Vietnam—The Eleventh Hour." *New Republic* 145 (December 4, 1961): 14–16.

Hall, Mitchell K. *The Vietnam War.* Rev. 2nd ed. Harlow, England: Pearson Longman, 2008.

Herring, George C. *America's Longest War: The United States and Vietnam, 1950–1975*, 4th ed. New York: McGraw-Hill, 2002.

About the Editor and Contributors

Mitchell K. Hall is a professor of history at Central Michigan University. He earned a PhD from the University of Kentucky in 1987. His publications include *The Vietnam War* (Longman, rev. 2008); *Crossroads: American Popular Culture and the Vietnam Generation* (Rowman & Littlefield, 2005); "Unsell the War: Vietnam and Antiwar Advertising," *The Historian* 58 (Autumn 1995): 69–86; and *Because of Their Faith: CALCAV and Religious Opposition to the Vietnam War* (Columbia University Press, 1990). He is a past president of the Peace History Society and a previous editor of the journal *Peace & Change.*

James M. Carter completed his PhD in 2004 at the University of Houston. He is currently an assistant professor of history at Drew University. His publications include *Inventing Vietnam: The United States and State Building, 1954–1968* (Cambridge University Press, 2008); "A National Symphony of Theft, Corruption and Bribery: Anatomy of State Building from Iraq to Vietnam," in *Vietnam in Iraq: Tactics, Lessons, Legacies, and Ghosts,* edited by David Ryan and John Dumbrell (Routledge Press, 2006); and "The Vietnam Builders: Military Construction, Private Contractors and the Americanization of U.S. Involvement in Vietnam," *The Graduate Journal of Asia-Pacific Studies* (November 2004): 44–63.

Joseph A. Fry is a professor of history at the University of Nevada–Las Vegas. He completed his PhD at the University of Virginia in 1974. His publications include "Unpopular Messengers: Student Opposition to the Vietnam War," in *The War That Never Ends: New Perspectives on the Vietnam War,* edited by David L. Anderson and John Ernst (University Press of Kentucky, 2007); *Debating Vietnam: Fulbright, Stennis, and Their Senate Hearings* (Rowman & Littlefield, 2006); *Dixie Looks Abroad: The South and U.S. Foreign Relations, 1789–1973* (Louisiana State University Press, 2002); and *John Tyler Morgan and the Search for Southern Autonomy* (University of Tennessee Press, 1992).

Jill K. Gill is an associate professor of history at Boise State University. She earned a PhD from the University of Pennsylvania in 1996. She wrote her dissertation on "Peace Is Not the Absence of War, but the Presence of Justice: The National Council of Churches' Reaction and Response to the Vietnam War, 1965–1972." Her publications include "The Political Price of Prophetic Leadership: The National Council of Churches and the Vietnam War," *Peace & Change* (April 2002): 271–300 and "The Politics of Ecumenical Disunity: The Troubled Marriage of Church World Service and the National Council of Churches," *Religion and American Culture* 14:2 (Summer 2004): 175–212.

Kenneth J. Heineman earned his PhD at the University of Pittsburgh in 1990. He is currently a professor of history at Ohio University–Lancaster. Among his numerous publications are *Put Your Bodies Upon the Wheels: Student Revolt in the 1960s* (Ivan R. Dee, 2001); *A Catholic New Deal: Religion and Reform in Depression Pittsburgh* (Pennsylvania State University Press, 1999); *God Is a Conservative: Religion, Politics, and Morality in Contemporary America* (NYU Press, 1998); and *Campus Wars: The Peace Movement at American State Universities in the Vietnam Era* (NYU Press, 1992).

Caroline Hoefferle is an associate professor of history and director of the women's studies program at Wingate University. She received her PhD in 2000 from Central Michigan University. Her publications include "A Comparative History of Student Activism in Britain and the United States, 1960 to 1975" (PhD diss., 2000) and "'Just at Sunrise': The Sunrise Communal Farm in Rural Mid-Michigan, 1971–1978," *Michigan Historical Review* 23:1 (Spring 1997): 70–104. She is currently writing *The Essential Historiography Reader* for Longman Publishers (forthcoming, 2009).

Rhodri Jeffreys-Jones is a professor emeritus of history at the University of Edinburgh. His PhD is from Cambridge University. His many publications include *The FBI: A History* (Yale University Press, 2007); *Cloak and Dollar: A History of American Secret Intelligence* (Yale University Press, 2002); *Peace Now! American Society and the Ending of the Vietnam War* (Yale University Press, 1999); and *Changing Differences: Women and the Shaping of American Foreign Policy, 1917–1994* (Rutgers University Press, 1995). He was founder and first chair of the Scottish Association for the Study of America.

Carol Reardon earned her PhD from the University of Kentucky in 1987. She is a professor of history at Penn State University and president of the Society for Military History. Her publications include "Writing Battle History: The Challenge of Memory," in *Civil War History* 53:3 (September 2007): 252–263; *Launch the Intruders: A Naval Attack Squadron in the Vietnam War, 1972* (University Press of Kansas, 2005); *Pickett's Charge in History and Memory* (University of North Carolina Press, 1997); and *Soldiers and Scholars: The U.S. Army and the Uses of Military History, 1865–1920* (University Press of Kansas, 1990).

Edmund F. Wehrle is an associate professor of history at Eastern Illinois University. He earned his PhD at the University of Maryland in 1998. His publications include *Between a River and a Mountain: The AFL-CIO and the Vietnam War* (University of Michigan Press, 2005); "Guns, Butter, Leon Keyserling, the AFL-CIO and the Fate of Full Employment Economics," *The Historian* 66 (Winter 2004): 730–748; "Labor's Longest War: Trade Unionists and the Vietnam Conflict," *Labor's Heritage* 11 (Winter/Spring 2002): 50–65; and "'A Good Bad Deal': John F. Kennedy, Averell Harriman, and the Neutralization of Laos, 1960–1962," *Pacific Historical Review* 67 (August 1998): 349–378.

James E. Westheider is an associate professor and the interim chair of humanities and social sciences at the University of Cincinnati–Clermont College. He earned his PhD at the University of Cincinnati in 1993. His publications include *The African American Experience in Vietnam: Brothers in Arms* (Rowman & Littlefield, 2007); *The Vietnam War* (Greenwood, 2007); and *Fighting on Two Fronts: African Americans and the Vietnam War* (NYU Press, 1997).

Clarence R. Wyatt earned his PhD at the University of Kentucky in 1990. He is the Claude D. Pottinger associate professor of history at Centre College. Among his publications are "The Media and the Vietnam War" in *The War That Never Ends: New Perspectives on the Vietnam War,* edited by David L. Anderson and John Ernst (University Press of Kentucky, 2007); "Peter Arnett: Reporting America's Wars from Saigon to Baghdad," in *The Human Tradition in the Vietnam Era,* edited by David L. Anderson, (Wilmington, DE: Scholarly Resources, 2000); and *Paper Soldiers: The American Press and the Vietnam War* (Norton, 1993).

Natasha Zaretsky is an associate professor of history at Southern Illinois University. She earned her PhD at Brown University in 2002. Her publications include *No Direction Home: The American Family and the Fear of National Decline, 1968–1980* (University of North Carolina Press, 2007); "Private Suffering and Public Strife: Delia Alvarez's War with the Nixon Administration's POW Publicity Campaign, 1968–1973" in *Race, Nation, and Empire in American History,* edited by James T. Campbell, Matthew Pratt Guterl, and Robert G. Lee (University of North Carolina Press, 2007); and "In the Name of Austerity: Middle-Class Consumption and the OPEC Oil Embargo of 1973–1974" in *The World the Sixties Made,* edited by Van Gosse and Richard Moser (Temple University Press, 2003).

Chronology

May 1941   The Vietminh is formed; it is a broadly based but communist-led organization that seeks Vietnamese independence from France.

September 2, 1945   Ho Chi Minh publicly declares a provisional government and Vietnamese national independence.

November 23, 1946   The French bombard Haiphong.

October 1949   Communists defeat the Nationalists in the Chinese Civil War.

May 8, 1950   The United States agrees to provide France with military and economic assistance in Indochina.

May 7, 1954   French forces surrender to the Vietminh at Dien Bien Phu.

July 21, 1954   The Geneva Conference concludes with the signing of the Geneva Accords.

September 8, 1954   The Southeast Asia Treaty Organization (SEATO) is established.

October 26, 1955   Ngo Dinh Diem is elected president of South Vietnam.

July 20, 1956   The United States supports Diem's refusal to hold national elections as the deadline established in the Geneva Accords passes.

October 1957   Small-scale civil war begins in South Vietnam between Diem's forces and communist-led insurgents.

December 20, 1960   Formation of the National Liberation Front (NLF), a South Vietnamese communist-dominated coalition against President Ngo Dinh Diem.

February 6, 1962   The United States establishes Military Assistance Command,

Vietnam (MACV) with General Paul Harkins as commander of American armed forces.

January 3, 1963   Battle of Ap Bac.

May–August 1963   Buddhist-led demonstrations occur in South Vietnam's largest cities.

November 1, 1963   Ngo Dinh Diem is killed in a coup and replaced by Duong Van Minh.

November 22, 1963   President John F. Kennedy is assassinated in Dallas, Texas.

December 1963   The North Vietnamese Army (NVA) sends its first regular units into South Vietnam.

January 30, 1964   Nguyen Khanh overthrows Duong Van Minh as head of South Vietnamese government.

June 20, 1964   General William Westmoreland succeeds General Paul Harkins as commander of MACV.

August 2, 1964   North Vietnamese patrol boats attack the *Maddox* in the Gulf of Tonkin near the North Vietnamese coast.

August 4–5, 1964   Both the *Maddox* and the *C. Turner Joy* report being under attack; U.S. naval aircraft conduct reprisal raids against North Vietnamese targets.

August 7, 1964   U.S. Congress passes the Gulf of Tonkin Resolution.

October 1964   General Khanh resigns as South Vietnam's president and is replaced by Tran Van Huong.

November 1, 1964   Vietcong forces attack Bien Hoa Air Base.

January 27–28, 1965   South Vietnamese president Tran Van Huong is ousted and General Khanh returns to power.

February 7, 1965   The Vietcong attack a U.S. military base near Pleiku. President Johnson orders retaliatory air strikes against North Vietnamese targets.

February 13, 1965   President Johnson orders a sustained bombing campaign against North Vietnam known as Operation Rolling Thunder. Actual bombing begins on March 2 and continues, with occasional pauses, until October 31, 1968.

February 25, 1965   South Vietnam's Armed Forces Council replaces General Khanh as head of state with Air Marshal Nguyen Cao Ky.

March 8, 1965   The first U.S. combat troops arrive in Vietnam.

April 6, 1965   President Johnson authorizes U.S. forces to conduct offensive operations to support Army of the Republic of Vietnam (ARVN) forces.

April 7, 1965   President Johnson's speech at Johns Hopkins University offers unconditional discussions with North Vietnam.

June 19, 1965   Air Marshal Ky becomes premier of the eighth South Vietnamese government since Diem was overthrown.

July 21–28, 1965   President Johnson makes a series of decisions that amount to committing the United States to a major war in Vietnam. Among the decisions he makes: draft calls are raised to 35,000 per month, 50,000 additional troops are sent to Vietnam with additional increases as the situation demands, and the air war against North Vietnam is expanded.

October 23, 1965   The battle of the Ia Drang Valley begins, the first major land battle between U.S. and North Vietnamese regular forces. It ends on November 20.

February 4, 1966   The U.S. Senate Foreign Relations Committee, chaired by Senator J. William Fulbright, holds televised hearings on the Vietnam War.

February 6, 1966   President Johnson convenes a conference in Honolulu on the Vietnam War.

March–April 1966   Vietnamese Buddhists and students protest against the Saigon government.

January 8–26, 1967   Operation Cedar Falls takes place in the Iron Triangle region northeast of Saigon.

February 22, 1967   Operation Junction City begins in War Zone C near the Cambodian border. It concludes on April 1.

September 3, 1967   Nguyen Van Thieu is elected president of South Vietnam.

September 29, 1967   President Johnson offers to stop the bombing of North Vietnam if it will agree to start negotiations, known as the "San Antonio Formula."

October 16–21, 1967   Antiwar activists hold antidraft demonstrations throughout the United States; the largest occurs at the Army Induction Center in Oakland, California.

October 21–23, 1967   In the March on the Pentagon, 100,000 people demonstrate against the Vietnam War in Washington, D.C.

November 30, 1967   Senator Eugene McCarthy announces his candidacy to challenge President Johnson for the Democratic presidential nomination in 1968.

January 20, 1968   North Vietnamese forces besiege an American Marine base at Khe Sanh. The siege is lifted on April 14.

January 30, 1968   NLF and North Vietnamese forces launch the Tet Offensive against cities throughout South Vietnam.

February 20, 1968   The Senate Foreign Relations Committee begins hearings on the 1964 Gulf of Tonkin incident.

February 28, 1968   General Earle Wheeler informs President Johnson that General Westmoreland needs an additional 206,000 troops.

March 12, 1968   Senator Eugene McCarthy pulls a near upset of President Johnson in the New Hampshire primary.

March 16, 1968   Senator Robert Kennedy announces his candidacy for the Democratic presidential nomination on an antiwar platform.

A platoon of U.S. soldiers slaughters hundreds of unarmed villagers in the hamlet of My Lai.

March 25–26, 1968   Johnson reconvenes the "Wise Men," who advise against additional troop increases and recommend a negotiated peace in Vietnam.

March 31, 1968   President Johnson announces a unilateral halt to all U.S. bombing north of the 20th Parallel and that he will seek negotiations with North Vietnam. He also announces his withdrawal from the presidential race.

May 12, 1968   Peace negotiations between the United States and North Vietnam begin in Paris.

June 5, 1968   Robert Kennedy is assassinated in Los Angeles.

June 10, 1968   General Creighton Abrams succeeds General Westmoreland as U.S. military commander in Vietnam.

August 26–29, 1968   The Democratic Party nominates Vice President Hubert Humphrey for president at the Democratic National Convention in Chicago. Riots occur between Chicago police and antiwar demonstrators.

October 31, 1968   President Johnson announces a complete bombing halt over North Vietnam, ending Operation Rolling Thunder.

January 25, 1969   The first four-way plenary session takes place in Paris among the United States, North Vietnam, South Vietnam, and the NLF.

March 18, 1969   President Nixon orders Operation Menu, the secret bombing of communist bases in Cambodia.

June 8, 1969   President Nixon announces that 25,000 U.S. troops will be withdrawn by the end of August, the beginning of Vietnamization.

June 10, 1969   The NLF announces the formation of a Provisional Revolutionary Government (PRG) to rule in South Vietnam.

August 4, 1969   Secret negotiations begin in Paris between U.S. special envoy Henry Kissinger and North Vietnam's Xuan Thuy.

September 2, 1969   Ho Chi Minh dies.

October 15, 1969   The Moratorium, the largest antiwar demonstration in American history, takes place across the country.

November 3, 1969   President Nixon's "Silent Majority Speech" defends his Vietnam War policies.

November 15, 1969   The Mobilization draws more than 250,000 people to Washington, D.C., in protest of the Vietnam War.

March 18, 1970   General Lon Nol ousts Prince Norodom Sihanouk as Cambodia's head of state.

March 27, 1970   ARVN forces attack communist bases inside Cambodia for the first time.

April 30, 1970   American forces invade the Fishhook region of Cambodia.

May 4, 1970   Ohio National Guard troops fire into a crowd of student demonstrators on the campus of Kent State University, killing four and wounding nine.

May 9, 1970   An estimated 80,000 young people, mostly college students, demonstrate peacefully in the nation's capital, protesting the Kent State Massacre and calling for the immediate withdrawal of all U.S. troops from Indochina.

May 20, 1970   More than 100,000 workers in New York City march in support of Nixon's war policies.

June 24, 1970   The U.S. Senate repeals the Gulf of Tonkin Resolution.

June 30, 1970   U.S. ground forces end their role in the Cambodian operation.

August 19, 1970   The United States signs a pact with Cambodia to provide Lon Nol's government with military aid.

January 1, 1971   Congress forbids the use of U.S. ground troops in Laos or Cambodia.

February 8, 1971   South Vietnamese forces invade Laos to cut supply routes down the Ho Chi Minh Trail. Communist counterattacks drive them out of Laos and inflict heavy casualties. The invasion ends on March 24.

March 29, 1971   Lieutenant William Calley is convicted of mass murder. His sentence is later reduced and he is paroled after three years.

April 19–23, 1971   Vietnam Veterans Against the War stage a demonstration in Washington, D.C.

June 13, 1971   The *New York Times* begins publication of what becomes referred to as the Pentagon Papers.

October 3, 1971   Nguyen Van Thieu is reelected president of South Vietnam.

December 26, 1971   President Nixon orders the resumption of U.S. bombing of North Vietnam.

February 21, 1972   President Nixon begins his historic visit to China, which ends on February 27.

March 30, 1972   North Vietnam conducts its Easter Offensive, a three-pronged attack across the demilitarized zone, into the central highlands, and northwest of Saigon that ends on April 8.

May 8, 1972   President Nixon orders the mining of all North Vietnamese ports and the Linebacker bombing campaign.

May 20, 1972   President Nixon and Leonid Brezhnev meet in Moscow for a summit conference.

June 1972   General Fred Weyand replaces General Creighton Abrams as commander of U.S. forces in Vietnam.

September 15, 1972   South Vietnamese forces recapture Quang Tri City.

October 8–11, 1972   Secret meetings in Paris between Henry Kissinger and Le Duc Tho produce a tentative settlement of the war.

October 22, 1972   President Thieu rejects the proposed settlement.

December 14, 1972   The United States breaks off peace talks with the North Vietnamese.

December 18, 1972   President Nixon orders renewed mining of North Vietnamese harbors and Linebacker II bombing campaign, known as the "Christmas Bombing."

December 28, 1972   Hanoi announces its willingness to resume negotiations if the United States will stop bombing above the 20th parallel; the bombing ends on December 31.

January 8–18, 1973   Henry Kissinger and Le Duc Tho resume negotiations in Paris and reach an agreement similar to the one reached the previous October.

January 23, 1973   President Nixon announces the signing of the Paris Accords, which go into effect on January 27, 1973.

January 27, 1973   The U.S. military draft ends.

February 1, 1973   Secret letter from Richard Nixon to Pham Van Dong promises postwar reconstruction aid to North Vietnam.

February 12, 1973   The release of U.S. prisoners of war begins.

February 21, 1973   A cease-fire formally ends the 20-year war in Laos.

March 29, 1973   The last U.S. troops and prisoners of war leave South Vietnam.

June 4, 1973 The U.S. Congress blocks all funds for any American military activities in Indochina, but the Nixon administration works out a compromise to permit continued U.S. bombing in Cambodia until August 15.

August 14, 1973 The U.S. bombing of Cambodia ends.

November 7, 1973 Congress enacts the War Powers Act over President Nixon's veto.

February 1974 South Vietnam launches a military offensive against PRG-controlled areas west of Saigon.

August 9, 1974 Richard Nixon resigns the U.S. presidency. Gerald Ford is sworn in as president.

September 16, 1974 President Ford offers clemency to draft evaders and deserters.

January 6, 1975 NVA forces overrun Phuoc Long Province. When the United States does not react, Hanoi concludes that America will not reintroduce its military forces to save South Vietnam.

January 28, 1975 President Ford requests an additional $722 million in military aid for South Vietnam. Congress refuses his request.

March 1975 NVA forces launch an offensive in the central highlands.

March 12, 1975 Ban Me Thuot falls to the communists.

March 14, 1975 President Thieu orders the withdrawal of ARVN from the central highlands.

March 25, 1975 Hanoi launches its Ho Chi Minh campaign to "liberate" South Vietnam before the rainy season begins.

April 8–21, 1975 Communists win the last major battle of the Vietnam War at Xuan Loc, about 30 miles from Saigon.

April 12, 1975 President Nguyen Van Thieu resigns and flees South Vietnam.

April 17, 1975 The Khmer Rouge accept the Cambodian government's surrender and occupy the capital city of Phnom Penh.

April 29–30, 1975 The last Americans and thousands of South Vietnamese are evacuated from Saigon.

April 30, 1975 Saigon falls to communist forces, ending the Vietnam War.

Divisions within the Containment Generation: U.S. Policy Makers and the Vietnam War

1

Joseph A. Fry

During the Lyndon Baines Johnson presidential administration, both those policy makers who supported U.S. involvement in Vietnam and those who opposed the war were charter members of the "containment generation." They had reached political maturity during World War II and the early years of the Cold War and had experienced the intense anticommunism of the McCarthy era of the early 1950s. More generally, these leaders had imbibed the lessons of American nationalism with its principal message that the United States was a unique and chosen nation with a duty to reform others in its image. They embraced the American faith in technology and had overseen the development of the nation's unequaled military power. Although most American policy makers and the nation were generally unwilling to acknowledge the imperial features of Cold War U.S. foreign policy, they agreed on the critical need to contain the Soviet Union and the People's Republic of China.

Despite this common intellectual and cultural heritage, shared foreign policy experience, and "generational mind-set," key Johnson administration and congressional policy makers disagreed fundamentally on the wisdom of U.S. involvement in Vietnam, the most important and costly U.S. foreign policy intervention during the Cold War. President Johnson and his secretary of state, Dean Rusk, considered Vietnam a crucial Cold War battleground where an American loss would trigger dire domestic and international repercussions. In contrast, Undersecretary of State George Ball and Senators J. William Fulbright (D-AR) and Albert Gore Sr. (D-TN) contended that the U.S. war in Vietnam was a misapplication of containment and a tragic waste of resources that was doing great damage to the nation's international standing. Examining why these key policy makers, all acting within the same political, cultural, and social milieu, responded so differently to the Vietnam War provides insight into the complexity of the issues they faced and the numerous considerations with which U.S. officials contended while arriving at policy positions and decisions.

Born between 1905 and 1909, all five of these policy makers had observed the arrival of World War II and had either been members of Congress, the military, or the national security bureaucracy as the Cold War followed in the mid-1940s. Having watched Adolf Hitler's march toward war and the futile European attempt to appease him with Czech territory at the 1938 Munich Conference, this generation of Americans concluded that aggressors had to be confronted rather than coddled. With the end of World War II, Americans perceived Joseph Stalin and Soviet communism as an even more threatening totalitarian menace. As the Soviets occupied the countries of Eastern Europe and probed in Iran and Manchuria, the United States adopted the policy of containment that, according to foreign service officer George F. Kennan (1984), entailed the "adroit and vigilant application of counter-force at a series of constantly shifting geographical and political points." This "long-term, patient but firm and vigilant containment" was necessary to repulse the Kremlin's drive to fill "every nook and cranny available to it in the basin of world power" (118–120).

Thereafter, seemingly decisive U.S. actions, such as demands for Soviet withdrawal from Iran in 1946 or aid through the Truman Doctrine to noncommunist forces in Greece in 1947, proved successful. In contrast, ostensibly more restrained policies failed in China, where Mao Zedong and communist followers prevailed in 1949, or Korea, where efforts to reunite the country under a noncommunist regime fell short by 1953. Based on these experiences, most members of the containment generation concluded that tough, forceful responses to perceived communist expansion were as appropriate for answering Soviet and Chinese challenges after World War II as they would have been for responding to the German, Italian, and Japanese threats in the 1930s.

In addition to agreeing on the need for toughness in enforcing containment, U.S. policy makers adopted two other key concepts that later proved central for Johnson era leaders as they assessed Vietnam. The first, "credibility," posited that U.S. failure to act decisively and appropriately in foreign crises would embolden enemies and engender doubts among allies. As Truman Doctrine aid was dispatched, State Department official Loy Henderson termed Greece "the test tube which the peoples of the world are watching" (Leffler 1992, 195). Over the ensuing 15 years, U.S. policy makers retained this concern for credibility, and their attempts to safeguard the U.S. reputation abroad played a prominent role in repeated crises over areas of seemingly marginal strategic importance, such as Vietnam.

Together with the elusive psychological concept of credibility, U.S. leadership during the early Cold War warned that communist victories in one country could breach the wall of containment and trigger a chain reaction of Soviet or Chinese gains in adjacent nations. President Truman voiced this assumption following the North Korean attack on South Korea in 1950: "If we let Korea down, the Soviet[s] will keep right on going and swallow up one piece of Asia after another. . . . If we were to let Asia go, the Near East would collapse and no telling what would happen in Europe" (Leffler 1994,

100). This concept became known as the "domino theory" in April 1954, when President Dwight Eisenhower emphasized the importance of maintaining a noncommunist South Vietnam. Were communist forces to prevail, Eisenhower warned, the "falling domino principle" would apply to Southeast Asia generally: "You have a row of dominoes set up, you knock over the first one, and what will happen to the last one is the certainty that it will go over very quickly" (McMahon 1995, 122).

Domestic political developments in the early 1950s reinforced the inclinations of U.S. policy makers to adopt tough anticommunist stands designed to enhance credibility and prevent the fall of dominos. Led by Sen. Joseph McCarthy (R-WI), critics of U.S. foreign policy charged the Truman administration with being soft on domestic communist spies, "losing" China to communism, and failing to prosecute the Korean War with sufficient vigor. These critics, primarily Republicans, asserted that the U.S. failure to prevail in all foreign policy encounters resulted from internal disloyalty rather than any external limits on American power. McCarthy contended that "highly placed Red Counselors" in the State Department were "far more deadly than Red machine gunners in Korea" (Sherry 1995, 185).

The search for disloyal Americans and the hysteria that accompanied it eventually assumed bizarre dimensions. High-profile prosecutions led to the execution of Julius and Ethel Rosenberg for atomic espionage and the conviction of former State Department official Alger Hiss for perjury; approximately 2,700 federal employees were dismissed between 1947 and 1956 for "loyalty-security" reasons; and virtually all of the experts on East Asia were driven from the State Department for allegedly facilitating the communist victory in China. In 1954, President Eisenhower recommended that communists be stripped of their U.S. citizenship based solely on their beliefs, regardless of their actions, and 80 percent of Americans agreed. In Oklahoma, a librarian was fired for daring to shelve the *New Republic, Consumer's Research,* and *Negro Digest;* and in Cincinnati, the professional baseball team changed its name from the Reds to the Redlegs. Having experienced this climate of fear and innuendo, policy makers emerged from the McCarthy Red Scare acutely aware of the hazards of being labeled soft on communism.

As they turned to the task of combating communist expansion, American policy makers and their constituents did so with the long-held nationalistic assurance that Americans were a "chosen people" who had been destined for "national greatness" from the time John Winthrop proclaimed that the Puritans were building a "City upon a Hill" in Massachusetts for all the world to emulate. Having never lost a war and having emerged from World War II as the world's strongest economic and military power, most Americans viewed themselves as having built uniquely successful political and economic systems that others would adopt if given the opportunity. Only "evil communists" blocked access to these superior American institutions (Baritz 1985).

American policy makers and their fellow citizens also harbored great faith in technology. Having opted as early as the 1930s for a general military strategy that emphasized using American technology to limit casualties on the ground, having been the first nation to develop both an atomic and a hydrogen bomb, and having achieved unparalleled domestic affluence in the 1950s,

Americans equated these technological achievements with their more general sense of uniqueness and superiority. They further assumed that superior technology guaranteed military success. In 1983, playwright Arthur Miller observed, "I'm an American. I believe in technology. Until the mid-1960s I never believed we could lose because we had technology" (Baritz 1985, 45).

Although most Americans in the 1950s shared the faith in the value of spreading their institutions and technology abroad, few would have acknowledged that along with containment U.S. policy makers oversaw an imperial foreign policy. Following World War II, American leaders were determined to maintain a "preponderance of power" sufficient to defeat all challengers (Leffler 1992, 15–19). The official policy of containment masked the simultaneous pursuit of empire as the nation sought to use its preeminent military and economic power to shape the world according to an American vision and guidelines. Such aggressive, expansive U.S. foreign policies were not a novel, post-1945 innovation, as Native Americans, Mexicans, Spanish, British, and other pre–World War II adversaries could attest. Consistent with the perceptions of virtually all previous empire builders, post–World War II Americans matched their grand ambitions with claims that their imperial actions were peculiarly defensive, that they sought only national security, and that they pursued no selfish objectives. Indeed, generations of Americans had been raised on a national "war story" that portrayed Americans as the repeated victims of unprovoked attacks by Indians, Japanese, and Germans. Having heroically repulsed these aggressors, Americans confronted communist foes in the 1950s and 1960s with the same conviction that unwelcome outside forces were pressing a peaceable, noninterventionist United States to assume an activist foreign policy.

Escalation Defended

Of the Johnson-era policy makers, the president was undisputedly the most important. This was true not only because he dominated Vietnam policy but also because he most fully embodied the nation's decisive Cold War perspective. Born in 1908 and a native of the Texas hill country west of Austin, Johnson attended a one-room school before graduating from high school at age 15 and Southwest Texas State Teachers College in 1930 at age 21. His personal family experiences, his teaching in rural Texas schools, his first important political job as secretary to a Texas congressman, and his service as director of the Texas National Youth Administration provided Johnson with firsthand knowledge of rural poverty and racial discrimination. Elected to Congress in 1937 and the Senate in 1948, LBJ strongly supported Franklin Roosevelt's New Deal legislation aimed at relieving suffering during the Great Depression. In addition to adopting a lifelong commitment to domestic reform, Johnson also backed the construction of containment under Truman. By the 1950s, Johnson had developed virtually unparalleled political skills and served as the Democratic Senate majority leader before reluctantly agreeing to run for the vice presidency on the 1960 ticket with John F. Kennedy. Despite his important role in carrying crucial southern

Lyndon B. Johnson, one of the most controversial U.S. presidents in modern times, fought for African American equality more than any president since Abraham Lincoln and sought to use the nation's wealth to eradicate poverty. Johnson also increased the U.S. commitment to one of the worst foreign policy disasters in the nation's history, the Vietnam War. (*Yoichi R. Okamoto/ Lyndon B. Johnson Library*)

states for Kennedy, Johnson endured as an awkward outsider in an administration dominated by self-consciously sophisticated northeasterners.

Clark Clifford, the longtime Democratic political activist who became Johnson's secretary of defense in 1968, described LBJ as "the most complex man I ever met" (Herring 1994, 16). Few contemporaries would have disagreed with Clifford's assessment. Truly larger than life, the hulking six-foot-four-inch Johnson combined towering ambition, a razor-sharp mind, an unquenchable thirst for politically related information, and enormous energy and drive. To these qualities he added a fervent commitment to aid the poor and aged of all races and unrivalled domestic political acumen. These qualities and his forceful leadership led to the passage of landmark legislation in the areas of civil rights, federal aid to education, medical care for the elderly, and antipoverty programs in 1964 and 1965. But the same Texas politician who could oversee such historic accomplishments could also be crude, boorish, vain, exceedingly mean to close associates, and terribly insecure. Having set "absurdly high" goals for himself and his administration, Johnson was a "tormented man" who periodically battled intense episodes of depression and self-doubt. He craved demonstrative gratitude and affection from the American public and was indignant when those for whom he had done so much failed to respond as he expected.

Much of the public's hostility toward Johnson resulted from the disastrous U.S. war in Vietnam. When Johnson assumed the presidency in November 1963, following John F. Kennedy's assassination, 16,300 U.S. military advisers were supporting the noncommunist South Vietnamese government. The Saigon regime had become an American client state when the United States assumed responsibility for its survival after the French withdrawal from its former colony in 1954. As LBJ took office, South Vietnam was in imminent danger of being overrun by communist-dominated insurgents known as the Vietcong. These insurgents were allied with the communist Democratic Republic of Vietnam located in North Vietnam and led by the legendary Ho Chi Minh. In addition to his communist ties to the Soviet Union and People's Republic of China, Ho had earned his standing as Vietnam's foremost nationalist and patriot by virtue of marshaling Vietnamese resistance to outside control by France, Japan, and finally the United States. North Vietnam and, in turn, the Vietcong received aid from the Soviet Union and the People's Republic of China in their battle against the United States. Faced with the prospect of a Vietcong–North Vietnamese victory, Johnson increased U.S. troop levels to 536,100 over the ensuing five years and oversaw the Operation Rolling Thunder bombing campaign that pummeled North Vietnam with 643,000 tons of explosives and inflicted $600 million in damage. To the intense frustration of the president and the American public, this enormous infusion of U.S. power had by the end of Johnson's administration in January 1969 produced only a stalemate at a far greater level of violence and death with no clear prospect of victory.

Johnson did not escalate the U.S. role heedlessly. In May 1964, he told National Security Advisor McGeorge Bundy, "I don't think it's [Vietnam] worth fighting for and I don't think we can get out. It's just the biggest damn mess I ever saw. . . . What the hell is Vietnam worth to me? . . . What is it worth to this country?" (Dallek 1998, 145). Even as he made the decisions for sustained bombing of North Vietnam in February 1965 and to dispatch massive numbers of U.S. ground troops in March and July, he worried prophetically that "airplanes" were not "worth a damn" and would not be decisive, that the enemy soldiers had greater staying power and "will last longer than we do," and that the American public might not remain supportive of the war "six months from now" (Woods 2006, 604, 611).

Despite his grave reservations and accurate predictions, Johnson chose war. This choice derived from a complex mix of strategic, political, and personal considerations. Like the majority of his fellow cold warriors, the president deemed tough, decisive responses the only way to repulse perceived aggression and contain communism. Convinced that a North Vietnamese–Vietcong victory would advance the cause of international communism at U.S. expense, he proclaimed there would be "no more Munichs" under his leadership (Goldman 1969, 490). LBJ believed that "if you let a bully come into your front yard one day, the next day he will be up on your porch and the day after that he will rape your wife in your own bed" (Logevall 1999, 393). Johnson also subscribed to the domino theory. In February 1965, the president warned a group of congressmen that the North Vietnamese "want to take South Vietnam, and . . . Thailand, and . . . Burma . . . and Sukarno-Indonesia . . . the Philippines, [and] Hawaii. They'd like to come right back to Seattle" (Fry 2006, 23–24). Also, U.S. credibility was at risk in Vietnam where losing a "war to communists" would cause the United States to "be seen as an appeaser" (Goodwin 1991, 252, 260) and lead the Russians and Chinese to think "we're yellow and don't mean what we say." Finally, Johnson's confidence in American economic and military might solidified his determination to demonstrate U.S. resolve. Like most other Americans, he could not conceive of the world's most powerful nation losing to what he described as a "damn little pissant country" (Hunt 1996, 79, 105).

Inextricably bound to these strategic calculations was Johnson's conviction that losing in Vietnam would preclude passage of his domestic reform program. Genuinely committed to social justice for all Americans, the president feared that deserting "the woman I really loved—the Great Society" for "that bitch of a war" would result in losing "everything at home" (Goodwin 1991, 251). In late 1964, he predicted correctly, "Those damn conservatives are going to sit in Congress . . . [and] use this war as a way of opposing my Great Society legislation." Congressmen unsympathetic to the poor and minorities would "take the war as their weapon" and argue that the first priority was "beating the Communists" (Woods 2006, 597). If fighting the war imperiled domestic reform, losing it would assuredly doom these measures by provoking "an endless national debate—a mean and destructive debate— that would shatter my presidency, kill my administration, and damage our democracy" (Goodwin 1991, 252). Or, as he phrased it less delicately, "If I don't go in now and they [southern conservatives] show later I should have, they'll push Vietnam up my ass every time" (Herring 2002, 136).

Ironically, when directed toward the Vietnamese, Johnson's commitment to reform further buttressed his decision for war. Randall Woods, Johnson's most recent biographer, has argued that the president's intervention in Vietnam derived from his "Christian idealism" and determination to aid the poor and dispossessed in Vietnam by effectively extending the Great Society to Southeast Asia. Although making Johnson's idealism primary in his foreign policy decisions is debatable, LBJ did believe "the average father and the average mother" in Asia had the same hopes for their children as American parents (Woods 2006, 385, 503). Based on this assumption, he proposed an American-funded, billion-dollar project to develop the Mekong River in South Vietnam on the model of the Tennessee Valley Authority. If North Vietnam and the Vietcong agreed to stop the war, Johnson pledged a grand gift of Western technology accompanied by a bounty of electricity, food, modern medicine, and education. The president was sure "Ho will never be able to say, 'No'" to this offer (Dallek 1998, 261). But, of course, he did. To the Vietnamese leader, Johnson's American prescription for Vietnamese political and economic development was the latest presumptuous, imperial effort to dictate to his country. Johnson later complained, "I keep trying to get Ho to the negotiating table. I try writing him, calling him, going through the Russians and Chinese, and all I hear back is 'Fuck you, Lyndon'" (Zeiler 2000, 171–172).

As Johnson decided for war, his own personality and sense of self were as decisive as any strategic, political, or humanitarian considerations. An enormously proud and competitive man, LBJ was determined to be a great president in both the domestic and foreign policy realms. He complained that northerners and the media criticized him unfairly because he was a southerner and lamented, "I don't think that I will ever get credit for anything I do in foreign policy because I didn't go to Harvard" (Goldman 1969, 490). Convinced that he faced "bigotry in the north against a southerner on . . . his ability to handle foreign relations," Johnson was determined to prove that he was a "world statesman" rather than a "Texas provincial" (Dallek 1998, 86, 90).

The most direct way to accomplish this was by prevailing in Vietnam. Upon becoming president, Johnson instructed his advisers that "Lyndon Johnson intends to stand by our word," and that "I will not lose in Vietnam" (Logevall 1999, 77). Four years and enormous American and Vietnamese losses later, Johnson reiterated that he was "not going to be the first American President to lose a war" (Dallek 1998, 500). Maintaining U.S. credibility was crucial. "The Chinese. The fellas in the Kremlin" would be "taking the measure of us" (Dallek 1998, 100). His concern for credibility was not confined to the nation's foreign policy; he also feared potentially negative perceptions of his personal honor and manliness. A "profoundly insecure man" (Herring 1993a, 108), he was terrified that losing in Vietnam would make him appear "a coward. An unmanly man. A man without a spine," and in a recurring nightmare he cowered before thousands of people who berated him as a "Coward! Traitor! Weakling!" Johnson so profoundly personalized the war that he could neither admit mistakes nor accept any outcome short of a U.S. victory (Goodwin 1991, 253).

Among Johnson's closest advisers, Secretary of State Dean Rusk provided the most sustained support for the president's Vietnam policies. Born in 1908 into a poor Georgia family, Rusk took his first job as a grocery clerk at age eight, worked his way through Davidson College, and earned a Rhodes scholarship to Oxford, where he graduated in 1934. After failing to secure a position with the State Department, he taught at Mills College in Oakland, California, leaving in 1940 to assume command of an infantry company preparing for war. He was soon transferred to military intelligence and over the course of World War II worked closely with Gen. George Marshall, attended several important wartime diplomatic conferences, and served as deputy chief of staff for the China-Burma-India theater. After the war, he moved to the State Department, where he rose to deputy undersecretary. With Republican Dwight Eisenhower's victory likely in the 1952 presidential election, Rusk accepted the presidency of the Rockefeller Foundation, where he remained until John Kennedy appointed him secretary of state in 1961.

Despite his rich foreign policy experience, Rusk was "never one of the 'Kennedy people' and never made the effort to become one" (Rusk 1990, 296). He did, however, form a close relationship with then Vice President Johnson, who was also relegated to the fringes of Kennedy's administration.

Dean Rusk was a quiet, loyal secretary of state in the administrations of John F. Kennedy and Lyndon B. Johnson. (*Yoichi R. Okamoto/ Lyndon B. Johnson Library*)

The two southerners swapped stories about who had been poorer and which family had been the first to get indoor plumbing and electricity. While still vice president, LBJ confided to his brother: "Some people around [Kennedy] are bastards," but not Rusk. Johnson pronounced him "a damned good man. Hard-working, bright, and loyal as a beagle. You'll never catch him working at cross purposes with his president. He's just the kind of man I'd want in my cabinet if I were president" (Schoenbaum 1988, 411). Johnson retained this assessment as he and Rusk completed their work together in 1969. The secretary had been a "loyal, honorable, hard-working imaginative man of conviction" who "stood by me and shared the president's load of responsibility and abuse" (Zeiler 2000, 133).

Like Johnson, Rusk did not rush to war thoughtlessly. He had opposed a 1961 recommendation to commit U.S. ground troops and had been uneasy about overcommitting to South Vietnamese president Ngo Dinh Diem, whom he considered a "losing horse" (Rusk 1990, 432). Similarly, he voiced reservations over the Americanization of the war in 1965, when Johnson initiated sustained bombing of North Vietnam and dispatched thousands of U.S. troops into the South Vietnam jungles. Still, Rusk also put aside such reservations in favor of a war he relentlessly defended. Although Rusk shared many of the president's strategic considerations, concern for national honor and credibility, and belief in the merits of toughness, the secretary's determination to fight and win in Vietnam was rooted in his devotion to constructing an international system based on Western law and maintained through collective security. Convinced that most of the people in the world "want the kind of world we want," Rusk deemed unchecked aggression the principal threat to a world of law, equality, and fairness (Zeiler 2000, 131). The failure of peaceful, democratic nations to challenge Germany and Japan in the 1930s had demonstrated that "aggression . . . allowed to gather momentum . . . can continue to build and lead to a general war" (Rusk 1990, 494). He considered the Chinese "militant Marxists" and had no doubt that they were directing North Vietnam's aggression against South Vietnam. Therefore, a resolute U.S. response was obligatory. Rusk never tired of lecturing antiwar protesters that dismissing Hitler's rhetoric in the 1930s had led to the murder of 6 million Jews. Those who failed to take seriously Chinese threats to spread revolution were also practicing appeasement. When opponents of the war protested that China and North Vietnam hardly constituted the same threat to the United States as Nazi Germany, Rusk responded "an airdale [sic] and a great dane are different but they are both dogs" (Fry 2006, 64, 66).

Based on membership in the Southeast Asia Treaty Organization (SEATO), Rusk argued that the United States was not just strategically but also legally obligated to repulse North Vietnamese aggression. The 1955 agreement called upon each member to respond "in accordance with its constitutional processes" to any act of "aggression by means of armed attack" against another member nation. This protection had been extended to South Vietnam, which was not a charter member. In Rusk's view, SEATO, like the North Atlantic Treaty Organization, was an essential collective security agreement designed to contain communism. As such, it had to be enforced. Following U.S. Senate ratification, SEATO had become the "law of the land and linked South Vietnam to the general structure of collective security." If the United States failed to live up to its "pledged word" and thereby impugned its honor and credibility, these treaties, the "pillars of peace in a dangerous world," would be fatally compromised. Abandoning South Vietnam, and with it SEATO and international collective security, could encourage aggression and threaten the very survival of the human race (Fry 2006, 30, 64, 66). Rusk also emphasized that if the United States ignored this small nation on the periphery, the "first thing you know the periphery is the center" (Gaddis 2005, 201). This emphasis on the importance of small, seemingly less important nations encouraged the assumption that all parts of the world were of equal strategic importance—that, in a zero-sum dynamic, anywhere communists gained the United States automatically lost.

Finally, Rusk voiced the American sense of uniqueness and selflessness in contrast with the selfish communist pursuit of world revolution. The United States, he asserted, sought no "territorial aggrandizement in South Vietnam" or elsewhere in Asia, "no permanent military bases, no trade advantages," and no ongoing alliance with South Vietnam. The Johnson administration was not attempting "to destroy the Hanoi regime" or to force North Vietnam to give up communism. Rather, the United States sought only to guarantee self-determination for the South Vietnamese. In short, Rusk rejected any suggestion that the United States harbored imperial intentions of imposing its will on others (Fry 2006, 66–67).

Dissenting Voices

If Rusk was Johnson's most steadfast supporter within the administration, George Ball was the most persistent critic of U.S. involvement in Vietnam. In contrast to Johnson and Rusk, Ball brought a much more privileged background to public service. The youngest of three brothers, Ball was born in 1909 in Des Moines, Iowa. As the son of a Standard Oil executive, he was "particularly cuddled and coddled" in a family that valued reading and education and regularly debated public issues at the dinner table. After earning a bachelor's degree in literature from Northwestern University in 1930, Ball graduated from Northwestern Law School three years later. The newly minted attorney then held posts in Franklin Roosevelt's Farm Credit Administration and Treasury Department before moving to a Chicago law practice in 1935. With the beginning of World War II, Ball served in the Lend-Lease Administration and ultimately headed the United States Strategic Bombing Survey, which assessed the impact of the bombing campaign against Germany. Following the war, he was a founding member of an international law firm with offices in New York, Washington, Paris, and Brussels. Ball thereafter made frequent trips to Western Europe and gained an excellent understanding of the most important European developments and political figures. With the advent

George Ball served as undersecretary of state in the John F. Kennedy administration. He was a strong opponent of the Vietnam War, arguing against the Vietnam policies of Kennedy, Lyndon Johnson, and Richard Nixon. (*National Archives*)

of the Kennedy administration, Ball was appointed undersecretary of state with primary responsibility for European and international economic affairs.

Despite these official responsibilities, Ball emerged as the most perceptive in-house skeptic regarding U.S. involvement in Vietnam until his resignation from the Johnson administration in September 1966. Ball voiced this skepticism as early as November 1961. He warned President Kennedy against U.S. military involvement: "Within five years we'll have three hundred thousand men in the paddies and jungles." JFK's response: "George, you're just crazier than hell. That just isn't going to happen" (Bill 1997, 19).

Ball thereafter challenged all of Johnson and Rusk's fundamental assumptions regarding U.S. involvement in Vietnam. He rejected Rusk's assertion that membership in SEATO obligated the United States to protect South Vietnam. The undersecretary stressed that South Vietnam had not been an original signatory to the pact and that none of the other SEATO members had concluded that South Vietnam was the victim of armed aggression by a foreign country or shown any inclination to act collectively to protect the Saigon government. The United States had adopted a unilateral and legally unjustifiable position. Reflecting his European ties and emphases, Ball also questioned South Vietnam's strategic significance. Unlike Johnson and Rusk, he did not consider small, less developed countries on the periphery nearly so important to the United States as more highly developed industrial nations such as West Germany or Great Britain. Nor did Ball believe military intervention in Vietnam would enhance American credibility. To the contrary, the major U.S. allies in Europe feared that America had become mired in a losing struggle that threatened to divert attention from the more eminent Soviet threat. Moreover, Ball argued, "what [the United States] might gain by establishing the steadfastness of [its] commitments, [it] would lose by an erosion of confidence in [its] judgment." Nor would the United States win many friends internationally by conducting a massive "white attack upon Asian people" (DiLeo 1991, 67, 70, 72).

Ball's disagreement with Johnson and Rusk reached beyond what he deemed the flawed rationale for intervention. He also predicted correctly in 1964 and 1965 that U.S. power and technology would not yield a military victory. Repeatedly referring to the French failure to subdue Ho and his followers, Ball asserted that the North Vietnamese and Vietcong were motivated more by nationalism than communism and that the United States would be viewed as the Western, imperial successor to the French. Based on examination of World War II bombing, he foresaw that strategic bombing of North Vietnam would not dissuade the Democratic Republic of Vietnam from aiding the Vietcong or effectively impede the flow of men and materiel south. Ball succinctly summarized in July 1965 what proved to be the decisive difficulties for U.S. ground troops:

> No one had demonstrated that a white ground force of whatever size can win a guerrilla war—which is at the same time a civil war between Asians—in jungle terrain in the midst of a population that refuses cooperation to the white forces (and the South Vietnamese) and thus provides a great intelligence advantage to the other side (Herring 1993b, 123).

Finally, the undersecretary cited the crucial weakness of the South Vietnamese. South Vietnam, he contended, was a "country with an army and no government" (Bill 1997, 162). Although he could see no prospects of a military victory against a formidable foe in a hostile terrain, climate, and culture, Ball understood that even military success could not compensate for South Vietnam's "fragile political base," led by men he dismissed as "clowns" (Woods 2006, 597).

Despite Ball's perceptive and persistent criticism of the administration's Vietnam policies, he remained on good terms with both Johnson and Rusk. The undersecretary was always careful to present his arguments in a respectful fashion, and he never challenged his colleagues' good faith. Johnson admired Ball's hard work and competence and assured him, "Don't worry, George, I know you ain't no half-ass egghead." Even more than competence and dedication, Ball's refusal to publicize his views kept him in Johnson's good graces. Placing loyalty and ambition before the public's right to know, Ball publicly defended the very policies to which he objected so perceptively in private (Bill 1997, 75).

Johnson responded far more harshly to other critics of the war. When he railed against "some goddamn senator" misleading the public, LBJ unquestionably had J. William Fulbright and Albert Gore Sr. in mind (Woods 2006). No member of Congress aggravated the president more than Fulbright,

Portrait of J. William Fulbright, U.S. senator from Arkansas (1905–1995). (*Library of Congress*)

whom Johnson dismissed as a "narrow-minded egotist" (Gibbons 1995, 228) and a "crybaby" (Dallek 1998, 289).

James William ("Bill") Fulbright was the fourth of six children born into a prosperous Fayetteville, Arkansas, family. With a successful businessman father and a socially and politically adept mother, Fulbright's path to prominence was rather smooth—experimental grammar and secondary schools at the University of Arkansas, graduation from the university at age 19 after starring in football, a Rhodes Scholarship to Oxford, completion of a law degree at George Washington University with honors in 1935, appointment as president of the University of Arkansas in 1939 (at age 34), and election to Congress in 1941 and to the Senate in 1944.

From his first days in Washington, Fulbright concentrated on foreign affairs, initially as a member of the House Committee on Foreign Affairs and after 1948 from his position on the Senate Foreign Relations Committee (SFRC). A strong proponent of U.S. membership in the United Nations, he favored international cooperation aimed at securing peace and economic prosperity. The senator endorsed and supported containment, even though he worried that U.S. policies precluded his ideal of a cooperative form of world government. During the 1950s, Fulbright's prominence as a Democratic foreign policy spokesman led then Senate Majority Leader Lyndon Johnson to declare, "Bill's *my* Secretary of State." Although frequently mentioned as a possible head of the State Department under John Kennedy, the senator's opposition to civil rights legislation precluded his appointment. Instead, he remained in the Senate where he had become chairman of the SFRC in 1959 (Fry 2006, 9).

From this crucial position, Fulbright initially supported Johnson's Vietnam policies out of party loyalty, a sense of personal obligation, and general devotion to containment. Most conspicuously, in August 1964 he managed the Gulf of Tonkin Resolution's passage in the Senate. This resolution authorized the president to take "all necessary measures to repel any armed attacks against the forces of the United States and to prevent further aggression" in Vietnam. The senator subsequently concluded that Johnson had withheld crucial information regarding the alleged North Vietnamese attacks on U.S. destroyers and had misled him with assurances that no wider war was contemplated. Therefore, part of Fulbright's later opposition to the war resulted from a sense of personal betrayal and from a desire to recoup the congressional role in foreign affairs that this resolution and other such Cold War "blank checks" had forfeited to the president. "For God's sake," he later exclaimed to a reporter, "I assume that this still is a democracy, that the Senate has a role to play in foreign affairs." These motives coincided with Fulbright's tendency to "dissent for dissent's sake." Observers described him as a "loner," as "bookish and sometimes supercilious," and other senators often referred to him as the "professor," a title and posture he readily embraced even as they just as readily infuriated Johnson (Fry 2006, 9, 32).

Policy differences were far more important than personal or constitutional considerations as the Arkansas senator emerged as the most conspicuous congressional opponent of the war by the fall of 1965. Fulbright was most apprehensive that U.S. escalation of the war would trigger the "real

William Fulbright Confronts President Johnson

By the summer of 1967, 450,000 Americans were serving in Vietnam, and more than 13,000 U.S. soldiers had died in this remote country. Numerous American observers declared that this massive U.S. effort had produced only a stalemate, a standoff with no military victory in sight. The American public had become increasingly frustrated at the nation's failure to defeat its seemingly weaker foes, the Vietcong and the North Vietnamese; by August, polls revealed that for the first time a majority of Americans believed intervention in Vietnam had been a mistake.

Against this tense backdrop, President Johnson held what he expected to be a routine meeting with the chairmen of the U.S. Senate committees on July 27. The opening pleasantries had hardly begun when William Fulbright, chairman of the Senate Foreign Relations Committee, boldly stated, "Mr. President, what you really need to do is stop the war. That will solve all your problems." The Arkansas senator declared, "The Vietnam War is a hopeless venture." As the president, who had shunned Fulbright socially and criticized him harshly over the past year, grew visibly angry and sought to move on through a discussion of for-

eign aid, Fulbright doggedly persisted. "We need a new look," he asserted. "The effects of Vietnam are hurting the budget and foreign relations generally" (Barrett 1993, 2).

Demonstrating uncharacteristic restraint, the now furious Johnson replied, "Bill, everybody doesn't have a blind spot like you do. You say don't bomb North Vietnam on just about everything. I don't have the simple solution you have." After defending his Vietnam policies, LBJ directly challenged Fulbright and the other senators. If critics of the war wanted him "to get out of Vietnam," they needed only to repeal the Gulf of Tonkin Resolution that had provided Johnson the authority to "prevent . . . aggression" in Vietnam, and, in so doing, "tell the troops to come home" and inform the American military commander "that he doesn't know what he is doing" (Woods 1995, 457).

This unusually direct and bitter exchange between the president and the most important congressional critic of the war provides clear insight into the divisions among members of the containment generation over the Vietnam War and the passions those divisions engendered.

catastrophe" of a land war with China or even a "third World War." Neither U.S. security nor the preservation of credibility warranted such a risk. Fulbright rejected the Johnson-Rusk claims of a "clear-cut case of aggression by North Vietnamese communists." He argued instead that Ho and his followers were "indigenous Vietnamese nationalists" who had begun their resistance pursuing "liberation from French colonial rule." The struggle was a "civil war" in which the United States had mistakenly intervened. As the obvious "intruders . . . we represent the old Western imperialism" to the Vietnamese. After all, he asserted, "Vietnam is their country" (Fry 2006, 32, 70–71). Fulbright perceived no U.S. "vital interest" at stake; instead, he contended, in direct response to Rusk's concern for nations on the periphery, that it did "not matter very much who rules in . . . small and backward lands" such as Vietnam (Woods, 1995, 559). He was equally certain that as a major power the United States was "quite strong enough to engage in a compromise without losing its standing in the world and without losing its prestige as a great nation" (Fry 2006, 72).

The senator also challenged the national conviction that the United States was a uniquely innocent and benign nation. While acknowledging that the Vietcong were "a very cruel, ruthless, and mean people," who had "engaged in all kinds of terrorism," he did not believe the United States could "claim any great superiority" by virtue of possessing sophisticated weapons that killed people at long range. Americans were certainly not "bad people," but neither were they "the only good people" because of "using weapons that we happen to have, and others don't." Fulbright further charged that by attempting to "impose our will unilaterally" in Vietnam, the United States was acting "the way great empires have done it in the past" (Fry 2006, 61, 71). Indeed, the Johnson administration was undertaking the impossible task of practicing imperialism abroad while sustaining republicanism at home. The Arkansan feared that "we are in grave danger of becoming a Sparta bent on policing the world" (Woods 2003, 161).

Albert Gore Sr., Fulbright's fellow member of the SFRC, provided an additional antiwar voice. Gore was born in 1907 into a farming family in central Tennessee near the village of Possum Hollow. After attending a one-room school, graduating from high school in 1925, and completing a teacher certification course, he alternately taught school and took courses at the University of Tennessee and Middle Tennessee State College. After a time of unemployment and work as a traveling salesman, he earned a law degree at the Nashville YMCA in 1935. An ardent New Deal Democrat, Gore

Albert Gore Sr. was U.S. senator from Tennessee from 1952 to 1971. (*Library of Congress*)

was elected to Congress in 1938 after more than a decade of active partici-pation in local and state politics. As a congressman and, after 1952, a U.S. senator, he favored an activist federal government and programs such as the Tennessee Valley Authority, the interstate highway system, federal funding for education and health care, and especially tax relief for the lower and middle classes. Gore backed Franklin Roosevelt's preparedness policies and aid to Great Britain before World War II, and he readily endorsed U.S. con-tainment policies after the war. Therefore, he came to the Vietnam issue from much the same liberal, internationalist perspective as Johnson and Rusk. However, by the early 1960s, the Tennessee Democrat had begun to voice privately the reservations he would make quite public by 1964.

Gore's opposition to U.S. intervention in Vietnam had its genesis in a 1959 trip to South Vietnam soon after he became a member of the SFRC. He returned convinced that U.S. support for South Vietnamese president Diem was misguided. Gore recognized correctly that Diem was not promoting democracy in South Vietnam, and the senator's criticism of Diem's dictatorial practices was part of a more general objection to U.S. backing of authoritar-ian regimes simply because they were noncommunist. This practice contra-dicted the professed U.S. goal of promoting freedom internationally.

As the U.S. role in Vietnam steadily escalated under President Kennedy, Gore broadened his critique but continued to do so privately with members of the administration or in closed SFRC hearings. Like Ball and Fulbright, he cited the French experience as an ominous forecast of future U.S. problems and expressed doubt that American technology and military power would prove decisive. The senator also agreed with Ball and Fulbright that the con-flict was far more complex than a simple Cold War confrontation with com-munism and that it would be "a great mistake for the United States . . . to pick up the chips of the disintegrating French colonial empire" (Hodges 1997, 136). Gore similarly disputed Vietnam's strategic importance. In late 1963, he told Secretary of Defense Robert S. McNamara, "I know of no strategic material that it [Vietnam] has. I know of nothing in surplus supply there except poor people and rice," neither of which the United States needed. A year later, Gore called publicly for a negotiated end to the war and thereafter openly repeated these objections, much to Johnson's conster-nation (Longley 2003, 209).

Consistent with his doubts about Vietnam's strategic importance, Gore charged that the war was preventing the United States from concentrating on far more important foreign policy issues, especially "cooperation with the two other major powers upon which the future of world peace depends—the Soviet Union and China." Protesting that Johnson suffered from an "Alamo complex in a nuclear age," Gore feared that U.S. bombing along the Chinese border in North Vietnam could be the "torch to the tinder box of World War III" (Hodges 1997, 142).

Gore's personal relations with President Johnson and, even more important, his domestic policy priorities solidified his opposition to U.S. involvement in Vietnam. Johnson and Gore had never been close person-ally, especially after Johnson became the Democratic leader in the Senate in 1954. LBJ, who sought to dominate every personal interaction, frequently remarked, "I want people around me who would kiss my ass on a hot summer's day and say it smells like roses" (Dallek 1998, 160). Gore, who was aptly described as a political "loner, a man not to be controlled," refused to assume such a posture. Gore was never a member of the Senate club, Gore's maverick instincts and not so "mysterious capacity" for aggravating Johnson reinforced his inclination to oppose the war. As one friend observed, "Show Albert the grain, so that he can go against it" (Longley 2003, 228, 231).

Finally, Gore protested that the war diverted attention and scarce funds from pressing domestic needs. For example, he noted that fiscal year 1966 war spending ran to nearly 50 percent of the reported $37 million in "unmet local, state and community [infrastructure] needs," such as hospitals, schools, and sewage systems. He also objected to increased taxes and higher interest rates, which he attributed to the war and considered disproportionately burdensome for the lower and middle classes. Thus, Gore, like Johnson, carefully calculated the war's domestic impact, but the Tennessee senator arrived at a contrary foreign policy conclusion (Fry 2006, 33).

Conclusion: Divisions within the Containment Generation

Gore and Johnson's disagreements embodied the divisions within the containment generation and personified those policy makers who did and did not surmount the American Cold War mentality in assessing the Vietnam War. President Johnson and Secretary of State Rusk perceived the Vietnam conflict as a clear case of outside aggression by the North Vietnamese that demanded a strong response rather than any form of compromise. Both acted on the assumption that an American loss would imperil U.S. credibility and trigger falling dominoes in Southeast Asia and beyond. Johnson also feared for his personal political credibility and the impact of a communist victory on the Great Society. Rusk, in turn, had no doubt that an American failure to enforce its SEATO obligations would fatally compromise collective security and endanger world peace. Ironically, both men's belief in America's benign influence abroad and duty to extend U.S. institutions to a grateful world reinforced these strategic calculations. Moreover, both had great faith in American technology and military power and could not conceive of losing to a far weaker and smaller adversary.

Once committed, Johnson, who personalized the war, could not bring himself to admit mistakes or to risk being the first U.S. president to lose a war. Always the good "company man," the secretary vowed never to differ publicly with the president. Finally, as the officials ultimately in charge of U.S. foreign policy, and therefore ultimately responsible for the domestic and international repercussions of an American defeat, Johnson and Rusk faced far greater emotional and intellectual obstacles to moving beyond the nation's majority views on containment and its application in Vietnam.

By contrast, Ball, Fulbright, and Gore could explore alternative ways of thinking about the war unencumbered by such ultimate responsibility. All three were personally inclined to be mavericks and to break with majority opinion: Ball because of his "imperious faith in his own abilities"; Fulbright because he also possessed no small opinion of his own intellectual abilities and, together with Gore, had a long habit of dissent and independent behavior in the Senate. The latter two's ambivalent personal relationship with Johnson also helped prompt their break with the administration. Fiercely independent, neither was comfortable with LBJ's relentless efforts at personal domination and manipulation. In addition to being the most intellectual of these five policy makers, Ball and Fulbright were the most cosmopolitan, which undoubtedly helped lead them to dispute their generation's thinking about containment and Vietnam. Nevertheless, such explanations have their limits. Gore, from Possum Hollow and with a YMCA law degree and proclivity for playing his fiddle on the campaign trail, adopted most of the same antiwar positions by starting from a more narrowly American position—the war's terrible impact on lower- and middle-class Americans.

Less restrained by their political positions, personally inclined toward independent thinking, and armed with their individual talents and motivations, these three dissenters mounted a devastating critique of the Johnson administration's handling of the war in Vietnam. All three questioned the core assumption of North Vietnamese aggression at the behest of the Soviet Union and China. They emphasized instead that Ho Chi Minh and his followers throughout Vietnam had opposed outside, imperial control since early in the 20th century—that they were motivated primarily by nationalism. The United States had stumbled into what was primarily a civil war among the Vietnamese, who viewed the United States as the latest imperial oppressor. Assessed from this perspective, U.S. Cold War credibility was hardly at stake; and even if it were, America's status as a great power would be little diminished by a compromise settlement that failed to preserve a noncommunist South Vietnam. These opponents of the war also questioned Vietnam's strategic importance and argued that the United States would lose nothing of substance by failing to enforce containment in this small, poor country. For Ball and Fulbright, this strategic assessment was reinforced by their lack of enthusiasm for nation building and lack of confidence in spreading American institutions abroad. Quite simply, they did not share Johnson and Rusk's more traditional American belief that other countries and cultures were eager to adopt American ways. Gore agreed and pointed especially at the contradictory nature of supporting authoritarian rulers as a tactic for preserving freedom against a communist assault. In the corollary to their minimizing the importance of the small, poor nation of Vietnam, all three of these antiwar policy makers stressed the far greater significance of avoiding war with the Soviets and Chinese.

These dissenters further challenged the majority American belief that its power and technology would win the war. Ball drew on his keen understanding of World War II bombing to predict that U.S. technology would not be decisive. Fulbright and Gore joined Ball in citing the French experience and highlighting the difficulty of fighting a guerrilla war in a jungle terrain among a hostile population. Declaring that as a southerner he understood the Vietnamese resistance to attempts at outside control in ways most Americans did not, Fulbright contended that U.S. efforts to impose its will on Vietnam would falter in the face of Vietnamese nationalist resistance.

Ball and Gore cited the corruption and incoherence of South Vietnamese culture and polity as another formidable obstacle to U.S. success. In short, all three accentuated the limits of American power in ways that conflicted with majority opinion among the leaders of the containment generation. Fulbright strayed even further from the Cold War consensus by challenging the American sense of uniqueness and superiority by declaring that U.S. attempts to impose its will abroad differed little from previous imperial powers, and that the use of technologically sophisticated weapons did not make the nation morally superior to those employing cruder methods.

Unfortunately, Ball, Fulbright, and Gore failed to convert either LBJ and Rusk or the American public to their antiwar positions during the Johnson presidency. Only in the wake of the U.S. loss in Vietnam did their arguments have great influence on U.S. policy makers. Sadly, that influence was only temporary. By the late 1990s, the nation had regained much of its traditional sense of uniqueness, innocence, and superiority, and a new generation of leaders, seemingly oblivious to the debate over policy in Vietnam, led the nation in another ill-advised intervention into an ostensibly weaker nation. Once again, issues of containment; presidential and national credibility; falling dominoes; guerrilla tactics; weak allies; nation building; illusive, fanatical foes, and exit strategies dominate the discussion of American foreign policy.

References and Further Reading

Baritz, Loren. *Backfire: A History of How American Culture Led Us into Vietnam and Made Us Fight the Way We Did.* New York: William Morrow, 1985.

Barrett, David. *Uncertain Warriors: Lyndon Johnson and His Vietnam Advisors.* Lawrence: University Press of Kansas, 1993.

Bill, James. *George Ball: Behind the Scenes in U.S. Foreign Policy.* New Haven, CT: Yale University Press, 1997.

Dallek, Robert. *Flawed Giant: Lyndon Johnson and His Times, 1961–1973.* New York: Oxford University Press, 1998.

DiLeo, David. *George Ball, Vietnam, and the Rethinking of Containment.* Chapel Hill: University of North Carolina Press, 1991.

Fry, Joseph A. *Debating Vietnam: Fulbright, Stennis, and Their Senate Hearings.* Lanham, MD: Rowman & Littlefield, 2006.

Gaddis, John Lewis. *Strategies of Containment: A Critical Appraisal of American National Security Policy during the Cold War.* Rev. ed. New York: Oxford University Press, 2005.

Gibbons, William Conrad. *The U.S. Government and the Vietnam War: Executive and Legislative Roles and Relationships.* Vol. 4. Princeton, NJ: Princeton University Press, 1995.

Goldman, Eric. *The Tragedy of Lyndon Johnson.* New York: Dell, 1969.

Goodwin, Doris Kearns. *Lyndon Johnson and the American Dream.* New York: St. Martin's Press, 1991.

Herring, George. *America's Longest War: The United States and Vietnam, 1950–1975.* 4th ed. New York: McGraw Hill, 2002.

Herring, George. *LBJ and Vietnam: A Different Kind of War.* Austin: University of Texas Press, 1994.

Herring, George. "The Reluctant Warrior: Lyndon Johnson as Commander in Chief." In *Shadow on the White House: Presidents and the Vietnam War, 1945–1975,* edited by David Anderson, 87–112. Lawrence: University of Kansas Press, 1993a.

Herring, George, ed. *The Pentagon Papers: Abridged Edition.* New York: McGraw Hill, 1993b.

Hodges, Robert. "The Cooing of a Dove: Senator Albert Gore Sr.'s Opposition to the War in Vietnam." *Peace and Change* 22 (April 1997): 132–153.

Hunt, Michael. *Lyndon Johnson's War: America's Cold War Crusade in Vietnam, 1945–1968.* New York: Hill and Wang, 1996.

Kennan, George. *American Diplomacy.* Chicago: University of Chicago Press, 1984.

Leffler, Melvyn. *The Specter of Communism: The United States and the Origins of the Cold War, 1917–1953.* New York: Hill and Wang, 1994.

Leffler, Melvyn. *A Preponderance of Power: National Security, the Truman Administration, and the Cold War.* Stanford, CA: Stanford University Press, 1992.

Logevall, Fredrik. *Choosing War: The Lost Chance for Peace and the Escalation of War in Vietnam.* Berkeley: University of California Press, 1999.

Longley, Kyle. "The Reluctant 'Volunteer': The Origins of Senator Albert A. Gore's Opposition to the Vietnam War." In *Vietnam and the American Political Tradition: The Politics of Dissent,* edited by Randall Woods, 204–236. New York: Cambridge University Press, 2003.

McMahon, Robert, ed. *Major Problems in the History of the Vietnam War.* 2nd ed. Lexington, MA: D.C. Heath, 1995.

Rusk, Dean, as told to Richard Rusk. *As I Saw It.* New York: Norton, 1990.

Schoenbaum, Thomas. *Waging Peace and War: Dean Rusk in the Truman, Kennedy, and Johnson Years.* New York: Simon and Schuster, 1988.

Sherry, Michael. *In the Shadow of War: The United States since the 1930s.* New Haven, CT: Yale University Press, 1995.

Woods, Randall. *LBJ: Architect of American Ambition.* New York: Free Press, 2006.

Woods, Randall. "Dixie's Dove: J. William Fulbright, the Vietnam War and the American South." In *Vietnam and the American Political Tradition: The Politics of Dissent,* edited by Randall Woods, 149–170. New York: Cambridge University Press, 2003.

Woods, Randall. *Fulbright: A Biography.* New York: Cambridge University Press, 1995.

Zeiler, Thomas. *Dean Rusk: Defending the American Mission Abroad.* Wilmington, DE: SR Books, 2000.

"The Needs Are Enormous, the Time Short": American Advisers and the Invention of South Vietnam, 1954–1960

James M. Carter

2

Commenting on the U.S. nation-building project in Vietnam in the 1960s, American adviser Frank C. Child wrote that southern Vietnam was in its "eleventh hour." The efforts to build democracy and promote economic development floundered. Meanwhile, southern Vietnam had become "a police state." Corruption, waste, incompetence, favoritism, and zealous and reaching government controls all plagued the project. All the effort to construct a new, modern, democratic state below the 17th parallel in Vietnam had instead brought this: "the shortcoming of [the] regime is not that it is undemocratic," Child (1961) wrote, "it is that it is a failure. It has neither of the two saving graces of an 'acceptable' dictatorship: it is neither benevolent nor efficient" (14). During the Vietnam War, similar criticism became commonplace. What is surprising and instructive about this critique is that it came when it did.

Years before U.S. policy in Vietnam expanded into wide-scale warfare and captured the attention of the nation, many advisers closest to the project already anticipated tragedy. Political science professor Wesley Fishel headed the Michigan State University Vietnam Advisory Group (MSUG), charged in 1954 with building the new state of South Vietnam. The United States entrusted President Ngo Dinh Diem to lead this new state, but advisers held few illusions regarding the magnitude of the task at hand. Shortly after arriving in Saigon, Fishel wrote with alarm, "I've never seen a situation like this. It defies imagination. . . . The government is shaky as all hell. It is being propped up for the moment only with great difficulty. Nothing can help it so much as administrative, economic, and social reforms. . . . The needs are enormous, the time short" (Carter 2008, 56). By the time Frank Child returned home in 1961, the United States had already spent around $2 billion in Vietnam. Child, a Stanford University economics professor, worked with the MSUG in Vietnam for two years. The experience left him pessimistic, as he concluded, "it has become clear that Diem can only post-pone defeat—he cannot win" (Child 1961, 14–16). Although American architects of the enormous war that followed were loath to admit failure, their colleagues responsible for building the new state in southern Vietnam in these early years had already conceded the point.

During 1954–1960, American advisers to Vietnam accepted the challenge of nation building, believing the United States was uniquely positioned to stem the expansion of communism and provide the model for national development in former colonies then moving toward independence. In the process, they faced the many inherent contradictions and obstacles in U.S. Cold War policy toward the Third World. As their efforts floundered in the face of these contradictions and mounting native resistance, they slowly alloyed their optimism with growing realism, skepticism, cynicism, and frustration, well before those sentiments became commonplace in the American media and in Washington in the 1960s.

Building "South Vietnam": The USOM and MSUG

After only a short time in Vietnam, Wesley Fishel enjoyed considerable support from and influence on Ngo Dinh Diem, and he eagerly assumed the role of presidential adviser. The relationship between Saigon leaders and Michigan State University (MSU) solidified quickly, and by spring 1955, Fishel and a number of other MSU specialists were working closely with a few Vietnamese to provide assistance in public administration, police and security, finance, and economics. Despite a near total lack of governmental

Wesley Fishel, head of the Vietnam Project at Michigan State University, with Ngo Dinh Diem. (*Michigan State University*)

infrastructure and the admittedly narrow base of support for Diem, American advisers remained optimistic that they could build a state around his leadership. They had their work cut out for them.

In 1954 all of Vietnam suffered from years of war, neglect, dislocation, and political chaos. In addition to political difficulties, the physical infrastructure and economy of southern Vietnam remained undeveloped, damaged, or abandoned. The political division of the country at the 17th parallel further aggravated the situation. While various military and governmental officials worked out the transition from French to American influence, Saigon became a veritable laboratory for development initiatives.

Wesley Fishel was uniquely positioned to influence events because of his personal relationship with Ngo Dinh Diem. Edward Weidner, chief adviser of the MSUG, recognized Fishel's importance to the program when he arrived in Vietnam in early October 1954. Cabling MSU president John Hannah, Weidner explained that "the situation here is extremely serious" and that according to the "highest authority . . . Professor Wesley R. Fishel is quite essential to American policy as long as Diem stays in power" (Carter 2008, 58). Fishel seemed to be especially proud of his relationship with a foreign head of state, writing to Weidner a couple of weeks earlier, "I go in and out of the palace so often these days I'm treated as one of his [Diem's] staff by the guards. Yesterday I was there for 15 hours, and on Saturday for 19 hours. Today is abnormal . . . I've not been in the place for five whole hours now" (Carter 2008, 58).

A team of university specialists spent that fall pasting together a political regime in Saigon. In addition to Fishel, this mission included MSU political scientist Edward Weidner, Arthur Brandstatter as a specialist on police administration, James Denison as a public relations specialist, and economics professor Charles Killingsworth. Of the group, only Fishel was considered an Asia expert. The rest read what they could at MSU and en route to Vietnam. The team conducted a brief two-week survey and pieced together an aid program based on its findings. The report, submitted in October, recommended emergency measures in public administration, police administration, and efforts to shore up the economy. With the aid of Fishel and MSU faculty, Diem and other Saigon leaders initiated a crash program to install a political structure that could ensure control over and development of the southern half of Vietnam.

In 1954–1955, Diem survived a number of serious challenges to his position. In spring 1955, he surprised his critics by effectively routing his political rivals with a show of force in the so-called Battle of Saigon. In doing so, he also provided a justification for continued U.S. support. The MSUG began its work in the immediate aftermath of that apparent triumph. To survive the Geneva-mandated national elections of 1956, the MSUG, the military, and others involved rapidly built a government infrastructure and aggressively promoted Diem to stabilize, popularize, and legitimize his rule.

The MSUG found the existing police system lacking proper authority, organization, trained personnel, buildings, and equipment. In July, Howard Hoyt recommended to Brandstatter that the MSU program scrap "everything else," such as the *Gendarmerie*, Sureté, "and all other various enforcement

Wesley Fishel

An otherwise obscure political science professor from Michigan State University, Wesley R. Fishel embodied many of the contradictions of U.S. Cold War foreign policy. He enthusiastically embraced the opportunity to transform southern Vietnam through nation building and at the same time approved strong-arm tactics for putting down the native resistance that the imposition of nation building brought about. As he played his part in building the new state in southern Vietnam, he was also uniquely positioned to set the kind of example so full of lessons for his era.

Only weeks after the French military defeat in May 1954, the United States embarked on an ambitious project in southern Vietnam, and Wesley Fishel was on the ground in Saigon offering advice and council to Ngo Dinh Diem, whom he had befriended in 1950 while in Japan. He and the others of the MSU team spent the next seven years diligently building, advising, cajoling, and nurturing the regime in Saigon. Along the way, Fishel remained more committed than most to the project even as developments took unforeseen and unwanted directions. Diem was an austere, contemplative, and personally sensitive leader who increasingly used force to quell opposition to his policies. As resistance mounted, Diem required larger amounts of military aid to protect his hold on power. Within a few short years, he presided over a growing police state and ruled it as a despot.

As Diem's American critics grew in number and outspokenness, Fishel steadfastly supported his friend. Publicly lauding developments in Vietnam while privately cajoling Diem to reform his regime, Fishel spent years attempting to reconcile what he had imagined for southern Vietnam and what was actually happening. Growing weary of mounting criticism, Diem allowed the MSU contract to expire in 1962, effectively firing the team and his friend Fishel. The following year, the administration of John F. Kennedy approved Diem's removal by Vietnamese generals, and Diem was subsequently murdered. Major escalation and war soon followed.

By the end of the decade, Fishel the professor had become controversial for his role in Diem's despotism and the subsequent chaos and war in Vietnam. Students regularly protested outside his classes. Some enrolled and stood silently during class holding "Vietcong" flags. Others held mock trials finding him guilty and hung "Wanted" posters of him around campus. For his part, Fishel eventually became an ardent critic of the American-sponsored regime and the massive war that followed. In a 1971 *New York Times* editorial, Fishel wrote, "The U.S. has sanctified in power a polished and ruthless military Machiavellian, heading a one-party military regime, authoritarian, institutionalized in its corruption, and lacking support among the people." Developments in the last few years of U.S. involvement in Vietnam made the former nation builder nostalgic for a return to the earlier years.

agencies." He believed they were all "going around in circles, stepping on one another's toes," and that the MSUG "should at least set the example" of how a police system ought to work (Carter 2008, 66).

The security apparatus needed far more than a fresh coat of paint. Chief adviser Weidner worried "about the future of democracy in Vietnam" because of the degree of insecurity and the inability of Saigon's leadership to address the problems (Carter 2008, 66). Reorganizing, training, and equipping a police force occupied much of MSUG's energy over the course of the next couple of years. Advisers almost completely rebuilt the police structure, updating equipment; importing modern fingerprinting methods; providing training in various police tactics and weaponry; and funding the construction of facilities such as vehicle garages, barracks, interrogation centers, detention centers, and crime laboratories. In 1956, MSUG further centralized the system by moving the Vietnamese Bureau of Investigation (VBI) to Saigon, where it received much of the police program's attention and funding and became a showpiece for the project.

At the same time, the various American groups held different priorities for nation building in Vietnam. Diem took advantage of the newly crafted police system to eliminate his political opposition through harassment and intimidation, and by imprisoning more than 20,000 by 1956. MSUG advisers criticized the increasing militarization of the civil police forces, the Civil Guard, but the regime ignored their advice and channeled equipment to favored units. Police engagement in combat operations and complaints of police brutality from ordinary Vietnamese mounted. Finally, in 1957, the MSUG cut off further funding for the Civil Guard. The United States Operations Mission (USOM) quickly filled the gap. With Washington's approval, the latter restored funding and the militarization of the regime's police system proceeded. This incident highlights the growing differences over the proper course of state building in Vietnam.

Besides the police project, the MSUG also spent considerable effort and resources on public administration. The program involved providing training in comparative administration, fiscal and budgetary problems, political science, public administration, comparative governments, and management of private enterprise. An additional facet of the program involved foreign training in such places as the Philippines, Malaya, Hong Kong, and particularly the United States. Additionally, around 325 foreign-educated Vietnamese returned to Vietnam after Diem ascended to power and filled positions in the civil service. As one MSUG member pointed out, however, the main "external source of trained civil servants is the study programs financed by the American government" (Scigliano 1963, 64–65).

Officially known as the Participant Program, MSUG and USOM sought out exceptional Vietnamese students to continue their education in the United States before, hopefully, returning to government service in Vietnam. Diem also prompted the MSUG to seek out Vietnamese students already in the United States to provide instruction at the National Institute of Administration (NIA) in Saigon, which trained people for careers in government. Adviser Stanley Sheinbaum described it as "primarily a technical assistance program not a cultural exchange" (Carter 2008, 71). Estimates of the number of participants vary greatly. Through 1961, the MSUG sponsored 179 Vietnamese and the USOM sponsored 1,705 more, most of them trained in the United States. According to MSUG adviser Robert Scigliano (1963), however, these numbers are only a fraction of the actual number of Vietnamese trained in the United States during the period. In any event, the NIA facilities in Vietnam trained a large number of students, enrolling between 200 and 300 per term (and about 500 per term in the evening school) and training thousands more through an in-service program.

Some MSUG members viewed the training project in Vietnam as only marginally successful. Advisers and instructors grew frustrated over the

Vietnamese reluctance to establish a school based on the American system. Some Vietnamese, for example, relied on the old French system that emphasized lecture and limited classroom interaction. MSUG personnel later complained that, while understandable, Vietnamese were "unwilling to sit in on classes taught by MSUG professors, and almost equally reluctant to offer courses jointly with them" (Ernst 1998, 51). The problems extended to more than just matters of style. There were also obvious cultural differences aggravated by language barriers. Furthermore, as in a number of other instances, the Diem regime insisted on very close scrutiny of the program and of potential candidates. Diem, either personally or through a designee, demanded ultimate oversight, creating a bureaucratic logjam and increasing the time required to fund, approve travel, train personnel, and fill positions in the government. Further, as Robert Scigliano (1963) later noted, the system was handicapped "by the government's insistence upon furnishing it with weak leadership, using its faculty positions as a convenient dumping place for civil servants not wanted elsewhere." Consequently, the NIA did not "enjoy a high reputation among high government officials and intellectuals generally" (65).

Despite the difficulties, the institute ultimately trained tens of thousands of people in conjunction with the in-service, participant, and other types of formal training. Over the course of the multiple programs inaugurated from 1955 until 1957, American aid projects created enough of a government to be relatively sanguine in progress reports. The Police Administration continued to train tens of thousands of new police, from VBI agents to municipal officers, despite MSU's suspending aid to the Civil Guard in 1957. Overall, personnel on the MSUG staff increased to a high of 182, excluding those employed directly by USOM (Carter 2008). Indeed, the program expanded considerably and events, despite occasional setbacks, seemed to justify increased effort.

By 1957, some of the more serious obstacles seemed less formidable. The October 1955 referendum effectively removed Bao Dai from power. Diem seated his National Assembly early the following spring with pomp and circumstance and little substance. Diem approved or handpicked 90 of the 123 members to ensure passage of a constitution drafted by him and his coterie of advisers (Anderson 1991). With the support of the United States, Diem was building all the accoutrements of a democratic government while retaining ultimate control. The date for the Geneva-mandated national unification elections came and went during 1956. Neither the United States nor Diem planned to comply with free elections that the communists would almost surely win.

By 1957, the American country team assured itself that the "newly created nation would survive successfully the series of crises which threatened its existence at the outset" (Carter 2008, 85). Beginning the following year, the aid mission, in conjunction with the Saigon regime, pursued a number of long-term projects. Most American advisers now assumed that the period of emergency had passed and that economic development and the creation of a modern national infrastructure would occupy the lion's share of their energies into the later years of the decade.

In addition to police and public administration training, the USOM oversaw substantial development aid to southern Vietnam for projects in a number of other fields. The USOM awarded lucrative contracts to numerous private firms to facilitate internal economic growth and build the necessary basic infrastructure in Vietnam. Director Arthur Gardiner told a Senate investigative committee in 1959, "You would be astonished . . . at the amount of business that has gone on in Vietnam under that [aid] program without any interference by the diplomats or the bureaucrats." His agency released $7.4 million to finance road and bridge construction in 1959 (Carter 2008, 89).

American firms Capitol Engineering and Johnson, Drake and Piper built a system of roadways stretching across southern Vietnam. National Route 21, completed in 1960 at a cost of $14 million, linked Ninh Hoa along the coast to Ban Me Thuot further inland and became the largest aid project since the resettlement of Catholic refugees during 1954–1955. Barely a road at all as late as 1957, the artery now boasted two well-surfaced lanes, built according to modern standards, that provided year-round access. The road dramatically reduced transportation costs and "greatly increased the exchange of commodities." The Saigon–Bien Hoa Highway consisted of nearly 20 miles of roadway, two major bridges (the two longest ever built in Vietnam), six intermediate bridges, drainage systems, and erosion and traffic controls. Surfaced in asphaltic concrete and more than 52 feet wide, complete with stable shoulders for heavy military traffic and built through swamp conditions, this road showcased the technological and individual hubris of the American mission. For these and other road projects, the American mission provided $18 million worth of tractors, power shovels, maintenance equipment, and spare parts. USOM trained thousands of Vietnamese for these jobs and contractors furnished technical manuals for the trainees (Carter 2008, 90).

To industrialize the country and integrate it into a market economy, in late 1957, the U.S. aid mission and the Saigon leadership established the Industrial Development Center (IDC). Southern Vietnam possessed only small-scale industrial concerns such as cigarette making, rice milling, small ship building, some sugar refining, and cottage industry textile manufacturing. The USOM saw possibilities in developing coal, limestone, iron, and gold and copper mines and in constructing hydroelectric dams in central Vietnam. Although resources turned out to be less abundant than initially hoped, advisers believed the economy had to diversify to survive a volatile world market. Relying on rice production and limited coal production left southern Vietnam vulnerable. The IDC fostered industrial diversity through financial and technical assistance, offering loans to would-be entrepreneurs. The Commodity Import Program (CIP) also financed imported capital goods for industrial projects, such as heavy equipment and machinery. The project oversaw the launch of a variety of businesses in industries ranging from textiles, ceramics, and soap to tobacco, pencils, and dinnerware.

Though initially ambitious, the IDC began with a number of entrenched and stubborn handicaps. The idea behind the scheme was, of course, to foster business and industrial growth, create an internal source of wealth, and wean the client from American aid. To increase private-sector industrial production would, in the eyes of American planners, encourage foreign and private investment and private ownership. Diem and his brother Nhu, however, emphasized government ownership of business enterprise. As Nhu explained to the American ambassador, he wanted to pursue a "third way" between the heavy state planning of communism and capitalism's emphasis on private ownership and market forces. A "mixed" economy of some government-owned enterprise and private ownership solved the lack of expertise, managerial skill, and risk capital because the government provided initial financing for capital ventures. Ultimately, as Nhu and Diem both pointed out, private concerns would take over these business enterprises.

From the outset, Saigon and the U.S. advisory mission clashed over these differences. Ironically, the compromise hammered out to begin the IDC undermined the program. The agreement kept American aid available to government firms, while making counterpart financing available to would-be importers. Through the CIP, the United States would use imports to make capital available to the regime, promote economic growth, and stymie inflationary pressures. Because commodity imports were entirely subsidized by the U.S. aid program, importers reaped enormous profits before any real exchange of commodity, thus discouraging manufacturing. Because the exchange rate alone guaranteed profit, and Diem tightly controlled access to funding, private foreign investment remained limited. Only 4 of the more than 100 loan applications received by the spring of 1959 received any assistance. Consequently, the IDC effectively became "a holding company for government enterprises," and the flow of American aid provided safe and certain profit to a business class eager to take the path of least resistance (Trued 1960, 258–261).

Industry remained a minor part of the overall economy. Although industrial enterprises such as coal, sugar, textiles, and glass expanded and were nurtured along by the regime, the industrial sector never approached the level necessary to reverse the constant trade imbalance. Imports fluctuated from $232 million in 1958 to $225 million in 1959 and back to $240.3 million in 1960, and imports continued to outstrip exports. Exports for the same years were $55.2 million, $75 million, and $84.5 million. From 1960 until 1972, in fact, the largest growth sector for the economy was government, which grew 10.6 percent. In contrast, agriculture grew by only 0.6 percent (Carter 2008).

Rice and rubber remained mainstays of the export economy, accounting for 80 to 90 percent of all exports through the 1950s and into the 1960s. Even these products, however, fell short of requirements based on population growth. Other crops, such as sweet potatoes, sugarcane, peanuts, and corn, steadily expanded, although they never contributed significantly to the trade imbalance (Fall 1967). The aid program nurtured greater dependency rather than modernization and eventual independence for the new state.

Vietnam had long been primarily an agricultural nation. Four-fifths of southern Vietnam's labor force worked in agriculture, and of a population of 13 million, 11 million lived in the rural environment. No more than an estimated 20 percent of American aid ever reached the countryside in a way that was recognizable to the people (Scigliano 1963). Southern Vietnam could not be effectively modernized and developed into a sovereign state if the vast majority of the people remained isolated in their villages and hamlets.

The aid mission envisioned transforming the Vietnamese agricultural economy by discarding "out-moded traditional production methods" and creating a "self-reliant nation of high proficiency" by implementing the most modern farming techniques and technology from the West. Soil analysis could determine the most efficient crops, while fertilizers and pesticides would reduce parasite damage. Introducing new varieties of fruits and vegetables, such as okra, eggplant, peppers, dry onions, potatoes, and garlic, would further diversify Vietnam's economy, and improved strains of sugarcane would replace and revitalize that crop. Individual farmers needed to become more efficient and the yield per hectare dramatically increased (Carter 2008, 93–94). With increased production Vietnam could boost exports of various commodities and ultimately become self-sufficient. Improved infrastructure, including roads and bridges, would provide farmers with an expanded market. The whole process would make peasants both more self-interested and interested in maintaining the new production system as their livelihood now depended on it. Furthermore, failure to reach out to the countryside threatened not only to fatally delay the ultimate goal of expanding agricultural production, but it also threatened the continued existence of the regime in Saigon.

For this reason, Diem continued to channel American aid to the countryside not only for road and bridge construction, but also for an increased military presence that harassed and jailed thousands of people and waged a propaganda campaign against his growing opposition. A number of officials believed Diem paid insufficient attention to industrialization or agriculture. As the situation in the countryside deteriorated during the late 1950s, economic development became less urgent. That deterioration created significant fissures within the American country team and between it and Saigon officials. By 1959, divisions over the proper use of American aid reached a critical juncture when key events drew a level of public attention and scrutiny not seen since 1954.

Nation Building and the Politics of Foreign Aid

As more policy makers, journalists, military figures, and advisers questioned the efficacy and use of aid monies, the added attention exposed numerous problems. Some leveled accusations of outright corruption; others charged enormous waste and inefficiency. Part of the problem stemmed from the inability of officials to identify substantive results. Many could quote specific numbers for railroad track mileage, roadways rebuilt, canals dredged, and police and military personnel trained, but reports on South Vietnam's self-sufficiency were less than glowing and riddled with inconsistencies and ambiguities. These problems came to light in a series of 1959 investigative articles written by Albert Colegrove for the Scripps-Howard newspapers.

Colegrove found evidence that substantially supported this negative view of American aid to Vietnam. He spent nearly three weeks in Vietnam turning up numerous examples of waste, mismanagement, favoritism, fraud, and widespread disinterest in the dispersal of American funding. Published under the title, "Our Hidden Scandal in Vietnam," the articles appeared in more than 15 newspapers with a nationwide audience of over 2.6 million. Colegrove charged the aid mission with losing 2,700 vehicles, failing to account for $34 million given to the Saigon regime, paying for more than a dozen nonexistent radio towers, subsidizing lavish living standards for Americans in country who never left the confines of Saigon, and losing $8 million in a 1955 fire, among others (Montgomery 1962, Appendix III). Not surprisingly, the articles caused a sensation in the media, and Congress quickly convened hearings to investigate the aid mission to Vietnam.

The U.S. mission immediately condemned Colegrove and the Scripps-Howard newspapers. USOM director Arthur Z. Gardiner testified to Congress that the claims were completely erroneous. Similar testimony came from Assistant Secretary of State for Far Eastern Affairs J. Graham Parsons, Ambassador Elbridge Durbrow, the Military Assistance and Advisory Group (MAAG) chief Lt. Gen. Samuel T. Williams, and others. Williams denied any record of the 2,700 vehicles mentioned; Durbrow claimed there was no cost-of-living allowance that provided "luxury" for the American mission; and Gardiner assured investigators there were no missing radio towers. Colegrove himself took the witness chair and maintained his ground, even offering to provide additional witnesses if needed (Carter 2008). The hastily convened hearings ended in a stalemate. No conclusive evidence emerged that the program was quite as corrupt as the articles had portrayed. Nor did officials manage to dispel suspicion of a broken aid program.

Diem's American advocates rallied and quickly scuttled the Colegrove exposé. The American Friends of Vietnam publicly denounced the reporting as "grist for the Communist propaganda mill." The organization's chairman, Gen. John "Iron Mike" O'Daniel, called Colegrove's effort "a disgraceful example," even "yellow journalism" larded with "misinformation" and "plain unvarnished sidewalk gossip." Meanwhile, Wesley Fishel attempted to discredit Colegrove's story by reporting his brief Vietnam itinerary to the American Embassy. Fishel dashed off a letter to Sen. Mike Mansfield, who had recently engaged in "increasingly frequent attacks" on the aid program, to inform him that Colegrove was merely a "malicious sensationalist" who would soon be discredited as the facts came out. The MSU professor also played the public relations angle, organizing a conference on Social Development and Welfare in Free Vietnam. He cajoled President Diem into allowing Vice President Nguyen Ngoc Tho to attend to increase the regime's visibility in the United States and to showcase "the progress which can be expected when a Southeast Asian country is well led and when its ideological guidons keep it stable, peaceful, and progressive." Fishel cited the Colegrove articles and the attention they attracted as threats to continued approval of aid monies from the U.S. Congress (Carter 2008, 101–102).

Almost simultaneously in Vietnam, however, the situation undermined the claims of these American mission officials. From May to July, for example, the periodical *Times of Vietnam,* noted for its pro-American perspective, reported the arrest of three well-placed Vietnamese officials for an array of crimes. Militia second lt. Tran Quoc Thai and Ngo Van Huan, an official of the Commissariat for Refugees, were convicted for embezzlement, and Capt. Dang Nhu Tuyet was convicted for embezzlement, false arrests, and receiving bribes. The Saigon government was so concerned with growing corruption that it made embezzlement of government funds punishable by death.

In October, the Scripps-Howard newspapers published a story that alleged fraud within the MSUG as well. What came to be termed the Rundlett Affair involved MSU adviser Lyman Rundlett giving contracts to Motorola, his former employer. The USOM reported that Motorola actually bid lower than competitors "on only two of the 31 items contained in the Invitation to Bid." Further, the American Justice Department had reportedly been investigating allegations that Rundlett received financial kickbacks for allowing the company to supply police radio equipment to the Diem regime (Ernst 1998, 75). Rundlett never faced charges, and he soon departed Vietnam and resumed employment with Motorola.

Following up on the investigation, a congressional delegation journeyed to Vietnam late in 1959 to conduct on-site hearings, interviews, and inspections. Heading the delegation were senators Albert Gore Sr., Gale McGee, and Bourke Hickenlooper, and representatives John Pilcher, Harris McDowell, Dante Fascell, Marguerite Church, and Walter Judd. Senators Gore and McGee sharply disagreed over what they saw. McGee observed "the most exciting and imaginative [aid program] of any . . . around the world." Gore was "shocked and disturbed" at the "slack-jawed laxness with which our tax money is being handled." The Saigon hearings also cast in relief the tense relations among all parties involved: the U.S. Congress seemed not to believe the official story given by aid mission members; the ambassador and the MAAG chief squared off over who actually was in charge; the Vietnamese were miffed at the arrogance of the delegation in assuming authority on Vietnamese soil; and the added scrutiny strained relations among the MAAG, the ambassador, the Saigon government, and the MSUG (Carter 2008, 102–104).

Senator Mansfield ultimately steered Congress away from the fundamental question of the efficacy of the current U.S. aid programs in Vietnam. Rather, he gave assurances that despite public statements by senators Gore and McGee, the issue "would be framed in such a way that its [the subcommittee's] recommendations would be generalized for the whole aid program rather than specifically directed toward Vietnam." Consequently, the final report is littered with detailed criticisms from the way contracts were awarded to the chain of command within the American mission. All recommendations, however, point to greater command and control, increased congressional oversight, and a general tightening of the budget. Mansfield explained to Senate Foreign Relations Committee chair J. William Fulbright that although "Vietnam has made a great deal of progress," the time had come for a "reshaping" of the aid program to make it more "efficient" and "effective" (Carter 2008, 104). Mansfield recognized that deeper questions and greater scrutiny of the program threatened Congress's ability to continue supporting the Diem regime and to control that support.

The Diem Regime and the Rise of the Insurgency

The Saigon regime had by this time a well-established presence beyond that city. Aside from the development of transportation and communication infrastructure, Diem had eliminated many elected village council posts in favor of direct appointments under his control. As he larded village and municipal councils with his own people—often outsiders—he eliminated an important degree of local autonomy and further centralized his administration. Saigon alienated many people by having these appointees implement denunciation campaigns aimed ostensibly at communists but reaching well beyond. By mid-1956, less than one year into the "denounce the communists" campaign, officials reported that more than 94,000 cadres "rallied to the government," more than 5,600 surrendered, and 15,000 to 20,000 were placed in camps. Between 1954 and 1960, almost 50,000 people were jailed. The official numbers reflect only a portion of the real damage done. As oppressive tactics became normalized, channels of political and social expression ceased to exist for ordinary Vietnamese. Local officials jailed hundreds of people without evidence so they could extort money or eliminate possible rivals for power. In Long An Province, for example, the Cong An security agents became notorious for inflicting terror and practicing extortion (Kahin 1987, 96–98).

Diem solidified his police state with the introduction of Law 10/59 in May 1959. This law reached well beyond earlier efforts in prescribing the death sentence, without right of appeal, for any act that could be construed as "sabotage" or as "infringing upon the security of the state" (Kahin 1987, 98). Diem's security forces rounded up suspected subversives, Viet Minh cadres, and those related to or suspected of supporting them; tried them before military tribunals; and sentenced them, all in three days. Although it disrupted the revolutionary effort in the countryside, this decree also caused a great backlash among villagers who feared and resented the regime. By 1959–1960, American observers were increasingly concerned that the whole experiment might be undermined by such policies. Even such indomitable supporters as Wesley Fishel warned Diem of the growing image within some circles in the United States of an emerging dictatorship in Vietnam, and the damage that would have on continued support. In a lengthy and thoughtful memorandum, Ambassador Durbrow also warned, "we should be prepared to acknowledge to ourselves that even over the longer term democracy in the Western sense of the term may never come to exist in Viet-Nam." Instead, the United States would have to learn to live with autocratic leadership and not attempt "to make over Viet-Nam in our own image" (Carter 2008, 106, 108). It was within the breathing space created by this contradiction that the Diem regime flourished and redoubled efforts to tighten security over the whole of southern Vietnam.

Diem based his increasing concerns over security issues on mounting evidence of a growing opposition. As early as 1957, assassins made a bold daylight attempt on the president's life at the opening of the Ban Me Thuot Economic Fair. Bombings, ambushes, and sabotage, as well as intimidation, harassment, and assassination of officials loyal to the Diem government had been escalating for several years. Assassinations of officials, for example, rose from approximately 700 in 1958 to 2,500 in 1960 (Herring 2002). The regime's aggressive security measures contributed to the opposition. The program of forced resettlement into agrovilles in 1959, for example, generated a great deal of resentment from the people. The first of many similar schemes to come over the years, the agroville program relocated large numbers of Vietnamese into concentrated zones along major transportation routes. Once concentrated, the peasants no longer provided the insurgency with a base of operations and sustenance. The effort smacked of the old colonial system of corvee labor as the government forcibly removed people from their farmlands and ancestral tombs to build their new quarters, occasionally out of materials from their dismantled former homes, and to construct the camp, all without recompense. Local officials took advantage of the confinement to extort money and goods, while meting out physical abuse and torture. Within the barbed wire surrounding these camps, not surprisingly, opposition only grew. Amid obvious failure and growing protest over the camps, the regime finally abandoned the effort, but not before it had demonstrated to large numbers of Vietnamese the necessity of resistance.

In April 1960, 18 well-placed officials demonstrated that government-generated hostility reached even into the cities. The group, including four former government ministers, issued their manifesto calling for a recognition and inclusion of opposition parties and asking the president to "liberalize the regime, promote democracy," and "guarantee minimum civil rights" to end the government's alienation of the people and stave off collapse. This Caravelle Manifesto was widely publicized, particularly in the United States, and caused considerable alarm among Diem's Vietnamese and American supporters. Wesley Fishel, who had warned his friend earlier of the betrayal of the intellectuals, advised "discrediting [the manifesto's] authors by presenting to the world their records of past collaboration with the French and with Bao Dai." Fishel urged Diem to forward brief biographies on each of the signers and promised he would "see what can be done" in the United States to counter their efforts. The regime immediately attacked the group as enemies of the state and moved to malign their individual reputations (Carter 2008, 108). Diem refused to allow publication of the manifesto and harassed and arrested some of those involved. As historian David Anderson has pointed out, however, "the complete ineffectiveness of the protest laid bare the truth of its charges." The government was not about to reform or to allow such criticism. The episode exacerbated tensions between different elements of the country team, with the ambassador, MAAG chief, and Diem increasingly at odds over how to proceed as the people grew restless and protests mounted (Anderson 1991, 184–186).

The regime became increasingly paranoid. The Can Lao, or Personalist, Party enveloped the president and his family to prevent encroachment from outsiders but also to prevent the intrusion of unwanted criticism and advice. Officially known as the Revolutionary Labor Personalism Party, this organization represented the ruling elite and served as an anticommunist, pro-Diem propaganda machine tightly controlled by Diem's brother, Ngo Dinh

Nhu. With its emphasis on conservatism, hierarchy, and position, personalism justified rigid and authoritarian rule. However, the doctrine mattered little because very few Vietnamese actually adhered to or even understood it. It became another in the panoply of weapons used to silence opposition and safeguard the Ngo hold on power.

By most accounts, security rather than democratic reforms motivated the Diem regime. The countryside teemed with opposition. Despite a variety of tactics aimed at destroying the insurgency, which Diem and others referred to derisively as the "Viet Cong," it continued to grow among the general population, which both joined and sustained it. That insurgency grew out of a decades-old revolutionary movement spanning all of Vietnam that had defeated the French and now opposed the Americans and Diem. By late 1960, this revolution, led by the Vietminh, attracted thousands of insurgents from all over southern Vietnam and formed itself into the National Front for the Liberation of Vietnam (NLF). Hanoi provided formal recognition by the close of the year for its aggressive opposition to Diem's rule. Additionally, a broad spectrum of workers, students, civil servants, and the military continued to oppose the government in a variety of ways.

Only weeks earlier, opposition reached crisis proportion as a coalition of military officers attempted a coup, and very nearly succeeded. Led by an elite parachute regiment and a marine battalion, in the early hours of November 11 the rebels stormed the presidential palace and took over army headquarters and the airport. As this fragile and divided coalition conferred about the composition of the new provisional government, Diem used phony concessions to stall for time. When loyal troops arrived the next day to surround the palace and its captors, the coup crumbled and its leaders fled to exile in Cambodia. On November 14, Diem announced, "The Government continues to serve the nation in accordance with republican and personalist principals" (Carter 2008, 110). The coup came and went quickly and seemingly without disturbing the balance of forces in Saigon. For the time being, Diem remained in power.

The coup did, however, expose an ominous trend. It revealed and even nurtured a politicized military, and it pitted that military against incompetent and, in many quarters, illegitimate political leadership. For the American mission, the event further divided Durbrow, who increasingly demanded reform, from now-retired MAAG chief Williams, who believed the ambassador had encouraged the plot or at least withheld wholehearted support for Diem in his hour of need. Diem clung to power in Saigon for the next several years, during which time the situation only worsened. The NLF gained more power, engaging increasingly in armed clashes with Diem's forces. Insurgent guerrillas became ubiquitous in numerous villages and controlled large areas of rural Vietnam as peasant dissatisfaction with the regime, now referred to derisively as "My-Diem," or *America's* Diem, grew. The Ngo family maintained its intransigence and continued to aggressively squash dissent and opposition. The American mission shifted as well, as circumstances drifted toward open armed conflict and away from any real focus on economic development. Indeed, the events of 1958–1960 in Vietnam set in motion tensions and divisions over American policy that became

Republic of Vietnam president Ngo Dinh Diem (1955–1963) casts a ballot in Saigon. Diem resisted democratization of South Vietnam and his dictatorial, often brutal, rule led to withdrawal of U.S. support, a coup d'état, and his assassination in 1963. (*Library of Congress*)

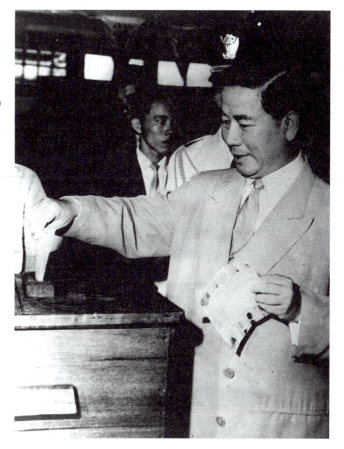

deeply entrenched and significantly informed U.S. policy toward Vietnam for years to come.

Conclusion: A Crumbling Bastion in Southern Vietnam

From the late 1950s into the early 1960s, the Eisenhower administration increased its aid to the Saigon regime in part to encourage its development but largely to stave off collapse. In the process, policy makers, both American and Vietnamese, invented a Vietnam below the 17th parallel that required constant aid and support to survive. By 1960–1961, the state invented below the 17th parallel, to the extent that it existed at all, was not what planners imagined. The Diem regime required increasing military aid as the revolution in the countryside became better organized and expanded its resistance. All the while, the aid program designed to build a modern state infrastructure around Vietnamese leadership had grown exponentially, although not uniformly.

Nevertheless, even as contrary evidence piled up, Senator Mansfield and others continued to believe that the Vietnam the United States wanted to create below the 17th parallel could only be built around Ngo Dinh Diem.

As the senator submitted his report after the congressional investigation, he was well aware that the regime in Saigon had earned the fear and hatred of many Vietnamese, and that, as far as some were concerned, the U.S. aid program made Diem's authoritarian rule possible.

Formerly enthusiastic American nation builders closest to the project also voiced their own grave concerns that the effort had veered onto the wrong track. MSUG economic advisers Adrian Jaffe and Milton Taylor believed the American aid program had overemphasized military concerns and had made the economy dangerously dependent. The two published a 1961 article warning that the project to build the new state in southern Vietnam was doomed. The authors believed Washington had deluded itself and the American people by touting the success of the U.S. aid program for Vietnam. Far from being a success story, according to Jaffe and Taylor (1961), "Vietnam is not stable, not viable, not democratic, and not a bastion" of the "Free World," as officials claimed. It was instead "a crumbling bastion" (17–20).

Other analyses found that of a population of more than 12 million, only about 15,000 paid any taxes. Of that number, approximately 12,500 were civil servants and military personnel. In short, the regime had little or no revenue-gathering capacity beyond American aid. The Commodity Import Program thwarted home production and the growth of manufactures as it continually expanded to meet inflationary pressures. This formula in southern Vietnam had mushroomed and become entrenched. The very structure of the program determined that the Americans could never cut it off and leave. These criticisms were sharply at odds with the more optimistic appraisals coming out of Washington. Not surprisingly, Diem rankled at such criticism and reacted strongly, expelling journalists, resisting reforms, and refusing audiences with key advisers. By 1962, Saigon leaders determined that they could afford to allow the MSUG contract to expire, and those advisers packed up and went home.

Over the course of these debates, hearings, and investigations the U.S. aid program for Vietnam hovered between $250 and $350 million annually. By 1961, total U.S. aid for the project climbed to $2.19 billion (Carter 2008). The massive and growing program in Vietnam could be either a showcase of U.S. Cold War state-building projects, or it could be an embarrassing failure. Some in Congress were keen to ensure the former.

This tendency to downplay or to conceal altogether the bad news or the ominous developments with the project became pervasive among American officials, both in Washington and Saigon. By the early 1960s, the U.S. aid program had nurtured the development of an utterly dependent regime. The point at which the Americans could have announced success, ended the aid program, and gone home continued to recede into the distance. Although those close to the project in Saigon and numerous others in Congress recognized this dilemma, they continued to limit their options as U.S. responsibility for the sustenance of the project expanded.

In that critical 1961 essay, advisers Jaffe and Taylor (1961) had already begun the now-familiar puzzling over how it all could have happened the way it did in Vietnam:

How was it possible for us to make so many mistakes, over so long a period of time? . . . We have sent to Vietnam, in large numbers, men of distinction in the academic and governmental world, professors and experts drawn from government agencies. . . . There have been few days when President Diem has not broken bread with at least one PhD and on good days, three or four. One of Diem's personal advisers . . . is one of the world's leading experts in the field of agricultural reform, and the Vice President of Vietnam is learning English at present from an American Chief of Mission. Another adviser, a political scientist with a PhD, has made some 22 trips to the Far East, and has written an article entitled "Vietnam's Democratic One-Man Rule." . . . But never in the history of our foreign affairs have we received more misinformation from a more qualified group (19).

Some of those experts and PhDs had, in the end, only limited influence. Many were surprised and disappointed to learn this. Despite their sober and earnest warnings, officials in Washington did not take heed, did not substantially shift course, and did not reform the aid program. Instead, they opted for greater levels of military force to provide security amid growing violence, instability, and resistance. That resistance coalesced late in 1960 as the NLF, in conjunction with Vietnamese above the 17th parallel, decided on overt, organized opposition to the U.S. effort and the American-backed regime in Saigon. Shortly after John F. Kennedy became president in early 1961, officials spoke of a "war" to be won in Vietnam. Meanwhile, that initial batch of advisers to Vietnam looked on from back in the United States as the nation-building effort gave way to open conflict and a set of military solutions to an array of nonmilitary problems. Shortly after numerous American advisers concluded that the project was hopelessly lost, military initiatives and open warfare supplanted nation building, and the successful creation of an independent South Vietnam receded further over the horizon.

References and Further Reading

Anderson, David. *Trapped By Success: The Eisenhower Administration and Vietnam, 1953–1961.* New York: Columbia University Press, 1991.

Carter, James M. *Inventing Vietnam: The United States and State Building, 1954–1968.* New York: Cambridge University Press, 2008.

Child, Frank. "Vietnam—The Eleventh Hour." *New Republic* 145 (December 4, 1961): 14–16.

Ernst, John. *Forging a Fateful Alliance: Michigan State University and the Vietnam War.* East Lansing: Michigan State University Press, 1998.

Fall, Bernard. *The Two Viet Nams: A Political and Military Analysis.* Westport, CT: Greenwood Press, 1967.

Herring, George. *America's Longest War: The United States & Vietnam, 1950–1975.* 4th ed. Boston: McGraw-Hill, 2002.

Jaffe, Adrian, and Milton Taylor. "A Crumbling Bastion: Flattery and Lies Won't Save Vietnam," *New Republic* 144 (June 16, 1961): 17–21.

Kahin, George. *Intervention: How America Became Involved in Vietnam.* New York: Anchor Books, 1987.

Montgomery, John. *The Politics of Foreign Aid: American Experience in Southeast Asia.* New York: Frederick A. Praeger, 1962.

Scigliano, Robert. *South Vietnam: Nation Under Stress.* Boston: Houghton Mifflin, 1963.

Trued, M. N. "South Viet-Nam's Industrial Development Center." *Pacific Affairs* 33 (September 1960): 250–267.

Vietnam Military Personnel | 3

Carol Reardon

A few iconic images of military service in Vietnam command a place in national memory: patrols of hollow-eyed "grunts" inching forward through triple-canopy jungle or rice paddies seeking an unseen enemy, helicopters dropping troops into hot landing zones, and the spectacular destructive effect of bombs and napalm. But these few scenes shed little meaningful light on what historian Christian R. Appy (1993) has called "the irreducible complexity of each life the war touched and the multiplicity of experiences the war comprised" (20). During America's longest war, from 1950 until 1975, no single set of shared motivations, expectations, and experiences frames the "soldier's story" of Vietnam. Only a mosaic of nearly 3 million tiles, each representing one individual's story, can do that.

The Advisory Stage

In September 1950, overshadowed by the Korean War, President Harry Truman sent the Military Assistance and Advisory Group-Indochina—a small number of American technical and logistical specialists—to French Indochina. The men served exclusively as inspectors, observing the distribution of American military equipment and supplies intended to help the French crush Vietnamese efforts to overthrow colonial rule. In October 1954, several months after Vietnamese insurgents—known as the Vietminh—defeated the French at Dien Bien Phu, the United States quietly changed its mission to training the new Army of the Republic of Vietnam (ARVN). This new Military Assistance and Advisory Group-Vietnam (MAAG-Vietnam) soon numbered more than 300 trainers, mostly career officers or veteran noncommissioned officers (NCOs) with combat service in World War II or Korea. In two- or three-man teams, they attempted to organize the new 150,000-man ARVN into the kind of army they understood best: a conventional force that could repel any North Vietnamese attack across the demilitarized zone (DMZ) that had come to serve as a border between North and South Vietnam. Strict rules of engagement severely proscribed when and where advisers could wear uniforms, carry arms, or accompany ARVN troops

Vietnamese soldiers take positions on a bridge during the Vietminh takeover of Haiphong in 1954. The Vietminh was formed by Ho Chi Minh in 1941 to seek independence for Vietnam from France. (*Corbis*)

on exercises outside training areas. Trainers gave only scant attention to counterinsurgency training. In 1957, as opponents of Ngo Dinh Diem's South Vietnamese government organized an armed resistance, the U.S. Army's 1st Special Forces Group trained only 58 ARVN soldiers in counterinsurgency tactics. A small number of advisers died—including, in 1959, Maj. Dale R. Buis and Master Sgt. Chester M. Ovnand, both U.S. Army, the first two names on the Vietnam Veterans Memorial Wall, or "the Wall"—but their loss forced no reconsideration of the advisory mission, because MAAG-Vietnam represented a miniscule portion of American armed forces posted overseas during the Eisenhower era.

The American military mission expanded further during the John F. Kennedy administration, fueled by concern about the ARVN's slow progress and the strengthening opposition to Diem's government within South Vietnam. In 1960, anti-Diemists organized the National Liberation Front, and its armed fighters—dubbed by Diem as "Vietcong," or Vietnamese communists—launched increasingly more frequent attacks on ARVN forces throughout the countryside. An advocate of counterinsurgency warfare, Kennedy now supported a dramatically increased role for the U.S. Army's Special Forces. In 1961, six- to twelve-man teams of these Green Berets began to train South Vietnam's ethnic minorities to resist attacks on their villages and to organize mobile strike forces to take the fight to the Vietcong. The U.S. Air Force's 4400th Combat Crew Training Squadron initiated Operation Farm Gate in November 1961 to train pilots for the South Vietnamese Air Force. In January 1962, Air Force crews flew the first Operation Ranch Hand missions in southern South Vietnam, spraying chemical defoliants on crops and dense vegetation to deny the Vietcong food and cover. Entire U.S. Army communications, medical, intelligence, aviation, and transportation companies of 100 men or more—no longer merely individual specialists in these fields—deployed to provide direct support to ARVN field operations. In 1962, the Pentagon replaced MAAG-Vietnam with a new headquarters—Military Assistance Command, Vietnam (MACV)—to coordinate the growing American presence, which jumped from 1,000 American advisers in Vietnam when Kennedy took office in January 1961 to more than 16,000 when he was assassinated in November 1963 (Appy 1993).

To some, the "brushfire war" presaged no long-term concern. In 1963, an Army radio technician recalled that, "If we wanted to go out and chase people around and shoot at them and get them to shoot back at us, we had a war going on. If we didn't do that, they let us alone. . . . There was no war after four-thirty. On Saturdays, no war. On Sundays, no war. On holidays, no war" (Santoli 1981, 5–6). But advisers who worked directly with the ARVN viewed affairs quite differently. Three American advisers died on January 2, 1963, when ARVN forces blundered into a Vietcong ambush at Ap Bac, a clash that raised troubling concerns about the capability—and even the loyalty—of the entire South Vietnamese military establishment. Green Beret captain Roger Donlon, the first winner of the Medal of Honor in Southeast Asia, realized as early as 1963 that he could count on only two-thirds of his Vietnamese strike force; when an attack started, he explained, the first thing the one-third who were "traitors did . . . was to slit the throat or break the neck of the person next to them" (Appy 2003, 14–15). By the end of 1963, the advisory mission in Vietnam had cost 120 American lives.

After the assassinations of Diem and Kennedy in November 1963, Lyndon Johnson understood little about the insurgency in Vietnam but, viewing the conflict in Cold War terms, was committed to denying a victory to communists there. In June 1964, he appointed Gen. William C. Westmoreland, a West Point–trained South Carolinian comfortable with conventional World War II–style warfare, to command MACV. After the August 1964 Gulf of Tonkin incident—an attack (then believed to be two separate attacks) by North Vietnamese patrol boats on American naval vessels in international waters—Johnson approved a limited number of airstrikes against specific North Vietnamese targets. He made no substantial increases in troop strength, however, until after the 1964 presidential election. Then, in early 1965, in the face of continuing political turmoil in Saigon and a substantial increase in Vietcong attacks, Johnson began to "Americanize" the fighting in Vietnam.

Getting to Vietnam

The most detailed studies of American military personnel who served in the Vietnam conflict slight the advisory period and stress the years from 1964 to the end of active combat operations in 1973. In raw numbers, of nearly 26.8 million American draft-eligible men during these years, 10.9 million ultimately entered military service. Only 2.1 million, however—less than 10 percent of the men in the war generation—actually served in Vietnam. With the inclusion of older veterans already in uniform, enlistees younger than 19, and an undetermined number of servicewomen, the total number of Americans who served in Vietnam reached nearly 3 million (Baskir and Strauss 1978).

Those whose paths led to Vietnam owed much of their fate to the vagaries of the Selective Service process. Even though the draft had operated continuously since the Korean War, a decade of comparative peace and low monthly quotas had lulled many young men into viewing it benignly. That changed in early 1965 when Johnson decided to "Americanize" the combat effort in Vietnam through dramatically increasing monthly draft calls rather than by activating Reserve or National Guard units. As a consequence, the Vietnam-era draft "cast the entire generation into a contest for survival" (Baskir and Strauss 1978, 6).

The men who served in Vietnam entered the armed forces for all kinds of reasons. Recruiters preferred true volunteers. In 1964, for instance, these include the 11.2 percent of Army enlistees who cited "patriotism"—to stop communism, to continue family tradition, or to accept Kennedy's challenge to action—as prime motivators. They also welcomed the 22.3 percent who joined that same year for "personal advancement," and the 28.8 percent who enlisted for "personal reasons" from peer pressure to escaping unhappy family situations. Standard enlistment periods varied. The Army required a three-year commitment—one year longer than a draftee served—but the Marine Corps offered a two-year option for volunteers; the Navy and the Air Force both required four-year enlistments. Recruiters also won recruits with promises of specialized training, specific duty stations, or a "buddy program" that allowed friends to go through basic training together.

The remaining 37.6 percent of 1964's Army recruits, however, fell into the category of "draft-motivated" volunteers, who enlisted to control the terms of their military service in ways that might be denied them if they waited for a Selective Service call-up. Some willingly joined for the same perceived guarantees to noncombat specialties used to lure true volunteers. Some decided not to enlist in the Army at all, opting instead for the Air Force or the Navy specifically to eliminate all possibility of being sent to Vietnam as riflemen. Still others sought slots in National Guard or Reserve units; indeed, a 1966 study showed that 71 percent of National Guard enlistees considered the draft to be their primary motivation for volunteering (Appy 1993, 29).

To meet unfilled personnel requirements, Selective Service ultimately drafted 2.2 million men during 1964–1972 for two years of service. Like those who enlisted voluntarily, each man made his own way through the system. Some simply waited for their summons. Others tried to evade service, failed, and made the best of it. Still others, resenting their fate, resisted from the day they reported for induction.

Whether volunteer or draftee, however, the transformation from civilian to military life began with a sharp, confusing, and frightening break from the past: recruit training. The arrival of John Rhodes (1996) at Parris Island was typical: "I've been here five seconds and I've already been kicked, yelled at and told I didn't have what it takes to be a Marine, great start. Get me out of here" (15). Eighty-nine percent of all American military personnel in Vietnam served in the enlisted ranks, and this eight- to twelve-week training cycle represented their single common experience. Most possessed no more than a high school education, had traveled little, and knew little about Vietnam. Nearly 80 percent of enlisted recruits came from working-class or poor families, separated by education and life experience from the overwhelmingly middle-class officer corps that led them (Appy 1993).

Recruit training stressed physical conditioning and weapons proficiency, working toward the goal of producing "general-service" personnel who had mastered appropriate basic military skills. Just before graduation, each received his MOS—his military occupational specialty. Recruits could submit personal preferences—the Army alone offered more than 300 MOSs—but service needs always came first. Army recruits assigned to the 11-B MOS, or "11-Bravo"—sometimes called "11-Bang-Bang" or even "11-Bulletstopper"—became infantrymen, highly likely to go to Vietnam. Future Marine infantrymen received a 0–3 designation. In some Army and Marine recruit classes from 1965 through 1968, nearly all graduates—even those who believed they had been promised other occupational training—received 11-B assignments. Appeals for a change rarely succeeded without an agreement to extend one's original enlistment for an additional year or more.

MOS instruction occurred during advanced individual training (AIT) after graduation from basic training. The common bonds forged in sweat during recruit training broke, as each individual mastered a specialty. Those assigned to the infantry or combat arms now practiced skills needed in Vietnam, even though they still did not know if their follow-on assignment would take them there. Not all training made sense. Army and Marine AIT infantry instruction did not include exercises in clearing villages until late 1965. At Fort Dix, New Jersey, some green-clad soldiers practiced jungle ambush tactics on snow-covered fields and forests in midwinter. Few AIT curricula included even basic instruction about Vietnamese culture, history, politics, and society.

For many in combat specialties, the end of AIT brought orders to Vietnam. Brief visits home ended with difficult leave-takings. The length of their tours represented their only real certainty now. Army troops—and most Air Force and Navy personnel stationed in country—calculated one calendar year from their date of arrival to determine their date of return from overseas (DEROS). Marines served 13-month tours. Air Force cockpit crews could rotate out of the combat zone after 100 missions, and sailors on aircraft carriers usually stayed for the varying length of an entire combat cruise.

Early on, some entire units sailed to Vietnam on old World War II and Korean War troopships, but most American military personnel subsequently flew as individuals by commercial airliner. As flight attendant Helen Tennant Hegelheimer noted, "At the top of the ramp was the world, at the bottom of the ramp was the war" (Appy 2003, 108). As the troop buildup of 1965 continued into 1966, newly arriving soldiers crossed paths at the bottom of the ramp with combat veterans returning home. Their gaunt look and haunted eyes invariably unnerved the new arrivals.

The haggard veterans presented only one shock. New arrivals quickly noted Vietnam's extreme heat and unique smells. The pungent fermented fish sauce called *nuoc mam,* rice paddies fertilized with water buffalo excrement, human waste, and the gasoline used to burn it all mixed to create a startling odor that rarely escaped remark. It disquieted many to learn that the wire grills on the windows of the buses taking them around the base kept out hand grenades tossed by Vietcong who blended in with noncombatants, their introduction to a war with no front lines.

For a brief period, sometimes up to a week, each new arrival awaited assignment to a unit. From this point on, four factors shaped his individual experience, but the most important was the timeframe of his in-country service. The war of 1965 differed from the war of 1968, which differed from the war of 1972. Branch of service, in-country duty station, and the requirements and duties of his MOS also mattered. It astounded many to learn that, although the most vivid Vietnam news stories back home centered on "grunts" who "humped the boonies"—infantrymen who patrolled through South Vietnam's jungle-covered mountains—only about 20 percent of new arrivals went to front-line combat units. Even at the height of the Americanization phase of the war—from 1965 through 1968—nearly 80 percent of all newly arrived troops worked in rear-area assignments (Appy 1993).

The American Buildup

The first large deployment of combat troops to arrive in Vietnam in 1965 enjoyed an important benefit denied to those who followed them. They trained in peacetime, and the presence of substantial numbers of "lifers"—World War II and Korean War combat veterans—among the senior NCOs had produced cohesive, professional units. The Marines who landed in Da Nang in March 1965 had trained together in Okinawa for months before they deployed to Vietnam. Much the same could be said for the Army's 173rd Airborne Brigade and 1st Cavalry Division, which arrived during the summer of 1965. Additionally, General William Westmoreland divided South Vietnam into four military regions, designated as I, II, III, and IV Corps, and assigned these skilled troops—as units—to specific areas of responsibility. Most Marines went to the five northernmost provinces just south of the DMZ designated I Corps, a rugged region that rose quickly from sandy beaches to jungle-covered mountains. Moving southward, II Corps included the central highlands, a mixture of grasslands and mountains crossed by valuable road networks; the 1st Cavalry Division served there. Still farther south, III Corps embraced the provinces north and west of Saigon, including areas long known for insurgent activity and tunnel complexes; as they arrived in country, the Army's 1st and 25th Infantry Divisions were assigned here. IV Corps included the southernmost reaches of South Vietnam, including the Mekong Delta, which required both the Army's 9th Infantry division and a significant naval patrol boat presence on the waterways.

The landing of ground combat troops occurred nearly simultaneously with the start of an ambitious and controversial air offensive. The air war of the 1965–1968 Americanization phase included several distinct elements. Fixed-wing aircraft and helicopters alike participated in the close-air-support mission to assist U.S. or ARVN troops in contact with enemy forces throughout South Vietnam. Beginning in June 1965, Air Force B-52s based in Guam and Thailand launched "arc light" missions against enemy troop concentrations in South Vietnam and along the Ho Chi Minh Trail, each aircraft capable of dropping 30 tons of ordnance. The early air war's most well-known effort, Operation Rolling Thunder, began in March 1965 as an interdiction effort against military targets just north of the DMZ. From the start, the White House and the Pentagon micromanaged target selection, expanding the list or calling for bombing halts as a means to apply diplomatic pressure. By 1966, with North Vietnam carved into seven "route packages," Air Force and Naval aviators—all volunteers—hit targets throughout the entire country. Still, concerns about communist bloc reaction shaped strict rules of engagement that put off-limits many important military targets, and frustrated aircrews repeatedly flew through increasing antiaircraft and surface-to-air missile batteries to hit unimportant points. "There's an incredible overestimation on the damage we do. It's mostly imagination or propaganda," wrote Lt. Frank Elkins (1991, 55), a naval aviator. Resolving the fates of airmen downed on Rolling Thunder missions—and Elkins joined them in October 1966—became one of the war's most emotional issues.

As the air war opened, ground combat operations in 1965 began with MACV headquarters establishing a defensively minded "enclave strategy" to protect American airstrips, supply depots, and other properties. The Marines in I Corps rejected this approach; it ran entirely counter to their offensively oriented doctrine. Thus, by summer 1965—with MACV approval—American ground troops adopted a more proactive strategy. Initially called "sweep and clear," but generally understood as "search and destroy," this attrition strategy required American troops to "find, fix, and finish" the enemy or to draw them out of concealment to be destroyed by supporting artillery or air power.

At first, search-and-destroy missions caused American deaths in ones and twos, too little to destroy unit morale or cohesion. By late summer 1965, however, Marine units in Operation Starlite in I Corps suffered more than 60 killed over a two-week period. The very nature of the war changed significantly in mid-November when elements of the 1st Cavalry Division clashed with North Vietnamese regulars in the Ia Drang Valley in the central highlands, the first large-unit action to pit U.S. ground troops against Hanoi's army. More than 300 American soldiers died in less than one week. Thomas Bird, an enlisted man, explained the battle's impact on his unit: "It took a long time to put the Cav back together again. It hit us extra hard because most of the units were stateside together. . . . We were friends of each other's families, dined together, entertained together, argued together" (Santoli 1981, 42). Deaths, illness, wounds, reassignments, and the one-year rotation system worked against reproducing the strong unit cohesion of 1965. No matter how badly a unit needed them, from 1965 until the end of armed hostilities, most new men arrived to cold receptions until they convinced veterans they were "shooters" and not "shakers."

By the end of December, the active combat operations of 1965 had cost at least 1,369 American lives, but those who fought still found it easy to rely on Cold War rhetoric to justify the cost (Appy 1993, 29). As Marine lance corp. Jack Swender wrote his family in September 1965: "I would rather fight to stop communism in South Vietnam than in Kincaid, Humboldt, Blue Mound, or Kansas City. . . . Last year alone 4,700 teachers and priests in South Vietnam were killed. This we are trying to *stop*—this is our objective" (Edelman 1985, 213).

Swender himself fell in December 1965 in a firefight that illustrated the style of ground combat that accounted for 83 percent of all American fatalities in Vietnam. By one estimate, an infantryman serving a typical 12-month tour during 1965–1970 stood a 3 percent chance of dying, a 10 percent chance of receiving a wound that required evacuation to a hospital, and a 25 percent chance of sustaining a wound that merited a Purple Heart (Vietnam Veterans Memorial n.d.; National Archives 2007). As Army veteran Billy Walkabout recalled, "A firefight is instant insanity. . . . They say war is hell, but contact is a sonofabitch" (Beesley 1987, 6).

To survive those firefights, the combatants mastered the tools and technology of their trade. In 1965, the Army and the Marine Corps adopted the new M-16 rifle. The new weapon was lighter than the M-14 it replaced, but troops carried 600 rounds instead of the standard 200 to compensate for the bullet's lack of penetrating power. The new weapon also jammed easily, and infantrymen died as they tried to clear a round stuck in the chamber. Indeed, many Americans preferred the AK-47 used by their enemy. For increased firepower, both Army and Marine patrols usually included troop-

After a firefight, two soldiers of the U.S. 173rd Airborne Brigade wait for a helicopter to evacuate them and a dead companion. (*National Archives*)

ers carrying the reliable M-79 grenade launcher and the unwieldy but indispensable M-60 machine gun.

Additional support required only a radio call. As Army first lieutenant Vincent Okamoto explained, "With that radio I was like God. I could call down from the heavens destruction on a massive scale. The radio connects you to eighteen howitzers that can fire shells from seven miles away. You got helicopter gunships with miniguns that could fire six thousand rounds per minute. And you got . . . air force fighter bombers who break in on the net and go, 'Bravo Six, I'm at your location and I've got eighteen thousand rounds of twenty-millimeter cannon and four five-hundred pound bombs. Where do you want 'em, over?' For a twenty-four-year-old lieutenant, it was really incredible" (Appy 2003, 359). This firepower came with an unfortunate downside, however. In firefights at close range, short rounds from artillery and bombs that skewed off target caused many friendly fire casualties.

During 1966 and 1967, military planners expanded the ground war by assigning larger units and more complex maneuvers to individual search-and-destroy operations. In the fall of 1966, entire battalions from both the 1st and 25th Divisions and the 196th Light Infantry Brigade took part in Operation Attleboro against enemy concentrations in War Zone C. In the same area in January 1967, Operation Cedar Falls began with 60 helicopters landing an infantry battalion in the town of Ben Suc and required five infantry battalions, two cavalry squadrons, and an artillery battalion—several thousand men in all—to complete the sweep. In February 1967, Operation Junction City included an airborne assault by the paratroopers of the 173rd Airborne Brigade.

Despite their best efforts, however, Vietcong or North Vietnamese troops invariably returned as soon as the Americans left, leading many American military personnel to question the effectiveness of these missions. Army historian S. L. A. Marshall described a typical sweep in 1966 as "incredibly boring, wasteful, and exhausting" (Appy 1993, 161). Soldiers sweated so much that their uniforms turned white from the salt leached out of their bodies. To ward off dehydration in the tropical heat, they drank any water they could find, often without using iodine tablets for purification. They suffered from ringworm, trench foot, plantar warts, jungle rot, malaria, and hepatitis. Leeches plagued them, but Sgt. Jerry Liucci found a solution: "The cocktail sauce they gave us for food wasn't edible but was great for leeches—you just squirt it on them, and they would drop off you" (Bergerud 1993, 19). Exhaustion took its toll. Marine PFC Raymond Griffiths wrote home in June 1966, "I tell you truthful I doubt if I'll come out of this alive. In my original squad I'm the only one left unharmed. . . . It seems every day another young guy 18 and 19 years old like myself is killed in action." Griffiths fell in combat on the Fourth of July (Edelman 1985, 118). He became just one of at least 5,008 Americans who died in 1966, and in 1967 the number jumped to 9,378 (Appy 1993).

The arbitrariness and violence of each individual death wore on survivors. Marine Warren E. Howe recalled a few brief seconds on June 26, 1967: "Jim Blakely never saw the mine he stepped on that morning. Nor did he live long enough to feel the wounds he would soon die from. The concussion of the mine's explosion detonated a 60mm mortar round carried on the back of Angel Correa. Angel never heard it. A piece of shrapnel caught Teddy (Doc) Hart in the chest. Doc was gone before his knees buckled. An instant in time for some, an eternity for others" (Palmer 1987, 205). Snipers took their toll. Soldiers and Marines found clever booby traps everywhere, some made from discarded cans of C-ration peanut butter. Some Marines learned the lethality of letting down their guard, when, after swimming in a pond, they returned the next day and watched as one man "dove in and ran a punji stick right through his chest" (Ebert 1993, 193).

Experiences such as this slowly eroded both troop morale and their moral fabric. The body count, the controversial measure adopted early on to assess progress, challenged common sense and institutional integrity. Capt. Howard Boone's commanding officer "used to ask me every day, as a measure of our effectiveness, 'How many gooks did you kill this morning?'" (Prashker 1988, 27). Common practice called for counting four Vietnamese body parts—even if they belonged to a single person who may or may not have been an enemy combatant—as four kills. More troubling, frustrated survivors found it increasingly easy to take revenge for comrades' deaths, with few qualms about crossing a moral or legal line. Soldiers and Marines cut off trigger fingers, scalps, and ears from enemy dead. As early as March 1966, Army sergeant George Barnett wrote home, "This war isn't by the Geneva Convention. Charlie doesn't take any prisoners nor do we. Only when the CO sees them first. We shoot the wounded." After he and his patrol found two of their missing comrades mutilated and hanging by their ankles from a tree, they decapitated enemy dead until officers took their hatchets away (Adler 2003, 28).

Additional frustration stemmed from the increasing inability of American military personnel to separate friend from foe, many coming to openly distrust the South Vietnamese they were sent to aid and protect. It stunned Marines who cleared a tunnel complex near Chu Lai to learn that the mayor of Da Nang was on a list of Vietcong double agents they found. American military personnel training or operating with ARVN units also grew increasingly frustrated. Advisers discovered early on that families of ARVN soldiers often followed them into the field, frequently bribing Vietcong patrols with information to get past them. Officers from all services in the South Vietnamese military establishment drew equipment for their men, and then sold it on the black market or abandoned it for the Vietcong to retrieve. To accomplish even small tasks, Karl Phaler concluded after his tour with the South Vietnamese Navy in 1966–1967, "You don't lead, you con" (Santoli 1981, 51).

By 1967, the absence of a clearly understood objective and an effective strategy to obtain it increasingly bothered American military personnel in Vietnam and stateside. Some, such as the Fort Hood Three, had already refused orders to deploy. Rants against senior military and political leadership became more common. As Marine captain Rodney Chastant wrote home in September 1967, "Johnson is trying to fight this war the way he fights his domestic wars—he chooses an almost unattainable goal with a

Carlos Lozada

Carlos James Lozada was born on September 6, 1946, in Caguas, Puerto Rico. His family moved to New York City in the early 1950s, and Carlos grew up in the Bronx. Soon after graduating from high school in 1966, Lozada enlisted in the U.S. Army. He hoped to use the G.I. Bill to go to college after completing his military service.

Lozada completed boot camp, won promotion to the rank of private first class, and received orders for Vietnam. Once in country, he was assigned to the 173rd Airborne Brigade and joined it in active operations in South Vietnam's central highlands. A physically strong young man, Lozada carried an M-60 machine gun, invaluable in close-contact firefights.

In November 1967, the 173rd Airborne Brigade undertook active operations in the central highlands. On November 20, on Hill 875 near Dak To, Lozada's unit had advanced halfway up the hill when stiffening North Vietnamese resistance stopped them. As enemy troops worked their way around the American position, Lozada and three other men were sent 35 meters back down the hill to watch for enemy movement. They had barely taken up their new position when the North Vietnamese attacked. As the other three soldiers pulled back up the hill to spread word of the new threat, Lozada covered them with suppressive fire. His actions killed at least 20 North Vietnamese soldiers and disrupted their attack long enough for his company to redeploy to counter the next enemy assault. Later, they found Lozada dead, slumped over his machine gun.

Carlos Lozada was buried with full military honors in Long Island National Cemetery, not far from his home. For his coolness under fire and saving the lives of his comrades at the cost of his own, PFC Carlos Lozada was awarded a posthumous Medal of Honor, the nation's most distinguished combat award. A playground in the Bronx is named for him.

scope so large it is virtually undefinable, and he attacks this goal with poorly allocated funds, minimum manpower, limited time, and few new ideas" (Edelman 1985, 219). Nonetheless, two months later, General Westmoreland addressed Congress and announced that he saw "a light at the end of the tunnel."

He could not have erred more. The North Vietnamese and Vietcong had already launched the opening phases of a highly organized operation that became known as the Tet Offensive. They hoped to draw American troops to South Vietnam's northern and western border areas to facilitate their own operations in urban centers. Thus, along the DMZ, when not out patrolling, Marines at Con Thien lived in underground bunkers to protect themselves from North Vietnamese artillery. At Khe Sanh, in the northwest corner of South Vietnam, Marines fortified and reinforced against a significant buildup of North Vietnamese regulars. In mid-November in the central highlands, troops from the Army's 173rd Airborne Brigade near Dak To lost heavily in a series of bloody battles.

American planners missed the significance of these actions. The Tet Offensive, which began on January 31, 1968, came as a surprise. Vietcong and North Vietnamese troops attacked nearly all of South Vietnam's province capitals and major military installations, and Vietcong sappers even breached the U.S. Embassy compound in Saigon. As American and ARVN troops fought to regain lost territory from I Corps to the Mekong Delta over the first five months of 1968, U.S. casualties neared—and then exceeded—500 dead each week, the war's highest toll.

The early war's firefights now seemed to pale in comparison with fighting during Tet. The bodies of Marines in plain green utilities appeared in I Corps grave registration units; they had not even been in country long enough to be issued their camouflage gear before they died. Reinforcements from the 101st Airborne came to the Marines' assistance in Hue, but the North Vietnamese pressure intensified so much, one trooper reported, "we had to get the hell out of there. . . . So we stacked all the weapons we couldn't carry in the middle of our perimeter and booby-trapped them. Then we buried the dead right there. We'd never done this before and never did it again—we buried our own men right there on the spot" (Appy 2003, 300).

Tet's high casualty rates shocked the nation and the servicemen who watched their brothers in arms die in greater numbers—and for no clear purpose—than ever before. As Spec. 4 Doug Johnson explained, "a lot of guys were leaving Vietnam with a CMH—no, not the Congressional Medal of Honor, but rather a casket with metal handles" (Grzyb 2000, 206). As casualty rates grew, officers pressed hard to exert their authority over their frustrated soldiers. Some failed. In March, 2nd Lt. William L. Calley Jr. commanded a platoon in the American Division on a sweep through My Lai; in the process, he gave the command that resulted in the deaths of an uncounted number of civilians. Other officers did all they could to exert a degree of moral leadership over their men. In June, Marine captain Rodney Chastant explained to his family why he extended his tour: "There are moral decisions made almost every day. My experience is invaluable. This job requires a man of conscience. The group of men that do this job *must* have a leader with a conscience. In the last three weeks we killed more than 1,500 men on a single operation. That reflects a lot of responsibility. I am needed here, Mom" (Edelman 1985, 130). Chastant stayed—and paid with his life.

Vietnamization and the Changing War

The year 1968 proved to be the costliest year of American military operations in Vietnam. The sense of loss, however, went much deeper than the loss of lives. The senior political leadership offered no workable plan to end the war. In late March, when President Johnson announced his decisions to end Operation Rolling Thunder, open negotiations, and pull out of the presidential race, many troops felt betrayed. As the 1968 primary season and the nominating conventions neared, Sgt. Edward Murphy cautioned restraint in effecting change: "In our country there are many ways to make ourselves heard. I hope that the legitimate means afforded us through the democratic process will be used. If the swifter and more dramatic means of violence are used, then history will have that much more reason to condemn us" (Edelman 1985, 145). By the end of the year, Johnson was out, Richard Nixon was in—and the war had claimed another 14,592 American lives (Appy 1993).

Before Johnson left office, however, General Westmoreland handed over command of MACV to Gen. Creighton Abrams. The general oversaw a new strategy designed, ultimately, to facilitate the withdrawal of American troops. As 1968 ended, the United States began backing away from large-scale field operations, returning to an advisory, training, and support role that would prepare the South Vietnamese armed forces to take full responsibility for their defense.

This process—called "Vietnamization"—began at a time when all branches of the American armed services felt the institutional effects of long-term deployment, political disaffection, and social disruptions on the home front. Combat units felt the stresses most directly. Because Johnson had refused to activate Reserves and National Guardsmen and built troop strength on draftees, the number of experienced soldiers in essential combat MOSs ran short. Without warning or retraining, thousands of individuals with noncombat MOSs received reclassification as infantrymen. To fill some needs, at least 15,000 National Guardsmen were activated in 1968 and 1969 and sent to Vietnam, triggering at least one court case that challenged the legality of the deployment. In 1966, Secretary of Defense Robert McNamara had initiated Project 100,000, a social betterment program for men who scored too low on the Armed Forces Qualifications Test for military service but would be accepted for occupational training they could use in civilian life. When these soldiers began arriving in country in 1968, however, detailers discovered nearly 40 percent of them had combat MOSs that would send them to front-line units (Appy 1993). A series of Selective Service reforms in the late 1960s—including the end of most education deferments and the start of the lottery system—brought into the Army a significantly higher percentage of new soldiers who ardently and openly opposed the war. By the end of 1968, the percentage of true volunteers citing "patriotism" as their primary reason for enlisting shrank to only 6.1 percent (Appy 1993).

Complicating matters further, racial concerns caused increasingly contentious confrontations in all the armed services. Studies of African American participation in Vietnam had produced troubling statistics. Although African Americans made up 12 percent of the U.S. population, estimates of black combat deaths in 1965 ranged between 22.4 and 25.0 percent. Additionally, draft boards accepted 30.2 percent of qualified African American men, but only 18.8 percent of qualified whites. Racial conflict rarely flared on the front lines, but in rear areas African Americans and whites clashed openly. Black soldiers clashed with officers over hair regulations and protocol issues, from saluting to the use of the "dap," an elaborate handshake ritual popular among black power advocates. African American service personnel filled a disproportionately low number of technical MOS slots and a disproportionately high number of cells in the military prison at Long Binh. Revisions to the personnel system resulted in a drop in African American combat casualties in 1966 to 16 percent, in 1968 to 13 percent, and in 1970 to 9 percent, but it had little effect in softening racial discord in the ranks (Appy 1993). Complicating the racial dialogue, military personnel of Hispanic background brought their own rising ethnic awareness into the ranks. As Army PFC Charley Trujillo explained, "Out in the bush I never felt such affinity and togetherness with men of other cultures and races as I did in

Vietnam." But that sense of brotherhood did not extend to the rear area, where some members of his unit threatened him with "'Hey, man, you better watch out because from behind you look like a gook" (Appy 2003, 368). Although no study has produced comprehensive statistics about the participation of Hispanic service personnel in Vietnam, at least 48,000 Puerto Ricans served in Vietnam, and 345 died (Appy 1993).

Drug use also rose dramatically after 1968. Soldiers and pilots took Benzedrine, Dexedrine, and other pharmaceuticals to remain alert. Far more turned to illegal drugs. A wartime study showed that marijuana use among American soldiers returning home in 1967 stood at 29 percent; by 1969 it had jumped to 50 percent and by 1970 to nearly 60 percent (Appy 1993). Most Vietnam veterans claim that they limited their marijuana use to camp, never in the field, but Army sergeant Bill McCollum admitted, "We'd go out on patrol just so we could smoke!" If they suffered a casualty, "we'd check to make sure no marijuana was found on him" (Grzyb 2000, 136). Efforts to curtail drug use produced few positive results. Soldiers sent to field hospitals for overdoses might be locked in large metal supply boxes for a few days, after which they would be rehydrated and sent back to their units. The availability of cheap heroin exploded in 1970, and by 1971 service personnel returning home underwent urinalysis—dubbed the "piss test"—to be cleared to get on their "freedom bird." A black market in clean urine samples flourished.

As the war continued, combat troops grew more vocal in their resentment of unfair personnel assignments. A unit of Army infantrymen complained directly to Nixon in April 1969 that "basically there are two different wars here in Vietnam. While we are out in the field living like animals, putting our lives on the line 24 hours a day, seven days a week, the guy in the rear's biggest problem is that he can receive only one television station" (Edelman 1985, 139). Enlisted "grunts," who usually spent their entire tours at the front, increasingly resented their officers, who usually served only six months in the field and then rotated to the rear to fill a staff billet with far less exposure to death, disease, and dismemberment.

Combat troops' concerns about their officers went far deeper than duty assignments, however. Even the Pentagon worried about a decline in the quality of their leadership. By 1967, Army Officer Candidate School programs lowered standards and commissioned men who would have been rejected earlier in the war. In 1968, for the first time, the Naval Academy's graduating class did not fill its quota for Marine second lieutenants. West Point accepted every eligible applicant to fill its plebe class that same summer. Some universities terminated their Army, Navy, and Air Force Reserve Officers' Training Corps (ROTC) programs, while others struggled to fill their ranks. The results could have been predicted. As one soldier in 1969 explained, his unit "had a gung-ho greenhorn ROTC platoon leader and nobody trusted his orders. It wasn't that they were refusing to fight, just to take orders from him. Eventually a PFC with more experience took over. The authority was given to him by the other men" (Appy 2003, 258). An Army War College study in 1970 deplored the pervasiveness of concern over personal advancement—so-called "ticket-punching"—among officers of all ranks. Just as troubling, increasing numbers of officers—including graduates from service academies—sought conscientious objector status while still serving in uniform; indeed, requests from all ranks jumped from 829 in 1967 to 4,381 in 1971 (Appy 1993).

These institutional weaknesses festered without resolution as the Vietnamization phase accelerated. Part of the new strategy called for an increased—and belated—effort by American military forces to help rally the South Vietnamese people's "hearts and minds" behind the Saigon government. American troops had attempted to train local defense forces since the advisory period, and in 1965 the Marines who served in I Corps began an aggressive program of civic action platoons (CAPs) that accompanied doctors and dentists into local hamlets to offer both protection and useful medical, educational, and occupational assistance. Although dangerous, CAPs attracted soldiers and Marines who, even late in the war, sought a constructive outlet. Jonathan Polansky of the 101st Airborne Division set up a school in 1969, feeling as though "I was a Peace Corps worker in this country, dealing with the classroom." After three months, however, he returned to find the village completely destroyed because the residents had accepted American help (Santoli 1981, 61).

Another element of the Vietnamization policy called for improving the South Vietnamese military's chances of defending its country by eliminating long-standing bastions of North Vietnamese Army (NVA) strength while American ground troops still remained in significant—if declining—numbers. At Ap Bia Mountain in the A Shau Valley in mid-May 1969, the NVA broke from its usual practice of avoiding extended contact to fight from bunkers and trenches for nine days, much of it in torrential rain. The 101st Airborne and other U.S. and ARVN troops finally took the hill—and, then, as happened so often before—abandoned it. The North Vietnamese immediately retook it. Heavy media coverage and congressional attention given to the fight—soon dubbed "Hamburger Hill" for the way the fighting ground down American troop strength—exaggerated the battle's importance, but it also illustrated a growing dissonance between the political promises of a reduced mission and the continuing loss of soldier lives.

In late April 1970, President Nixon approved a joint incursion by 30,000 U.S. troops and 50,000 ARVN soldiers into Cambodia's Fishhook region to eliminate a suspected North Vietnamese command center there and to test the progress of South Vietnamese military readiness. The action polarized popular opinion at home and compromised troop morale on the battlefront, but not always in predictable ways. Army specialist 4 Gregory Lusco, mourning lost comrades, objected to memorials for the students killed at Kent State University in protests spawned by the incursion: "So why don't your hearts cry out and shed a tear for the 40-plus thousand red-blooded Americans and brave, fearless, loyal men who have given their lives so a bunch of bloody bastard radicals can protest, dissent, and generally bitch about our private and personal war in Vietnam and now Cambodia?" He concluded, "I am coming home soon. Don't shout and preach your nothingness to me. I am ashamed to be fighting to keep you safe, the rest of the loyal Americans" (Edelman 1985, 240–241).

Not all servicemen shared Lusco's opinion, of course. Army medic Keith R. Franklin, killed in Cambodia on May 12, left a last letter with his family that read in part: "The war that has taken my life and many thousands before me is immoral, unlawful and an atrocity unlike any misfit of good sense and judgment known to man" (Emerson 1985, 101). Antiwar sentiment in the ranks increasingly affected field operations. Individual soldiers "ghosted"— faked illnesses or injuries to stay out of the field. Patrols "sandbagged" by only pretending to complete risky missions, even supplying fabricated reports and faked coordinates marking their position. In some units, soldiers overtly refused orders for missions they deemed useless or excessively dangerous. The once reliable 1st Cavalry division experienced 35 cases of combat refusal in 1970 alone. Officers and senior sergeants found little incentive to interfere. In 1969, military courts considered 129 cases of alleged fragging—murder of officers or senior NCOs by one's own troops, often by fragmentation grenade— and the numbers jumped to 270 cases in 1970 and 333 in 1971 (Appy 1993). Few cases resulted in a conviction. As marine James Hebron recalled, "A friend of mine put sixteen rounds in a staff sergeant's back. . . . The staff sergeant received a Purple Heart, was put in a green bag and packed home. No autopsy or anything else" (Santoli 1981, 95).

By mid-1971, military journalist Robert Heinl offered this assessment: "By every conceivable indicator, our army that now remains in Vietnam is in a state of approaching collapse, with individual units avoiding or having refused combat, murdering their officers and noncommissioned officers, drug-ridden and dispirited where not near-mutinous" (Appy 1993, 247). It did not help that the Lam Son 719 campaign into Laos in February 1971, designed once again to test the readiness of the ARVN troops, ended in abject failure. Although no American ground units took part, Air Force, Marine, and Navy aircraft attempted to provide air support. At least 253 Americans died in the effort, which exposed the continued incapacity, even unwillingness, of the ARVN to fight. As Bill Poffenberger, an adviser with the South Vietnamese riverine force in 1971 complained: "My closest friends were the Cambodians" who "were wanting to win the damned war." By contrast, the South Vietnamese "who were supposed to be with us would run the other way. It really pissed me off" (Beesley 1987, 58).

By March 1972, most American ground combat troops had left South Vietnam. Only advisers and support personnel remained when the several prongs of the North Vietnamese Army's Easter Offensive swept across the DMZ, into the central highlands, and toward Saigon. Unwilling to risk his reelection by increasing American ground troops but still committed to helping South Vietnam, Nixon turned to "the air weapon." Air Force units withdrawn at the end of Operation Rolling Thunder in March 1968 redeployed to Guam and Thailand, and A-6 Intruders and A-7 Corsairs launched from Yankee Station initiated Operation Linebacker in early May by mining Haiphong Harbor. With an intensity absent from the air war since 1968, the interdiction campaign targeted North Vietnamese bridges, warehouses, and other logistical targets. The air strikes helped stop the North Vietnamese offensive by midsummer, but diplomacy did not result in a negotiated settlement despite a premature announcement in October 1972 that "peace is at hand." Nixon ordered Linebacker II, often called "the Christmas bombings," to begin on December 18. For 11 days, Air Force and Navy missions hammered military targets near Hanoi and Haiphong long off limits to American airmen. For the first time, the Air Force's B-52s hit military targets near North Vietnam's biggest cities, losing at least 15 of the big bombers and their crews in the process. Although global and domestic protest exploded—and a few Air Force air crews refused missions—other aviators took professional satisfaction in challenging one of the strongest air defense systems in the world to hit difficult targets. One naval aviator even wrote home, "you have to respect" Nixon "for the courage and ability to make a decision and stick to it, even if he is endangering my own neck!!" (Reardon 2005, 330).

The Paris Peace Accords that followed called for a ceasefire on January 27, 1973. As part of the agreements, all remaining American service personnel had 60 days to leave South Vietnam. From the war's beginning, soldiers could not wait for their departure. Each man knew his DEROS and counted the days. As one bit of soldier doggerel went: "Eighty days have September, April, June, and November. All the rest have ninety-three except the last month which has one hundred and forty" (Ebert 1993, 214). In February and March, the North Vietnamese repatriated 591 American prisoners of war in Operation Homecoming but did not follow through with the required accounting for at least 2,500 other Americans listed as missing in action. Over the course of America's longest war, some career military personnel went through the process of deploying to Vietnam and returning home after second, third, and even fourth tours. Some even deployed after the Paris Peace Accords, returning in civilian clothes as part of military materiel missions to transfer equipment and supplies to the South Vietnamese and Cambodian armed forces. The last American military personnel officially left in late April 1975, when Saigon finally fell to the North Vietnamese.

Not all sevicemen returned safely to their families, of course. Statistical studies reveal casualty rates by branch, race, religion, home state, marriage, rank, age, and more. At least 58,193 American military personnel died in Vietnam. At least 38,502 were killed in combat and another 5,264 died of wounds. At least 3,524 servicemen "died while missing," many of them members of Air Force and Navy aircrews. Nonhostile causes—from vehicle accidents to malaria—accounted for more than 10,700 deaths. The Army lost 38,209 soldiers, but the 14,838 Marine Corps dead represented a much higher percentage of that service's wartime strength. Officers made up 13.2 percent of the dead; eight were Army or Air Force nurses. Project 100,000 casualties accounted for 4.1 percent of the dead. But statistical tables reveal little about the human bonds broken with each death. Beallsville, Ohio—population 475—lost six young men in Vietnam. Thomas Edison High School of Philadelphia lost at least 54 of its former students. Dan Bullock lied about his age to enlist in the Marine Corps and died in Vietnam at age 15. At least 29 sets of brothers died in Vietnam; two families lost both a father and a son (Vietnam Veterans Memorial n.d.; National Archives 2007).

As he contemplated his return home in 1971, Army captain James Gabbe wrote, "my sojourn here has been a very personal, very complicated

John McCain

John Sidney McCain III, the son and grandson of U.S. Navy admirals, was born in the Panama Canal Zone on August 29, 1936. After a childhood marked by frequent moves, he entered the United States Naval Academy. Preferring history and literature to the engineering core of the academy's curriculum, McCain graduated fifth from the bottom of his class and gained a reputation for flaunting authority.

After commissioning, McCain entered pilot training at Pensacola Naval Air Station and later became a flight instructor. As the air war in Vietnam heated up, however, he requested a combat assignment. Deployed first on the USS *Forrestal*, McCain was nearly killed on the carrier deck on July 29, 1967, when a Zuni rocket on another aircraft accidentally fired and hit the full fuel tanks of his A-4 Skyhawk. He escaped the cockpit with shrapnel wounds, but the ensuing conflagration killed 132 others. McCain transferred to the USS *Oriskany*.

During an October 26, 1967, strike on the Hanoi thermal power plant, a surface-to-air missile downed McCain's aircraft. Two frac-

tured arms and a broken leg made escape impossible, and he became a prisoner. He was initially denied medical care, but his treatment improved briefly in July 1968 when the North Vietnamese realized that McCain's father was the new commanding officer of the Pacific Command and offered the aviator an early release. Accepting the offer would violate the Prisoner of War Code of Conduct, so McCain turned it down and was beaten and tortured for his refusal. McCain was taken to Hoa Lo Prison—the "Hanoi Hilton"—in late 1969, where he continued to resist his captors by refusing to meet American antiwar activists. After five and a half years, McCain was repatriated on March 15, 1973.

Despite his injuries, McCain returned to the cockpit and retired from the Navy in 1981 as a captain. He later won election as a U.S. senator from Arizona and became a strong advocate of normalizing relations between the United States and Vietnam. In 2008, he became the Republican Party's nominee for president of the United States.

experience for me" (Edelman 1985, 283). The staccato sentiments of Army veteran Billy Walkabout cast light on the complexity of individual experience: "I volunteered to serve. I saw a lot. Men died. Friends died. I got hurt. It was shit. It was awesome" (Beesley 1987, 122). In the end, each Vietnam veteran—regardless of rank, date of tour, branch of service, MOS, or in-country location—had to decide for himself the most important personal legacy of his service. Even before he rotated home in early 1966, Army PFC George Robinson wrote his family, "Any combat GI that comes here doesn't leave the same. . . . Don't ask any questions. When I come home, if I feel like talking about it I will, but otherwise don't ask" (Beesley 1987, 122–123). For many, closure still remains elusive.

References and Further Reading

Adler, Bill, ed. *Letters from Vietnam.* New York: Random House, 2003.

Appy, Christian. *Patriots: The Vietnam War Remembered from All Sides.* New York: Viking Penguin, 2003.

Navy pilot John McCain (bottom right) poses with members of his squadron in 1965. (*Library of Congress*)

Appy, Christian. *Working-Class War: American Combat Soldiers and Vietnam.* Chapel Hill: University of North Carolina Press, 1993.

Baskir, Lawrence, and William Strauss. *Chance and Circumstance: The Draft, the War and the Vietnam Generation.* New York: Vintage Books, 1978.

Beesley, Stanley. *Vietnam: The Heartland Remembers.* Norman: University of Oklahoma Press, 1987.

Bergerud, Eric. *Red Thunder, Tropic Lightning: The World of a Combat Division in Vietnam.* New York: Penguin Books, 1993.

Ebert, James. *A Life in a Year: The American Infantryman in Vietnam.* Novato, CA: Presidio Press, 1993.

Edelman, Bernard, ed. *Dear America: Letters Home from Vietnam.* New York: Pocket Books, 1985.

Elkins, Frank. *The Heart of a Man: A Naval Pilot's Vietnam Diary.* Edited by Marilyn Elkins. Annapolis, MD: Naval Institute Press, 1991.

Emerson, Gloria. *Winners and Losers: Battles, Retreats, Gains, Losses, and Ruins from the Vietnam War.* New York: Penguin Books, 1985.

Grzyb, Frank. *A Story for All Americans: Vietnam, Victims, and Veterans.* West Lafayette, IN: Purdue University Press, 2000.

National Archives. "Statistical Information about Casualties of the Vietnam Conflict." http://www.archives.gov/research/vietnam-war/casualty-statistics.html (accessed November 27, 2007).

Palmer, Laura. *Shrapnel in the Heart: Letters and Remembrances from the Vietnam Veterans Memorial.* New York: Random House, 1987.

Prashker, Ivan. *Duty, Honor, Vietnam: Twelve Men of West Point Tell Their Stories.* New York: Warner Books, 1988.

Reardon, Carol. *Launch the Intruders: A Naval Attack Squadron in the Vietnam War, 1972.* Chapel Hill: University of North Carolina Press, 2005.

Rhodes, John. *Rejoice or Cry: The Diary of a Recon Marine, Vietnam, 1967–1968.* Danbury, CT: Economy Printing, 1996.

Santoli, Al. *Everything We Had: An Oral History of the Vietnam War by Thirty-Three American Soldiers Who Fought It.* New York: Ballantine Books, 1981.

Vietnam Veterans Memorial: The Wall-USA. n.d. "Names on the Wall." http://thewall-usa.com/names.asp (accessed November 27, 2007).

Antiwar Activists 4

Rhodri Jeffreys-Jones

In his defiance of those in authority, Harry Bridges had few equals. His leadership of the San Francisco general strike of 1934 provoked demands for deployment of the U.S. Army and Navy against his longshoremen, and there followed prolonged efforts to deport Bridges to his native Australia on account of his communist sympathies. By 1962, the veteran leader claimed to be a Republican and seemed to have mellowed. Not so. In May of that year, he bluntly criticized President John F. Kennedy for sending American troops to Thailand and South Vietnam.

The Bridges protest suggests a need to look beyond the popular image of 1960s antiwar activists, that of long-haired students who began the serious challenge to the war policy of President Lyndon Baines Johnson only when major military escalation began in 1965. After all, American involvement in Vietnam and objections to it ran all the way back to the late 1940s, when the government decided to block the expansion of communism by supporting the French attempt to reassert colonial control over Indochina.

Furthermore, antiwar protest and civil disobedience were rooted in a tradition supported by some of the nation's greatest literary figures. Henry David Thoreau had refused to pay his taxes because he opposed the Mexican-American War of 1846. In the 1930s, there had been widespread condemnation of the "merchants of death," the arms manufacturers accused of maneuvering America into World War I. Antimilitarist sentiments of this type prepared America for allegations that a sinister military-industrial complex had groomed Washington to opt for war in Vietnam.

Yet the truth remains that Bridges and his longshoremen were considerably in advance of public opinion in the early 1960s. While the longshoremen celebrated Labor Day in 1965 with a demand for "Peace and Pork Chops," other maritime workers feared that the former could not be achieved without sacrificing the latter, for the Vietnam War apparently made workers rich. The Sailors' Union of the Pacific pointed out in 1968 that 98

Activist Harry Bridges (left) leaves the county jail in San Francisco, 1950. (*Library of Congress*)

percent of war supplies and 66 percent of military personnel went to Vietnam in American ships that created American jobs. The vast majority of the labor movement lined up behind the war in its early phases, with AFL-CIO (American Federation of Labor and Congress of Industrial Organizations) president George Meany leading the military parade (Jeffreys-Jones 1999).

Emerging Dissent

If the force of the antiwar movement and the reasons for it are to be appreciated, support for the war must first be understood. Popular endorsement of the war came about not just because of greed but for other reasons, too. One of the most important was the American nation's solid opposition to communism. America's opponents in Vietnam were communists, and thus, fighting them could be squared with the American people.

More immediately, the Tonkin Gulf episode afforded the justification for U.S. military escalation. On August 5, 1964, President Johnson asked Congress to pass a joint resolution giving him the powers he needed to counter aggression from the Vietnamese communists. He stated that, in the Gulf of Tonkin the previous evening, torpedo boats from communist North Vietnam had attacked two U.S. destroyers, the *Maddox* and the *C. Turner Joy*. America has always retaliated against aggression, and on this occasion the president achieved a near declaration of war by an overwhelming majority, with only two senators voting against the Gulf of Tonkin Resolution. According to Harris opinion samplers, before this resolution only 42 percent of Americans supported Johnson's handling of Vietnam. After the Gulf of Tonkin incident, 85 percent approved of his response to the crisis, and 72 percent supported his general policy (Moise 1996).

Underlying these particular circumstances, another phenomenon was at work. Americans tend to rally behind their president when he confronts threats from abroad, and none more so than in the cases of those who might otherwise have a grievance against society. For example, laborers who might engage in militant strike action in more peaceful times line up with the Stars and Stripes when the fighting starts; women who are pacifists in peacetime support the military when there is a serious conflict; African Americans who have bitterly cried out against injustice are among the first to volunteer when America confronts an enemy. Such responses indicate not just patriotism but also a hope that conformity will bring acceptance and a breakthrough in terms of social and political status. This breakthrough syndrome operated powerfully in creating support for the Vietnam War.

Yet the American people ultimately turned against their nation's involvement in the Vietnam War. In one of the great social movements of modern times, antiwar protesters led the way. There is some debate about the consequences of protest. Because the *image* of the typical protester was that of a long-haired student with scant respect for the law or conventional morality, public opinion tended to be hostile to protest even as it turned against the war, so the White House was able to use protest as a justification for continuing the war. Some argue that protest was counterproductive and prolonged, even as it doomed, the war.

According to another school of thought, Hanoi and its communist allies in South Vietnam took courage from the antiwar movement and fought longer and harder as a result. However, finally and much more convincingly, there is the argument that the policy makers listened. Just as the Republican president William McKinley had abandoned his imperialist agenda to undermine the appeal of the Democrats in the election of 1900, so President Richard Nixon withdrew from Vietnam to hang on to political office. When Joan Baez sang in New York's Central Park to celebrate the war's end, she and her supporters believed they were also rejoicing in their own victory as protesters. So did the neoconservatives who saw America's withdrawal as mistaken, premature, and tragic, the action of pusillanimous politicians who bent the knee to unpatriotic protesters. To the theory that protest forced American withdrawal from the war, there is a bipartisan ring of truth.

One could explain with deceptive ease why protest occurred and how it succeeded. Many of those in Congress who had voted for the Gulf of Tonkin Resolution came to believe they had been tricked into doing so and felt betrayed. Senator J. William Fulbright (D-AR) was chairman of the Senate Foreign Relations Committee and had led the push for the resolution, but with doubts setting in both about the resolution and about the war, he instigated inquiries into Tonkin.

It emerged that the U.S. Navy had been engaged in intelligence and covert operations in the Tonkin Gulf. The way in which the administration denied their existence provoked anger. Even more upsetting, the communist attack of August 4 simply had not taken place. In an understandable error on a dark and stormy night, U.S. naval gunners had shot at phantom targets. Confronted with more evidence about this event, critics concluded that the Johnson administration had duplicitously blown the incident up into a case of North Vietnamese aggression. The White House offered further provocation when it tried to block the Fulbright inquiry. In the course of the cover-up, it even had a key witness, a naval officer from the Pentagon, locked up in a mental ward to prevent him from testifying.

A simple explanation of the antiwar revolt would thus seem to be at hand. Not so, however. Although the Tonkin justification of war had unraveled by 1968, it was not until June 30, 1973, that Congress voted to cut off funds for all military operations in and over Indochina. Although Fulbright was constitutionally the second most powerful formulator of foreign policy in the nation after the president, he could not act until public opinion was on his side. He was ill equipped, however, to offer the kind of leadership that might swing opinion. His urbanity and internationalism may have pleased his admirers, but they did not make him a popular figure. Even more debilitating was his stubborn opposition to civil rights, the one cause that united the diverse liberal crusaders of the 1960s. Marginalized for this reason, Fulbright could not lead the antiwar campaign.

Mass opposition nevertheless developed, and antiwar activists supplied a multiplicity of reasons for their opposition to the war. Most activists expressed themselves in terms of principle, and a few in terms of ideology. Citing the First Amendment guaranteeing free speech, activists demanded the right to speak out against the war and fought against restrictions imposed by college authorities and security services such as the Federal Bureau of Investigation (FBI). In the name of democracy they denounced their nation's support for the Saigon government, which was just as dictatorial as the Hanoi regime that directed the enemy. As the Vietnamese were a nonwhite people, they denounced American policy for being neocolonialist and racist. Additionally, a small minority of activists saw the antiwar movement as an opportunity to frustrate global neocolonialism and to destabilize capitalism in America.

As the war progressed and the fighting claimed more lives, psychology and emotion became entangled with principles. The American philosophy on war was to avoid it if you can, but, if you must, fight all out to win. However, Hanoi and its allies in South Vietnam fought a war of attrition in which neither side could win obvious victories. Then came Tet, the January 1968 surprise communist offensive that sent Americans and their allies in South Vietnam scuttling for cover, with television cameras showing ignominious scenes, such as communist guerrillas racing through the grounds of the U.S. embassy in Saigon. No matter that U.S. and allied forces counterattacked so effectively that they almost destroyed enemy fighting power. The communists had struck a psychological blow that shook American faith in the wisdom of its cause.

In disturbing numbers America's bravest patriots were coming home in body bags, 58,000 of them by the war's end. Not only this, but some of those patriots were committing atrocities, leading activists to question exactly what values America was defending. The most notorious outrage was that at My Lai on March 16, 1968, in which an American infantry company attacked a group of unarmed civilians, destroying their property, raping the women, and killing between 175 and 400 men, women, and children. The crime came to light the following year and has caused Americans anguish ever since. In the stress of battle soldiers do very often lose their humanity. Only the previous month, on February 25, 1968, troops of America's allies, the South Korean expeditionary force, had massacred 135 elders, women, and children in the village of Ha My, subsequently desecrating their graves and reburying them en masse to destroy the evidence (Kwon 2006). American discourse did not recognize Ha My then or has not recognized it since—what shocked Americans was the spectacle of *American* boys turning into savages.

Visual images recorded by television cameras brought the war home to Americans in their living rooms and pricked their consciences. The media were not antiwar. If anything they were anti-protest. To make an impact, however, they did not have to be biased; they just had to be there. Because the American military campaign in Vietnam was authorized only by a joint congressional resolution and not by a full declaration of war, the American government could not use censorship to shield its citizens from the crimson-hued horrors of maimed American soldiers and little Vietnamese girls burnt

Former residents of My Lai hamlet who were killed by U.S. soldiers. During the most notorious publicly acknowledged military atrocity of the Vietnam War, between 200 and 500 Vietnamese civilians were massacred by U.S. soldiers at My Lai hamlet on March 16, 1968. A cover-up kept the massacre a secret for a year, after which 14 soldiers were charged with the crime and only one was found guilty and sentenced to prison. (*Ronald S. Haeberle/Time Life Pictures/Getty Images*)

alive by U.S. Air Force napalm attacks. All of this happened in an era when color television first swept the nation and had its maximum impact.

Violations of American principles were not in themselves enough to provoke effective protest. Other factors came into play to give them an irresistible force. Young men began to think of their self-interest. They opposed, resisted, and avoided the draft. The war economy went from boom to bust, another good reason for antiwar activism.

Groups within American society whose leaders had seen it as being to their advantage to support the war began to think differently. This caused serial problems, as they rebelled at spaced-out intervals, giving the White House no rest and a constantly shifting political adversary. African Americans began to protest in significant numbers approximately at the time when Martin Luther King Jr. attacked the war in April 1967. The popularity of women's crusade against the war peaked the following year, and, by 1970, the possibility of a wage earners' revolt against the war caused serious policy reappraisals within the Nixon administration. Each for its own reasons, these social groups rejected the conformist mentality that goes with the social breakthrough syndrome, and, inconveniently for the war makers, they did so at unpredictable times.

Yet the group that first dissented on a significant scale had never had status worries in the first place. In an article on the student Left in the May 1965 issue of *The Nation*, reporter Jack Newfield wrote of a "new generation of radicals" that had been spawned from the "womb of affluent America" and took its inspiration from Bob Dylan, not Karl Marx (Anderson 1995, 147–148). The following year he described this middle-class New Left as a "prophetic minority." His perception that the protesting students were from affluent backgrounds was perhaps only partly correct, but certainly the campus protesters had access to future middle-class status. They did not have to worry about making political compromises to consolidate their standing, which perhaps helps to explain why students protested against the Vietnam War well before the majority of off-campus America stirred from its complacency.

Students

Like other groups in American society, students operated within a cultural tradition. Until the Twenty-Sixth Amendment lowered the voting age to 18 in 1971, people of campus age could not vote. Thus, they were tempted by "direct action" of the type most famously employed by the Progressive-era revolutionary socialist organization, the Industrial Workers of the World. The IWW had fought on behalf of disenfranchised groups, African Americans, migrants, and women as well as youth, and, with its advocacy of strikes, sabotage, and free speech fights, the group inspired study on 1960s campuses. Taking a leaf from more recent history, campus rebels were even more deeply moved by the struggle for voter registration and civil rights in the American South. Here, too, the direct action tactic of nonviolent resistance gave antiwar activists a model that could be emulated.

Student protesters raged against the establishment. In 1964, the sociologist E. Digby Baltzell had discerned a decline in the "authority of an establishment which is now based on an increasingly caste-like White-Anglo-Saxon-Protestant (WASP) upper class" (9). If the WASPs were on the way out, the 1960s rebels tilted at a new foe that might be conceptualized as the WORM, or White *Old* Rich Men. It was nothing new for young folk to rebel against their parents, but the sixties generation cast the whole of the governing elite of America as an oppressive and hypocritical parental entity. The refrain of the 1965 Phil Ochs song "I Ain't a Marchin' Anymore" captured the complaint: "It's always the old who lead us to war; it's always the young who fall."

The reasons why this attitude was more acute in the sixties than before or since are open to conjecture. Were the nation's foreign-policy leaders more debilitated by advancing years than usual? The evidence is not persuasive. The average age of secretaries of state in their last year of office in 1949 to 1973 was 62.8, not a great increase on the figure for 1892 to 1905, which was 61.5. In real health terms, given medical advances, the secretaries were more vigorous than their earlier counterparts. As average life expectancy in 1900 was only 47.3, compared with 69.7 in 1959, one can say that, relatively speaking, diplomacy was in the hands of the aged in the early period but was conducted by men in the full vigor of late middle age in the 1960s (Jeffreys-Jones 1999, 46).

Young people felt emboldened and empowered for a number of reasons. John F. Kennedy was the charismatic young president who challenged the campus generation to serve society and who first announced his plan for a Peace Corps in the course of a campus address at the University of Michigan in October 1960. He and his glamorous wife, Jacqueline, stamped the sixties with the imprint of youth in a way that his tragic death only enhanced. In the 1960s, the post–World War II baby boom hit campuses at a time when university education was rapidly expanding. The college population grew from 3 million in 1960 to 10 million in 1970. The impact of this on antiwar activism was not automatic. Only 300 of the nation's 2,000 campuses experienced unrest (Heineman 2001), yet it can be said that the unrest affected a variety of campus types, thus permeating a broad section of the nation at a time when educational expansion had ensured that just about everyone knew a college student. If the elite campuses led the way, they had a significant following.

The campus antiwar movement threw up charismatic leaders who conveyed in eloquent terms the discontents of their generation. Tom Hayden recorded in his memoir that he came from Detroit, where his father was an accountant and life was mundane. Then Hayden attended the prestigious University of Michigan at Ann Arbor, an institution he boasted was "the birthplace of Students for a Democratic Society (SDS), the Peace Corps, and the Vietnam Teach-ins" (Hayden 1988, 25). Hayden was president of SDS in 1962–1963, and the main author of the Port Huron Statement, which outlined the group's principles. The statement expressed the ideology that propelled America's middle-class youth to fight racism, nuclear weapons, and poverty and pressed for community spirit and participatory democracy.

On March 24–25, 1965, the SDS organized the nation's first teach-in against the Vietnam War. It took place in Ann Arbor and supplied a model followed in 35 other universities. Three thousand students, community activists, and professors took part in discussions and lectures about the war, with a heavy emphasis on dissent. Hayden had by this time left Ann Arbor to become a nationwide activist. When the Johnson administration illegally tasked the Central Intelligence Agency (CIA) with spying on Hayden and his friends, it submitted an awestruck report that described them as "tireless, peripatetic, full-time crusaders" (Jeffreys-Jones 1989, 168). Hayden kept on hitting the headlines. In 1968, for example, he was one of the Chicago Seven, arrested on flimsy charges for conspiracy at the Democratic National Convention. Not everyone admired him, least of all the feminists who saw him hand his dirty laundry to the nearest woman on hand. His marriage to the movie actress Jane Fonda helped improve his image even in that quarter.

Though the University of Michigan had a pioneering role in what came to be known as "The Movement," the teach-in against the Vietnam War echoed a protest that was already taking place on the campus of the University of California at Berkeley. This was another publicly funded institution, which carried the prestige—according to nationwide polls of professors—of being the best university in America. Trouble had brewed in the fall of 1964 when the Berkeley authorities tried to enforce a regulation that prohibited political meetings on campus. Students who were already unhappy about the Vietnam War now vehemently attacked the University of California president. Clark Kerr was a liberal with a reputation for supporting the

Demonstrators protest the trial of the Chicago Seven (also known as the Chicago Eight). The Chicago Seven, antiwar activists arrested for protests during the Democratic National Convention held in Chicago in 1968, drew attention to their cause during a lengthy and often bizarre trial. (*Library of Congress*)

rights of organized labor, but in a fiery speech at Sproul Plaza on December 4, campus rebel Mario Savio denounced him as a "two-faced hypocrite" (Rorabaugh 1989, 40).

The Free Speech Movement (FSM) grew out of the fall 1964 confrontations. Savio, the son of a Sicilian factory worker and recently active in civil rights work, was one of its organizers. So was Bettina Aptheker. Like several in her radical group, Aptheker was Jewish, came from a family victimized by McCarthyism, and had been a "red diaper" baby (i.e., had communist parents) but now favored the tenets of the New Left. Aptheker once said, "I've got a last name that's dynamite" (Rorabaugh 1989, 24). Her father, Herbert Aptheker, had written a landmark book. Challenging widely held racial assumptions, it claimed that African Americans had not enjoyed slavery and had consistently rebelled against it. Bettina was a communist like her father, but unlike communists of the Old Left type, she did not respect the Communist Party line, and finally left the party because of its conservative stance on homosexuality.

Jerry Rubin was another Berkeley figure who helped put antiwar activism on the political map. The son of a labor union official, Rubin had majored in sociology at the University of Cincinnati. He arrived in Oakland via an Israeli kibbutz and a sojourn in communist Cuba and helped give intellectual shape to student protest. Taking his cue from left-wing intellectuals such as C. Wright Mills, Herbert Marcuse, and Ronald Radosh, Rubin denounced organized labor as racist, reactionary, and no longer capable of being a catalyst of reform. He challenged students to pick up the discarded torch of American radicalism. Building on the base established by the FSM, he organized the Vietnam Day Committee. Neglecting his studies—he dropped out of his graduate course—he organized a teach-in at Berkeley in May. He also helped launch a new form of direct action—in October 1965, several hundred people gathered outside the Oakland Army Terminal in an unsuccessful attempt to block incoming trains full of troops destined for the passage to Vietnam. Unarmed students could not hope to succeed in this tactic, but they did capture the headlines.

This was just the start of a string of direct actions by the nation's students. They included strikes, mass demonstrations and marches, teach-ins, sit-ins, draft resistance, tantrum tactics (smashing windows and other property), and the occupation of university buildings—SDS students closed down Columbia University's campus for a week in April 1968. To put that in perspective, the loosely termed "generation of '68" was less active in America than in other countries—the London School of Economics scarcely functioned in 1967, and Paris's prestigious university, the Sorbonne, never quite recovered from the confrontations of 1968. Vietnam was at best a marginal issue in those international upheavals. Nevertheless, American students' antiwar activism had a dramatic impact in the context of U.S. politics, and their tactics were sometimes devastatingly imaginative, as when they targeted the offspring of senior policy makers and converted them to their cause. Craig McNamara, the son of Robert McNamara, who as secretary of defense from 1961 to 1968 was the architect of U.S. military escalation, smashed windows in protest and then emigrated. Robert McNamara's

Republican successor, Melvin Laird, had a similar problem with his niece. Men such as McNamara and Laird fought the war from their offices, but when they went home their children reminded them who was dying.

Over time the character of student protest changed. Some critics have pointed to the increasing frivolity of some of the protest and to the descent of the SDS into ideologically driven factionalism in 1969. The problem that affected a far greater number of students was the draft. The Selective Service Act of 1948 applied to young men in the 18–26 age bracket, with deferments for those in full-time study. But the expansion of the war meant an escalation in the number of troops needed. President Johnson's first escalation call in July 1965 was for 50,000 men; in June 1966, he requested 431,000. To ensure greater manpower and in the name of social justice, the administration now abolished deferment for graduate study. This had two effects. First, it greatly increased the degree of student support for ending the war. Second, it made the student movement less idealistic in character.

Disillusioned by Tet, President Johnson refused a request from the military for a further 206,000 troops. The Nixon administration introduced a draft lottery in 1969 to ensure greater fairness, but this became irrelevant because the government reduced American troop numbers as part of its policy of "Vietnamizing" the war. Now there was no incentive for students of draft age to oppose the war for purely selfish reasons, and the campus protest movement swung back to its former, idealistic character. By this time, however, it had yielded its primacy in the antiwar movement to other groups.

African Americans

The African American revolt spelled trouble for the war leaders. Speaking in Mississippi in December 1964, black nationalist leader Malcolm X accused the United States government of hypocrisy for declaring itself in favor of democracy. How could that be when it sent black soldiers to fight for freedom in Saigon while at home African Americans still found it difficult to "vote without getting murdered" (Westheider 1997, 18–19)? Within two months, Malcolm X would be dead, the victim of a brutal assassination. His removal helps to explain why students held center stage in the opening phase of the antiwar movement, yet his critical remarks had prepared the ground for a black revolt.

African Americans were at first loyal to the war effort. If any section in American society needed help and recognition, it was the oppressed and poor black minority. The Democratic administration may have been escalating the war, but it did seem committed to ending discrimination and poverty. These were prime goals of Lyndon Johnson's Great Society programs, and the president himself was committed to the reforms. Why rock the boat by complaining about a distant war, even if that war was repugnant? This was the philosophy of prominent black leaders such as Ralph Bunche and Whitney Young. National Association for the Advancement of Colored People (NAACP) president Roy Wilkins explained his view in an address at Yale University: "The better plan is to stick with the civil rights issue and leave foreign policy to individuals who feel a strong urge and to organizations working in that field" (Jeffreys-Jones 1999, 116–117).

From the point of view of the young black man from a typically impoverished background, the pay and skills training in the armed forces were attractive. In the early years of the war, such men volunteered in significant numbers for military service, and then for dangerous combat assignments that paid even better money. Like black soldiers in previous wars, they welcomed the pay but also looked beyond it. They hoped a demonstration of loyalty and valor would lift up their race and enhance their personal prestige. They were heroes when, and if, they returned to their communities. Even after the outbreak of discontent, most black Americans were conspicuous by their absence from mass demonstrations. Urban deprivation remained the prime cause of grief in their lives.

That grinding inequality also contributed to the undoing of the Johnson administration. At a speech in New York's Riverside Church on April 4, 1967, Martin Luther King Jr. advocated unilateral withdrawal from the Vietnam War. A Baptist minister, King had won national fame by leading the Montgomery, Alabama, bus boycott of 1955–1956 aimed at ending discrimination against African Americans in public transportation. One of America's greatest-ever orators, he had delivered the "I have a dream" speech in front of the Lincoln Memorial in Washington, D.C., at the culmination of the mass march for jobs and freedom in 1963. Aged only 38 in 1967, he epitomized the sixties spirit of youth and was America's most prominent civil rights leader.

King had been opposed to the war since March 1965 but had kept relatively silent despite pressing reasons to oppose the conflict. His civil rights campaign in the South had been based on nonviolence, he had received the 1964 Nobel Peace Prize, and he wanted to condemn the mid-sixties race riots sweeping America without seeming hypocritically to condone a foreign war. Above all, by early 1967, he could see that the ever more expensive war was sucking the lifeblood out of the Great Society and that already impoverished black people would be the first victims of this. Eighty billion dollars per annum went to the military, compared with "a pittance here and there for social uplift" (Mullen 1981, 79).

When President Johnson heard about the Riverside speech his face "flushed with anger" (Rowan 1989, 2). He felt personally betrayed and deeply indignant. He had done so much to help black Americans, and now he was being treated in this way. Johnson was right to be anxious. African Americans had been a dependable part of the Democratic coalition that had been mostly successful since the Franklin D. Roosevelt administration of the 1930s. The King speech was a real stab at the self-esteem of those liberal politicians who ran the Vietnam War and complacently thought themselves to be, in the devastating words of journalist David Halberstam, "the best and the brightest" (Halberstam 1972).

King's speech was not immediately popular. A Harris poll suggested that only 25 percent of African Americans favored his antiwar stance, and 34 percent were worried about its alienation of civil rights supporters (Jeffreys-Jones

President Lyndon B. Johnson meets with civil rights leader Martin Luther King Jr. at the White House in March 1966. Under Johnson important civil rights gains were made, including the passage of the Voting Rights Act of 1965 and the introduction of federal affirmative action. (*Lyndon B. Johnson Library*)

1999). King had a lot of persuading to do. When he fell to an assassin's bullet on April 4, 1968, black protest lost its most articulate voice.

However, support for King's views increased steadily. Black discontent was nowhere so critical as in the armed forces. It stemmed from the racial statistics of the Vietnam War. In 1967, about 11 percent of the U.S. population was black, yet 14.5 percent of the enlisted men in the Army were black and only 3.8 percent of the officers serving in Vietnam were black. Furthermore, the latest figures showed that 22.4 percent of battle fatalities were black (Jeffreys-Jones 1999). The perception grew that African Americans— as well as Hispanic Americans and Native Americans—were being used as cannon fodder while being denied promotion. Poorer than their white contemporaries, black youths could not escape the draft by going to college. By the end of the war the statistical anomalies had balanced out, and it could be argued that the American armed forces were much better integrated than, say, their British equivalents. However, inspired by King and other outspoken African American leaders, black consciousness had been aroused. The sight of a brave black soldier advancing against enemy fire still inspired pride, but it had also become a source of anger.

Racial disorders in army camps mirrored the riots taking place in civilian America, and desertions were another serious problem. Black soldiers complained about being taunted by displays of the Confederate flag and even cross burnings to remind them of the Ku Klux Klan. White G.I.s were disturbed by "dapping," the African American way of greeting another "brother" or "blood," a handshaking ritual that seemed deliberately to exclude nonblacks. Their commanders were even more disturbed by "frag-ging," the practice of throwing a fragmentation grenade into a promotion-hungry officer's tent to ensure that, come dawn, there would be no order for a perilous advance against the enemy.

Although King's Riverside speech may have marked a high point in black antiwar protest, African Americans never ceased to contribute to the rising swell of activism. Their protests often had a distinctively racial character, but they also contributed to a common thrust, notably to objections by military personnel in general to the war's continuation. In Congress, too, black rep-resentatives such as Ron Dellums (D-CA) contributed to the debates that would reverse the Gulf of Tonkin Resolution and starve the war of funds.

Another such antiwar activist was Shirley Chisholm (D-NY), the first African American woman elected to Congress. In 1972, this daughter of West Indian parents would run for the Democratic presidential nomination. However, Chisholm did not consider the color of her skin to be the greatest impediment to her career. "Women," she wrote in 1970, "are a majority of the population, but they are treated like a minority group. . . . Of my two 'handicaps,' being female put many more obstacles in my path than being black" (Chisholm 1970, xii). Many women agreed with this assessment of the low status of their gender in American society, and it prompted them to launch a distinctively female campaign against the Vietnam War.

Women

In the early phases of the Vietnam War, women's minority mentality caused them to exercise restraint. At a time when students and African Americans were already protesting, women did not wish to risk unpopularity and fur-ther loss of standing by pressing for the peaceful foreign policy their gender characteristically favored. As in previous conflicts, women seemed to aban-don their peaceful outlook once war broke out. A character in Mary McCarthy's perceptive 1963 novel *The Group* noted of one woman that she was a pacifist only in peacetime. The League of Women Voters refused to come out against the Vietnam War. Margaret Chase Smith (R-ME), the ranking minority member of the Senate Armed Services Committee, sup-ported the war in spite of her private reservations.

From the beginning, nevertheless, some women did challenge the status quo. On November 1, 1961, women had demonstrated against nuclear test-ing, advancing the "nurturant motherhood" argument that the resultant radioactive fallout would harm children. These women were typically middle-class mothers and housewives. Potentially they could draw on the support of many millions of others just like them. A few of them sent a chill up the spine of male America by going on strike—no ironing, washing, or cooking for an entire day. Thus was born Women Strike for Peace (WSP), an organization that contributed to support for the 1963 treaty banning atmospheric testing. WSP then opposed the escalation of America's presence in Vietnam.

A new wave of feminism was beginning to take hold in 1960s America. This did not necessarily bode well for antiwar activism. Some of the new

Eartha Kitt Shatters White House Decorum

In the wake of recent urban riots, law and order had become a matter of public concern when, on January 18, 1968, Lady Bird Johnson hosted 50 influential women at a White House luncheon. Their aim was to brainstorm about the crime problem. Once the ladies had eaten, President Johnson entered the room. Mothers, he declared, should accept their own responsibility to fight juvenile delinquency.

Eartha Kitt suddenly rose to her feet. She told Johnson, get real. How could single mothers who had to go out to work be expected to police their kids? The president said they should make child care arrangements and left the room. With discussion under way, the irrepressible Kitt spoke again. As a "mini-mommy of America," she blamed the war, not mothers. Young men were deliberately acquiring criminal records because it disqualified them from military service and that meant they would not have to join the disastrous conflict in Vietnam: "It pays to be a bad guy" (Jeffreys-Jones 1999, 2).

Though other celebrities protested against the war, Kitt's outburst was especially significant because she spoke not just for women, but also for America's racial underclass. Her mother was of mixed African American and Cherokee ancestry. She had grown up in Harlem, and, as she put it, had "lived in the gutter." In 1950, she starred as Helen of Troy in an Orson Welles movie; her sexy 1953 rendition of "Santa baby" gave her instant fame as a singer; she was a household name in the 1960s because of her role as Catwoman in the TV series *Batman*. But talent, not privilege, had accounted for this rise to fame.

The reactions to Kitt's remarks were nationwide, vivid, and vicious. The Republican George Bush called from Texas to condemn Kitt and support the first lady. A woman from Maryland telephoned the White House to say "my heart and the hearts of millions of other white women in America go out to Mrs. Johnson to think that she had to invite people such as Eartha Kitt to her home and then be treated like that" (Jeffreys-Jones 1999, 163). The press all of a sudden discovered that Kitt was a fornicator and denounced her as a "Tobacco Road" exhibitionist. Nightclubs cancelled Kitt contracts.

However, if Kitt was disgraced, she was not defeated. Sammy Davis Jr. and Martin Luther King Jr. were among the African Americans who sprang to her defense. Then, 12 days after the White House fracas, the Vietcong and their North Vietnamese allies launched a psychologically devastating offensive in Vietnam. In the wake of that attack, most Americans began to believe the war had been a mistake. President Johnson stopped the military escalation and withdrew his candidacy for reelection, tacit acknowledgments that Kitt may have been right after all.

As for Eartha Kitt, she paid a price for her principles. She had to leave the country to find work and made a second career for herself as a cabaret diva on the European circuit. However, in 1978, she returned to America to appear in the Broadway spectacle *Timbuktu!* She was an instant success and resumed her position as an American superstar.

feminists wanted a more robust approach to war, on the principle that the image of feminine passivity was holding women back in society. The male chauvinism of some antiwar activists was repugnant to women—why should women do the cooking while men made the decisions? When in 1967 Joan Baez posed for an antidraft poster that proclaimed "Girls Say Yes to Boys Who Say No," some feminists objected to the implication that women were no more than a sexual service industry within the antiwar movement (Baez 1987).

Gradually, however, feminists were able to play their part in female opposition to the war. Attitudes began to change. Perhaps remembering that franchise leaders had achieved the vote by withdrawing their opposition to World War I, some women may at first have supported the Vietnam War to achieve gains, or at least to avoid loss. Toward the end of the decade, however, it was clear that the reverse had happened. In an interview in 1969, India Edwards, director of the women's division of the Democratic National Committee, noted that women were "at a lower ebb in the political life of this country" than at any time in her long career (Jeffreys-Jones 1999, 144). In the 1960s, female representation in Congress declined from 20 to 11; the number of women in the foreign service declined from 8.9 to 4.8 percent of the total. In spite of new feminist expectations, it became all too apparent by the late 1960s that the Vietnam War was masculinizing America by eroding the status of women in society. The time had come for women to be not just peacetime pacifists but wartime pacifists as well.

In 1967, 14 women associated with the Hollywood movie industry formed the organization Another Mother for Peace (AMP). As the name suggests, this emphasized maternal reasons for being opposed to war. Donna Reed, Oscar winner for *From Here to Eternity* (1953) and mother of a draft-age son, was one of the cochairs. The antiwar movement now attracted a galaxy of stars, including Joanne Woodward and Jane Fonda, as well as female writers such as Frances FitzGerald, Mary McCarthy, and Susan Sontag. By 1968, the Beverly Hills–run AMP was achieving mass support. It had 100,000 members, a similar number to WSP, and by the early 1970s, its newsletter had a circulation of a quarter of a million.

On January 15, 1968, the recently formed Jeanette Rankin Brigade marched, 5,000 strong, on Capitol Hill where Congress was about to convene. Rankin had been the first woman member of Congress and had voted against American entry into World War I. In 1941, she had repeated the act, this time the only member of either house to vote against World War II. Now, at age 87, she headed the Brigade's march to protest the Vietnam War. This event dramatized the distinctive role of women as antiwar activists. It also illustrated the tensions within the women's peace movement—a splinter group of younger women broke off from the main demonstration to conduct a ceremonial burial of "traditional motherhood" at Arlington cemetery.

The evidence of distinctively female dissent was plain. Men, too, were losing faith in the war, but at a slower rate. Gallup polls indicated that in 1965, 58 percent of men supported the war; in 1968, 48 percent; and by 1970, only 41 percent. For women the pro-war figures were significantly lower at 48 percent in 1965, 40 percent in 1968, and 30 percent in 1970 (Levy 1991). The gender gap peaked in 1970. In that year the election to Congress of the fiery Bella Abzug (D-NY) promised no-compromise opposition to the war and its funding.

The Nixon White House had no answer to these developments. In the case of students and African Americans, it could appeal to populist sentiment through backlash tactics, denouncing them as unrepresentative and disorderly—law and order was a main theme of the 1968 presidential election that put Nixon in office. But no such tactic was at hand with which to discredit the middle-class mothers of America.

A Divided Nation

On May 8, 1970, about 200 construction workers marched into the financial district of New York City, where students had congregated to protest the extension of the Vietnam War to Cambodia. The tough guys shouted "All the Way USA." They sang "The Star Spangled Banner." After beating up a few students they dispersed. The episode became known as the "hard hat demonstration" after the yellow safety hats worn by the marchers (Appy 1993, 39–40).

President Nixon took a big interest in the event. His aides organized a photo shoot in the White House in company with the low-level union leaders who had organized the demonstration. Nixon was forming a plan to build a new political majority in America to end the long domination of the Democratic majority. His appeal would be to those who cared about "a strong United States, about patriotism, about moral and spiritual values" (Mason 2004, 182). If he could attract some votes from the traditionally Democratic ranks of organized labor, his prospects would be improved.

Blue-collar workers felt a powerful affinity with the G.I.s in Vietnam, who were typically their sons and brothers, young men who had not had the privilege of going to college and qualifying for draft deferral. The leadership of the AFL-CIO was steadfastly behind the war effort, and had even been involved in it, attempting to marshal South Vietnamese workers into U.S.-style labor unions with assistance from the CIA. With the economy unraveling because of war-induced inflation, there were ever-louder rumblings of discontent among rank-and-file workers against the AFL-CIO's stance on the war. What the White House now had in mind was capitalizing on the New York demonstration by hard-hat rank-and-filers to get workers not just to support the war but also to vote Republican.

However, after further political pondering, the Nixon administration made a different call, one that was more consistent with the "peace with honor" policy it had always proclaimed. Playing the war and patriotism card was all very well, but the astute president realized this would have to be combined with an effort to woo the labor vote by promising an end to the war. Whether they were African American, women, or labor unionists, those who had been reluctant to oppose the war for fear of losing respect and power now had a different calculus because of the war's adverse effects, and because the changing mood of the nation meant they would be out of step with the majority if they continued to support the war.

The demonization of protest would not work any more. In fact, antiwar activists were becoming respectable. One sign of this was the arrival in Congress of committed antiwar legislators. The students had been too young to achieve this, but women and African Americans sent antiwar representatives to join the growing peace cohort on Capitol Hill.

There were other telling signs, too. Notably, though Nixon wanted to appeal to the nation's sense of morality, he could no longer rely on the support of Christians. Clergy and Laymen Concerned About Vietnam (CALCAV) formed in January 1966. Among its leading voices was William Sloane Coffin. Coffin came from a privileged background, his family having owned stock in the W. & J. Sloane Company, which ran a store for the rich in New York City. By the 1960s, however, he was chaplain of Yale University and a radical who encouraged students to resort to direct action and to burn their draft cards.

CALCAV challenged institutional religion's silence on the Vietnam War and included Jews as well as Christians. Devout Americans who had moral doubts about the war could now feel they were not alone. CALCAV members deliberately targeted the American mainstream, providing a counterimage to that of the long-haired student. With this end in view, when its members attended antiwar demonstrations, they wore coats and ties.

Another powerful injection of respectability into the antiwar movement came from veterans of the fighting, patriots against whom no effective backlash tactic was possible. White soldiers as well as African Americans became disillusioned by what they saw in Vietnam, by what they considered to be an incompetent and unsympathetic military leadership, and by a poor reception back home generated both by inconclusive results on the battlefield and disapproval of the war. In November 1967, protests by soldiers of varying ranks culminated in the formation of Vietnam Veterans Against the War (VVAW). Membership remained small until 1970, but then VVAW began to attract support and attention. Its 1970 advertisement in *Playboy* drew 12,000 responses. In a heart-stopping display of contempt and defiance, on April 23, 1971, 700 veterans threw their medals and ribbons over a barricade onto the Capitol steps. Most servicemen were proud to have fought for America, but a majority also thought that the war had been a mistake, and an estimated 20 to 25 percent of them protested against it (Moser 1996).

In the case of Vietnam, people's reasons for supporting the war simply broke down, partly because of the nature of the war itself, and partly because of the war's impact on different components of American society. The antiwar activists won the day and raised questions about war and society that would remain on the national agenda for years to come.

The author would like to thank Fabian Hilfrich and Robert Mason, University of Edinburgh colleagues who critiqued an earlier draft of this essay.

References and Further Reading

Anderson, Terry. *The Movement and the Sixties.* New York: Oxford University Press, 1995.

Appy, Christian. *Working-Class War: American Combat Soldiers and Vietnam.* Chapel Hill: University of North Carolina Press, 1993.

Baez, Joan. *And a Voice to Sing With: A Memoir.* New York: Summit Books, 1987.

Baltzell, E. Digby. *The Protestant Establishment*. New York: Random House, 1964.

Chisholm, Shirley. *Unbought and Unbossed*. Boston: Houghton Mifflin, 1970.

Halberstam, David. *The Best and the Brightest*. New York: Random House, 1972.

Hayden, Tom. *Reunion: A Memoir*. New York: Random House, 1988.

Heineman, Kenneth J. *Put Your Bodies Upon the Wheels: Student Revolt in the 1960s*. Chicago: Ivan R. Dee, 2001.

Jeffreys-Jones, Rhodri. *Peace Now! American Society and the Ending of the Vietnam War*. New Haven, CT: Yale University Press, 1999.

Jeffreys-Jones, Rhodri. *The CIA and American Democracy*. New Haven, CT: Yale University Press, 1989.

Kwon, Heonik. *After the Massacre: Commemoration and Consolation in Ha My and My Lai*. Berkeley: University of California Press, 2006.

Levy, David. *The Debate over Vietnam*. Baltimore: Johns Hopkins University Press, 1991.

Mason, Robert. *Richard Nixon and the Quest for a New Majority*. Chapel Hill: University of North Carolina Press, 2004.

Moise, Edwin. *Tonkin Gulf and the Escalation of the Vietnam War*. Chapel Hill: University of North Carolina Press, 1996.

Moser, Richard. *The New Winter Soldiers: G.I. and Veteran Dissent During the Vietnam Era*. New Brunswick, NJ: Rutgers University Press, 1996.

Mullen, Robert. *Blacks and Vietnam*. Washington, DC: University Press of America, 1981.

Rorabaugh, W. J. *Berkeley at War: The 1960s*. New York: Oxford University Press, 1989.

Rowan, Carl. "Martin Luther King's Tragic Decision." In *Martin Luther King, Jr.: Civil Right Leader, Theologian, Orator*. Vol. 3, edited by David Garrow. Brooklyn, NY: Carlson, 1989.

Westheider, James E. *Fighting on Two Fronts: African Americans and the Vietnam War*. New York: New York University Press, 1997.

The Silent Majority | 5

Kenneth J. Heineman

O n November 3, 1969, President Richard M. Nixon appealed to Americans for patience as he sought to extricate the United States from the Vietnam War. Addressing himself first to antiwar partisans, Nixon asserted that he respected their right to dissent and granted that most were patriotic. However, to the radicals who demanded immediate withdrawal, denounced the United States as a source of oppression in the world, and threatened violent social disruption, he was less charitable:

> For almost 200 years, the policy of this nation has been made under our Constitution by those leaders in the Congress and the White House elected by all of the people. If a vocal minority, however fervent its cause, prevails over reason and the will of the majority, this nation has no future as a free society (Nixon 1969).

Setting aside the militant vocal minority, Nixon coined a memorable phrase: "And so tonight—to you, the great silent majority of my fellow Americans—I ask for your support" (Nixon 1969). In short order, the Silent Majority (usually written with capitals) became, variously, a political epithet, a sociological category of analysis, and a dark Hollywood subtext. Actor Peter Boyle, for example, chewed scenery in the 1969 film *Joe*, portraying a racist, flag-waving member of the Silent Majority who killed nonconformist youths.

Those in academe, the news media, and Hollywood who depicted the white working-class supporters of Nixon's Vietnam policy as, in the *New York Times'* formulation, "the most reactionary political force in the country," were never able to resolve the central political paradox that had arisen by the end of the 1960s: the members of the Silent Majority, just like their most heated critics, were *Democrats* (Polenberg 1980, 224). Republicans such as Nixon did not instigate the Democrats' civil war over Vietnam, campus unrest, and urban crime, but they hoped to reap the political benefits from the destruction of the New Deal–Cold War electoral coalition.

To understand the Democratic Party's divisions over American foreign policy in the late 1960s and the rise of the Silent Majority, it is useful to examine the origins of the electoral coalition that dominated national politics for a generation. There are several historical points to keep in mind. Each point provides a context for the divisive politics that gave rise to the Silent Majority.

The New Deal Coalition

Popular memory has recalled the Great Depression as an era of unity in which Americans rallied behind President Franklin D. Roosevelt. The historical record demonstrates something different. Far from embracing the New Deal, millions of Americans reacted against social welfare policy initiatives and collective bargaining rights for workers. For instance, the violent strike wave of 1937 that hit Illinois, Michigan, Ohio, and Pennsylvania particularly hard contributed to a conservative electoral backlash a year later in those states.

The party of Roosevelt was a coalition of minorities: northern urban Catholics and Jews, rural southern white Protestants, northern urban black Protestants, and labor union members. Although Protestants were the doctrinal majority in the United States, only a small fraction voted Democratic— southern whites and northern blacks. Collectively, blacks, Catholics, and Jews could deliver key political battleground states in the industrial heartland, but usually only by narrow majorities of 51 to 52 percent. Defections or declining turnout among any single bloc of voters spelled doom for the Democrats in Congress and the Electoral College.

National Democrats were heavily dependent on the urban centers where the bulk of northern blacks, Catholics, and Jews resided. In 1940, 45 percent of all Illinois voters lived in Chicago and 51 percent of New York voters called one of the boroughs home. The overwhelming majority of Michigan Democrats and labor union members lived in Wayne County (Detroit). Without the support of the 12 largest cities in 1940, Roosevelt's electoral vote tally would have been 237, rather than 449. Two hundred and sixty-six electoral votes were required to win the presidency (Erie 1988).

The New Deal electoral coalition was glued together by shared poverty and sacrifice in depression and world war. However, cultural cleavages could not be ignored. Racial segregation and voter disenfranchisement in the South made civil rights a dangerous issue to Democrats. Roosevelt's solution was to practice color-blind hiring on federal works projects in the North where blacks had the vote and to remain silent on segregation and disenfranchisement in the South.

There were also religious and racial divisions over union enrollment with which Democrats had to contend. Southern whites were generally hostile to unions, embracing a Protestant individualist ethos that disdained collective action, viewed poverty as a product of sin rather than of low wages, and looked upon government power with a suspicion born of a lost Civil War.

A National Recovery Administration (NRA) poster displayed by businesses to show support for the government program. The NRA was considered the cornerstone of the New Deal and was often controversial in its regulation of industrial codes of competition. (*National Archives*)

Even northern black Protestants, who were more inclined than southern whites to see poverty as a social justice issue and to embrace government intervention, had their own ambivalent relations with organized labor. Most union leaders and the rank and file were Catholics who embraced collective action and government assistance, except when state authorities pushed for the racial integration of their neighborhoods and schools.

So far as foreign policy was concerned, 80 percent of the public in late 1941 opposed going to war to stop Nazi German aggression (Cantril 1951). Only the Japanese bombing of Pearl Harbor induced Americans to support Roosevelt's interventionist foreign policy. Even then, most Americans would not have supported a war against Nazi Germany—the enemy Roosevelt feared more than Imperial Japan. If Hitler had not first declared war on the United States, it is doubtful that Roosevelt could have received congressional and public support to intervene militarily in Europe.

In addition to a strong streak of isolationism, the New Deal coalition experienced small ideological fissures on foreign policy before World War II. Many Catholics viewed communism as a more compelling foreign threat than fascism. Some American Catholic clerical and lay leaders shaded their anticommunism with anti-Semitism. At the same time, large numbers of Jews regarded Nazi Germany as the real enemy and were prepared to join an alliance of convenience with the Soviet Union to stop Hitler. The bitter arguments between American Catholics and Jews over which side to support in the Spanish Civil War (1936–1939)—the Soviet-backed Madrid government or the Nazi-supported Francisco Franco—echoed into the 1960s with Saigon taking the place of Barcelona.

Looking back on the early 1950s, sociologist Seymour Martin Lipset detected a class rift within the Democratic Party. In the 1952 presidential election, Lipset observed that two-thirds of the 2,000 social science faculty he surveyed voted for Adlai Stevenson, the Democratic nominee whom, they believed, would pull the United States back from the Cold War contest with the Soviet Union. At the same time, half of working-class whites and union members voted for Dwight Eisenhower. Such Democratic voters thought the Republican presidential nominee's anticommunism and military credentials were not in question—unlike Stevenson's. Nearly as bad as being weak on national defense, in their minds, Stevenson had not served in World War II. Veterans occupied the White House between 1945 and 1992; eight had been in the military during World War II (Lipset 1981).

Political scientist James Q. Wilson similarly documented a cultural divide within the Democratic Party. According to Wilson, 1950s America experienced the rise of "amateur Democrats." These amateur Democrats were largely social science professors, public school teachers, public or foundation-employed social workers, and defense and civil liberties attorneys. They were offended by labor union leaders and urban politicians, complaining that such Democrats supported increased defense expenditures and resisted the racial integration of their neighborhoods (Wilson 1966).

Amateur Democrats could most often be found near prestigious universities and affluent urban neighborhoods. Few Catholics belonged to the political reform clubs that the amateur Democrats established. As Wilson contended, the best predictors of the relative strength of the reformers were the proportion of the overall population holding a bachelor's degree and the size of the Jewish community.

In 1950 New York, where Wilson reported the existence of a strong Democratic reform movement, 26.0 percent of the population was Jewish and 10.2 percent of residents over the age of 25 had a college degree. Chicago, with 14.0 percent of its population being Jewish and 5.7 percent claiming a college education, had a weaker reform organization that was centered in the Gold Coast neighborhood as well as the University of Chicago and Hyde Park environs. In Pittsburgh, which in 1950 had a small Jewish population—8 percent—and a low proportion of college-educated residents—3.6 percent—there were no amateur political clubs (Wilson 1966).

Vietnam and Party Divisions

The tensions between reformers and rank-and-file Democrats might have remained more of a nuisance than an actual agent of electoral disaster but for the escalating Vietnam War in the 1960s and concurrent campus and inner-city unrest. For many white working-class Democrats, the Vietnam War set in motion debates over the draft and patriotism. A fair amount of cultural conservatism and economic populism became intertwined with these debates, helping to dissolve the bonds that had held the New Deal–Cold War coalition together.

Perhaps the most divisive issue confronting the Democratic coalition was the class bias inherent in the operation of Selective Service. Because college student draft deferments were provided through 1968, millions of youths avoided military service. Nearly all of these students were middle class as just 17 percent of college students in the 1960s came from working-class and lower-middle-class families. Student draft deferments helped place the burden of combat on working-class youths who made up 80 percent of the U.S. soldiers fighting in Vietnam (Appy 1993).

Given the demographics of American military service in the 1960s, the backgrounds of those who made the ultimate sacrifice were overwhelmingly blue collar. In 1969 Long Island, of the 400 killed in Vietnam only one in eight had ever set foot on a college campus. Nearly all were white and working class. In an analysis of 1,300 Illinois troops killed in Vietnam, social scientists concluded that the risk of death increased as income declined (Polenberg 1980). Nationally, Catholics, who were 24 percent of the overall U.S. population in the 1960s, accounted for 30 percent of those killed in action. As journalist Michael Lind later observed, Catholics were the only group, including African Americans, to be consistently overrepresented in combat ranks throughout the 1960s. The group next most likely to see combat were southern white Protestants (Lind 1999).

When journalists interviewed working-class whites in the North, their anger with the draft and student antiwar protesters sprang from the newspaper pages. "Here were these kids, rich kids who could go to college," said one critic of antiwar demonstrators in 1970 New York, "who didn't have to fight, they are telling you your son died in vain. It makes you feel your whole life is shit, just nothing" (Rieder 1985, 157). Another white working-class interviewee informed a reporter that "we can't understand how all those rich kids—the kids with beads from the fancy suburbs—how they get off when my son has to go over there and maybe get his head shot off" (Levison 1974, 162).

If northern white workers expressed loathing for collegiate protesters, by the end of the 1960s they were also registering disgust with the Vietnam War. In 1968, national public opinion polls, along with local antiwar referendums held in such blue-collar communities as Dearborn, Michigan, confirmed what many newspaper reporters were finding: there were numerous targets of working-class ire as well as dissatisfaction with the conduct of the war. One white working-class member who lost a son in Vietnam at first condemned the peace movement. This individual's next observations, however, were a perfect mix of populist scorn for Republican stock brokers and Democratic faculty:

> It's people like us who give up our sons for the country. The business people, they run the country and make money from it. The college types, the professors, they go to Washington and tell the government what to do. Do this, they say; do that. But their sons, they don't end up in the swamps over there in Vietnam (Polenberg 1980, 228).

Such class resentments also had an ethnic component. In the Canarsie neighborhood of New York, for instance, the local amateur Democratic club had a large middle-class, antiwar Jewish membership. This reflected the fact that, nationally, by the end of the 1960s, Jews were nearly twice as likely to oppose the war as Catholics. Even earlier, in 1956, Canarsie's Democratic Italian Catholics and Jews had parted company over Cold War American foreign policy. Where 70 percent of ethnic Italians voted for Eisenhower, 85 percent of Jews embraced Stevenson (Rieder 1985).

At a peace rally sponsored by Canarsie's Jefferson Democratic Club in the early 1970s, working-class ethnic Italians from the Catholic War Veterans and the Veterans of Foreign Wars descended with fists flying. Bringing the ethnic divide into focus, an Italian member of the Canarsie Knights of Columbus observed: "All Americans should know their heritage, but we are Americans first. That's what annoys me when Jews rally for Israel, but they wouldn't even do it for the Korean War, and they tried to keep their kids out of Vietnam" (Rieder 1985, 41, 161–162).

On college campuses, which served as important locales of antiwar organization in the 1960s, there were ethnic and religious divisions similar to those afflicting Canarsie. As sociologist Nathan Glazer observed in 1969, anywhere from one-third to half of the membership of the most radical student antiwar organizations came from Jewish families (Glazer 1969). Catholics were nearly invisible in radical campus ranks at secular institutions such as the University of California at Berkeley and the University of Wisconsin. At Catholic universities from Canisius in Buffalo, New York, to Notre Dame in South Bend, Indiana, there were but handfuls of antiwar activists and nearly all were moderates, not radicals.

The first major rupture within the Democratic Party over the Vietnam War came in the run up to the 1968 presidential election. Former Alabama governor George Wallace, who had earned notoriety in the early 1960s for his opposition to racial integration, made an independent race for president. Redirecting his fire away from civil rights advocates, Wallace targeted student and faculty activists:

> I'm going to ask my Attorney General to seek an indictment against every professor in this country who calls for a communist victory and see if I can't put them under a good jail somewhere. I'm sick and tired of seeing these few college students raise money, blood, and clothes for the communists and fly the Vietcong flag; they ought to be dragged by the hair of their heads and stuck under a good jail also (Page and Brody 1972, 992).

Representing a region that was home to many military bases and defense contractors, and whose sons filled the ranks of the armed forces, Wallace's ridicule of campus demonstrators played to the home crowd and won fans in northern Catholic enclaves. Southern white transplants to the factories of Akron, Columbus, and Detroit also cheered Wallace. Giving the lie to the mass media depiction of a generation gap in which youths protested against the war while their parents embraced it, Wallace picked up notable support among voters under the age of 30. These were youths who did not go to college.

Even as the Democratic Party experienced defections by frustrated cultural conservatives who demanded a crackdown on demonstrators and a decisive military victory in Vietnam—or a withdrawal—progressives moved against Johnson's designated heir, Vice President Hubert Humphrey. Mounting their challenge from the reform clubs, white-collar activists gained control of the Americans for Democratic Action (ADA). Founded in 1947 by intellectuals, labor leaders, and politicians such as Humphrey, the ADA embraced civil rights and the Cold War. A generation later, however, reformers repudiated the organization's anticommunism and dedicated themselves to securing the Democratic presidential nomination for Minnesota senator Eugene McCarthy. In response, labor leaders pulled their financial support from the ADA and reaffirmed their commitment to Humphrey.

Unlike the victory progressives claimed in changing the ideological orientation of the ADA, the success of the amateur Democrats at the state level varied greatly. In 1968, the Democrats in North Carolina affirmed, "We oppose draft card burning, interference with the proper activities of our educational institutions by students and outsiders, refusal to serve our country when needed, and expressions of disloyalty to state and nation." Wisconsin's Democratic state organization, having come under the influence of Eugene McCarthy loyalists in 1968, identified America's "real enemy" as "white racism," not communism (Paddock 1990).

In spite of the defections of many culturally conservative Democrats to Wallace and the determination of antiwar progressives not to vote for either Humphrey or Nixon, the 1968 election was extremely close. The very closeness of this election helped determine President-elect Nixon's foreign policy and 1972 reelection strategy.

Nixon and Humphrey understood that regardless of who won the election, Johnson's successor would have limited military and political options. Public opinion had turned against the war as U.S. casualties mounted without any apparent progress toward victory. The North Vietnamese had timed the January 1968 Tet Offensive to coincide with the American electoral cycle. Although the United States largely destroyed the communist insurgency in South Vietnam and transformed the war into a more conventional—and winnable—contest with the North Vietnamese Army, it was politically too late. The news media, and the public at large, interpreted the Tet Offensive as a U.S. military defeat. Two-thirds of the citizenry condemned the president's conduct of the war in March 1968. Johnson subsequently announced that he would embrace peace negotiations with Hanoi (Barone 1990).

Both Nixon and Humphrey favored ending the war. Neither, however, desired an immediate withdrawal that would lead to a collapse of South Vietnam and, they feared, encourage Chinese and Soviet aggression elsewhere. Nixon and Humphrey also appreciated one more aspect of public opinion that many in the peace movement failed to digest: if Americans, and especially white working-class voters, wanted to end the war, they were also willing to accept a withdrawal *or an escalation* of the air war. The majority of Americans in 1968 still desired a victory—they just wanted it accomplished quickly and with few U.S. casualties.

Close examination of the 1968 election returns yielded vital data that Nixon would use to advantage in 1972. First, 1968 was one of the most racially polarized elections in American history. Where 97 percent of blacks voted Democratic, just 35 percent of whites followed suit. Wallace, not

Nixon, had made deep inroads among white Democratic voters, particularly with Southern Baptists. Forty-five percent of Southern Baptists, a once reliably Democratic voting bloc, supported Wallace (Orum 1970). A promise to slow down the pace of racial change, and appeals to sectional pride and patriotism, would form the cornerstone of Nixon's 1972 "Southern Strategy" in pursuit of Dixie's Wallace voters.

Second, the 1968 election returns revealed that Wallace had made gains in the North at the expense of the Democrats. Several United Automobile Workers (UAW) locals in New Jersey and Illinois supported Wallace. In Buffalo, New York, traditionally Democratic precincts that bordered black neighborhoods or student communes at the State University of New York in Buffalo voted for Wallace or Nixon. These precincts were populated by ethnic Poles and Italians. Democratic Party leaders were aghast.

Frank Rizzo and George Wallace: The Silent Majority's Odd Couple

At first glance a Deep South governor and a Philadelphia police officer would seem to be improbable allies. First impressions, however, were misleading. Both Alabama governor George Wallace (1919–1998) and Philadelphia mayor Frank Rizzo (1920–1991) were combative, socially conservative Cold War Democrats who grew sickened with the direction progressives were taking the party of Franklin Roosevelt. In the divisions in the 1960s and early 1970s over the Vietnam War, crime, and civil unrest, Rizzo and Wallace became significant voices of the Silent Majority.

Wallace grew up the son of poor Alabama farmers, and he worked his way through college during the Great Depression. Although he could

Alabama governor George Wallace holds a picture of "known agitators" while speaking to a Citizens Council group in Atlanta in 1963. (*Library of Congress*)

Nixon and the Silent Majority

Although academics and journalists had spent much of the 1960s exploring discontent among middle-class student activists and blacks, few had considered that northern white working-class Americans might have cause for complaint. Greater numbers of working-class whites worried about their declining living standards and worsening urban neighborhoods. They also began to express resentment for bearing nearly the entire burden of combat service. Here was a foundation upon which Nixon could build a "Northern Strategy."

Nixon's 1969 inauguration was the first in U.S. history to be disrupted by violent protest. Many congressional Democrats, although willing to criticize the Vietnam War now that a Republican occupied the White House,

---

have received an officer's commission during World War II, Wallace chose to serve in the ranks of the Army Air Corps. Wallace had postwar political ambitions and realized the common people of Alabama would feel more kinship with a sergeant than a lieutenant. His subsequent political career until the late 1950s revealed him to be a racial moderate and advocate of government spending to improve the quality of education and infrastructure in Alabama.

Like Wallace, Frank Rizzo endured hardship during the Great Depression. The son of Italian immigrants, Rizzo grew up in the blue-collar ethnic enclave of South Philadelphia. To help his struggling family, Rizzo dropped out of high school and joined the U.S. Navy in 1938. The navy discharged him on medical grounds before the United States entered World War II. Rizzo worked at various construction jobs until he was able to follow his father into the Philadelphia police department in 1943. The younger Rizzo impressed his supervisors and received swift promotion. By 1959, Rizzo was a police inspector and popular figure among local Irish and Italian Catholic Democratic office holders. Philadelphia's upper-middle-class Protestant and Jewish progressives, on the other hand, disliked Rizzo's law-and-order mantra.

Rizzo and Wallace entered the 1960s along racially charged paths. Most famously, Wallace, who had concluded that the way to advance in the Alabama Democratic Party was to embrace segregation, achieved infamy by personally blocking the entrance of black students to the University of Alabama. Meanwhile in Philadelphia, Rizzo, as the deputy police commissioner, seemingly placed his officers on the side of working-class whites seeking to block black settlement. Philadelphia experienced numerous neighborhood racial riots that Rizzo quashed.

Although Rizzo, who thought the universe existed between the Delaware and the Schuylkill rivers, had only local political ambitions, Wallace set his sights much higher. Wallace had entered the 1964 Democratic presidential primaries as the anti–civil rights movement candidate. Four years later Wallace shifted his attention toward antiwar demonstrators and urban criminals. Although progressives claimed, with some justice, that the criminals Wallace targeted were often black, their failure to acknowledge the legitimate public order concerns of working-class city dwellers meant that their charges of racism fell upon deaf ears.

(continued on following page)

Frank Rizzo and George Wallace: The Silent Majority's Odd Couple (continued)

In 1971, Rizzo, having risen to the lofty position of Philadelphia police commissioner, found himself being begged by local Democratic leaders to run for mayor because he was the only member of the party who had any public credibility on law-and-order issues. He won in a landslide and then, with much fanfare, journeyed to Washington to confer with President Richard Nixon.

Although Wallace and Rizzo heaped abuse on the Democratic Party's growing activist base, and were in turn objects of progressive scorn, conservative Republicans did not welcome either into their camp. As conservative intellectual William F. Buckley Jr. argued, Wallace was an unreconstructed New Deal Democrat; a man who, as governor, had no problem taxing the affluent to benefit the poor—both whites and blacks, though the governor kept this last fact as quiet as possible. So far as Rizzo was concerned, he expected federal assistance to help his city cope with deindustrialization and mounting unemployment. Nixon did not disappoint Rizzo.

Paradoxically, Wallace and Rizzo, who both loomed so large in the public mind in the 1960s and early 1970s, had little further personal impact on national politics. In 1972, Wallace, having scored a few victories in the Democratic presidential primaries, was paralyzed by an assassin's bullet. He reentered Alabama politics in the 1980s, making two successful runs for governor as an economic populist and friend of civil rights. Paralysis led to an epiphany for Wallace. Rizzo would have liked to have made more runs for mayor after having served two terms, but he found his ambitions thwarted by Philadelphia's demographic changes. As Catholics moved to the suburbs, Philadelphia's black and white progressive voters gained sufficient clout to sideline Rizzo.

To the end of their lives, Rizzo and Wallace remained Franklin Roosevelt Democrats, even as many of their allies in the Silent Majority migrated to the Republican Party. They would also have the satisfaction of being courted by Nixon and detested by progressive foes of the Cold War and conservative enemies of the New Deal.

cringed. They knew that violence further alienated the public, making the peace movement at least as unpopular as the war. In addition to being upset with leftist violence, working-class citizens were decidedly patriotic and resentful of those they deemed to be less so. New York journalist Pete Hamill, whose brother had been decorated for valor in Vietnam, wrote in 1969 that:

> Patriotism is very important to the working-class white man. Most of the time he is the son of an immigrant, and most immigrants sincerely believe that the Pledge of Allegiance, the Star-Spangled Banner, [and] the American Flag are symbols of what it means to be Americans. They might not have become rich in America, but most of the time they were much better off than they were in the old country. On "I Am an American" Day they march in parades with a kind of religious fervor that can look absurd to the outsider (imagine marching through Copenhagen on "I Am a Dane" Day), but that can also be oddly touching. Walk through any working-class white neighborhood and you will see dozens of veterans' clubs, named after neighborhood men who were killed in World War II or Korea. There are not really orgies of jingoism going on

inside; most of the time the veterans' clubs serve as places in which to drink on Sunday morning before the bars open at 1 p.m., or as places in which to hold baptisms and wedding receptions (Hamill 1969, 24).

In 1969, the general public's patriotism and dislike of social disorder permitted Nixon to adopt a sorrowful tone that embraced much of the sentiment expressed by Wallace a year earlier, but without the threat of retribution that disturbed moderate voters. "We live in a deeply troubled and profoundly unsettled time. Drugs, crime, campus revolts, racial discord, draft resistance—on every hand we find old standards violated, old values discarded." Nixon left it up to Vice President Spiro Agnew to play the Wallace "bad cop" role when he characterized radicals as "rotten apples" that should be thrown away (Rieder 1985, 154–156).

If, as *Time* magazine reported in a 1969 poll, 80 percent of the public thought the Vietnam War had been a "mistake," just 36 percent demanded an immediate withdrawal (Lunch and Sperlich 1979). This seeming confusion in the public's mind provided an opening for supporters of the war. Voices that had been relatively silent on the war emerged in 1969. W. A. Criswell, the president of the Southern Baptist Convention, declared:

Richard Nixon visits troops in Vietnam in July 1969. Many soldiers who were deemed fit to be drafted into the Vietnam War did not have the right to vote because they didn't meet the legal voting age of 21. It wasn't until 1971 with the passage of the Twenty-sixth Amendment that the voting age was lowered to 18. (*National Archives*)

The communist aggressor can go just so far and no further. Where are you going to draw that line? Are we going to draw it in Thailand and South Vietnam? Or are you going to pull back and draw it in the Philippines . . . at Hawaii . . . at the western coast of California . . . at the western line of Texas, or are you going to pull back still further and draw it at the Mississippi River? Somewhere—sometime—America has to stand! (Blevins 1980, 238).

The contending voices of war and peace clashed most spectacularly in 1970. In response to the U.S. incursion into Cambodia in April 1970 to interdict North Vietnamese Army supply lines, hundreds of campuses erupted. On May 4, 1970, demonstrators at Kent State University squared off against elements of the Ohio National Guard, leading to the deaths of four students. Protests at other universities escalated, causing hundreds of thousands of dollars in property damage and injuring scores of students and police officers.

When antiwar activists rallied in New York City and St. Louis in solidarity with the "Kent State 4," construction workers responded savagely. Thousands of working-class whites demanded that Mayor John Lindsay, a Nixon foe, not lower the American flag in honor of the killed and injured Kent State students. A full-scale riot erupted at City Hall and the voices of the "hardhats" choked with emotion: "I am an American and America wasn't made to have these pansy-assed creeps running around wild," said one construction worker. "I don't mind people demonstrating, but when these brats rip, spit on and chew up the flag, what are we supposed to do, stand around and kiss them?" (Cannato 2001, 448–452).

Two weeks later, 100,000 New Yorkers staged a demonstration in support of the troops and against the antiwar movement. Some of their signs would not have passed muster with the Southern Baptist Convention: "Lindsay Drops the Flag More Times Than a Whore Drops Her Pants." Nixon, who took his allies where he could find them, welcomed Peter Brennan, the leader of the New York Building and Construction Trades Council, and other labor heads to the White House. Having helped orchestrate the New York march, Brennan happily gave Nixon a hard hat (Cannato 2001).

Paradoxically, by the time the 1972 presidential election season rolled around, Nixon had persuaded the general public that the Vietnam War was no longer a major issue even while peace activists succeeded in making it nearly the only issue for the Democratic Party. In 1972, public opinion polls reported that the great majority of Americans regarded the most important issues facing the country to be, in order, inflation, crime, violence, and drugs. The Vietnam War occupied a more distant fifth place among public concerns—a dramatic shift since 1968 (Wattenberg 1976).

Nixon's decision to abolish student draft deferments and go to a Selective Service lottery helped defuse campus unrest. Because students had assigned numbers in the lottery they knew that, with declining troop calls, only a few would be drafted. Once the threat of the draft receded campus antiwar protest collapsed. The Kent State shootings revived campus protest but only briefly.

The president's policy of "Vietnamization" of the war also worked to quell American qualms. By replacing U.S. ground forces with South Vietnamese troops, while escalating the air and naval war against North Vietnam, American casualties declined. South Vietnamese casualties, of course, increased, but even Nixon's supporters thought they should have been bearing more of the fight all along. With Nixon's overtures to China and the Soviet Union, on top of deadlier American bombing runs, North Vietnam felt pressured to accept, at least temporarily, the existence of an independent South Vietnam.

Since taking the oath of office, Nixon had courted high-profile Democratic political and labor leaders. Peter Brennan was but one of many. Nixon had felt a strong attraction to Philadelphia police commissioner, and then mayor, Frank Rizzo. A stalwart law-and-order man, Rizzo, according to Nixon, "was a leading member of what I called The Silent Majority." Rizzo did not disappoint the president. The outspoken Philadelphian effusively praised Nixon's May 1972 decision to mine North Vietnam's Haiphong Harbor—disrupting supplies needed for the spring communist offensive: "Your forthright and decisive action will shorten hostilities and pave the way for the return of our troops and prisoners. Your honest and courageous decision has spurred the hopes of all who seek an early and just end to the war." Rizzo supported Nixon for reelection (Paolantonio 1993, 145–148).

Nixon ardently pursued American Federation of Labor and Congress of Industrial Organizations (AFL-CIO) president George Meany but did not achieve the same level of comity he had with Rizzo and Brennan. Meany did not trust the historically anti-union Republican Party. At the same time, however, Meany had never valued the judgment of professors, whether in the 1950s when they voted for Stevenson or the 1970s as they cast about for an anti–Cold War crusader.

Most important to Nixon, Meany was committed to creating a democratic South Vietnam and did not want the United States withdrawing without first securing that nation from communist aggression. The culturally conservative, Irish Catholic Meany also assumed the mantle of godfather of the Silent Majority, using choice words for the progressives who were gaining control of the presidential nomination machinery. As Meany caustically observed after the 1972 Democratic National Convention when he declined to endorse his party's presidential nominee:

> We listened for three days to the speakers who were approved to speak by the powers-that-be at that convention. We listened to the gay lib people—you know, the people who want to legalize marriages between boys and boys and legalize marriages between girls and girls. . . . We heard from the abortionists, and we heard from the people who look like Jacks, acted like Jills, and had the odors of johns about them (Robinson 1981, 294, 322–323).

To Meany's disgust, and Nixon's delight, progressive reformers, led by South Dakota senator George McGovern, were successfully redirecting the Democratic Party away from the Cold War and toward social liberalism. Antiwar student and faculty activists from Morgan State and Johns Hopkins universities in Baltimore helped defeat a somewhat conservative incumbent congressman in the 1970 Democratic primary and replaced him with a black peace partisan. For their part, North Dakota Democrats in 1972 proclaimed that:

> We should abandon war or the threat of war as an instrument of national policy. We support phasing out nationalism as an ultimate long-range objective because we recognize that until we have an international society, war, racism, and exploitation will continue to plague us (Paddock 1990, 181–190).

The repudiation of American Cold War foreign policy by North Dakota Democrats and Baltimore's primary voters, however, was not a sign of a mass populist uprising on the prairie or in the city. North Dakota was a Republican state that, with the exception of 1964, handed Democrats lopsided defeats. Humphrey only received 38 percent of the North Dakota vote in 1968. Most North Dakota Democrats were white-collar professionals concentrated in university communities. Paradoxically, they were more influential in the national party than they were in their home state. The same was true in the East.

Within the Democratic Party there was some resistance to the progressives. Andrew Greeley, a Catholic priest with a sociology PhD, decried the "snobbery" of upper-class liberals who held culturally conservative members of the working class in contempt (Greeley 1972). If working-class Catholics were wrong to regard blacks as less than human, Greeley argued, then college-educated progressives should be ashamed to harbor similar feelings toward misguided, less-educated whites. Given their own class blinders and bigotry, Democratic reformers, Greeley concluded, should not be surprised that working-class Catholics were lumping progressives together with such traditional class foes as the corporate executive:

> A Harvard graduate is, after all, a Harvard graduate, whether in a picket line or in a boardroom of a large corporation. The peace movement was seen as an establishment movement, working against the values, the stability, and the patriotism of the American masses—which masses, incidentally, were seen as footing the bill for establishment games and amusements (Greeley 1974, 375–376).

Michael Novak, a Slovak Catholic son of Johnstown, Pennsylvania, experienced the confusion of class and ethnic tensions that Greeley described from a vantage point within the 1972 Democratic presidential campaign. A long-time peace activist, Novak had already begun to express his revulsion with radicals when Democratic vice presidential nominee Sargent Shriver contacted him to become a speechwriter. Novak enthusiastically plunged into the campaign, having long admired Shriver for his work in the Peace Corps, the Office of Economic Opportunity, and earlier efforts against racial discrimination in Chicago with the Catholic Interracial Council. It did not take long for Novak to realize that something was going horribly wrong with the Democratic Party:

> Mr. Shriver was greeted with scarcely veiled disdain, I thought, by workers at the gates of the Homestead [Pennsylvania] Steel mills—my own kind of folks,

who would normally be with us by upwards of 89 percent. In Joliet, Illinois, on a factory floor where I encountered dozens of Slovak faces that made me think of my cousins in Johnstown, workers did not want to shake McGovern-Shriver hands. Trying to find out why, I met our "advance person"—a young woman wearing a miniskirt, high white boots, and a see-through blouse, with a large pro-abortion button on her collar. On that factory floor in 1972, the clash of social classes and cultural politics could scarcely have been more discordant (Novak 1988, 257).

There were other signs that the Silent Majority was preparing to hand antiwar Democrats a massive electoral defeat. A Louis Harris Poll in the spring of 1972 reported that 59 percent of Americans approved of Nixon's decision to mine Haiphong Harbor. That September, 55 percent of the public supported increased U.S. bombing of North Vietnam. When Gallup asked who would handle the Vietnam War better, Nixon received the endorsement of 58 percent of the public. Just 26 percent thought McGovern would do a credible job, and the remainder either claimed no opinion or expressed skepticism about both candidates (Wattenberg 1976).

The Silent Majority, which had not been all that quiet for the past several years, roared on Election Day 1972. Nixon received 61 percent of the popular vote and carried every electoral vote but those belonging to Massachusetts and the District of Columbia. McGovern even lost his home state of South Dakota. For the first time since the Great Depression, the Democratic presidential candidate performed miserably among white working-class voters and Catholics. Nixon carried 60 percent of such voters. McGovern also decisively lost the South; 80 percent of white evangelical Protestants, long the backbone of the Dixie Democrats, opted for Nixon. McGovern did carry the student body of Harvard Law School 698 to 131 and swept Harvard Law professors 34 to 4 (Heineman 1998).

Pennsylvania's election returns were particularly telling. In a state that had been a crucible of the industrial union movement and a center of Catholic Democratic mobilization, McGovern was able to win just a single county: Philadelphia. Even then, Frank Rizzo's Catholics defected to Nixon, leaving it up to blacks and Jews to deliver for McGovern. At the other end of the Keystone State, in the overwhelmingly Democratic Allegheny County (Pittsburgh), McGovern performed poorly. Nineteen percent of Allegheny County Democrats sat out the election, refusing to vote for either McGovern or Nixon. Another 11 percent of Allegheny County Democrats chose Nixon (Heineman 2004).

Nixon's 1972 victory proved fleeting after revelations that a few of his campaign staffers had conspired to break into national Democratic headquarters at the Watergate Hotel in Washington, D.C. His resignation in 1974, followed a year later by a North Vietnamese offensive that broke the 1973 truce and destroyed South Vietnamese resistance, cheered progressive Democrats. With Nixon disgraced and America's Cold War foreign policy in ruins, progressives thought a stake had been driven through the heart of the Silent Majority. Subsequent developments proved such hopes to be false.

Southern white Protestants returned to the Democratic fold in 1976 by voting for Jimmy Carter. Disgust with Soviet expansionism, inflation, the Iranian hostage crisis, and the freewheeling lifestyle revolution of the 1970s, however, turned Dixie whites against their fellow Democrats. Republican Ronald Reagan reached out to southern whites and to socially conservative Catholics in the North. The Silent Majority became reborn in the 1980s as "Reagan Democrats." Southern whites and northern Catholics, mostly blue collar, voted Republican in presidential contests but continued to support Democrats at the congressional and state level. It took a generation, until 1994, for white southerners to abandon the Democrats from top to bottom.

Republican electoral success since Nixon's presidency depended on destroying the New Deal electoral coalition. To an extent, but only to an extent, Republicans were successful. Southern whites ultimately withdrew from the Democratic Party, but Catholics fractured along class and educational lines. Affluent Catholics resisted conservative overtures. Rather than achieving an electoral realignment, Nixon, and then Reagan, had made the Republicans competitive but not safely dominant. In many ways the conservative majority of the 1990s, built on the foundation of the 1970s Silent Majority, floated between 48 and 52 percent, just as had been the case with the New Deal Democrats.

If conservatives came away from the 1960s with the shaky support of the Silent Majority, progressives had firm ownership of the national Democratic Party. Democrats became the peace party, denouncing Reagan's military buildup in the 1980s and driving opposition to the War on Terror in the 21st century. Antiwar activists in the 1960s, notably McGovern's 1972 Texas campaign director, Bill Clinton, assumed leadership positions in the Democratic Party in the 1990s. At the dawn of the 21st century, the publisher of the influential *New York Times* (Arthur Sulzberger Jr.), the chair of the National Democratic Party (Howard Dean), and the 2004 presidential nominee (John Kerry), had demonstrated against the Vietnam War. Only Kerry had served in Vietnam. However, his charges that U.S. troops routinely committed war crimes, and his leadership in the Vietnam Veterans Against the War, tempered whatever goodwill working-class whites might have had toward Kerry.

It was thus the fate of Americans in the new century that if the specter of Vietnam hovered over the War on Terror, Nixon and McGovern cast enormous shadows over the Republicans and Democrats as well. How much longer this situation will remain is open to debate. If the history of the New Deal and the Roosevelt presence is any guide, the Vietnam War and the politics that created the Silent Majority should be put to rest around 2030—or about the time the partisans of the 1960s Left and Right expire.

References and Further Reading

Appy, Christian. *Working-Class War: American Combat Soldiers in Vietnam.* Chapel Hill: University of North Carolina Press, 1993.

Barone, Michael. *Our Country: The Shaping of America from Roosevelt to Reagan.* New York: Free Press, 1990.

Blevins, Kent. "Southern Baptist Attitudes Toward the Vietnam War in the Years 1965–1970." *Foundations* 23(1980): 231–244.

Cannato, Vincent. *The Ungovernable City: John Lindsay and His Struggle to Save New York.* New York: Basic Books, 2001.

Cantril, Hadley, ed. *Public Opinion, 1935–1946.* Princeton, NJ: Princeton University Press, 1951.

Erie, Steven. *Rainbow's End: Irish-Americans and the Dilemmas of Urban Machine Politics, 1840–1985.* Berkeley: University of California Press, 1988.

Glazer, Nathan. "The Jewish Role in Student Activism." *Fortune* 79, January 1969: 111–113, 126, 129.

Greeley, Andrew. *Building Coalitions: American Politics in the 1970s.* New York: New Viewpoints, 1974.

Greeley, Andrew. "Political Attitudes Among American White Ethnics." *Public Opinion Quarterly* 36 (Summer 1972): 213–220.

Hamill, Pete. "The Revolt of the White Lower Middle Class." *New York Magazine* 2, April 14, 1969: 24, 26, 28–29.

Heineman, Kenneth J. "Reformation: Monsignor Charles Owen Rice and the Fragmentation of the New Deal Electoral Coalition in Pittsburgh, 1960–1972." *Pennsylvania History* 71 (Winter 2004): 53–85.

Heineman, Kenneth J. *God Is a Conservative: Religion, Politics, and Morality in Contemporary America.* New York: New York University Press, 1998.

Levison, Arthur. *The Working Class Majority.* New York: Coward, McCann & Geoghegan, 1974.

Lind, Michael. *Vietnam, The Necessary War: A Reinterpretation of America's Most Disastrous Military Conflict.* New York: Free Press, 1999.

Lipset, Seymour Martin. *Political Man: The Social Bases of Politics.* Baltimore: Johns Hopkins University Press, 1981.

Lunch, William, and Peter Sperlich. "American Public Opinion and the War in Vietnam." *Western Political Quarterly* 32 (March 1979): 21–44.

Nixon, Richard. "The Pursuit of Peace: An Address by Richard Nixon," November 3, 1969. Washington, DC: U.S. Government Printing Office, 1969.

Novak, Michael. "Errand into the Wilderness." In *Political Passages: Journeys of Change Through Two Decades, 1968–1988,* edited by John Bunzel, 239–272. New York: Free Press, 1988.

Orum, Anthony. "Religion and the Rise of the Radical White: The Case of Southern Wallace Support in 1968." *Social Science Quarterly* 51 (December 1970): 674–688.

Paddock, Joel. "Beyond the New Deal: Ideological Differences between Eleven State Democratic Parties, 1956–1980." *Western Political Quarterly* 43 (March 1990): 181–190.

Page, Benjamin, and Richard Brody. "Policy Voting and the Electoral Process: The Vietnam War Issue." *American Political Science Review* 66 (September 1972): 979–995.

Paolantonio, S. A. *Frank Rizzo: The Last Big Man in Big City America.* Philadelphia: Camino Books, 1993.

Polenberg, Richard. *One Nation Divisible: Class, Race, and Ethnicity in the United States Since 1938.* New York: Viking, 1980.

Rieder, Jonathan. *Canarsie: The Jews and Italians of Brooklyn Against Liberalism.* Cambridge, MA: Harvard University Press, 1985.

Robinson, Archie. *George Meany and His Times.* New York: Simon and Schuster, 1981.

Wattenberg, Ben. *The Real America: A Surprising Examination of the State of the Union.* New York: Capricorn Books, 1976.

Wilson, James. *The Amateur Democrat: Club Politics in Three Cities.* Chicago: University of Chicago Press, 1966.

Religious Communities and the Vietnam War | 6

Jill K. Gill

Religious organizations are not political entities. Although they may speak to sociopolitical issues, they exist to point human beings toward transcendent truths and concepts of morality. When they look at problems, they place them against the backdrop of their own spiritual teachings and understandings of the Divine's wishes for humankind. Therefore, for most religious communities, the Vietnam War was always about more than the war. They tended to see it as a symptom or manifestation of something greater, and this shaped their responses and priorities. Yet because religious communities disagreed about the will of the Divine, they sometimes fought one another and jockeyed for influence through their responses to the conflict. The war occurred during a time of traumatic transition for America's religious organizations, adding stress and high stakes to their choices. Their desired relationships with the government and mainstream culture also affected their actions on Vietnam as "church" and "state" struggled to woo, and even use, each other for their own desired ends.

With the exception of such groups as the Jehovah's Witnesses, which eschew political involvement and patriotic loyalties as idolatrous, most religious communities fell into one of four "camps" with respect to the war. The first can be called "religious crusaders," for its adherents viewed the Vietnam War as part of a larger spiritual crusade against Satan's scheme to control humankind. America was God's mighty arm called to crush the forces of evil, especially communism. They saw the war simplistically as one front in America's global struggle against communism, ignoring Vietnam's own history, desires, and culture as irrelevant. They deemed the war "good," and urged using all necessary means to ensure victory. Seeing God on America's side, they conceived of no possible reason to lose this fight other than sheer lack of will to win. They equated dissent with opposing God, and therefore actively organized against the antiwar movement like crusaders on a mission (Pratt 1988).

Protestant separatist fundamentalists made up the bulk of this camp, the loudest of whom was defrocked Presbyterian minister Carl McIntire, who founded an organization for fundamentalist groups called the American Council of Christian Churches (ACCC). McIntire spearheaded most of the planned responses for religious crusaders to the Vietnam War. Other spokespersons included fundamentalist preachers Billy James Hargis and Edgar Bundy. They remained a small but vocal group that mastered the media and made their message more influential than their numbers might suggest.

Protestants by no means stood alone here. The stridently anticommunist Roman Catholic archbishop of New York, Francis Joseph Cardinal Spellman, added his considerable influence. So too did Father Patrick O'Connor, the key correspondent stationed in Vietnam for NC News Service, the American bishops' official news organization. Like many Protestants, Catholics viewed atheistic communism as a threat to their churches. Because South Vietnam's first president, Ngo Dinh Diem, was an anticommunist Catholic who drew many Vietnamese Catholics into the top ranks of his military and government, the U.S. Catholic community was especially drawn to his cause. Some—usually Orthodox—Jewish Zionists also aligned closely with this camp. They described communist advances anywhere as threats to Jewish freedom and Israel's survival, and they saw communists in league with Israel's Arab enemies. As Meir Kahane (2004) asserted in the Orthodox newspaper the *Jewish Press,* "the State of Israel is a bitter target of the communists in general and the Chinese and Vietcong in particular" (150).

Francis Cardinal Spellman is flanked by presidential candidates John F. Kennedy (left) and Richard M. Nixon at a memorial dinner event in New York City, October 19, 1960. (*Associated Press*)

The second camp, the "religious nationalists," shared the basic anti-communist worldview of the crusaders. They were not, however, as militant about the war, nor as blind to its historical and cultural factors. They supported America's Vietnam policy, especially when presidents asked them to, but they did not demand victory at all costs. They were far more devoted to preserving their notion of faith and nation as righteous partners than to winning the war. Only saving souls counted as a higher priority. They also viewed their uncritical blend of piety and patriotism as the remedy for whatever ailed the United States in the 1960s. When the war went well, they waved flags and cheered. When it went poorly, they kept waving flags while chastising clergy who would not muffle their criticisms, advising clerics to stick to spiritual matters and to trust government and military experts. Most remained officially disengaged from the specifics of the war because these threatened to spark critical examination of American perceptions; rather, they promoted anticommunism, patriotism, and the purely spiritual activities of religious communities. This patriotic avoidance strategy became a way to hold together their vision of a godly nation amid a bad war. Dissenters drew the rebuke of religious nationalists, not for being wrong on Vietnam, but because they did not submit to the worldly authorities God had placed over humans to restrain sin and preserve order. Religious nationalists showed little interest in the Vietnamese other than converting them or dispensing occasional relief supplies. When the war seemed all but lost, some religious nationalists interpreted America's troubles as divine punishment for its ingratitude and disobedience. The solution became more flags, revivals, conversions, and prayer, not analyzing the war itself.

Most conservative Protestants, Catholics, and Mormons in America fell into this group, making it the largest of the four. So, too, did some Jews, generally from Orthodox and Conservative traditions. White middle-class Americans often felt most comfortable with this ideology. Religion had boomed in 1950s suburbia, often marching in lockstep with what came to be known as the "American way of life." Evangelist Billy Graham became the poster boy for conservative evangelicals, popularizing the posture, language, and arguments of this camp in prominent venues. So, too, did the well-known evangelical magazine *Christianity Today* and the National Association of Evangelicals, the main umbrella organization for evangelical churches. Dr. J. A. O. Preus, conservative president of the Lutheran Church-Missouri Synod (LCMS), echoed similar sentiments. For Catholics, Jews, and Mormons who were moving rapidly into the mainstream of American life, patriotic expressions became badges of inclusion, inoculating them against accusations of radicalism or "foreignness." Even when the Vatican came out early against the Vietnam War, American Catholic bishops generally stood behind U.S. government actions. Catholic and Mormon beliefs about deference to state authority added impetus. The Catholic journal *America* often voiced the religious nationalist position. Although many religious nationalists grew disillusioned with the war after 1968 for practical reasons, seeing it as mismanaged rather than mistaken, they remained supportive of America's objectives and righteous intentions.

The third camp, called "religious dissenters," consisted of those religious bodies and individuals who judged U.S. policy in Vietnam to be misguided, unjust, and immoral. Although nearly all disliked communism, they analyzed the war within the historical context of Vietnamese history and U.S.–Vietnamese relations, not purely in ideological terms. In fact, they criticized the American government's simplistic bipolar view of communism, the domino theory, and containment policies based on them. More important, they put their transnational spiritual ties with brethren overseas ahead of bonds to country. They saw the war as symptomatic of an "arrogance of power" stemming from an overly nationalistic, militaristic American worldview that defied God's higher values of love, justice, reconciliation, community, and peace. They also believed the war presented a *"kairos"* or teachable moment that could expose and transform destructive worldviews into ones better suited for living and leading in a justice-based international community. To them, this was vital religious work. They stood in the tradition of the ancient Jewish prophets, calling for loyalty to God and neighbor before nation. They urged religious bodies to remain separate from the state and, as the Quakers often said, "speak truth to power." As Rabbi Abraham Heschel asked, "Do they [government leaders] have the wisdom? . . . Can I turn over my soul and conscience to them?" (Friedland 1998, 59). In these ways, the religious dissenters directly challenged what the religious nationalists wanted most to preserve: the fusion of Americanism and faith.

The moderate to liberal mainline (i.e., long-established) Protestant churches such as the Methodists, Presbyterians, Episcopalians, Congregationalists, and American Baptists produced the greatest number of dissenters. Most held membership in the National Council of the Churches of Christ in the USA (NCC), which often spearheaded official antiwar statements and actions on behalf of its large membership. Two popular Protestant periodicals, *The Christian Century* and *Christianity and Crisis,* remained strong prophetic voices for debate and action on Vietnam. Unitarian Universalists also lined up largely with the dissenters. So, too, did many Jews, especially from the Reform and Reconstructionist traditions. A Catholic minority also moved into these ranks as the war increasingly defied Catholic principles of "just war theory," and Vatican II reforms invited Catholics to engage the world more actively. *Commonweal* and the *National Catholic Reporter* carried Catholic concerns about the war. When the dissenters' religious bureaucracies moved too slowly, individual Protestant, Jewish, and Catholic leaders came together to create independent action groups such as Clergy and Laymen Concerned About Vietnam (CALCAV). Rounding out this camp were a handful of theologically conservative yet socially conscious evangelicals who echoed the basic concerns of the dissenters while staying within the evangelical fold and usually at arms length from liberal Protestants. Oregon senator Mark Hatfield became an evangelical antiwar spokesperson, as did clergy such as Jim Wallis, the founder of *Sojourners,* and several professors at Calvin College who penned articles for the *Reformed Journal.* By and large, religious dissenters maintained some distance from radical, secular, New Left antiwar groups. They did so to preserve their respectable images, access to middle America, and separate identities as religious groups driven by spiritual, not ideological, motivations.

The fourth group, the pacifists, echoed the dissenters' religious arguments on the war, but they brought unique concerns and preferred strategies. First, they rejected all war and violence as ungodly, not just U.S. actions in Vietnam. Second, the most radical of them insisted that nonviolent civil disobedience was essential to force the government's hand and refuse cooperation with evil. In contrast, most religious dissenters only opposed wars deemed unjust, and saw civil disobedience as a method of last resort. Many members of the traditional peace churches, such as the Society of Friends (Quakers), the Mennonites, and the Brethren, worked through the system—respecting legal channels preferred by dissenters. However, radical pacifists within these groups often confronted the political establishment in dramatic extra-legal ways that made dissenters uncomfortable, yet prodded them further. No one pushed this envelope more than Philip and Daniel Berrigan, two Catholic priests. Radical pacifists collected in several groups, including the Fellowship of Reconciliation (FOR), the War Resisters League (WRL), the Catholic Peace Fellowship (an offshoot of the Catholic Worker Movement), and other peace fellowship groups situated within religious denominations.

It is useful to examine the specific responses of religious communities within each of these camps as the war progressed through four stages: the buildup (1954–1965), the escalation (1966–1967), the turning point (1968–1969), and America's struggle for disentanglement "with honor" (1970–1973).

The Buildup, 1954–1965

With rare exception, like the rest of the nation, religious communities paid little attention to troubles in Vietnam before the deployment of U.S. combat troops in 1965. In the mid-1950s, religious groups established relief operations for Vietnamese refugees when Diem withdrew from scheduled elections and split south from north. The Mennonite Central Committee, Catholic Relief Services, and Church World Service (a branch of the NCC) each dispensed aid, much of which the U.S. government donated along with transportation and logistics support. Diem invited church assistance, and, before 1965, the churches saw little danger in collaborating with the U.S. or South Vietnamese governments. Helping the needy was God's work. The fact that the churches were working within the U.S. government's Food for Peace program, which granted relief only to anticommunist allies in the effort to win their populations' "hearts and minds," seemed acceptable. Warning signs foreshadowed later trouble as Mennonites chafed against American government attempts to control their personnel, and the Vietnamese assumed mistakenly that church and state were one and the same. The U.S. government intentionally co-opted relief organizations into doing its diplomatic nation-building work. The militaries swung the sticks, while the churches doled out the carrots.

As a religious distress call in 1963, Buddhist monks self-immolated (burned themselves to death) in Vietnam's streets while Diem responded with repression. In June, about a dozen concerned Christian and Jewish clergy formed a Ministers' Vietnam Committee. Through full-page ads in the *Washington Post* and *New York Times,* the group criticized America's alliance with Diem's undemocratic regime, as well as the use of defoliants and strategic hamlets. It also questioned U.S. military involvement in a civil war that required political solutions. By August, this committee boasted having more than 17,000 unnamed supporters for its ads, but few clergy would challenge the president outright.

Between 1963 and 1965, the civil rights movement was in full swing, and clergy advocates—both black and white—feared alienating Lyndon Johnson by criticizing the war when they sought his cooperation on civil rights legislation. Many had supported his election in 1964 over Republican Barry Goldwater, who seemed ready to introduce nuclear weapons into Vietnam. Nevertheless, Johnson's approach to the conflict made liberal and pacifist clergy increasingly uneasy. By 1965, waves of critical voices, both domestic and from overseas, converged within the more liberal religious communities, sparking several condemnatory statements by year's end from major religious bodies.

Within liberal Protestant circles, pressure built for prophetic church criticism of the war. Nationwide, young adults within the Student Christian Movement began speaking and organizing for this within church denominational meetings. Asian Christians overseas, especially those in the East Asia Christian Conference and Japan's Christian Council, sought meetings with the NCC to educate American church leaders about Vietnamese nationalism, resistance to Western imperialism, and the improper blurring of church/state identities in dispensing relief. The editorial boards of *Christianity and Crisis* and *The Christian Century* published a flurry of articles questioning the Johnson administration's explanations of the conflict. They called the NCC to step up and lead the churches in a prophetic response to the war similar to its efforts on civil rights. Pacifists such as A. J. Muste urged the NCC to stop "marking time" on Vietnam. The NCC dispatched a study team to Southeast Asia and gathered information from other Christians making fact-finding trips there. In these ways, religious communities accessed data independently from the U.S. government.

Meanwhile, pacifists began demonstrating against the war. In April 1965, FOR created the Clergymen's Emergency Committee for Vietnam, which published ads on behalf of "2,500 ministers, priests, and rabbis" asking the president to, "in the Name of God, STOP IT!" (Friedland 1998, 148–149). It then formed an Interreligious Committee on Vietnam, which brought about 1,000 Protestants, Catholics, and Jews together for a silent May vigil at the Pentagon. The well-known Trappist monk Thomas Merton published essays about peace and mentored a few priests who had just formed the Catholic Peace Fellowship, including Daniel Berrigan. Daniel Berrigan's brother Philip criticized the racist aspects of the war. The Catholic Church silenced Merton from publishing on peace, and both Berrigans were transferred suddenly to different parishes when they got too controversial.

Some suspected Cardinal Spellman's hand behind the latter move and picketed his chancery.

Pacifists also began addressing the draft. Both the Catholic and Jewish Peace Fellowships distributed information on attaining conscientious objector status; CPF's New York offices fielded more than 50 inquiries a week. Pacifist groups such as the CPF, WRL, and American Friends Service Committee (AFSC) united with others to organize antiwar demonstrations in Berkeley, Chicago, and New York. Some sponsored controversial draft card burnings (Friedland 1998).

When three religious persons in America self-immolated to express their distress over the war and empathy for the Vietnamese, they stunned the nation. The first, Holocaust survivor Alice Herz, did so in Detroit's streets in March 1965. In early November, the Quaker Norman Morrison turned his body into a torch within feet of the Pentagon. A week later, Catholic pacifist Roger LaPorte self-immolated in front of the United Nations. He lived long enough to tell paramedics that "I did this as a religious action" (Friedland 1998, 160). Clerical leaders noted the spiritual anguish caused by the war. Others dismissed the three as kooks.

Between November 1965 and January 1966, important bodies within the Protestant and Jewish communities released official statements critical of U.S. policy in Vietnam, and Pope Paul VI condemned the hubris that led to war without mentioning Vietnam. The NCC reminded its flocks that "the reason Christians have a specific responsibility to speak and to criticize is that they have a loyalty to God which must transcend every other loyalty. . . ." (NCC Message 1965). The Union of American Hebrew Congregations, the NCC, and the Synagogue Council of America each called for a bombing halt and questioned the unilateral military means rather than the goals of U.S. policy. The statements were mild by later standards. Nevertheless, these gave their organizations official marching orders to begin taking action against the war. National church bodies, such as the NCC and its member denominations, could not move without them, and it often took time to build enough consensus among their leadership to pass them.

Responding to this rising tide of religious dissent, President Johnson called Billy Graham and Cardinal Spellman for support and got it. Graham railed more frequently against communism's global agenda and implored clergy to stay silent on specific foreign policy issues, especially Vietnam. Johnson pressed dissenting Jews to see parallels between Israel and South Vietnam and to reconsider their criticism. Soon Israeli president Zalman Shazar praised Johnson's military defense of small nations. Orthodox rabbis tried unsuccessfully to coerce dissenters such as Rabbi Abraham Heschel to desist. Jewish acquiescence to the war pained Heschel deeply, for he remembered how the silence of "good Germans" allowed the Holocaust to happen. "To speak about God and remain silent on Vietnam is blasphemous," he asserted (Kimelman 1983). Overall, religious nationalists followed Graham's lead, remaining overtly patriotic and quietly supportive of the president's Vietnam policy.

Religious crusaders became more active. Their vocal support for the war grew in proportion to Johnson's bombing campaign and the dissenters' criticism. In October 1965, Carl McIntire's ACCC produced its own resolution declaring the Vietnam War a noble part of America's fight against global communism. He and fundamentalist John Stormer visited South Vietnam in November and returned convinced of the rightness of their cause. Stormer's book, *None Dare Call It Treason* (1964), which sold several million copies, had accused the liberal churches of being conduits for communist infiltration in America. By the end of 1965, the crusaders, the religious nationalists, the religious dissenters, and the pacifists had each crafted the basis for their positions on the Vietnam War.

The Escalation, 1966–1967

As the war escalated, so did the positions and actions of religious communities within their respective camps. Religious dissenters launched multipronged efforts to stimulate "debate and action" at the pew level, among religious denominations, and within the government. The newly born CALCAV, which blossomed rapidly with 100 local chapters nationwide, aimed to educate, train, and activate local religious people from all faith traditions on the war and help bring their voices to government. The prominent names among its leadership—such as Reverends Martin Luther King Jr., John Bennett, Daniel Berrigan, William Sloane Coffin, and Rabbi Abraham Heschel—and its close relationship with the NCC imbued it with legitimacy and respectability. King's famous April 1967 antiwar speech at New York's Riverside Church gave the entire antiwar movement a boost. CALCAV also gave clergy, who might feel unable to act within their official religious bodies, an outlet for quick collective action. It organized vigils, fasts, workshops, marches, book projects, literature drops, and lobbying sessions. As frustrations with the war grew, the group gradually embraced draft resistance. In 1967, Yale chaplain and CALCAV leader William Sloane Coffin was arrested for collecting draft cards in a church, thereby "aiding and abetting" violations of Selective Service laws. The former World War II veteran and Central Intelligence Agency officer embraced civil disobedience as a way to call attention to God's higher laws that address peace with justice; he hoped his later court appearance would allow him to put the war on trial instead. Philip Berrigan went further. He and others poured blood on draft card files at Baltimore's U.S. Customs House. Both Berrigans quit CALCAV for being too cautious. Philip even left the CPF, calling it overly "safe, [and] unimaginative" (Friedland 1998, 193–207).

At its first annual religious "mobilization" in February 1967, CALCAV brought more than 2,000 participants to the nation's capitol. As they marched respectfully before the White House, McIntire led 100 heckling counterprotesters waving signs declaring "God and the Devil Don't Co-Exist" and "Fight to Win in Vietnam" (Friedland 1998, 177–179). Meanwhile Carl Henry, editor of the evangelical magazine *Christianity Today,* peered disapprovingly from his office window and urged both sets of ministers to go home. McIntire dubbed such detachedness "cowardice," while the liberal *Christian Century* said Henry "looked down in sanctimonious aloofness and serene neutrality" at the marchers below (Pratt 1988, 195, n. 118). This painted a perfect picture of the opposing postures struck by the crusaders, nationalists, and dissenters.

Whereas CALCAV rallied individuals, the NCC and its denominations worked to mobilize education, discussions, and action within congregations and denominational structures on the war. This proved difficult for many reasons. Laity tended to be more conservative theologically and politically than mainline Protestant church leadership, creating what some called the "clergy-laity gap." In addition, the 1960s mantra to question authority had reached the churches, and laity grew increasingly reluctant to follow clergy blindly. Finally, the war was highly divisive, and congregations resisted discussing it for fear of disrupting parish unity. Therefore, church leaders tended to be far more vocal and antiwar than laity—which resulted in several denominational statements against the war—while many laity echoed the religious nationalist stance and denied that their leadership spoke for them. One member of the Lutheran Church in America asked if the NCC sought "peace at the price of an atheistic (Godless) form of government [in Vietnam]" (Settje 2007, 109). Many would have preferred their church executives to mimic Graham in 1966: visit the troops—on General William Westmoreland's invitation—trust national leaders, and hold one's tongue on the war. LCMS president J. A. O. Preus affirmed the patriotic preferences of such laity when he asserted that "we owe much more to our soldiers in Viet Nam than we do to irresponsible clergy [who urge bombing halts over Vietnam]" (Settje 2007, 109).

The NCC also sought to convert members of the Johnson administration, not only with respect to Vietnam policy but also to a whole new set of assumptions about peace, security, and power based on liberal religious principles. NCC international affairs director Robert Bilheimer targeted Secretary of State Dean Rusk, a fellow Presbyterian. Rusk, in turn, sought to woo the influential NCC back onto the side of the administration, for politicians wanted religious authorities to provide an appearance of godly blessing over national actions. In the summer of 1967, Bilheimer led a team of highly respected, moderate, denominational leaders on a "Mission of Concern" to Vietnam to study the situation and express care for peoples on both sides. He had Rusk's support, for Rusk hoped the trip would help bend the churches toward embracing U.S. policy. Bilheimer, in turn, hoped his team's report would convince Rusk to look more critically at his deepest assumptions about the war. Both failed to persuade the other. From that point on, the NCC found it increasingly difficult to get respectful White House audiences—once easy for mainline churches to do—as the White House courted conservative religious nationalists for blessings in exchange for access to power. Meanwhile, seeking to counter every dissenter action, McIntire's ACCC sent his own delegation to Vietnam. He created Vietnam resolutions contradictory to those produced by the NCC and encouraged letters from laity admonishing its positions.

For religious moderates seeking a less radical outlet than CALCAV or the pacifist groups, Negotiations Now! formed in 1967. It refrained from blaming either side for the war. It merely urged a negotiated rather than military settlement, and did not push for an immediate withdrawal. Its "realistic" mild tone drew a few U.S. Catholic bishops for the first time into the movement, along with religious anticommunists seeking to keep South Vietnam independent and free from communist control. In spite of the pope's 1966 encyclical *Christi Matri,* which urged a diplomatic peace in Vietnam, American bishops stated that "our [military] presence in Vietnam is justified" (Friedland 1998, 175). Therefore, this move by a few was significant, especially after Cardinal Spellman declared the Vietnam conflict to be a "war for civilization" and distributed Christmas cards with photos of himself standing next to U.S. bombers. He was not alone. Archbishop John Cardinal Cody of Chicago sprinkled holy water on tanks headed for the war zone. The 60 Catholic seminarians who protested the ceremony with signs reading "Stop Blessing Death" were directed by superiors to undergo psychiatric examinations (Friedland 1998, 175).

Two events in 1967 divided religious communities with respect to the war. First, scandal erupted when the *National Catholic Reporter* broke the story about Catholic Relief Services' (CRS) humanitarian aid being given as payment to Popular Forces units within South Vietnam's army. The payments happened at General Westmoreland's request. This, in effect, made the Catholic Church part of the war effort and a pawn of the U.S. military, defying injunctions on separation of church and state, as well as marring the church's mission to care for all who hunger and thirst regardless of political or ideological boundaries. Speaking for many, the *National Catholic Reporter* demanded that CRS "Get Out of the War," while others said that the Popular Forces were needy too and that CRS had to obey America's "Trade with the Enemy Act" forbidding relief to the Vietcong (Flipse 2002).

Protestant relief agencies found themselves in a similar bind. Vietnam Christian Service (VNCS), a joint project of the Church World Service, the Mennonite Central Committee (MCC), and Lutheran World Relief, received pressure from military commanders to become "part of the team" and stop its workers, such as the young Mennonite David Hostetter, from giving relief to both sides. Aided by his fluency in Vietnamese, Hostetter followed VNCS guidelines to preserve independence from U.S. officials and the military; he associated most closely with locals, and refused official U.S. protection. He also sent relief aid to local churches operating in enemy-held territory, aided four U.S. Army deserters, and became increasingly outspoken against the war. Hostetter told the MCC's Peace Section leaders that he was most concerned about "how much of our God and gospel . . . we [are] willing to withhold or have perverted to stay in Vietnam" (Bush 2002, 210). A U.S. colonel called for his transfer, asserting that no American who questioned U.S. policy should be working in country. U.S. ambassador Ellsworth Bunker pressured VNCS director Paul Leatherman to stop relief workers from aiding potential Vietcong, warning that "if you're helping VC, that is treason." Leatherman retorted that "there is no treason in the church" (Bush 2002, 210). But VNCS leaders also tried to hush Hostetter. The NCC ran into additional trouble with Asian Christian partners overseas who questioned its integrity for condemning the war on one hand while apparently assisting U.S. military imperialism via VNCS's charity work on the other. Like Hostetter, many Christian aid workers ultimately quit or ignored

U.S. laws. Called "the politics of charity," these dilemmas created boiling arguments over church relationships to governments and their responsibilities to war victims on all sides.

Second, when Israel crushed an Arab attack and then took control of Palestinian territory in the Six-Day War, American Jews quieted dramatically on Vietnam. How could Jews criticize one war when they desired U.S. military support for another? Further, because liberal Christians often felt sympathy for displaced Palestinians, tension erupted between Jews and Christians who had marched together for peace in Vietnam. Interfaith relations cooled, and Jews found it suddenly awkward to be part of the antiwar movement. Divisiveness within the nation worsened over the next two years, exacerbating splits within and between religious communities, even as the population began to sour on the war.

Turning Point, 1968–1969

The year 1968 commenced with a surprise Vietcong attack called the Tet Offensive. Tet exposed the U.S. government's credibility gap on the war and convinced Johnson to seek a diplomatic end to the conflict. Except for the crusaders, who preferred military conquest, optimism rose among religious communities for a quick settlement. Hope blossomed further when Johnson pulled himself out of the presidential race, clearing the way for a new leader who might offer a fresh peace policy. With strong leadership supplied by the Methodist Church, the NCC and CALCAV pushed hard for congressional and presidential candidates to include peace planks in their platforms, and they urged electoral support of those who did. Church World Service even began planning to aid postwar reconstruction. By the end of 1969, however, these hopes were dashed as newly elected president Richard Nixon revealed his desires to win the war and to crush the peace movement.

Many religious communities were willing to give Nixon's policies a chance. The evangelical dissenter Senator Hatfield supported Nixon's candidacy but grew quickly disillusioned. Hatfield's 1968 book, *Not Quite So Simple*, urged Americans—especially fellow evangelicals—to take a more complex view of the war. He and writers for the *Reformed Journal* were often lonely voices among evangelicals, who rarely questioned Vietnam policy. The NCC also approached Nixon optimistically at first, for Nixon had invited its input. In addition, NCC president Arthur Flemming knew Nixon and Secretary of State William Rogers personally, for they had all served together at top levels of President Dwight Eisenhower's administration. Therefore, the NCC assembled a prestigious group of experts on a wide variety of subjects related to the war and wrote up recommendations for Nixon. However, the president and Secretary of State Rogers ignored the document and criticized the NCC for not using its influence to promote Nixon's policies. FOR received similar treatment when it—along with CALCAV, the Disciples of Christ, the Episcopal Church, and the Brethren—sent a high-profile study team to South Vietnam to explore issues of religious and political freedom. Its report condemned U.S. support of the repressive regime in South Vietnam. The Nixon administration gave it detached acknowledgment, but no more. Team member, Congressman John Conyers, later read it into the *Congressional Record.*

As Nixon threw the polite religious dissenters a cold shoulder, he opened White House doors warmly to religious nationalists. Billy Graham sat with Nixon's family at the 1968 Republican Convention and led the first of many Sunday worship services at the White House. Theologian Reinhold Niebuhr noted disapprovingly "what a simple White House invitation will do to dull the critical faculties" (Friedland 1998, 216). The services had a political purpose: to court and reward conservative religious supporters and to provide Nixon with an aura of religious blessing. Discerning religious dissenters blasted them for their partisanship and for blurring the line between church and state.

CALCAV continued offering annual February religious mobilizations in Washington to lobby elected officials and to train the faithful to organize action on Vietnam at home. Carl McIntire brought counterprotesters to each one. Along with pacifists, CALCAV also heightened attention to the draft. It began a ministry to deserters in Sweden and helped draw the NCC into a joint ministry with the Canadian Council of Churches to serve U.S. war resisters who had fled to Canada. Various American congregations situated near the Canadian border already participated in an "underground railroad" of sorts, helping young men make their way north to avoid the war. Pacifists continued urging draft resistance and staging draft card burnings. The radical Berrigans even torched draft files in Catonsville, Maryland, with homemade napalm. Although many radical pacifists applauded their motives, not all approved of this particular action, which bordered on a type of violence. Even Merton wondered if it crossed a line. When the Berrigans later fled the law rather than turn themselves in, religious dissenters criticized their abandonment of a key principle of civil disobedience: paying the penalty. Religious nationalists had little sympathy for lawbreakers, period. When members of the Catholic Left joined civil disobedience protests of Dow Chemical's napalm production, evangelicals defended napalm as justified in defending the free world and urged obedience to law as God's means of preserving order.

The issue of civil disobedience challenged religious communities. Many believed their faiths' calls to be peacemakers included respecting the system and the law, but peaceful civil disobedience also had long historical roots in many religious traditions. White clergy gradually accepted the tactic when used by black churches against Jim Crow statutes in the South. However, civil rights protesters had the backing of federal laws in their pursuit of justice. By contrast, civil disobedience against the Vietnam War stood against the U.S. government in its appeal to higher justice, making it harder for some to do. By the late 1960s, however, religious dissenter groups largely, albeit cautiously, embraced nonviolent civil disobedience, provided that protesters submitted to legal penalties as part of their witness. They also stood strongly in favor of selective conscientious objection. Some even argued with draft board administrators that churches, not the government, should be authorized to judge their members' consciences in making conscientious objector determinations, for the state did not specialize in matters

James Rubins

Young draft-aged parishioners challenged their churches to do more than pass resolutions supporting selective conscientious objection and civil disobedience. They sought shared complicity. The Reformed Church in America (RCA), a conservative denomination within the NCC, faced a spiritual and legal crisis when five seminarians asked its General Synod to hold their draft cards and thereby stand with them in defiance of the law. Because Christian principles forged their spiritual opposition to the Vietnam War, the seminarians urged their church to put itself in legal jeopardy with them. Agonizingly, the synod declined their cards; however, it endorsed civil disobedience based on conscience, and promised to provide them with spiritual and legal aid. Later, a group of RCA leaders created an independent committee to accept their cards (Gill 1996, 389–394).

The NCC faced the same challenge when 21-year-old Hope College student and RCA member James Rubins made a similar request at its 1969 General Assembly. The earnest young man argued compellingly that the church should stand with those whose con-sciences it had sculpted. Although a majority of delegates voted to accept his card, the vote fell shy of the two-thirds needed for passage. When it failed, a Christian activist group called Jonathan's Wake, who judged the NCC to be too moderate on the war, stormed the speakers' table. Rev. Jack York of the Free Church of Berkeley took the microphone and hollered something like, "The blood of the Vietnamese is upon you!" Then he doused the table with red paint (Gill 1996, 389–394). Papers were dripping, and the NCC officers seated there left coated with paint, clothes destroyed. Rubins remained respectful. He said simply, "I hold no grudge against people who did not stand with me. I believe in the church. I stand by the church. May God help us all" (Geyer 1969). When some NCC delegates voted independently to hold Rubin's card, Carl McIntire's ACCC telegrammed U.S. Attorney General John Mitchell, imploring him to instigate "an immediate investigation of this criminal act which is a subversion of national security" (Geyer 1969). As this story reveals, liberal religious dissenters were often rebuked by both the right and the left on Vietnam.

of "conscience." Some urged as well that military chaplains be placed under the authority of their churches, not the military, so that they could be freer to counsel potential objectors without military pressure against doing so. In lieu of this, the NCC worked in conjunction with the General Commission on Chaplains to develop materials for conscientious objector counseling that denominations could distribute to chaplains.

The close of 1969 brought a series of some of the largest nationwide protests against the war, and religious communities were thoroughly involved with them. Former seminarians David Hawk and Sam Brown organized the Moratorium, which called for a one-day general strike on October 15 to reflect on the war in various local ways across the nation; each month a strike day would be added until the war ended. Although the sequential observations lost steam, the first Moratorium was massively successful. The solemn call to reflection drew religious participation. The NCC, CALCAV, Committee for a Sane Nuclear Policy(SANE), FOR, the Central Conference of American Rabbis, Boston's Catholic bishop Richard Cardinal Cushing, and several denominational leaders supported and observed the

Moratorium. Churches, chapels, and synagogues opened their doors for vigils, special masses, educational events, and prayers. Evangelical dissenters also took part. Even *Christianity Today's* editors applauded its dignified tone. However, 10 days later about 7,000 religious crusaders responded disdainfully with a "Bible-believer's March" in New Jersey to "call for victory in Vietnam" (Pratt 1988, 223). Nixon countered too by appealing for a national day of prayer for October 22. He then swung popular support his way with his famous "Silent Majority" speech on November 3, and proclaimed November 9 "national unity day," whose patriotic spirit was reinforced by Veterans Day on November 11. Although regretting the war's destructiveness, religious nationalists applauded Nixon's speeches and policy, echoing support for the nation.

The New Mobilization Committee to End the War in Vietnam (New Mobe) and second Moratorium antiwar protests that followed in mid-November were the largest to date. Although more radical than the October observances, they remained largely nonviolent, thanks in part to Quakers who trained thousands of peacekeeping marshals. Religious groups took part in numerous ways, even though they may not have agreed with every aspect of the Mobe's platform. They helped coordinate the March Against Death, a highly spiritual ceremony that honored and mourned war dead from all sides. William Sloane Coffin and president of the World Council of Churches Eugene Carson Blake led a powerful ecumenical prayer service at the Washington Cathedral during the 36-hour march. Of course, McIntire appeared at both with about 100 counterprotesters in tow. He tried but failed to disrupt the prayer service (Pratt 1988). Jewish groups participated in Mobe and Moratorium events, too. The National Jewish Organizing Project set up antiwar resource centers at various places around Washington, read names in the death march, and demonstrated in front of the White House. About 150 Jews marched around Nixon's residence seven times blowing the shofar and singing "Joshua Fought the Battle of Jericho," intimating that its walls should come tumbling down (Masch 2004).

Through his speeches, Nixon cleverly managed public perceptions, painting the protesters as the nation's larger threat, not the war. Religious nationalists did the same, and it worked. Average Americans denigrated and detested protesters more than the war, and in their minds religious dissenters were no better. The religious activists' efforts to distinguish themselves from the New Left failed to resonate with the masses.

Disentanglement "with Honor," 1970–1973

Nixon went to war against the peace movement, and his enemies list included the dissenting religious communities. The Internal Revenue Service targeted both the NCC and CALCAV for punitive audits, the NCC's phones were bugged, and the Federal Bureau of Investigation included CALCAV in its "Internal Security Investigations." All audits and investigations came up clean. Vice President Spiro Agnew also threw verbal spears at the NCC, mocking progressive preachers as ones "more interested in fighting pollution than fighting evil" (Cornell 1970).

Ironically, Nixon's Vietnamization policy inspired McIntire's ACCC to question the president's own commitment to fighting evil. Vietnamization aimed to return greater combat responsibilities to the South Vietnamese while increasing U.S. training and air support. Whereas religious dissenters condemned the policy for merely changing the color of the bodies, religious crusaders pilloried Nixon's lack of will to use U.S. military might to its fullest. McIntire led his most successful pro-war March for Victory in April 1970, which drew between 50,000 and 100,000 participants. He wanted South Vietnamese vice president Nguyen Cao Ky to give the keynote address, but the U.S. government prevented Ky from doing so. McIntire read Ky's talk aloud instead. Crusaders repeatedly complained that U.S. soldiers were deployed to war "with their hands tied, with orders to die, but not to win. . . ." Most thought a U.S. victory could be ensured in six to eight weeks if its military were freed fully to fight. When Nixon visited communist China seeking détente, McIntire demanded that he "apologize to the Christians of this country" for shirking his duty to crush communism (Pratt 1988, 275–277, 286).

Religious nationalists rallied around Nixon and boosted patriotism by raising the prisoner of war issue. LCMS president Preus was so zealous in doing so that Nixon rewarded him with preaching engagements at the White House. Antiwar Lutherans accused both men of political motives, charging that "the Nixon administration began this business of turning the prisoner issue into a trick to arouse world opinion against Hanoi." They noted that "within a week of this [Preus's] news-release, he [Preus] becomes the guest preacher at the White House" (Settje 2007, 140–141). Other religious nationalists, buoyed by Nixon's affections and rising Silent Majority, turned their attention away from the war and onto America's own cultural upheavals. This included targeting dissenters as dangerous to the nation's values, fabric, and traditions, which also suited Nixon's purposes. Nixon was photographed with Billy Graham at a revival as both bowed their heads in prayer. Graham then hosted an Honor America Day, seeking patriotism as a salve for the nation's scars. Although he harbored private concerns about the war, he concealed them. This frustrated the handful of fellow evangelicals, such as Jim Wallis and Lewis Smedes, who wanted this icon to separate God from nation and become more prophetic on the war. Hatfield explained that, "even if they [evangelicals] had misgivings about past policies, [they] found it difficult to break with their allegiance to President Nixon" (Pratt 1988, 323).

Meanwhile, religious dissenters sought to make their break as visible and vocal as possible. Like others in the antiwar movement, they excoriated Nixon when he appeared to expand the war into Cambodia and Laos. Twenty-six Lutheran seminarians told him that "such increased entanglements can only prolong this already fruitless and disastrous conflict and . . . further undermine our confidence in your professed desire for peace." Frederick A. Schiotz, president of the American Lutheran Church, urged Nixon to negotiate,

Evangelist Billy Graham in a 1966 photograph. (*Library of Congress*)

reminding him that "God has not ordained that the U.S. shall always 'win'" (Settje 2007, 126). Along with holding more public vigils, prayer services, and marches, groups such as CALCAV got more creative. It participated in an advertising project to "Unsell the War," running ads in magazines highlighting its destructiveness. It also conducted protests in stockholders' meetings at Dow Chemical and Honeywell to condemn their manufacture of napalm and antipersonnel weapons. Many CALCAV members shifted to the Left, getting more radical, while sacrificing some of their appeal to the mainstream parishioners that it had originally sought to attract (Hall 1992).

Along with 23 other religious groups, CALCAV supported a new organization called "Set the Date," which pushed the administration to declare a troop withdrawal date. The NCC and many of its denominations backed it, too. The NCC also created an Emergency Ministries Program to aid ailing Vietnam veterans who showed up at church doorsteps seeking help. It was highly successful, using local churches and experts in a variety of cities. Along with other antiwar activists, religious dissenters also put greater pressure on Congress to stop the war through legislative means.

Realizing that neither practical critiques of war policy nor discussions of presuppositions and worldviews had any effect on the White House, the NCC switched to making a strong moral argument against the war. It did this to deprive Nixon of moral cover for his war policies. In January 1972, it sponsored a huge Ecumenical Witness conference, which the *New York Times* called "the most comprehensive religious gathering ever assembled in the United States over the peace issue" (Fiske 1972). It boasted more than 132 official sponsors and drew about 650 high-profile delegates from Protestant, Catholic, Jewish, and Orthodox communities worldwide (Gill 1996). The conference focused specifically on making theologically grounded moral arguments against the war, as well as challenging the fusion of patriotism and piety nurtured by Nixon and the religious nationalists as doctrinally unsound and spiritually damaging. The war, therefore, became a religious battleground over morality, worldviews, and the relationship of church and state. The NCC sought to swing the mainstream faithful to its side, but its impact largely missed the pews.

The Paris Peace Agreement of January 1973 got America's military out of Vietnam without ending its civil war. Each religious camp responded differently. Religious crusaders were angry, deploring it as a sellout that stopped short of victory. Evangelist Billy James Hargis's book, *Our Vietnam Defeat! What Happened: A Study in International Defeat, Shabby Betrayal, Shameful Retreat* (1975) presented this view. Religious nationalists applauded the president, as did Preus when he said, "Let me add my congratulations to those I hope will come from millions of our fellow countrymen for bringing peace with honor" (Settje 2007, 103). Nationalists also expressed relief, urged detachment from the subject and recommended that the nation move forward to deal with domestic issues. Conversely, religious dissenters pressed the point that America had sinned in Vietnam and called for national repentance, reflection, and worldview transformation. To them, this was how the war might yet redeem America from its hubris and juvenile sense of innocence. Although by the early 1970s most Americans wanted the war ended, and judged it a failure for practical reasons, they resisted moral criticisms that implied America had sinned. Thus, although the religious dissenters were largely correct in their analysis of the war from 1965 forward, they lost the battle for the hearts and minds of average citizens who, like the nationalists, wanted to preserve their blessed image of America and themselves.

Conclusion

In 1970, Rev. Richard John Neuhaus, a CALCAV founder who became a leading religious neoconservative in the 1980s, predicted correctly which of the four religious camps would "win" the war of public opinion. If America failed in Vietnam, he foresaw that religious groups that remained officially neutral on the war, while staying in the public's good graces, "would feel confirmed . . . and be in a position to congratulate themselves." However, those who opposed the bad war and critiqued the systemic causes would be rejected by a public seeking to hang on to its self conceptions (Pratt 1988,

349–350). He was right. In the 1970s and 1980s religious nationalist groups boomed, especially conservative evangelicalism, which became part of the Republican political establishment. Mainline Protestant groups, which made up the bulk of religious dissenters, lost much of their previous cultural, political, and financial clout. Their underlying goal of using the war as a self-reflective mirror to help transform American self understandings and ways of interacting in the world failed.

When U.S. soldiers returned home, Americans wanted to forget, not reflect on, the war. Because few Americans had explored the war's causes beyond simple administration rhetoric about containing communism, and most wanted to retain their assumptions about the nation's righteousness, they were vulnerable to flawed interpretations that supported these desires. Besides, the war had not dramatically shaken up the lives of Americans not directly involved in it, and the disaster in Southeast Asia had not significantly altered America's superpower status. This made it easier to perpetuate old worldviews. When Ronald Reagan became president in 1980, in part by wooing religious nationalist voters, he helped resurrect and confirm the crusaders' explanations for the war's failure. Along with bitter generals such as Westmoreland, Reagan implied that America could have won had the military's hands been untied by the weak-kneed politicians who lacked the will to stay the course. He also demonized dissenters as traitorous and the media as sellouts. These interpretations, which ignored historical evidence, have become mainstream in part because religious nationalists adopted them, too. These became the "lessons" that future president George W. Bush echoed as he waged an ill-begotten war in Iraq. They were not, however, the deeper lessons dissenters tried to teach. They knew the Bible's warning that prophets are rarely accepted by their own country; yet they believed a religious group's real power resided in its independence and willingness to speak its truth, regardless of popularity.

For religious communities, the struggle over the Vietnam War was always about something bigger than the war. It embodied a larger clash over worldviews, religious values, visions of God and country, the relationship between church and state, and the influence of conservative and liberal religious visions in America. These struggles continue.

References and Further Reading

Bush, Perry. "The Political Education of Vietnam Christian Service, 1954–1975." *Peace and Change* 27 (April 2002): 198–224.

Cornell, George. From AP Newsfeatures, *Religion in the News,* June 17, 1970, RG 6, box 30, folder 16, NCC Archive.

Fiske, Edward. "Religious Assembly Terms Vietnam Policy Immoral." *New York Times,* January 17, 1972.

Flipse, Scott. "The Latest Casualty of War: Catholic Relief Services, Humanitarianism, and the War in Vietnam, 1967–1968." *Peace and Change* 27 (April 2002): 245–270.

Friedland, Michael. *Lift Up Your Voice Like a Trumpet: White Clergy and the Civil Rights and Antiwar Movements, 1954–1973.* Chapel Hill: University of North Carolina Press, 1998.

Geyer, Alan. "Joy Box with No Joy: The NCC at Detroit." *Christian Century,* December 17, 1969: 1601–1605.

Gill, Jill K. "Peace Is Not the Absence of Conflict, but the Presence of Justice: The National Council of Churches' Reaction and Response to the Vietnam War, 1965–1973." Ph.D. diss., University of Pennsylvania, 1996.

Hall, Mitchell K. "CALCAV and Religious Opposition to the Vietnam War." In *Give Peace a Chance: Exploring the Vietnam Antiwar Movement,* edited by Melvin Small and William D. Hoover, 35–52. Syracuse, NY: Syracuse University Press, 1992.

Kahane, Meir. "The Jewish Stake in Vietnam." In *The Jewish 1960s: An American Sourcebook,* edited by Michael E. Staub, 150–152. Lebanon, NH: Brandeis University Press, 2004.

Kimelman, Reuven. "Abraham Joshua Heschel: Our Generation's Teacher." *Melton Journal* 15 (Winter 1983). http://www.crosscurrents.org/heschel .htm (accessed November 14, 2007).

Masch, Mike. "Antiwar Marchers Turn Out En Masse in Washington." In *The Jewish 1960s: An American Sourcebook,* edited by Michael E. Staub, 153–156. Lebanon, NH: Brandeis University Press, 2004.

NCC Message. "A Message to the Churches on Viet-Nam," General Board, National Council of Churches, December 3, 1965 RG 4, box 36, folder 15, NCC Archive.

Pratt, Andrew LeRoy. "Religious Faith and Civil Religion: Evangelical Responses to the Vietnam War, 1964–1973." Ph.D. diss., Southern Baptist Theological Seminary, 1988.

Settje, David. *Lutherans and the Longest War: Adrift on a Sea of Doubt about the Cold and Vietnam Wars, 1964–1975.* Lanham, MD: Lexington Books, 2007.

Women and the Vietnam War   7

Natasha Zaretsky

When Americans today recall the Vietnam War era, certain iconic images come to mind: young, fresh-faced soldiers being sent overseas; national leaders such as Lyndon B. Johnson and Richard Nixon justifying the war to an increasingly skeptical public; and antiwar activists burning their draft cards in protest. Women do not loom very large in our collective memory of the Vietnam War, and when they do appear, it is often in the context of haunting photographs of Vietnamese civilians burned, maimed, and killed by U.S. bombing raids. Yet American women too played a role in both the execution of the war and the broader politics that surrounded it, and this essay explores their relationship to the war in three different capacities: as military personnel and civilians who served and worked in Vietnam during the war; as protesters on the home front who became increasingly vocal in their opposition to the war; and finally, as the wives, mothers, and sisters of American prisoners of war (POWs) in Southeast Asia. By tracing their roles in all of these capacities, women's complex position vis-à-vis the war comes into fuller view: they were both enablers of the war and resisters to it; executors of the war and, increasingly, protesters against it; actors who challenged official narratives of the war and, at times, crucial shapers of those narratives. Hardly on the sidelines, American women—both on the home front and the war front—were at the center of the military conflict.

American Women in Vietnam

Between 1962 and 1973, approximately 55,000 American women lived and worked in Vietnam, and somewhere between 7,500 and 11,000 of them served on active military duty. These women worked in a range of capacities: as clerical workers, air traffic controllers, cartographers, intelligence specialists, missionaries, teachers, journalists, photographers, and flight attendants. Almost all of them were volunteers. For women in the military, nursing was by far the most common occupation. One historian estimates that nurses represented a full 80 percent of women who served in Vietnam (Jeffreys-Jones 1999). The Navy, the Air Force, and the Army all enlisted nurses, who had to be at least 20 years old and were generally expected to complete a one-year tour of duty. In addition, civilian women worked in Vietnam under the auspices of several organizations, including the Red Cross, the United Service Organizations (USO), the American Friends Service Committee, and Catholic Relief Services.

Although nurses were officially excluded from the combat zone, the brutal, haphazard nature of the military conflict often placed them in perilous situations. As the Vietnam Women's Memorial Foundation (formerly the Memorial Project) later recalled, "There was no front. There was no such thing as safe behind our lines" ("During the Vietnam Era"). Naval nurses worked on hospital ships that sailed along the Vietnamese coast; Air Force nurses administered aid to the wounded on evacuation flights; and Army nurses worked in field hospitals, surgical hospitals, evacuation hospitals, mobile army surgical hospitals, and POW hospitals throughout the war. They often did this work in the midst of chaos. Writer Keith Walker, who interviewed several women who had served in Vietnam, recalled the various stories women had told him: "Red Cross women being fired upon in helicopters on their way to fire bases and outposts or stranded in a jungle clearing with no help in sight; nurses routinely working twelve-hour shifts six days a week and often much longer during mass casualties while rocket attacks went on outside their hospitals; a Special Services worker being flown out to a safe area during the Tet offensive, her helicopter lifting off as the mortar rounds walked in across the field" (Walker 1985, 4–5).

Women who made the decision to go to Vietnam had not always been adequately prepared for these risks. As Army nurse Lynda Van Devanter recalled, she had gone to Vietnam under the fallacious assumption that she would be safe. That assumption was soon debunked: "No sooner had I met some other nurses than I began hearing the stories. At least six U.S. Army nurses had died in Vietnam before I arrived—two in '66 and four in '67, all in helicopter crashes. And there were plenty of doctors, corpsmen, and other medical personnel who had been sent home in body bags." She recalled an older woman major mocking her earlier naiveté. Whoever told her she would be safe, the woman said, "should be horsewhipped. There might not be many nurses dying, but there are enough being wounded to discourage anyone with half a brain from being here" (Van Devanter 1983, 85).

In their capacity as nurses, women bore witness to the extraordinary violence unleashed by the war. Throughout the military conflict, both the North Vietnamese and American forces relied on small arms that were designed to inflict massive, mutilating injuries on the enemy. The relatively small size of Vietnam meant that injured soldiers could be taken relatively quickly to base camps, which maximized their chances of surviving injuries that undoubtedly would have killed them in earlier wars. It also meant that nurses routinely confronted the bloodshed and brutality of war as they, along with doctors and surgeons, conducted triages, performed amputa-

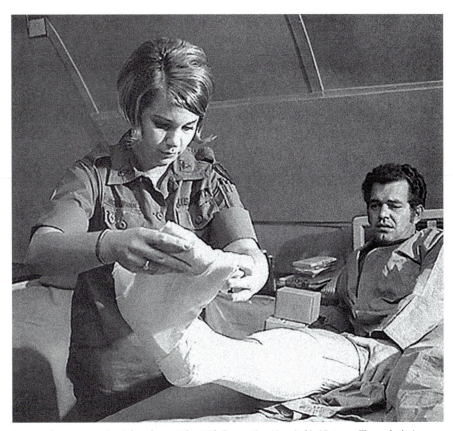

A nurse changes a patient's bandage at the 24th Evacuation Hospital in Vietnam. Through their involvement in the Vietnam War, nurses began to practice specialties and take more independent action. In 1966, Congress authorized the recruitment of male nurses, who eventually comprised one-fourth of the nurse corps. (*National Archives*)

tions, and inserted tracheotomies and breathing tubes. In their recollections of the war, nurses noted not only the split-second decisions they had to make in makeshift emergency rooms but also the remarkable youth of the soldiers they tried to save. One Army nurse who served for a year in two evacuation hospitals recalled that she "had to make the decision about those people who were wounded so bad that no matter how much time you would spend on them, they wouldn't live. They were called 'expectants,' and you would have to put them in an area behind a screen to die—these 19 year old kids" (Walker 1985, 13).

This intimate proximity to the violence unleashed by the war had a transformative effect on many American women in Vietnam. Women went to Vietnam in the first place for a variety of reasons. Those who worked for relief organizations chose to go there out of a broad commitment to humanitarianism. For young nurses from working-class backgrounds, the choice to join the military meant they would be able to avoid going into debt for an education. Still others went to Vietnam out of a sense of patriotic duty and a desire to make a contribution to the war effort. Lynda Van Devanter

(1983) remembered her early decision to go to war: "we were saving a country from communism. These were brave boys fighting and dying for democracy . . . And if our boys are being blown apart, then somebody better be over there putting them back together again" (47).

Many women found themselves forever changed by their wartime experiences in ways that were not unlike the transformations later described by male Vietnam veterans. They adopted coarser language and started using profanity, and some smoked marijuana and drank alcohol to numb themselves against the unrelenting violence they encountered. Perhaps most significantly, some women changed their views about the war. In the summer of 1969, Van Devanter (1983) wrote in a letter to her parents that it hurt "so much to see the paper full of protestors" (127). As the months passed, however, her attitude toward the war began to change. She found herself "cursing the people" who had brought American troops to Vietnam, and she soon viewed the protesters as allies rather than adversaries: "I wished I could march with them to make the politicians understand the terrible price Vietnam was extracting from our young" (Van Devanter 1983, 184). Not all women lost faith in the war effort, however. Over the course of her year in Vietnam, one woman who served in the Special Services oscillated between being very pro-war and doubting the direction of U.S. policy. By the end of her tour of duty, she had come full circle: "I was convinced we were doing the right thing and I supported it totally" (Walker 1985, 34). Much like the position of men who served, women's position regarding the war defies easy political categorization.

Although there were parallels between men's and women's experiences in Vietnam, there were also marked differences. Despite the extraordinary trials of wartime, women were expected to maintain standards of moral and sexual propriety while overseas that men were not. Van Devanter summarized the Army's oppressive double standard: "If the guys wanted to go carousing to all hours of the night and screw 97 prostitutes in a day, it was to be expected," but "if we [women] wanted to have a relationship, or to occasionally be with a man we cared deeply about, we were not conducting ourselves as 'ladies' should." Condoms were routinely available to GIs, she recalled, but birth control pills were rarely dispensed (Van Devanter 1983, 138). The denial of women's sexual freedom—particularly compared with men's—was overshadowed by a more pervasive problem: sexual harassment. Although the dynamic of sexual harassment did not enter the realm of public awareness in the United States until after the war was over, women who served in Vietnam later related their vulnerability to unwarranted sexual advances. In one particularly vivid account, a civilian airline flight attendant who flew in and out of Vietnam remembered that men routinely masturbated on her flights. More often, the harassment was subtle, as women encountered lonely, emotionally starved men who pushed the line between flirtation and coercion. One nurse described going to a local officers club after working a 12-hour shift and having "one guy after another" pressuring her to dance and complaining when she would decline a request (Walker 1985, 10). Another woman who worked at a communications center explained that as the only woman on her shift, she "got a lot of comments. . . . It was always sort of that fine line between flattering popularity and sexual harassment. And there were times when you really couldn't distinguish between the two." At the same time, she described her male colleagues as "like brothers," whom she tried to nurture as best she could over the months. "The few women that were there," she explained, "had to fill in as mother, sister, sweetheart, confidante . . . we filled every gap we could" (Walker 1985, 23).

After the war was over, the unique challenges women confronted in Vietnam remained largely obscured. Male soldiers who had fought in Vietnam did not receive a hero's welcome upon their return, in part because of the failures of U.S. foreign policy in Southeast Asia and in part because of the growing domestic opposition to the war. The war deeply divided the country, and returnees came home to a nation that, in many respects, wanted to put a contentious and unpopular war behind it as quickly as possible. Thus, for many years returnees were rendered invisible, and this invisibility was even more acute for women. Throughout the late 1970s, there was no public recognition that women had played an active role in the military conflict. This failure of recognition could have dire consequences, as many returning women suffered from the same psychological fallout described by many male returnees: depression, suicidal tendencies, difficulty holding down a steady job, and post-traumatic stress disorder. Despite these shared experiences, women found themselves excluded from various forms of veteran mobilization. Lynda Van Devanter, who had turned against the war while overseas, attended a meeting of Vietnam Veterans Against the War shortly after her return to the United States. Upon learning she was a nurse, a member of the group praised her and her fellow nurses for having saved men's lives, but the same man nonetheless hesitated when Van Devanter asked if she could participate in a protest march being planned by the group. Even though she was a veteran, the man explained, she did not look the part: "You don't look like a vet . . . If we have women marching, Nixon and the network news reporters might think we're swelling the ranks with nonvets" (Van Devanter 1983, 272). The man excluded her not out of a sense of malice but rather because he thought her participation might undermine the legitimacy of an organization that was already embattled.

By the early 1980s, this picture began to change as women veterans shared their experiences with one another, advocated for themselves, and asserted a greater role in the public sphere. Rose Sandecki, a nurse who had served in two evacuation hospitals in Vietnam between October 1968 and October 1969, later became a strong advocate for women veterans. By the 1980s, Sandecki was traveling to veteran centers throughout the country to educate male veterans, counselors, and psychologists about women's experience in Vietnam. Dubbing herself a "social activist for women in the military," she described her calling: "I let them know that women are in the military, that women veterans have needs as well as men. People are starting to pick up the fact that women were in the war and were in combat even though they didn't carry guns" (Walker 1985, 16). No less important than educating the wider public, women returnees made contact with one another and shared their experiences. When one woman veteran told her story—through publishing a memoir, giving a public lecture, or being interviewed on the radio—other women listened and discovered they were not alone in their traumas. An Army nurse explained the experience of meeting two other women nurses at a conference on post-traumatic stress disorder in 1982. The women "practically talked nonstop for three days," she recalled. Talking with other women, in her words, "[brought] out a lot of stuff and [helped] with filling in some of the gaps in memories" (Walker 1985, 121).

Perhaps the most tangible physical symbol of the growing visibility of women veterans is the women's memorial at the Vietnam Veterans Memorial on the mall in Washington, D.C. In 1984, a group of women founded a nonprofit organization called the Vietnam Women's Memorial Project. The mission of the group was to identify military and civilian women who had served in Vietnam, to enlighten the public about them, and to facilitate psychological and sociological research on their experiences. No less important, the organization led the fight to ensure that women received their proper place in the collective memory of the war itself through the creation of a national monument. Located about 300 feet south of artist Maya Lin's

Detail of the Vietnam Women's Memorial in Washington, D.C. Located at the site of the Vietnam Veterans Memorial, the statue commemorates the many women who served in the armed forces during the Vietnam War. (*Defense Visual Information Center*)

memorial wall, the bronze sculpture was dedicated in November 1993. Designed by sculptor Glenna Goodacre, the multifigure piece depicts three women caring for a wounded male soldier. On the day of its unveiling, 25,000 veterans and family members gathered at the site. More than two decades after the end of the Vietnam War, Mary Beth Newkumet, the memorial's spokeswoman stood before the crowd and remembered what women had done: They "bore the intensity and carnage of war. . . . Three hundred fifty thousand wounded soldiers went through their hospitals, airplanes, and ships. Thousands died with a nurse beside them—she was the last person many of them saw. Many thousands more were saved because of quick, effective medical care" (Roberts 1993).

Women War Resisters

As some American women supported the war effort overseas, others on the home front tried to stop the war. Women's position concerning the war proceeded in three stages between 1960 and 1973: early indifference, maternalism, and, after 1970, increased militancy. According to historian Rhodri Jeffreys-Jones, in the early to mid-1960s, women's groups showed few signs of dissent in the face of the war's escalation. Mainstream organizations such as the League of Women Voters and the Young Women's Christian Association (YWCA) adopted what he describes as a position of "quiescence": they urged the Johnson administration to work with the United Nations to end the conflict but went no further. In addition, the 12 women who served in Congress between 1967 and 1969 were relatively quiet when it came to speaking out against the war. Antiwar activist—and the first U.S. congresswoman—Jeannette Rankin condemned women's silence on the home front, arguing that they had prioritized the economic benefits of war over the lives of their own children. "They've been worms," she accused, "They let their sons go off to war because their husbands will lose their jobs in industry if they protest" (Jeffreys-Jones 1999, 148–150).

By the mid-1960s, women did begin speaking out against the war, but they frequently did so in specifically maternalist terms—that is, they drew on traditional ideas about motherhood to condemn war and promote peace. Two organizations were particularly effective at mobilizing maternalist rhetoric to condemn the war during this period: Women Strike for Peace (WSP) and Another Mother for Peace (AMP). WSP was founded in 1961 by a small group of women that included children's book illustrator Dagmar Wilson. An organization that developed a powerful critique of Cold War militarism, the group was not launched in opposition to the Vietnam War, but rather it began by seeking to call public attention to the risks of nuclear testing on the part of both the United States and the Soviet Union in the context of the arms race. Relying heavily on marches and street demonstrations to spread their message, the group was made up of mainly married, white, middle-class mothers of young children who resided in the nation's growing suburbs. Initially, the group focused on the multiple dangers that attended the arms race, but after 1965 it increasingly turned its attention to the war in Vietnam.

Over the next five years, it engaged in a range of tactics to sway public opinion against the war: it protested the use of defoliants such as napalm that injured Vietnamese children, it demonstrated in front of the Pentagon in January 1967, and it launched a letter-writing campaign to the White House that urged President Johnson to seek peace in Vietnam "for the sake of our children" (Jeffreys-Jones 1999, 157). Finally, it turned to legislative politics and sought to create an explicit peace platform within the Democratic Party. In the midterm elections of 1970, members of WSP celebrated as several antiwar candidates—including Rep. Bella Abzug—won seats in Congress. The congressional victory was due at least in part to the increased mobilization of women voters by this time.

The second organization that mobilized maternalist rhetoric to end the war was AMP. Founded in 1967, this group was even more explicit than WSP in its appeals to traditional motherhood. Spearheaded largely by women in the entertainment industry, this nonpartisan group developed the famous slogan "War is not healthy for children and other living things" and urged women to send their congressional representatives Mother's Day cards that demanded an end to the war for the sake of motherhood and peace. In the cases of both WSP and AMP, the reliance on maternalism was complex. On the one hand, it legitimated women's roles in the public sphere solely on the basis of their traditional identities as mothers and protectors of young children. It was only in their capacity as mothers, in other words, that women could act as moral arbiters in the growing domestic debate about the war. On the other hand, as Rhodri Jeffreys-Jones suggests, these groups helped to legitimize the antiwar movement as a whole and move the movement from the margins to the center of American society in the late 1960s.

After 1970, however, women began shedding this earlier maternalism and adopting a more overtly militant position toward the war. There were several reasons for women's increased militancy and prominence in the antiwar movement by the early 1970s. First, as we have already seen, women voters became increasingly mobilized in electoral politics and contributed their efforts to the congressional campaigns of several peace candidates. Indeed, the growing significance of women voters was apparent in the 1972 campaign of George McGovern, who made a point of courting them. Second, certain high-profile women in the entertainment industry, most notably actress Jane Fonda and folk singer Joan Baez, used their celebrity status to publicly condemn the war and speak out against U.S. foreign policy. In 1972, Fonda famously traveled to Vietnam and was photographed sitting at a communist antiaircraft gun—an image that made her a villain in the eyes of military hawks who supported the war effort. Third, women writers such as Frances FitzGerald, Susan Sontag, and Mary McCarthy also traveled to Vietnam and wrote arresting accounts of their experiences there. In 1972, Fitzgerald published *Fire in the Lake*, in which she simultaneously chronicled her travels through the country and condemned what she saw as the misguided nature of U.S. foreign policy in the region. The book was awarded both the Pulitzer Prize and the National Book Award.

Women's growing militancy regarding the war after 1970 also had its origins in the rise of the women's liberation movement. By the early 1970s,

Activist and actor Jane Fonda sits behind a North Vietnamese antiaircraft gun while the gun crew looks on. The film and images of Fonda's July 1972 trip to Hanoi were a propaganda coup for the North Vietnamese and an affront to many Americans. (*AP/Wide World Photos*)

women who had first become politicized through their involvement with the civil rights movement and the New Left turned to the themes of women's oppression and male patriarchy. The struggles for racial freedom and equality, coupled with the New Left attention to the theme of alienation, compelled women to question their own marginalization in the larger society. They also developed a critique of the antiwar movement. Although white, middle-class mothers in the 1960s had spearheaded organizations such as WSP, young women became involved in groups such as Students for a Democratic Society, a student-based organization that had become increasingly involved in anti-war activism. Yet women activists later complained that patterns of male oppression had been reproduced within the movement itself. Male activists gave the speeches, led demonstrations, and dramatically burned their draft cards, while women activists did clerical work, cooked food, and provided male leaders with sexual companionship. By the early 1970s, women antiwar activists were rejecting both the appeals to traditional motherhood that animated WSP and AMP *and* the ways student radicals unwittingly reproduced patterns of women's oppression that pervaded the culture at large. Thus, women activists condemned the war neither as mothers nor as male help-mates but rather as their own moral and political agents, and some feminists even condemned the war explicitly as both a manifestation and symptom of global patriarchy. The growing militancy of women protesters after 1970 was evidence of a developing feminist consciousness.

In many respects, the women who opposed the war on the home front were worlds apart from the women who worked, lived, and served in the combat zone, even though some American women in Vietnam gradually turned against the war. Yet both groups of women had one thing in common: a tendency to be left out of the public's collective memory of the Vietnam era. Women who served in Vietnam were rendered invisible in accounts of returning veterans, and women antiwar activists were also obscured by images of the antiwar movement, which consistently featured male protesters clashing with police and burning their draft cards. In many respects, the emphasis on male protest is not surprising, as it was young men who were being conscripted into war. By rejecting the war, these young men were simultaneously revising prevailing definitions of masculinity by attempting to decouple manhood from military service. Yet women had also helped to bring an end to the war—as mothers, as voters, as public figures, and ultimately as feminists. In the process, they played a crucial role in moving the antiwar movement from the margins to the center of American life.

Women Relatives of U.S. POWs in Southeast Asia

There was a final group of American women who played a crucial role in the public debate about the war in Vietnam: the wives, sisters, and mothers of U.S. POWs in Southeast Asia. These women assumed prominence in the late 1960s, as the plight of POWs and their families became the subject of growing public attention. Before that time, the government had pursued what it called a policy of "quiet diplomacy" concerning the POWs, which was later dubbed the "keep quiet policy" by one disillusioned POW wife (Stockdale and Stockdale 1984, 307). Premised on the assumption that publicizing information about POWs might jeopardize their safety and derail ongoing negotiations with the North Vietnamese, this policy advised the families of captured and missing men to stay out of the public eye and refrain from contacting the press.

Beginning in 1966, a number of forces began to undermine this policy. As the government received reports of prisoner mistreatment, the Johnson administration became more proactive on the POW issue, establishing a Committee on Prisoner Matters within the State Department in April 1966. But the demand for greater attention to the plight of POWs also came from the wives, sisters, and mothers of prisoners themselves. By the late 1960s, many relatives of POWs had grown frustrated, not only by the dearth of information coming out of Vietnam but also by the policy of quiet diplomacy, which they now saw as an excuse for government inaction. Sybil Stockdale, whose husband, naval commander James Stockdale, had been captured in 1965, met on numerous occasions with officials in the Department of the Navy and the State Department and reached the disheartening conclusion that "official silence and secrecy can cover up incompetence and just plain inertia" ("At Least" 1970). In October 1968, she defied the government's policy and went public with her husband's story in the *San Diego Union Tribune*.

Stockdale was not acting alone; she was part of an informal network of POW wives, parents, and siblings who took matters into their own hands and engaged in grassroots organizing, many for the first time in their lives. They launched letter-writing campaigns to members of Congress and the White House, appealed to the press, attempted to establish direct contact with Hanoi in the hope of gathering information, and sent POW wives to Washington, D.C., and to the Paris peace talks to demand North Vietnamese compliance with the terms of the Geneva Convention. Swayed in part by the growing assertiveness of these relatives, Defense Secretary Melvin Laird ended the policy of quiet diplomacy in May 1969, publicly charging Hanoi with prisoner mistreatment and demanding that if the Vietnamese did not release the prisoners, they at least had a humanitarian obligation to disclose information about their condition. The policy of quiet diplomacy was subsequently replaced with a coordinated "go public" campaign—spearheaded by both government officials and POW relatives—that aimed to generate sympathy for POWs and their families.

Over the next four years, this campaign featured stories of the loyal wives, grief-stricken parents, and uncomprehending children of American POWs. Editorials blamed the North Vietnamese for transforming the home front into a "fatherless world," one of sons and daughters who, according to one editorial in the *Armed Forces Journal*, had "a right to know if their fathers [were] dead or alive" ("A National Disgrace" 1969). In December 1970, *Life* and *Look* magazines featured photo essays documenting POW children growing up without their fathers, contrasting early family photographs of cheerful, intact families with more recent, somber photographs in which the father was absent. Meanwhile, the POW wife was left with the nearly impossible task of explaining her husband's disappearance to a child with no understanding of war. As Frank Sieverts, the State Department's top official on POW and missing in action (MIA) matters, reported during the same period, "The telephone rings all the time. In the holiday season, it is especially bad. Wives call up asking me what to say to their children, how to explain that they don't know where their husbands are, whether they are dead or alive, when all the other kids have their fathers" ("Living with Uncertainty," 20). Through its policy of secrecy, according to these accounts, Hanoi had placed innocent women and children in a cruel state of suspension, generating enormous uncertainty within the family. "It's a very lonely existence," revealed one POW wife whose husband had been shot down in 1967. "You're married but you're not married. You're not single. You're not divorced or widowed. Where does that put you in society? That puts you in your own world" ("Living with Uncertainty," 19).

The wives, sisters, and mothers of POWs who were at the center of the publicity campaign shared certain features with both the women who served in Vietnam and those who fought to end the war at home. Like some of the women who chose to go to Vietnam, many of them had spent their entire lives in military communities, and they strongly supported the war in Southeast Asia. But, like the women who formed WSP and AMP, they mobilized a maternalist rhetoric, one that appealed to essentialist ideals of motherhood to make political demands on the state. Although the maternalism of WSP and AMP was aligned with pacifism, however, these women were hawks who emphasized their roles as wives and mothers to condemn

Delia Alvarez

On August 5, 1964, 26-year-old naval lieutenant Everett Alvarez Jr. was shot down over the Gulf of Tonkin, becoming the first U.S. fighter pilot taken prisoner in North Vietnam. His family initially expressed their faith in the U.S. government and their support of the war effort. "We all used to have great respect for the flag and the uniform," Delia Alvarez recalled about her family in a 1973 interview. "I believed in the domino theory, fighting communism and killing the enemy" (Alvarez 1973). Delia had "cursed her gender for disqualifying her from a combat role" when she learned of her brother's capture (Alvarez and Pitch 1989, 155). Yet by the time Everett Alvarez returned to the United States in 1973, his family had publicly denounced the Nixon administration, and his sister Delia had emerged as an outspoken critic of the war.

Delia Alvarez's evolution from cold warrior to dissenter was shaped by local, national, and international forces. Like other relatives of POWs, Delia was frustrated by Defense Department officials who provided little information about captured and missing men. The more she read about Vietnam's history, the more convinced she became that the United States was on an errant mission. Delia's growing critique of the war also emerged from what she witnessed at home. Working for the Santa Clara County welfare department, she observed young Mexican American men who should have been enrolled in college being sent to Vietnam in disproportionate numbers. Her growing awareness of Chicano racial politics went hand-in-hand with her disillusionment with the war effort. As she explained in a 1973 interview, "My involvement with the Chicano movement has done more than anything to open my eyes to things as they really are" (Alvarez 1973, 36–37).

Spurred on by the Chicano movement, Delia Alvarez gradually took action against the Vietnam War. In May 1971, she helped form POW-MIA Families for Immediate Release, which advocated complete U.S. withdrawal. As Alvarez explained, "The only way the prisoners are going home is by the cessation of hostilities" ("Sister" 1971, 19). By July 1971, approximately 300 relatives had joined the group and accused the Nixon administration of using the prisoners to justify prolonging the war. Delia Alvarez emerged as one of a handful of POW relatives who openly condemned the war. Between May 1971 and her brother's repatriation in February 1973, she spoke at protest rallies, appeared with high-profile antiwar activists such as Jane Fonda, participated in press conferences, and met in Paris with a peace delegation from Indochina. These actions entailed personal risk and violent confrontation. Other POW relatives ridiculed her at public appearances, and she received hate mail and anonymous phone calls that accused her of being a communist traitor (Alvarez and Pitch 1989, 273). Once a staunch supporter of the war, she now blamed her brother's lengthy captivity on the failure of political leadership within the United States. Ten months before her brother's repatriation, she reflected on the prerequisite for his safe return: "Everett will return when Vietnamese children will be able to look at the sky and clouds and not fear that a bomb will drop that will burn and tear their bodies. Everett will return because the Vietnamese will live! Because the Vietnamese will win! (Ruiz 1972, 30–32)." At a time when the Nixon administration was urging the American public to direct its sympathies to the children of American POWs, Delia Alvarez insisted that Vietnamese children deserved not only sympathy but justice.

the North Vietnamese and demand more American military intervention, not less. Above all, the POW wife and mother hoped for the POW's safe return while simultaneously wanting him to wage and win the war.

Just as some women who served in Vietnam gradually turned against the war, so, too, did some POW wives, sisters, and mothers. In May 1971, several relatives formed a group called POW-MIA Families for Immediate Release, which adopted an overtly antiwar position by demanding the immediate withdrawal of U.S. troops. By July of that year, approximately 300 POW relatives had joined the group, claiming that the Nixon administration was using the prisoners as a justification for prolonging the war and insisting that the president negotiate the prisoners' release without regard to the political fate of South Vietnam. As one member of the group exclaimed, "They cannot use my husband to spread the blood of 45 young men a week on Viet Nam." These relatives insisted that their missing men had by this point become the political hostages of both Hanoi and the Nixon administration. Although some of them aligned themselves with the antiwar movement primarily for pragmatic reasons—believing that ending the war would be the quickest way to get the prisoners home—others believed American military involvement in Vietnam was morally wrong, above and beyond the POW issue.

The wives, mothers, and sisters of American POWs were thus another group who played a pivotal role during the Vietnam War era. Although the women who went to Vietnam helped to execute the war, and women war protesters on the home front sought to end it, the women relatives of POWs did something else: they helped shape an official narrative of the war that indicted the North Vietnamese for humanitarian crimes and constructed the POWs—and by extension their families—as innocent victims rather than aggressors in the wider war. Yet over time, as opposition to the war gained momentum, some women relatives of POWs questioned this official narrative and eventually challenged it from within. The shifting story of the wives, mothers, and sisters of POWs thus reminds us that women are not only the subjects of the stories Americans tell about the Vietnam War but also that women both construct and contest those same stories.

This essay has traced women's relationship to the Vietnam War in three different capacities: as both civilians and military members who chose to live and work in Vietnam for the duration of the war; as protesters who fought to end the war on the home front; and finally, as the wives, sisters, and mothers of POWs who waged a campaign to call public attention to the plight of captured men and their families. These three positions reveal the difficulties inherent in making blanket generalizations about the role women played in the conflict: they waged the war and fought against it; they protested against the government in some instances and collaborated with it in others. No less significant, women's positions changed over time: some women executors of the war evolved into protesters; protesters who condemned the war as mothers later did so as autonomous moral agents; other women who had helped craft official stories about the war later became critics of those same stories. Not coincidentally, many of these transformations took place in an era of women's liberation, when women increasingly claimed more power and autonomy in the public sphere. Taken together, these stories leave little doubt that women played a constitutive role, not only in the war's execution and opposition but also in shaping the collective memories of the military conflict that we have carried into the present.

References and Further Reading

Alvarez, Delia. "Interview with Delia Alvarez, POW Sister." *La Raza: News and Political Thought of the Chicano Struggle,* February 1973.

Alvarez, Everett, Jr., and Anthony Pitch. *Chained Eagle.* New York: Donald I. Fine, 1989.

"At Least I Know Jim's Alive." *Good Housekeeping,* February 1970: 78–79, 215–222.

"During the Vietnam Era," Vietnam Women's Memorial Foundation, http://www.vietnamwomensmemorial.org/vwmf.php (accessed December 16, 2008).

Jeffreys-Jones, Rhodri. *Peace Now! American Society and the Ending of the Vietnam War.* New Haven, CT: Yale University Press, 1999.

"Living with Uncertainty: The Families Who Wait Back Home." *Time,* December 7, 1970: 20.

Marshall, Kathryn. *In the Combat Zone: An Oral History of American Women in Vietnam, 1966–1975.* Boston: Little, Brown, 1987.

"A National Disgrace." *Armed Forces Journal,* September 27, 1969.

Roberts, Roxanne. "New Vietnam Memorial Readied on Mall—Honoring the Women," *Washington Post,* November 2, 1993, http://www.vietnamwomensmemorial.org/dedicat.php (accessed December 16, 2008).

Ruiz, Raul. "The POW: News and Political Thought of the Chicano Struggle," *La Raza,* April 1972: 30–32.

"Sister of Longest-Held POW Starts Protest." *Regeneración* 1 (10 (1971)).

Stockdale, Jim, and Sybil Stockdale. *In Love and War: The Story of a Family's Ordeal and Sacrifice During the Vietnam War.* New York: Harper & Row, 1984.

Van Devanter, Lynda. *Home Before Morning: The Story of an American Nurse in Vietnam.* New York: Warner Books, 1983.

Walker, Keith. *A Piece of My Heart: The Stories of 26 American Women Who Served in Vietnam.* Novato, CA: Presidio Press, 1985.

Wartime Journalists | 8

Clarence R. Wyatt

The role of the news media remains one of the most controversial aspects of American involvement in Vietnam. Understanding what the press did—and did not do—and why is important to achieving a clearer sense of how and why American society approached the conflict in Vietnam, and the parallel conflict at home, as it did.

This issue of the press and the Vietnam War had lasting implications. The issue of government information policy, especially regarding national security, is still very much with us. From the 1983 Grenada operation through the Persian Gulf War to the conflict in Iraq and the global War on Terror, information policy and press access have been a major part of government and military planning. The degree to which the public has confidence in the information that it receives, whether from the government, the military, or news organizations, greatly affects the degree to which it will support any military conflict.

In addition, ideas about the role of the press are an important part of the mythology that has developed around the Vietnam War. As it has for all of the United States' previous major military engagements, American society has developed a kind of public "consensus of memory" that designates certain topics and conclusions as safe, while dismissing or ignoring others altogether. That consensus has evolved over time, but at each step it has limited the questions that we can ask of that experience and the answers that might help us view current and future conflicts more clearly.

Since the end of the Vietnam War, two images of the press have appeared in this public memory. The first appeared only briefly, toward the end of the war and immediately afterward. In that conception, the press was something of a deliverer, dispelling government lies and enabling the American people to bring an ill-advised, unjust war to an end. That image was soon replaced by that of betrayer. In this manifestation, individual journalists and entire news organizations deliberately distorted news of the war to suit their own political biases. In this view, the press downplayed or ignored progress in the conflict and emphasized—or invented—negative reports. Over time, this barrage of bad news eventually sapped the public's will to bring the "noble cause," as President Ronald Reagan called it, to a successful end. Thus, the news industry became a villain that misled the American public, dishonored the sacrifice of American soldiers, and abandoned the people of South Vietnam to communist oppression.

Neither image, however, is based on a real understanding of two larger issues. First, they are not based on a thorough sense of the institution of U.S. journalism. During the 20th century, the news media in America underwent significant changes. The institutional characteristics that developed derived from economic and cultural issues rather than the supposed political motivations incorporated in the public images of the press. Second, during the Cold War a "national security mentality" developed. The potential Armageddon represented by a Soviet Union in possession of nuclear weapons encouraged and justified a culture of official secrecy. The ability and willingness of the federal government, especially the executive branch, to control and manipulate information—often for legitimate security reasons, but frequently for more self-interested political reasons—grew dramatically. An exploration of the relationship between the press and government and the role that relationship played in American involvement in Vietnam should include these two elements.

Journalism in the United States possessed several key characteristics during the Cold War and the war in Vietnam. The first is *ethnocentrism*—the belief in the superiority of one's own culture—what Herbert Gans described as the tendency of news organizations to focus on stories featuring the members of their "home" societies as one of the "enduring values of the news" (Gans 1979, 42–43). For American editors and news directors, this meant a story was really news only if Americans were somehow involved. Stories that did not directly affect or involve Americans were shunted to the background, if they were covered at all. American news organizations were not alone in exercising such judgments. A British editor once declared that it would take the deaths of 1,000 Africans or 50 Frenchmen to equal the newsworthiness of the death of one Englishman; "1,000 wogs equals 50 frogs equals one Englishman" in his more colorful phrasing (Wyatt 2007, 267).

This ethnocentrism affected how news organizations allocated resources. Believing that coverage of domestic issues and domestics stories was what readers, listeners, and viewers wanted, and that this was where the profits were, editors and news directors kept the bulk of their resources at home. This meant devoting relatively little attention to foreign coverage, especially of Asia, in the late 1950s as the United States became involved in Vietnam. Most of the meager foreign assets were devoted to Europe. For example, *Time* had 14 overseas bureaus, but only two—Hong Kong and Tokyo, with a total of three reporters between them—were in Asia. That same year, *Newsweek* had two reporters in Tokyo and *U.S. News* covered all of East Asia with one regional editor. The *New York Times* had 28 foreign offices, but only three in Asia.

The danger of this practice was not lost on news and media professionals, even at the time. A 1960 study of public relations work in the United States on behalf of foreign governments concluded that "the economics of U.S. news coverage" resulted in "hordes of reporters" following the American president's every move while "the ranks of American journalists covering the rest of the world are remarkably thin . . . The facts we need to know are often concealed from us or get to us too late. All of a sudden there may be a blow-up in a country with which we have been deeply involved" (Cater and Pincus 1960, 20). Otto Friedrich, working for United Press during the French war in Vietnam, said: "The basic fact is that it would have cost a lot of money to support one of those red-blooded American reporters in Vietnam. Figure at least $100 a week in salary and at least $50 a week in expenses, and is it worth it? It might be, if an American newspaper really wanted to know what was going on in Indo-China. . . . But that is not what American editors wanted. They wanted stories of good guys fighting Reds, and that is what they got" (Friedrich 1959, 474–480).

During this post–World War II period, growing national literacy, mobility, and prosperity led to two other important changes in the economics of American journalism. First, news became a big and profitable business. Newspapers evolved from being the creatures of single owner/publishers to being publicly owned, corporate entities. This transformation to big business was particularly true in television. Also, journalism changed from being a barely respectable craft to being a profession. It developed a canon of standards and a system of professional education. Reporters were increasingly college and graduate-school trained, the professional and social peers of the political leaders whom they covered.

The Rise of the National Security Mentality

From the beginning of the Republic, American officials had attempted to conduct certain business in private. Because the federal government was so limited for most of the nation's history, however, there was little concern over the maintenance of government secrets. This began to change in the 1930s and 1940s as the power of the federal government increased, especially with the advent of the atomic age and the Cold War. With the fear of subversion from within and the profound threat from without, with massive death and destruction just hours or minutes away, presidents felt the need to control information lest any slip signal weakness or overaggressiveness. This led the press and public to defer to the presidency, especially on matters of national security. Presidents Harry Truman and Dwight Eisenhower greatly expanded the ability to classify information and hold it from public, even congressional, view. In late 1945, the McMahon Act severely restricted access to information about nuclear technology. In September 1951, President Truman issued Executive Order 10-290, giving hundreds of executive branch employees authority to classify information. Executive Order 10-501, issued in November 1953 by President Eisenhower, created 30 new levels of classification and formed the basis of federal information policy for the next 15 years.

These developments raised concerns among congressional leaders, the press, and public figures. *U.S. News* editor David Lawrence called Truman's order "our own iron curtain" and predicted that "the only information the public may get officially will be that which the President and his political advisors deem good for the Administration's political fortunes" (Lawrence 1951, 6). Responding to Eisenhower's order, Sigma Delta Chi, the press fraternity, declared: "The imposition of secrecy on the broad and undefined ground of 'Executive Privilege' has reached a new peak . . . posing the most serious threat to the theory of open government so far in U.S. history" ("Journalism Group" 1959, 12).

Although this increased control did serve legitimate security concerns, it also provided political cover for administrations. A prominent example is the May 1960 U-2 incident, in which American pilot Francis Gary Powers was shot down and captured while flying photo reconnaissance missions over the Soviet Union. Such flights had gone on for years; the Soviets knew about them, as did key journalists and congressional leaders. Still, Eisenhower hoped to avoid embarrassment. Assuming the pilot was dead and the plane destroyed, the White House issued a cover story that described the mission as NASA (National Aeronautics and Space Administration) weather research. However, when Soviet premier Nikita Khrushchev produced pictures from the plane's cameras and a live pilot before the Supreme Soviet, it became clear that only the American public had been deceived.

President John F. Kennedy raised information management to a high art. He understood how journalism had changed and how journalists worked much better than did his immediate predecessors. After all, he had worked as a reporter himself; he listed his occupation on his National Press Club bio as "a former newspaperman now in politics" (Wyatt 1993, 27). Kennedy understood reporters' need for access and a steady supply of information.

Kennedy cultivated relationships with key news organizations and journalists. During the 1960 presidential campaign, he met several times with Henry Luce, hoping to at least neutralize the staunchly Republican publisher of *Life* and *Time*. His attentions had at least some effect—Luce told an aide that Kennedy "seduces me. . . . When I'm with him I feel like a whore" (Halberstam 1979, 352–355). Ben Bradlee of *Newsweek* and the *Washington Post* was JFK's neighbor and drinking buddy. Charles Bartlett, the Washington correspondent for the *Chattanooga Times*, was a long-time Kennedy intimate, having introduced him to Jacqueline Bouvier. One White House reporter, in describing Bartlett's close relationship to Kennedy, called Bartlett "a tomb of secrets" (O'Brien 2005, 827).

Kennedy also understood the rising influence of television and the ability it gave him to bypass the press. On January 25, 1961, Kennedy held the first presidential press conference to be broadcast live on television, and the event represented a major change. Kennedy moved the event from the Indian Treaty Room, where reporters could see every grimace and twitch in the presidential face, to the State Department auditorium, which created a physical distance between the president and the press and was much better suited to the needs of television. Reporters were told not to identify themselves or their employers when asking questions, supposedly to save time and allow more participants. Of course the practice also kept the focus on the star of the show, Kennedy himself. Many journalists hailed the live press conference as a move to greater openness, but it actually gave a president, especially a natural performer such as JFK, even greater ability to shape the news and public perception.

If this program of control through the appearance of spontaneity and candor did not work, Kennedy also showed a willingness to clamp down. He once denied Hugh Sidey, *Time*'s White House correspondent and Washington's most influential reporter, access to the White House for weeks in retaliation for an irksome story. He also used federal investigators to find sources of unauthorized leaks.

Despite Kennedy's personal relationships with key journalists and his understanding of the journalistic process, his information practices eventually created resentment. His attempts to suppress the *New York Times* story on the Bay of Pigs invasion and the Cuban Missile Crisis brought critical responses. New policies regulating contacts between executive branch officials and reporters also drew fire, even from Kennedy's friends. In a private letter to the president dated November 24, 1962, columnist Joe Alsop, whose home had been the Kennedys' last stop on inauguration night, decried the regulations, saying that openness was "the chief safeguard of the public interest" (Wyatt 1993, 46). Less friendly critics also weighed in. A Republican Party publication quoted a joke involving Defense Department spokesman Arthur Sylvester and presidential press secretary Pierre Salinger that was making its way around Washington: "When Sylvester says the government is lying, he's telling the truth. When Salinger says the government is telling the truth, he's lying" (Meyer 1963, 513).

The American Press Comes to Vietnam

President Kennedy brought these approaches to information management to his handling of the Vietnam conflict. The Vietcong had become much more aggressive in 1959 and 1960, putting greater pressure on the increasingly fragile regime of South Vietnamese president Ngo Dinh Diem. Two major priorities shaped Kennedy's policies toward Vietnam: don't lose South Vietnam, but don't appear to be taking over the effort. After the October 1961 fact-finding mission by military adviser Maxwell Taylor and special assistant Walt Rostow, Kennedy responded to the higher level of insurgent activity by increasing military and financial aid to Diem, as well as increasing the number of American advisers working directly with South Vietnamese combat units.

The increased combat activity sparked greater interest among the American public. Combat reporting—simple, direct, and dramatic—appealed to editors and readers. Vietnam also emerged as a more prominent part of the continuing Cold War drama between Kennedy and Khrushchev. This heightening U.S. involvement made Vietnam more of an "American" story, and the increased press commitment in South Vietnam paralleled that of the Kennedy administration. In 1961 and early 1962, major news organizations established full-time offices in the South Vietnamese capital of Saigon.

CBS News anchor Walter Cronkite (left) interviews President John F. Kennedy about U.S. involvement in Vietnam at the president's summer home in Hyannis Port, Massachusetts, on September 2, 1963. (*Library of Congress*)

Among the early group were Homer Bigart for the *New York Times,* Peter Arnett and Malcolm Browne for the Associated Press, Neil Sheehan for United Press International, Nick Turner for Reuters, François Sully for *Newsweek,* and Charles Mohr and Mert Perry for *Time.*

However, Kennedy also did not want Vietnam to be seen as an American war. To create the appearance of distance, in November 1961 his administration ordered U.S. officials to provide the press with no information regarding military or political activity and to refer all inquiries to South Vietnamese officials—who were usually reluctant to speak with reporters. Admiral Harry Felt, commander in chief of U.S. forces in the Pacific, tightened access even more in early 1962 when he banned reporters from helicopter combat missions piloted by Americans. This made it more difficult for reporters to assess the effectiveness of this new tool and the effectiveness of the South Vietnamese troops it took into battle.

On February 20, 1962, a cable from Dean Rusk to Frederick Nolting codified the State Department policy of stonewalling, issuing a cable that established an information policy for U.S. government and military personnel in South Vietnam. The policy urged Americans not to "grant interviews or take other actions implying all-out U.S. involvement," and declared that stories on civilian casualties "are clearly inimical to national interests." Additional points emphasized the need to support Diem, claiming "articles that tear down Diem only make our task more difficult."

The final guidelines held the key to the whole memorandum and provided the muscle by which the U.S. government could withhold or manipulate information. Item six said:

"Operations may be referred to in general terms, but specific numbers—particularly numbers of Americans involved—and details of material introduced are not to be provided. On tactical security matters, analyses [of] strengths and weaknesses and other operational details which might aid the enemy should be avoided." The last point said: "Correspondents should not be taken on missions whose nature is such that undesirable dispatches would be highly probable" (Wyatt 1993, 92).

These two statements essentially denied the American people information on the greater role that their fathers, sons, and brothers were playing in the conflict, while also preventing them from hearing of any but the most favorable stage-managed operations.

In the meantime, President Ngo Dinh Diem also cracked down on reporters. Government officials refused to speak with them, military commanders denied them access to their areas of operations, and they were followed and harassed by Diem's secret police. The regime even expelled reporters such as *Newsweek*'s François Sully on trumped-up charges of being a Vietcong spy, an opium smuggler, and a patron of sex orgies.

At this point most of the mythology surrounding the press's role in Vietnam began to take shape. Reporters such as Bigart, Sheehan, and Browne represented a significant commitment of human and financial resources by their employers, who expected steady coverage of the conflict in return. Needing to satisfy this demand, but being shut off from American and South Vietnamese official information, reporters turned to the only available sources—American advisers in the field.

It was not surprising that a partnership developed between the Saigon press corps and the young captains, majors, and lieutenant colonels who made up the advisory force. They were peers in age, mainly in their twenties and early thirties. Advisers and reporters also shared a background of advanced professional training in their respective fields; they were all rising stars. Shaped by the legacy of World War II, they held similar views regarding the need to oppose aggression early and firmly, as well as the U.S. responsibility to lead the way. They also shared similar ideas on American power and, by extension, their own capabilities, sharing a sense of "candoism." The reporters and advisers were committed to drawing the line against communism.

Each group satisfied professional needs of the other. The advisers, frustrated with the ineffectiveness of U.S. policy, especially the commitment to the increasingly isolated Diem regime, needed an outlet to publicly air their concerns. Reporters needed reliable sources to support the coverage their employers demanded. The journalists did not want South Vietnam to fall to the communists, nor did they have an innate desire to criticize U.S. policy. They were motivated not by political or ideological bias but rather by the need to satisfy the imperatives of the American news industry.

The best-known example of this relationship involved Lt. Col. John Paul Vann, Neil Sheehan, and David Halberstam. Vann, the chief adviser to the commander of the South Vietnamese army's Seventh Division, was a star among the American advisers, and the press gravitated toward him and the Seventh Division's success against the Vietcong. That success quickly unraveled, however, as Huynh Van Cao, commanding general of the Seventh, grew cautious, fearing that aggressive action and the resulting casualties might jeopardize his political ambitions. Vann voiced his frustrations, particularly to Sheehan of United Press International and Halberstam of the *New York Times,* who had won Vann's confidence by sharing the hardships of life in the field.

Reflecting the perspectives of these sources, coverage of the conflict grew more critical of the Diem regime and the U.S. commitment to it. The U.S. and South Vietnamese governments responded by continuing to stonewall the Saigon press corps. Kennedy sought to divide the press and discredit the reporters working in Vietnam. He cultivated editors and prominent columnists, encouraging them to reassign bothersome reporters or to dismiss them as inexperienced and their coverage as overly dramatic. For example, Joe Alsop received access to helicopter missions during a visit to Vietnam in the spring of 1962, an opportunity denied resident reporters. On a similar VIP tour in July 1963, *New York Herald-Tribune* columnist Marguerite Higgins enjoyed access to top American and South Vietnamese officials, including a rare interview with Diem himself. On the basis of these sources, Higgins concluded that the effort in South Vietnam was going quite well and that reporting to the contrary by the resident press corps was due to its collective inexperience and gullibility.

Otto Fuerbringer, the managing editor of *Time,* went so far as to disavow his reporters' coverage in the very pages of the magazine. Charles Mohr and Merton Perry had been working in Vietnam for months. Their reporting, which had grown increasingly critical, was repeatedly rewritten to reflect a more positive tone. In the fall of 1963, Fuerbringer asked the two to file a status report on the conflict. Seizing the opportunity, Mohr and Perry filed a major assessment of the state of the South Vietnamese government and the effectiveness of the American effort. Holding no punches, the piece began: "The war in Vietnam is being lost." An enraged Fuerbringer rejected the dispatch, and then dictated a story for *Time*'s Press section. "The newsmen themselves have become a part of South Vietnam's confusion," he wrote. "They have covered a complex situation from only one angle, as if their own conclusions offered all the necessary illumination." In the resident press's eyes, Fuerbringer said, Diem was automatically "stubborn and stupid," while his critics were treated with "sympathy." The reporters also downplayed South Vietnamese successes as contrary to "the argument that defeat is inevitable as long as Diem is in power" (Wyatt 1993, 121–122). Not surprisingly, Mohr and Perry resigned.

Diem took a more direct approach. His brother and chief adviser Ngo Dinh Nhu unleashed his secret police on reporters. Halberstam and Sheehan discovered that their names were on an assassination list kept by Nhu. On July 7, police attacked reporters, including Peter Arnett of the Associated Press, who were covering an anti-Diem demonstration. Four policemen knocked Arnett to the ground and kicked him viciously until Halberstam, yelling "Get back, get back you sons of bitches, or I'll beat the shit out of you," rescued him (Sheehan 1988, 352–353, 356–357).

Peter Arnett

It was one of those summer days in Saigon that, back in 1962, when he was a 26-year-old Associated Press correspondent fresh in Vietnam, could almost have made Peter Arnett forget there was a war going on.

The war seemed far away. The city's population of 600,000 had yet to feel the influence of the growing but still small American presence. Sitting on a park bench, Arnett could watch the Vietnamese girls, demure yet alluring in their close-fitting *ao dais,* go by. He could smell the jasmine blossoms as their scents competed with the joss sticks burning in family altars and the charcoal fires of the outside food stalls.

But it wasn't 1962. It was summer 1970, and even in Saigon it was harder and harder for Arnett to forget about the war. Saigon had become a refugee camp, its population swollen to nearly 2 million by peasants who had fled the fighting. Vietnamese bar girls in halter tops and miniskirts had replaced the schoolgirls in traditional dress. The odor of exhaust fumes and garbage overwhelmed the fragrance of the trees. And, after eight and a half years in Vietnam, Arnett had decided that, at 35, he was too old to cover the war any more.

As they sat together in a Saigon park, Arnett's old friend Morley Safer asked him if he had become hardened to the killing. After all, Arnett had probably seen more death than any American soldier. "No," Arnett said, "I probably was a reverse case. . . . I've seen as many as 120 Americans on a battlefield in the Nha Trang Valley, and I've seen 200 at a time North Vietnamese just chopped to pieces by artillery, and I've always tried to look past that." But by the time he covered the spring 1970 invasion of Cambodia, he had had his fill. He told Safer about what he found in the Cambodian town of Snoul. "The North Vietnamese had dug in," he said. "We went in on the tanks next morning and the enemy had fled. Left in the marketplace were five bodies, a woman, looked like three kids, and a man, [who] had sort of been all fused together by napalm." It was at that moment, Arnett said, that he decided, "I just don't want to see any more bodies" (Wyatt 1993, 190).

From January to September 1963, the conflict between American reporters and American officials in Vietnam became acute. At the beginning of the year, an operation near Ap Bac in the Mekong Delta had been designed as a showpiece of South Vietnamese prowess. When it failed owing to the incompetence of the South Vietnamese commander, American officials tried to claim it as a success and dismiss media coverage of the battle. Admiral Felt, visiting Vietnam at the time of the operation, characterized Neil Sheehan's coverage as an example of "bad news . . . filed immediately by young reporters without checking the facts." On seeing Sheehan two days later, Felt snapped "So you're Sheehan. You ought to talk to some of the people who've got the facts." "You're right," Sheehan shot back, "and that's why I went down there every day" (Sheehan 1988, 314).

Over the following weeks, tensions increased. Upon hearing that John Mecklin, the U.S. Information Agency chief in Saigon, had returned stateside for surgery, one reporter said, "I hope the son of a bitch dies" (Moyar 2006, 453, n. 52). Reacting to news that a reporter had narrowly avoided being shot, one embassy staffer snapped his fingers and said, "Darn." The press corps created a little jingle, sung to the tune of "Twinkle, Twinkle, Little

Star"—"We are winning/This I know/General Harkins told me so/If you doubt it/Who are you/McNamara says so, too" (Wyatt 1993, 104).

The crisis for the Diem regime and within the American community came to a head in the summer and fall of 1963. In May, a parade in Hue celebrating the anniversary of Archbishop Ngo Dinh Thuc's appointment to the bishopric included the display of Vatican flags. Ngo Dinh Diem, Thuc's brother, attended the parade and reminded his brother of the law against flying any flag but that of South Vietnam. Diem even issued a statement saying that the Vatican flags had flown in error. A few days later, when denied the right to display their flags during the celebration of the Buddha's birthday, Buddhist priests launched nationwide protests. Within days, what became known as the "Buddhist crisis" attracted opponents of the Diem regime from across South Vietnamese society. The Kennedy administration was shaken by the depth of the anti-Diem actions, illustrated most vividly by photographs of a Buddhist monk burning himself to death at a Saigon intersection on June 11.

When Diem and his brother Nhu struck back by beating and arresting hundreds of Buddhist monks on August 21, Kennedy realized that the Diem regime was self-destructing. Kennedy replaced discredited Ambassador Frederick Nolting with Henry Cabot Lodge. Lodge privately indicated to a group of Vietnamese generals that the United States would recognize a new government in South Vietnam, giving the green light to a coup. More publicly, Lodge signaled a new relationship with the Saigon press corps. Immediately upon arriving in Saigon, Lodge began to meet with reporters, and exchanged blunt questions and candid answers. Lodge agreed with the reporters' assessment of Diem and, as a savvy politician, knew the value of a sympathetic press. The embassy took a much tougher stand in response to attacks on reporters by the police, and Lodge even allowed reporters to use the embassy's communications equipment to file stories when Diem shut off the government facilities.

Various plans by South Vietnamese officers finally came to fruition on November 1, when Diem's government was overthrown. Despite U.S. calls for safe passage for Diem and his family, Diem and his brother Nhu were murdered. Exactly three weeks later, an assassin would kill President Kennedy.

The Rise of Maximum Candor

In its last days, the Kennedy administration realized that its policy of denying reporters access to official information only drove them to other, less controllable sources. A shift in approach was evident by the time of President Kennedy's death. As the United States became more deeply and directly involved in the war in Vietnam under President Lyndon Johnson, that new policy, known as "maximum candor," formed the basis of information policy until U.S troops began their gradual withdrawal from Vietnam in 1969.

Although several officials in the government and military argued for a change in press policy, Assistant Secretary of State for Public Affairs James

Greenfield was the most forceful and articulate advocate. In a memo dated December 8, 1964, he told his counterparts at the Defense Department and the White House that "the press will write whether we brief or not. You can't prevent stories by not providing information. . . . Whenever we have taken pains to keep the press abreast of what is happening it has worked to our advantage" (Wyatt 1993, 158).

Beginning in the summer of 1964, the new policy sought to remove the chief irritants between the resident press and American officials in Vietnam. Barry Zorthian, a senior U.S. Information Agency official, was named coordinator of information for the entire U.S. effort in Vietnam, and significantly increased the staffs of the civilian and military information operations. The Military Assistance Command, Vietnam (MACV) expanded its briefings, distributed a much greater volume of information, and made access to top officials easier. Reporters received more help in getting out to the field, and the press received improved facilities in Saigon and other locations.

Over the following months, a coordinated information effort, operating as the Joint U.S. Public Affairs Office (JUSPAO) evolved. Working under Barry Zorthian was a small army of information officers, all the way down to provincial and battalion levels. This apparatus quickly became extremely effective at furnishing the American press what it needed most—the information and logistical support necessary to report the hard news of American activity in Vietnam.

To work in Vietnam, a journalist had to receive accreditation from JUSPAO and the South Vietnamese government. This required only a valid passport and visa, a letter of employment, and a current immunization card. Accreditation gave journalists access to the full range of facilities provided by the U.S. effort in South Vietnam—commissary and post exchange stores, officers' clubs, military transportation, and press facilities. At the height of U.S. combat involvement, more than 600 people held official press accreditation.

In addition to such assistance, the press in Vietnam worked under extremely light official restrictions. Formal military censorship was considered briefly in the spring of 1965 but was rejected as legally unworkable and politically problematic. Instead, reporters in Vietnam agreed to abide by a set of ground rules detailing the types of information that could and could not be released. Although the rules changed slightly from time to time, restricted information generally fell into the following categories: (1) future plans, operations, or strikes; (2) information on or confirmation of rules of engagement; (3) amounts of ordnance and fuel on hand in combat units; (4) exact number and types or identification of casualties suffered by friendly units; (5) during an operation, unit designations and troop movements, tactical deployments, name of operation, and size of friendly force involved, until officially released by MACV; (6) intelligence unit activities; and (7) a variety of information about air operations against North Vietnam.

As the number of American troops and the level of combat action grew, the press corps faced an increasingly daunting task. The war spread across the difficult terrain of South Vietnam and consisted mainly of small unit actions that lasted a few minutes or hours. Even with access to military transportation, it was hard for reporters to reach many of these engagements while in progress. Although the number of accredited news personnel eventually grew to more than 600, that figure does not accurately reflect the press corps' news-gathering capability. Everyone who worked for a news agency, from the bureau chief to the driver, had to be accredited. Even at the height of the press presence in Vietnam, probably no more than 30 or 40 people were actually involved in gathering and producing news for organizations with national audiences. Finally, American editors and producers made covering the day-to-day action of Americans in combat their first priority. All of these factors made it impossible for news organizations to gather and verify independently all information about combat action. As a result, they depended on the flood of information provided by the official U.S. information machine.

All of this points to the central factor—and the central problem—of the relationship between the American press and the American government and military over Vietnam information. Taking advantage of the characteristics of the American news industry, the maximum candor approach largely achieved its goals. It made the press dependent on the government for information concerning the war and, consequently, allowed the government to shape the news. As one of James Greenfield's aides wrote to him on April 30, 1965,

> The preoccupation of the press with each day's story can be made to our advantage to minimize the impact and duration of unfavorable events, but only if we tell the story whole, all at once. It's never a good idea to conceal from reporters what they may find out for themselves—because in Viet-Nam they will. And when they do they'll write it *their* way, not in a context of our choosing (Wyatt 1993, 163).

To be sure, some minor incidents occurred. In the summer of 1965, reporters were denied access to the airbase at Da Nang, a chief staging point for the bombing campaign against North Vietnam. Later that year, military efforts to downplay growing American casualty rates and inflate those of the enemy, especially after the fierce fighting in the Ia Drang Valley, inspired anger and sarcasm from reporters. In June 1968, John Carroll of the *Baltimore Sun* had his accreditation suspended for six months for violating a news hold on Operation Pegasus along the demilitarized zone. One of the most famous incidents occurred in August 1965. Morley Safer of CBS filmed a group of Marines setting fire to thatched huts. On the morning after the film had aired, CBS president Frank Stanton was awakened by a phone call. "Frank, are you trying to fuck me?" the voice bellowed. "Who is this?" asked the groggy Stanton. "Frank, this is your president and yesterday your boys shat on the American flag." Lyndon Johnson followed up his tirade with an investigation into Safer's background, as well as pressuring Stanton to reassign Safer from Vietnam (Halberstam 1979, 490). Many journalists expressed growing concern and frustration over this dependence and its consequences. In a 1967 assessment of the press's performance, *Newsweek* lamented the fact that "coverage of Vietnam . . . suffers from undue reliance on centralized sources." *New York Times* Saigon bureau chiefs repeatedly asked their editors to allow them to stop writing a daily summary of combat action—"a tedious collection of largely meaningless scraps," as Charles Mohr called it. The emphasis on the "bang-bang," Mohr continued, "severely limits our ability to do the deep, thoughtful, interesting, funny, investigative, and analytical reporting which will be our real record here." When he made a similar request, R. W. Apple was told that "we get an arbitrary space allotment and the spot news has to be covered" (Wyatt 1993, 141).

All of this added up to a sense of near helplessness on the part of many journalists. "It's the only story I've been on in my life where I get a hopeless feeling when I try to get on top of things," said CBS's Dan Rather. William Tuohy of the *Los Angeles Times* complained that "we're drowning in facts here, but starved for information" ("Crud" 1966, 53).

Despite these frustrations, the journalistic/information system in Vietnam gave each participant what it needed in a largely complementary relationship—not the adversarial one that has come down to us as conventional wisdom. For example, from 1965 through 1972, fewer than a dozen reporters had their accreditation suspended or revoked for violating the ground rules. For several reasons, major news organizations had become, as institutions, more cautious and conservative. Especially as regarded stories involving foreign policy and national security, the press was reluctant to appear disloyal in the face of the threat from the Soviet Union. The professionalization of journalism, with its quest for objectivity, was part of this trend, as was the need to maintain access to sources within the government. Major news organizations had become big, profitable businesses subject to all of the pressures stockholders and the marketplace brought to bear. This was particularly true for the television networks, which were subject to Federal Communications Commission regulation and licensing.

A number of examples illustrate this caution. In late 1966 and early 1967, Harrison Salisbury, veteran foreign correspondent for the *New York Times,* became the first reporter from a major American news organization to visit North Vietnam. In his dispatches he acknowledged that his hosts showed him what they wanted him to see. Still, fellow *Times* correspondent Hanson Baldwin, concerned about "the effect that these stories will have upon the country and upon the *Times,*" wrote a refutation of Salisbury's reporting and pressured editors into publishing it on the front page of the paper. Among other attacks, he referred to Salisbury's reports as "grossly exaggerated." A few days later a *Times* editorial further distanced the paper from Salisbury, and editor Clifton Daniel instructed his staff to "do everything we can in the coming weeks to balance the Salisbury reports" (Wyatt 1993, 155–156).

Reluctant to jeopardize access or profits, major news organizations also approached the big stories that supposedly defined the adversarial relationship between the press and the government with similar caution. The My Lai Massacre took place on March 16, 1968, in a small village on the northern coast of South Vietnam. According to charges later filed against Lieutenant William Calley, American troops murdered several hundred Vietnamese civilians. No reporters were present that day, only Army photographer Sgt. Ronald Haeberle. After the incident, officers, including the division commanding general, invoked a conspiracy of silence that held

Harrison Salisbury, foreign correspondent for *The New York Times,* became the first reporter from a major American news organization to visit North Vietnam during the Vietnam War. (*Bettman/Corbis*)

for more than a year. A soldier named Ron Ridenhour, who had not been present at My Lai, pieced together enough bits of stories from other troopers to conclude that something terrible had happened. He wrote to President Nixon, the secretaries of state and defense, the chairman of the Joint Chiefs, and several members of Congress. His letters led to an Army investigation and the filing of charges against several officers involved in the alleged incident, principally platoon commander Calley.

Even then, no major news organization picked up the story, leaving the field to former Associated Press reporter Seymour Hersh. From interviews with Calley and other participants and witnesses, Hersh put together a detailed account of the day. However, no major news outlet would touch the story. Only after the tiny Dispatch News Service, an alternative media organization based in California, marketed the story did the big organizations, now able to blame any problems with the story on Dispatch, pick it up.

A second example of caution involves the Pentagon Papers. In 1967, Secretary of Defense Robert McNamara grew increasingly concerned about the direction and prospects of U.S. policy in Vietnam. Hoping to figure out how the situation had reached its current point, he authorized the compilation of a top-secret documentary history of U.S. involvement that became known as the Pentagon Papers.

One of the authors of the Pentagon Papers was political scientist Daniel Ellsberg, who had worked in the Pentagon and in Vietnam as a pacification analyst. Before going to Vietnam, Ellsberg had been an ardent supporter of the war, but his exposure to the war turned him into a similarly passionate opponent. By 1971, he was convinced that if the Pentagon Papers were released to the public, a popular outcry would bring the war to a quick end. Still possessing his security clearance, Ellsberg copied significant portions of the papers and looked for an outlet. He began with antiwar members of Congress, none of whom would touch the papers. He finally found a kindred soul in Neil Sheehan, who now worked for the *New York Times.* Sheehan convinced his editors and *Times* publisher Arthur Sulzberger to authorize a series of articles based on the Pentagon Papers. Sulzberger devoted a team of reporters and more than $100,000 to the series, which began on June 13, 1971. The *Times* endured immense political and economic pressure, as well as a legal challenge by the Nixon administration, to continue publishing the series.

As dramatic as these stories were, and as courageous as were the journalists involved, they still indicate the limits on reporting the Vietnam story. First, neither of these stories broke in Vietnam. Reporters there, committed to covering the day-to-day action of the war, did not have time to take on long-term investigative projects. Second, insiders broke both stories. Seymour Hersh and Neil Sheehan displayed significant courage and industry, but without Ron Ridenhour, the massacre might yet be unknown to all but a few Americans. Without Daniel Ellsberg, the Pentagon Papers could well be gathering dust in the bowels of the National Archives.

Even with these stories, public interest in Vietnam began to wane. Richard Nixon came into office determined to stabilize American power in the world by achieving some degree of rapprochement with the Soviet Union and the People's Republic of China. The war in Vietnam represented a major inconvenience to achieving this goal. Nixon first attempted to end the war quickly through increased bombing of North Vietnam. When that failed, in November 1969, he initiated a gradual withdrawal of U.S. troops and a buildup of the South Vietnamese military. As this process of "Vietnamization" continued, the number of American troops—and of American casualties—steadily declined. Declining with them was the press and the American public's interest in the conflict. The antiwar movement lost momentum and fractured. A survey of college freshmen in the fall of 1970 revealed that the environment, not the war, was their top public policy concern. News organizations reduced or eliminated altogether their presence in Vietnam. The elaborate information apparatus that had once issued daily reams of statistics and summaries had less American activity to report. On January 9, 1971, a MACV press officer took the podium at the daily briefing in Saigon and announced there would be no morning release that day. "Normally we report B-52 strikes in Vietnam," he said. "There were no indirect fire attacks. Normally we report ground action involving U.S. troops. There were no ground actions. There just wasn't anything to report" ("U.S. Command" 1971, 2).

The war would, of course, continue for another four years and on occasion still intrude into the headlines: later in January 1971 with the failed invasion of southern Laos by the South Vietnamese military; the Easter Offensive in spring 1972, when the North Vietnamese seized control of the northern provinces of South Vietnam; and the final, tragic collapse of South Vietnam in March and April 1975. The press enjoyed a temporary glow of public acclaim during the Watergate period. However, news organizations proved not to be immune as the public lost confidence in the major institutions of American life—government, big business, education, and the press. With the end of the war, the process of assigning blame and drawing lessons began. With the conservative ascendancy of the 1980s, criticism of a supposedly liberal press became the conventional wisdom and shaped assessment of the press's role in the failure of American will in Vietnam.

Basing their thinking about the press on this characterization, military and civilian leaders determined to keep the press on a tight leash in future conflicts. During the October 1983 invasion of Grenada, the government banned the press entirely for the first two days. Reporters who approached the island on their own in small boats were turned away at gunpoint. Under great pressure, the military allowed 15 reporters, out of the 700 staging on Barbados, access to the island. After Grenada, Chairman of the Joint Chiefs Gen. John Vessey appointed a commission headed by former MACV chief information officer Winant Sidle to draft a press policy. The main result was the development of the National Media Pool, an "emergency response team" of press from major media organizations. Panama was the first test of this new policy, and it did not work well, as the military deliberately did not mobilize the pool until after the initial invasion. The pool was mobilized at the beginning of Operation Desert Shield/Desert Storm in August 1990, and accompanied the first troops into Saudi Arabia, but as U.S. troops poured into the region, so did journalists. The press corps soon exceeded 1,600, and the pool arrangement crashed and burned. Reporters had very limited pool access to the battlefield, and then only under the most tightly controlled conditions. Most coverage came from reporters at the briefings by commanding general "Stormin' Norman" Schwarzkopf. This stonewall approach worked in Grenada, Panama, and Desert Storm only because the periods of intense combat were short, and journalistic and public attention shifted elsewhere before the controls began to crack. Even in Desert Storm, journalists struck out on their own to reach the battlefield. The most notable case was CBS's Bob Simon, who was captured and held for 40 days by Iraqi troops.

Beginning in 2002, officials in the Defense Department came to the same realization that Assistant Secretary of State James Greenfield had back in late 1963 and early 1964. They understood that any war in Iraq aimed at removing Saddam Hussein and instituting new political and social structures would be longer than Desert Storm. They also understood that the characteristics of American journalism that had operated in Vietnam—the draw of covering American troops under fire, the "police beat" approach that the media took, justifying the massive economic investment that ensued, and the need to fill the even bigger news hole created by 24/7 news networks and the Internet—were still present and gave the government and military the same opportunity to shape the story. Assistant Secretary of Defense for Public Affairs Victoria Clarke and her deputy Bryan Whitman developed an approach that greatly resembled Operation Maximum Candor. The heart of this approach was the embedded media policy—assigning reporters to units for extended periods. This eventually placed more than 600 reporters with units, with ground rules calling for relatively few limits on what could be reported, similar to the ground rules used during Vietnam.

As was also the case in Vietnam, the American public's support for this conflict rests ultimately upon some hardheaded judgments. Is the goal achievable, and is it achievable at a price the public is willing to pay? In Vietnam, the reality of a complex struggle with no simple solutions eventually led the majority of Americans to answer "No."

For a brief period at the end of the Vietnam War, Americans engaged in a consideration of the appropriate uses, and the limits, of American power. In a few years, the desire for simple answers to complex questions won out, and citizens began to compartmentalize and sanitize their experience in Vietnam. Americans eventually made the veterans of that war the focal point of their shared memory of Vietnam. Of course, honoring the service and sacrifice of these men and women is more than appropriate, but it also allowed us to ignore the hard questions that we confront yet again. The American people have a right to expect their government, their military, and, yes, their press to provide honest information. But the answers regarding the right or wrong, the worthiness, and the effectiveness of the sacrifice of blood and treasure rests ultimately with a wary, skeptical citizenry.

References and Further Reading

Cater, Douglass, and Walter Pincus. "The Foreign Legion of U.S. Public Relations." *Reporter,* December 22, 1960, 15–22.

"Crud, Fret, and Jeers." *Time,* June 10, 1966, 53.

Friedrich, Otto. "How to Be a War Correspondent." *Yale Review* 48 (Spring 1959): 474–480.

Gans, Herbert. *Deciding What's News: A Study of CBS Evening News, NBC Nightly News, Newsweek, and Time.* New York: Pantheon, 1979.

Halberstam, David. *The Powers That Be.* New York: Alfred A. Knopf, 1979.

"Journalism Group Scores U.S. Secrecy." *New York Times,* November 12, 1959, 12.

Lawrence, David. "Our Own 'Iron Curtain.'" *U.S. News and World Report,* October 5, 1951, 6.

Meyer, Karl. "Kennedy and the Press." *New Statesman,* April 12, 1963: 513.

Moyar, Mark. *Triumph Forsaken: The Vietnam War, 1954–1965.* Cambridge, UK: Cambridge University Press, 2006.

O'Brien, Michael. *John F. Kennedy: A Biography.* New York: St. Martin's, 2005.

Sheehan, Neil. *A Bright, Shining Lie: John Paul Vann and America in Vietnam.* New York: Random House, 1988.

"U.S. Command Finds Nothing to Report." *New York Times,* January 10, 1971, 2.

Wyatt, Clarence. "The Media and the Vietnam War." In *The War That Never Ends: New Perspectives on the Vietnam War,* edited by David Anderson and John Ernst, 265–288. Lexington: University Press of Kentucky, 2007.

Wyatt, Clarence. *Paper Soldiers: The American Press and the Vietnam War.* New York: Norton, 1993.

African Americans and the Vietnam War

James E. Westheider

9

Wayne Smith was 18 and just out of high school when he enlisted in the Army in 1968. Smith hoped to go to medical school some day, and became a medic so he could do good things for people. In 1963, Albert French also enlisted straight out of high school; in his case it was the Marines, and his reasons were markedly different from Smith's. "It wasn't to go save America," French recalled. He was 19 and "I was not college material at the time." Largely, it was to get away from home, "Something you are supposed to do to become a man" (French 2007). Dennis Hughes did not have a choice. He was 19 when he was drafted into the Army in 1966. Neither did Quinton Johnson, who was drafted in 1969. Despite their different routes into military service, Hughes, Smith, French, and Johnson would share a common fate; they would be four of the roughly 300,000 African Americans to serve in the Vietnam War.

Military Service

African Americans had long sought military service as a way to earn their just civil rights and prove to whites that they were equally as brave, patriotic, and capable, but they had to contend with officially sanctioned segregation, racism, and second-class status in the armed forces. Conditions changed after President Harry Truman issued Executive Order 9981 in July 1948 ordering fair treatment and equal opportunity in the armed forces regardless of race. After initially resisting the order, the armed forces found that mixing the races did not hamper efficiency or lead to violence. Quite the contrary. An integrated military was more cost efficient and excellent propaganda at home and abroad. By the time French, Smith, Hughes, and Johnson were inducted into the armed forces in the 1960s, the military was probably the most racially egalitarian institution in America. The Department of Defense was proud of its achievement, and boasted in its annual report for 1968 that institutional racism had been eliminated from the armed forces.

American media and politicians often held the military up as a model in race relations for civilian society to emulate. "The U.S. Army has achieved a revolution in integration," remarked the *New York Times* in 1969 (Sulzberger 1969, 46). Writing in *Ebony,* David Llorens characterized the armed forces as the "most productive, rewarding, and racially congenial experience that [African Americans] can have" (Llorens 1968, 87). Most African Americans in the services also commended the military as a model for civilian society to imitate. Stating a widely held belief, Captain Sylvian Wailes remarked, "Basically, the Army affords you as good an opportunity as you can find . . . there is at least a better, or more of an equal opportunity" (Grove 1966, 7).

It also paid better than most of the civilian alternatives open to young black men in the 1960s and 1970s. Charles Cato hoped to return to his old career of jeweler's apprentice after his three years in the Army and a tour in Vietnam. He liked the work and it paid a decent $55 a week, but there were no jobs available to him, and he ended up on $33 a week unemployment pay. In contrast, in the mid-1960s, an enlistee could hope to make corporal or E-4 after three years of service and earn $60 a week after taxes as well as free room and board. Married military personnel received even higher allotments. Serving with an elite unit brought additional rewards; men in airborne units received $55 a month in jump pay, for example. Service in a combat zone such as Vietnam meant yet an additional $65 a month. The military was also eager to keep trained personnel and paid relatively lavish reenlistment bonuses. Depending on rank and one's military occupational specialty (MOS), first-time reenlistees could earn as much as $1,400 for "re-upping." African Americans showed their appreciation by enlisting, and reenlisting, in large numbers. In 1966, for example, only about 12 percent of eligible whites chose to remain in the armed forces after their enlistments were up, but for African Americans it was more than two-thirds (Foner 1974).

Not all blacks believed in the racial fairness of the armed forces. Before Dennis Hughes joined the Army he "had some uncles in WWI, WWII and Korea. They had parades for the WWI and WWII veterans, but treated the Korean veterans the way they would later treat Vietnam veterans." He saw "at an early age that they did not care for their troops" (Hughes 2007). Hughes's skepticism was justified. The military had made great strides in combating racism and proving equal opportunity, but conditions were still very far from ideal. Despite the Pentagon's claims that it had eradicated institutional racism, African Americans encountered both personal and systemic racism in virtually every aspect of their service careers.

Unequal treatment for many African Americans started with their induction into the armed forces. One of the most contentious aspects of the Vietnam War was the use of the draft to supply much of the manpower needed for the conflict. Because of inequities in the draft, eligible men from the middle and upper classes could normally find ways of avoiding service, or at least service in Vietnam, meaning the burden of the draft fell on working-class whites and minorities. Consequently, African Americans were drafted in disproportionately higher numbers than were whites. African Americans of

An African American soldier peers cautiously into a tunnel during an ambush patrol near Cu Chi. The draft and Project 100,000, which aggressively recruited underprivileged youths, hit the African American community particularly hard, leading Martin Luther King Jr., who believed that disproportionate numbers of African Americans were being sent to Vietnam, to describe the conflict as "a white man's war, a black man's fight." (*National Archives*)

draft age made up about 11 percent of the general population, but from 1965 to 1970, approximately 14 percent of all draftees were black. To illustrate the problem another way, in 1967 nearly one-third of eligible whites were drafted, but for African Americans it was nearly 64 percent (Murray 1971).

There were several major reasons for this. The Selective Service Act under which the Vietnam era draft operated allowed for educational deferments, so someone in college or a trade school was usually exempted from the draft. Though this applied equally to men of all races, black families were on average poorer than whites and could not normally afford a college education. In 1967, the median income was $8,274 a year for the average white family, but only $5,141 a year for a black family. Only about 5 percent of draft-age black men were enrolled in college at the height of the war, for example. Second, although the draft itself was legally color-blind, the men that sat on the 4,080 local draft boards were not. The local draft boards had tremendous power in deciding whether a young man deserved an exemption or would be drafted, and some of them, such as Jack Helms, a Ku Klux Klan grand dragon in New Orleans, were avowed racists. Even those members who would not have considered themselves racist often harbored racial stereotypes, and few were black, as the average board member was white, male, conservative, over 40, and a veteran of either World War II or Korea. Early in the war in 1966 there were only 230 African Americans on local draft boards, or 1.3 percent of the total. The demographics improved slightly, but not greatly, and by the end of the war there were 1,265 African Americans, or 6.6 percent of the total, on local boards. Finally, it was also easier for many whites to avoid active service by getting into the Reserves or the National Guard, both of which were heavily white and had long waiting lists to get in.

Many African Americans resisted induction. In 1967, for example, 15 members of the Student Nonviolent Coordinating Committee (SNCC), including its chairman, Stokely Carmichael, and its national program director, Cleveland Sellers, refused induction into the armed forces. Probably the most famous black draft resister of the war was the boxer Muhammad Ali, who refused to be inducted in April 1967. In June, Ali was convicted and sentenced to five years in prison for draft evasion, but in 1971 the Supreme Court overturned his conviction on a technicality. Carmichael and Sellers also avoided service when their New York draft boards ruled them physically unfit for service. Few black draft resisters, however, had the resources of an Ali or a Carmichael or a Sellers to fight the system. Fellow SNCC member David Bell received two years in a federal prison, and Walter Collins received a 25-year sentence for draft evasion.

Ironically, despite the huge disparities in the Selective Service System, at least early in the war a higher percentage of African Americans than whites supported the draft. A Harris poll in late 1966 found that only 48 percent of

Stokely Carmichael, an effective leader of the Student Nonviolent Coordinating Committee (SNCC), brought the concept of black power into the U.S. civil rights struggle. In 1967, Carmichael, an advocate of militancy rather than nonviolent cooperation, broke with SNCC and joined the more radical Black Panthers. (*Library of Congress*)

whites but 63 percent of blacks believed the system was fair. A Gallup poll in *Newsweek* that same year found an even higher percentage of blacks—75 percent—thought the draft was racially fair. As the war progressed, however, and the racial and class inequities inherent in the selective service system became apparent, black Americans turned against the draft.

Many African Americans encountered racism during basic training or boot camp. "It was pretty damn racist," recalled Wayne Smith of boot camp at Fort Dix, New Jersey. "The sergeants talked about the 'gooks.' And they would call brothers 'niggers'" (Vietnam Veterans Memorial Fund Forum 1992). "I would say yes, they were all racists . . . there was a racial tinge to all the basic training—less so in AIT [Advanced Individual Training]" (Smith 2007). Many African Americans were shocked to discover that the black drill instructors could be harder on them than the white ones. "The black DIs [drill instructors] were just as tough on African Americans," recalled Wayne Smith. "There was one African American from Newark that the black sergeants focused on to provoke. There was no sense of solidarity between black NCOs [noncommissioned officers] and enlisted" (Smith 2007).

The drill instructors were rough and often cruel to the trainees to prepare them for the rigors of combat, and sometimes this included, or was misinterpreted to include, racism. Wayne Smith believed a lot of the abuse involved "power and intimidation. They would use anything, even against the whites. They were pretty bad. I had joined with a white, a white Irish friend. One of the basic training sergeants picked on him a lot. I thought it was atrocious. They tried to bully us; it was almost insulting." Smith was disappointed with his basic training; it did not prepare him for Vietnam nor did it foster any cohesion and camaraderie among the men. "You know," Smith recalled, "there's a lot of racial stuff being mixed up and that blew my mind, first of all, because, you know, I thought we'd kind of be all in this together" (Smith 2007). Others resented the treatment given them during basic training but felt it paid dividends later on. Quinton Johnson thought his DIs at boot camp were "mean and a little hard on you," until he was sent to Vietnam, and "then I think the training really done some good" (Carper, Martinez, and Johnson 1999).

The Vietnam Experience

Many African Americans did not think much about being sent to Vietnam. Albert French, one of the first Marines to go ashore at Da Nang in 1965, was typical of some of the early combat soldiers, white or black. "At that time I had no idea of what this war would become, and how history would show it," he remembered. "I don't think I did think about it; been in the Marines for two years already so it was no big deal. We just went. Not a lot of talk about whether we should be there or not. No flag waving but no dissent. Just salt of the earth kids without a political agenda. I never believed I was saving the United States of America in Vietnam" (French 2007).

At least early in the war, however, Vietnam was generally viewed as another favorable opportunity for African Americans to prove themselves.

In 1968, *New York Times* correspondent Thomas Johnson wrote that "the Negro fighting man has attained a sudden visibility—a visibility his fore-fathers never realized while fighting in past American wars" (Johnson 1968, 1). Cpl. Lawrence E. Waggoner believed "the Negro warrior has distin-guished himself in Vietnam. This is to be looked on with pride and commit-ted to memory as he presses on to distinguish himself in his own country" (Waggoner 1968, 77). Army major Beauregard Brown considered that ser-vice in Vietnam represented the best prospect for advancement for a black career officer.

Patriotism was a motivating factor for many African Americans. Women were not required to serve in Vietnam, but 17-year Army veteran Doris "Lucki" Allen volunteered for duty in Vietnam in 1967, considering it her patriotic duty. Dennis Hughes "thought we were doing the right thing" when he was sent to Vietnam in February 1967. "I didn't really want to go but did not have a choice," Hughes recalled. "Me and the rest of the guys thought we were doing something for our country. We thought people would respect that, but they didn't" (Hughes 2007). Some were idealistic, such as Wayne Smith. Smith went to Vietnam to save lives and not take them: "I was naive. I thought I could make a difference" (Smith 2007).

Smith the idealist, like many, became disillusioned with the war after experiencing its realities. "I rejected the war after 18 months in Vietnam," he remembered. "I could no longer go along with the game. . . . You see the massive waste of life, people I knew. Their lives squandered for what? Lies cut me to the bone. It was a devastating sense of betrayal" (Smith 2007). Dennis Hughes was "disappointed in the politics of the war" after serving in Vietnam, but most particularly he was upset with the waste of the "58,000 lives on the wall in DC" (Hughes 2007). Jerry Brown went to Vietnam "believing strongly in the war," but he "came out believing it to be immoral and futile" (Dalglish 1970, 11). For some, the impact of the war sunk in later. "Years later I thought differently about it when I became more politi-cally aware," explained Albert French. "I became against the war, not to the extent of protesting it. After awhile I believed we were fighting on the wrong side" (French 2007).

French, like many of his countrymen, had little regard for America's South Vietnamese allies, the Army of the Republic of Vietnam (ARVN). He recalled that "on one patrol once ARVN brought bright colored umbrellas with them because it was raining. . . . We just stayed back because that's a damn target and a half. Most were local militia" and lacked decent training, motivation, or leadership (French 2007).

French may not have thought much of "Marvin the ARVN," as Ameri-cans derisively labeled their erstwhile allies, but like many he liked the peo-ple. Children would hang out near his machine gun emplacement; one day it was "a four or five year old kid smoking a cigarette, and I didn't want him around the machine gun, so I told him 'didi' [go, go]." The kid stunned and amused the Marine by replying, "I live here." French got to "know the local kids and they came around a lot . . . there was no reason not to trust them. I treated the Vietnamese like humans and they treated me like a human." Unlike many Americans, French "didn't use the word gook—to me it was too much like nigger. It was too ugly, too racist" (French 2007). Wayne Smith also got to know and like the Vietnamese people and refused to demean them with racial pejoratives. "I was part of a civic action team working with the Vietnamese, and I saw their humanity," he reminisced. "I knew them as human beings. Some were good and some were not. I was very fond of some of the people" (Smith 2007).

Albert French was not under any illusions and understood the ambiguous nature of most Vietnamese in the war. Sometimes the same children that played around the American encampment would stick a "Y shaped stick in the ground during the day—that night the sniper can find it easily in the dark, and be right on target" (French 2007). Some Americans despised all Vietnamese as duplicitous and cowardly. African American Sp/4 (Specialist 4) Ray Ambrose believed that "with all due respect . . . I don't think that a young man . . . should come over here and die for a country that is so worthless and unconcerned" (Ambrose 1968, 71).

Initially, many Americans also had little respect for their enemies, the Vietcong (VC) and the North Vietnamese Army, also known as the People's Army of Vietnam (PAVN). Wayne Smith said that "in military training, before I knew them, the military trained us to think of them as gooks and slants," but Smith was sensitive to the racist implications and "I resisted all that. Had we been sent to the Congo it would have been niggers. That's how they in fact trained us—the Vietnamese were less than human so you could kill them easier" (Smith 2007). Albert French would watch the Vietnamese fishing in their sampans and ask, "How could they attack the U.S. in those things." Time and experience convinced him otherwise and he developed a grudging admiration for both the VC and the North Vietnamese. "South Vietnam had a puppet government," French declared. "The VC and PAVN were very good, and we respected them. They believed in their cause, whereas the South Vietnamese did not believe in it that much" (French 2007). Wayne Smith also grew to admire the men trying to kill him. "We called them Charlie. As you fought against them you saw these average people with less experience than we had, they were very brave taking on the American army. Ultimately we called them Sir Charles" (Smith 2007). Mutual respect did not translate into kindness or restraint, and Vietnamese and American did their best to kill each other, often without mercy.

Though African Americans made up only around 10 to 11 percent of the American military establishment in Vietnam from 1965 to 1973, a disproportionate number were concentrated in combat units. Marine Albert French, who was stationed at Chu Lai, described a somewhat typical day-to-day existence. "Chu Lai was a hole. We had tents and ate C rations. There was a cafeteria, usually got a hot meal each day, but the food was terrible. We were either in a foxhole, tent or on patrol. On the average day it would be at least three patrols or ambushes. If you did not go out you were on the line. I looked forward to going out to the outpost—Scalawag—to get some sleep. Spend a week or so there. About five men manned the outpost. We never got hit at Scalawag. Fortunately they were not good shots" (French 2007).

Many of the enemy, however, proved to be decent enough shots. Four months into his tour in Vietnam in 1965, French was shot and wounded in

U.S. Army soldiers fire at a suspected Vietcong position during a search-and-destroy mission. African American soldiers were assigned to combat at higher rates than whites and also suffered a disproportionate number of casualties in the war's early years. (*National Archives*)

his throat. As more Americans poured into Vietnam, casualties mounted, and black casualties early in the war were unusually high. The same year French was wounded, one out of every four American deaths in Vietnam was black. By late July 1966, African Americans were 15 percent of American forces in Vietnam but represented 22 percent of the total casualties. The alarmingly high death rate for blacks in Vietnam declined after 1967, and by the end of U.S. involvement in 1973, the 7,257 African Americans killed in Vietnam constituted 12.6 percent of all U.S. deaths in the war (Department of Defense 1985).

As the war progressed, blacks in the armed forces questioned why African Americans were fighting and dying to preserve the freedom of the South Vietnamese when the civil rights movement was still struggling hard to win equal rights back at home. Albert French had met a girl from Los Angeles, and they wrote back and forth. He recalled watching a major Marine operation known as Operation Starlite, "and she was writing to me about Watts. What am I doing here," he thought to himself, "when I can't go on one side of Jackson, South Carolina" (French 2007).

The fight for equality was very important to African Americans in Vietnam, but some were torn between their desire to be good soldiers and their obligations to the black community back home. Wayne Smith explained that "while many of us thought, I believe, that it was necessary to show our

Albert French, Dennis Hughes, and Wayne Smith

Despite initially having their own readjustment problems after returning home from Vietnam, Albert French, Dennis Hughes, and Wayne Smith did more than just put their lives together; in different ways all three have dedicated their lives to helping fellow veterans. Albert French did so by telling their story. After the war French taught himself photography and worked as a medical photographer and then as a photojournalist for 13 years for the *Pittsburgh Post-Gazette* before cofounding a women's magazine, *Pittsburgh Preview*. But he also wanted to leave a record of his—and other veterans'—experiences in the war so they would not be forgotten. He started writing and published his first novel, *Billy,* in 1993, and is the author of five books, including the widely acclaimed *Patches of Fire,* French's account of his own experiences in Vietnam.

Dennis Hughes "has been helping people my whole life," a character trait he credits to his mother. He is a block watch captain for his neighborhood in Pittsburgh and is instrumental in aiding senior citizens, but he has also become a shoulder for other veterans to lean on, "to make the quality of life better for veterans, helping them with their benefits, medications, things like that," particularly in the area of mental health. He serves on numerous boards and committees, such as the Mental Health Behavioral Sciences Committee, the Allegheny Coalition for Recovery, National Organization on Mental Illness, and the Coalition of Veteran's Advocates. Since 2003, he has been chairman of the Mental Health Consumer Council in Pittsburgh, which oversees the three veterans' hospitals in the Pittsburgh area (Hughes 2007).

Wayne Smith has also dedicated his life to helping other veterans. "After the war, clearly all of us, white brothers as well, and sisters, it was evident that we had fallen through the cracks. America had abandoned Vietnam veterans, in general, all of us" (Vietnam Veterans Memorial Fund Forum 1992). In 1998, Smith was one of 20 U.S. veterans who returned to Vietnam and met with 20 former enemy soldiers on a mission of peace and reconciliation, and in 1999 he was featured in the Emmy Award–winning documentary, *Vietnam: A Long Time Coming.* He became president of the Black Patriots in Washington, D.C., and was a longtime therapist in the Veterans Administration's Vietnam Veterans Readjustment Counseling Program. Later Wayne Smith was director of development at the Vietnam Veterans Memorial Fund. Today he is a special assistant to the president of the Vietnam Veterans of America Foundation in Washington, D.C., and program manager for Civil Liberties, of the Unitarian Universalist Service Committee.

ability to be effective and responsible and, indeed, heroic and doing our duty, there were other brothers who had the feeling that it was a white man's war, it was not our war. Our war was back home in the United States, struggling to advance our people and to eliminate the crime, the drugs, and other related problems that were assaulting the black community. So, it was a subject of constant discussion among us" (Vietnam Veterans Memorial Fund Forum 1992).

Increasingly the war and the movement were linked. "American Negro soldiers in Vietnam used to consider the war and the civil rights movement as separate things but the past three years have had an exacerbating effect," wrote C. L. Sulzberger in the *New York Times* in 1969. "Now, a small minority wonders if black troops should fight for their country at all" (Sulzberger 1969, 46). It was becoming more than a small minority. Discontent was spreading among black troops to the point that just one year later, journalist Wallace Terry could assert that "a majority of black GI's . . . feel they have no business fighting in Southeast Asia" (Terry 1970, 7). Vietnam veteran Jerry Brown was typical. "Why fight a war for freedom in a country far away," he asked, "when at home the civil rights war is not yet won" (Dalglish 1970, 11)?

Black military personnel were not only dissatisfied with the war, but with the treatment accorded them in the armed forces. Many blacks were convinced that far from being a model for civilian society, the military was just as racist as the rest of America. The military may have superficially eliminated institutional racism, but vestiges of it still plagued African Americans in many areas, particularly in testing and assignments. For example, the Armed Forces Qualification Test (AFQT), the exam given to all incoming recruits, contained a European cultural bias that in the words of one black sergeant was "a bonus for growing up white" (NAACP 1971, 3). A recruit's performance on these exams largely determined his or her career options; a high score meant a recruit could choose one of the more lucrative and rewarding "hard core" military occupational specialties such as military intelligence or one of the technical programs, whereas a low score relegated one to a "soft core" area such as service and supply or combat infantry. In 1965 and 1966, 40 percent of all African Americans tested into the lowest acceptable category on the AFQT. As late as 1970, the Department of Defense was alarmed over the high number of minority enlistees that tested poorly on the exams. Consequently, as late as 1972, blacks made up 16.3 percent of the enlisted personnel assigned to combat specialties and nearly 20 percent of the service and supply troops. Interestingly, that same year the Defense Department replaced the AFQT with a new test, the Army Classification Battery, which eliminated much of the cultural bias suspected in the older exam. Whites' scores remained the same but the number of African Americans now testing into the higher classifications rose considerably.

Probably no single area of military life elicited more complaints from black service personnel than did the administration of military justice. In the armed forces, justice is dispensed on two discreet levels. Minor infractions such as a uniform code violation or tardiness were handled through nonjudicial punishment, known more commonly as a Captain's Mast in the Navy and Marines and an Article 15 in the Army and Air Force. The accused was given a hearing presided over by his or her commanding officer. The accused could speak and bring a personal representative, but the commanding officer made the final determination, and most enlisted personnel believed guilt was predetermined anyway. Punishment could range from a written reprimand in your service file to 30 days in the stockade, loss of pay, and demotion in rank. More serious transgressions, such as rape, murder, or cowardice in the face of the enemy, were adjudicated through courts-martial. A court-martial is similar in most respects to a civilian trial, but the jury is usually composed of commissioned officers and not the defendant's peers, and the rights of the accused, particularly the right to appeal, is far more limited. Punishment, if convicted, can include years at hard labor or even execution.

The problems plaguing military justice were partially institutional; the judge advocate general's (JAG) office was overwhelmingly white, meaning a black defendant would likely face prosecution by a white officer in a trial presided over by white judges and heard by an all-white jury; his defense counsel would almost assuredly be white as well. In 1972, for example, Captain Curtiss Smothers was the only African American judge advocate out of 123 captains assigned to the JAG offices in West Germany.

The real problem with military justice was not institutional as much as it was personal; the system gave officers and NCOs a lot of discretion, and many bigots abused the system. Dennis Hughes found that "some white officers were fair, but then you had others that still had a southern mentality" (Hughes 2007). A double standard existed under which African Americans were charged and punished for infractions for which whites were not. One white captain in Vietnam noticed that an inordinate number of black soldiers in his unit were being given Article 15s for being late to their duty stations. He discovered that his white sergeant was waking up the whites in the barracks but not the African Americans. Another problem in Vietnam had to do with uniform code violations and hair length. Out in the field many commanding officers often relaxed what were called "Mickey Mouse" or "chickenshit" regulations, allowing their men a little latitude to adorn their uniforms with such things as peace symbols or personal mementos. In many cases infractions by whites were ignored but black soldiers were written up.

Racism also affected an African American's chances at promotion. "Black people are the last to be promoted as far as rank goes," concluded a dejected Lionel Anderson in a letter from Vietnam to the *Black Panther* in September 1969 (Anderson 1969, 10). Dennis Hughes went to Vietnam as a spec four and returned "still a spec four." He was denied promotion because a captain yelled "hey" at him, and he did not respond. The captain yelled it again. Hughes finally replied, "Hay is for horses." He was then berated by a colonel for insubordination and held back from making sergeant. "I knew my job and I did it well, and I knew others that it happened to" (Hughes 2007). Wayne Smith also believed there was racism in most aspects of military life, including promotion. "The military is a microcosm of our larger American society," he reflected, but Smith also believed that for black careerists to some extent it "was largely based on merit promotion. It was not like affirmative action—the military was desperately in need of people. The lifers, the ones willing to eat a lot of shit got promoted" (Smith 2007).

Racist sergeants in charge of duty assignments often picked on African Americans. "For whatever reason," recalled Dennis Hughes, "for specific duties, KP [kitchen police], guard duty, it seemed that your name kept coming up, too often" (Hughes 2007). This personal bigotry was often subtle, "the northern gentility of race," explained Wayne Smith, "No overt racism but it was skin deep" (Smith 2007). Many blacks believed they were not only given the worst jobs but the most dangerous ones as well. Blacks in Vietnam called active combat zones "Soulville" because there were so many brothers there. Steven Carper, who was in the same unit with Quinton Johnson, recalled that the unit's senior NCO, a sergeant named Ard, "did not like black or Mexican people," and "he would make them walk point just so he could get them eliminated" (Carper, Martinez, and Johnson 1999, 25).

African Americans reacted to racism, real and perceived, to an unpopular war, and to feelings of isolation in a white-dominated military by finding strength and comfort in racial solidarity. "It was one of the most beautiful and memorable experiences that still give me enormous strength and character," recalled Wayne Smith about the racial solidarity that prevailed in his unit in Vietnam. "We are a brotherhood. We were all connected." They called one another "brother" or "blood" or "soul" and greeted each other with a clenched fist "black power salute" or, more commonly, by dapping. A dap was a ritualized handshake, with numerous variations and permutations, in which each of its many and often intricate moves had a meaning. "It was purely improvisational, imaginative and creative," explained Wayne Smith. "Some used it for pride and others showing off, and others, a sincere symbol of respect" (Smith 2007). Many African Americans wove "slave bracelets" out of their boot laces and wore them as a sign of cultural pride, while others carried ebony black power canes. Wayne Smith, for example, wore a slave bracelet and a braided necklace but did not carry a cane.

When one served in Vietnam was very important because the outward manifestations of black solidarity and black power did not appear until later in the conflict. "We didn't dap in 1965," remembered Albert French. "There were no slave bracelets or black power flags. Just talk; references were usually about what was going on in the states, especially events down south" (French 2007). Dennis Hughes, who was in Vietnam in 1967–1968, did not wear a slave bracelet or carry a cane, but he remembers others in his unit who did. When Wayne Smith served in Vietnam from May 1969 to November 1970 "there were signs of solidarity. We dapped all of the time—longest time many times to the song "Black Magic Woman." It was getting into this whole mentality of not just shaking hands but telling a story" (Smith 2007).

Smith also discovered that not all African Americans believed in racial solidarity. Smith hitched a ride in a truck to Tan Son Nhut Air Base to pick up supplies, but when he arrived with "mud on my shoes and carrying an M-16" he had forgotten his pass to get on base. Unconcerned he "threw up the black power sign to two MPs guarding the gates," only to be told, "We're not your brothers—where is your pass?" (Smith 2007).

Black officers in particular were suspect. There were not many; during the Vietnam War only about 5 percent of the officer corps was black. Dennis Hughes had a cousin who was in Vietnam as a first lieutenant, William Webb, but he personally had "never seen that many black officers." When Webb visited him at his company "it was the first time I had seen a black officer" in Vietnam (Hughes 2007). Albert French could recall seeing "only one black officer in Vietnam, and very few back in the states" (French 2007). Wayne Smith encountered "a handful, maybe . . . I remember an African American major, maybe a lieutenant colonel, some Hispanic officers. They were not nice at all, the career officers. African American careerists—we thought of them as Uncle Toms. There was not a lot of respect for them. They tried to get promotion at the expense of their own men" (Smith 2007).

The Impact of the Civil Rights Movement

Like many young black men entering the armed forces at that time, Smith had come out of a more radical civilian world; and like many, he had lost faith in the civil rights movement. Although he "admired Dr. King's vision," he "did not see it as practical, and did not believe that America would move to equality peacefully" (Smith 2007). Some, such as Dennis Hughes, failed to see any tangible results. "Civil rights" for African Americans, he observed, were "still not accepted by many white southerners" when he was stationed at Fort Jackson, South Carolina. "The Voting Rights Act and the Civil Rights Act passed, but people were not ready to openly accept that." Hughes believed that to deny African Americans their just civil rights "stunk and it still stinks today. Even to this day I think a lot has been taken away" (Hughes 2007).

Many African Americans gravitated toward more aggressive, militant heroes. Like scores of his contemporaries, Wayne Smith idolized "first and foremost Malcolm X. I admired his ferocity, his truth speaking and his warrior spirit" (Smith 2007). Malcolm X's message of black pride, separatism, and self-defense appealed to a younger generation of African Americans brought up in the promise of the civil rights movement but discouraged by its results. More than 70 percent of the black troops interviewed in Vietnam by journalist Wallace Terry in 1970 expressed admiration for Malcolm X, and he inspired at least two radical organizations that developed in the armed forces, the Malcolm X Society and GIs United against the War.

Another group held in high esteem by African Americans in the military was the Black Panthers. More than a third of the men interviewed by Terry claimed they would join the Panthers or a similar black nationalist organization when they left the military. Some did not wait to leave and formed Panther-inspired self-defense organizations within the armed forces, such as the Movement for a Democratic Military, the Blackstone Rangers, the Ju Ju, or the Black Mau Mau. Actual membership in any of these organizations was relatively small. Neither Albert French nor anyone he knew of in his company belonged to one. Dennis Hughes "did not join any organizations, I didn't even join the Army," but there were a few members of the Mau Mau in his unit (Hughes 2007). Wayne Smith "never encountered any organizations; but people talked about it, the ideology" (Smith 2007).

The ideology was often very infectious, and many African Americans adopted one major tenet of black nationalism in particular—separation from whites. As the war progressed, racial separation became increasingly common within the armed forces. One sign of growing racial polarization in Vietnam was the rising number of all-white or all-black living quarters. When Albert French served in 1965 his "hooch" was integrated, but as early as 1967 white helicopter pilot Dan Furman said they were allowed to stay "in whatever hootch we wanted to," resulting in largely racially exclusive quarters. "It was almost like we segregated ourselves" (McMichael 1998, A4).

Not all African Americans embraced self-segregation. Like most blacks, Wayne Smith was not a separatist, but he respected the black nationalists. "I saw it as a step towards self-pride, self-actualization," he remembered. "I was not a segregationist, I did not think that African Americans should be separate, but I respected people who had this black power. It was nothing I really embraced as my own" (Smith 2007). "[I] always felt that people had their beliefs and their rights," agreed Dennis Hughes, "even if they weren't mine, I could not knock them" (Hughes 2007).

Many African Americans found it easy to shift back and forth between a black and an integrated world. Albert French admitted that "if you get with a bunch of black kids you could get back to home a bit. For a moment you could go home. Back in tent time, we would hang out together more so," French explained, but "we also accepted whites. We played a lot of whist— if a white could play and wanted to, he was in. I looked at the individual— if they were cool fine" (French 2007). "No, our hooch was not segregated," remembered Wayne Smith, although it was self-selective in another way; "it was nonlifers. Those were the dividing lines. We had some isolation from white people but it was not wholesale, and we hung out with people who shared some kind of values; those who were stuck in the war but saw the folly in it" (Smith 2007). It was the same for black officers. Lt. Col. Maurice L. Adams was glad that the military was integrated, "and we can mix, though we often sit apart just to look at each other in our pride" (Dalglish 1970, 11). For Colin Powell, his days at the Command and General Staff College at Fort Leavenworth "represented integration in the best sense of the word. . . . We had our own parties, put on soul food nights, and played Aretha Franklin records," he recalled, but "we had the ability to shift back into the white-dominated world on Monday morning" (Powell 1995, 124).

Not all African Americans could transition smoothly from one world to another, however. Many chose not to, going beyond racial separation into the realm of racial hatred and violence. In 1972, for example, the Department of Defense's Task Force on the Administration of Military Justice saw "evidence of blacks separating themselves from their nonblack comrades in hostile ways, going beyond affirming their racial and cultural solidarity" (Department of Defense 1972, I, 61–62). Many used the outward symbols of racial pride to provoke or antagonize whites. Dapping in particular was the cause of a lot of racial friction in the ranks. What was a sincere and meaningful experience for its participants would often cause racial animosity, especially when it occurred in, and held up chow lines. Wayne Smith admitted that lengthy daps could "stall the chow line," and cause resentment.

For most African Americans, black pride and black power did not necessarily translate into hatred of, or separation from whites. Wayne Smith did not experience overt racism growing up in Rhode Island, where African Americans made up only 3 percent of the state's population. "I had to get along early with different people," recalled Smith. "Few people ever called me nigger." He knew from experience "some whites who were decent and some not, and some blacks that were decent and some that were not" (Smith 2007). But many African Americans brought their resentment of whites and white society with them into the military from the civilian world. "Some brothers from the south . . . had not dealt with whites much and they had some resentment. Their attitude was that no one is going to disrespect me," observed Wayne Smith (Smith 2007). James Daley's friend in Vietnam,

Willie Watkins from South Carolina, for example, "had a lot of hatred in him, and I knew he didn't trust whites much" (Daly and Bergman 2000, 121).

Racist whites naturally brought their particular prejudices with them into the military as well. "Some of these guys a few months earlier were throwing stones at freedom riders," explained Wayne Smith. "Now they have to take orders from a senior black sergeant from Detroit who was not going to take any shit" (Smith 2007). Vietnam veteran Donnel Jones found many officers and NCOs from the Deep South "who think the Afro-Americans should still be in slavery, and treat us soul brothers as such" (Jones 1968, 6). Many whites commonly referred to their black brothers in arms as niggers, spearchuckers, coons, or boy; often they brought the trappings of white supremacy into the military with them as well. Confederate flags—always a source of extreme antagonism for African Americans—flew defiantly over American bases in Vietnam, and the Ku Klux Klan operated openly on many installations. Many African Americans reported finding Klan or white supremacist literature in barracks and guard houses. Even the traditional cross burning found its way to Vietnam. In 1969, white sailors burned a 12-foot-high cross in front of a predominantly black barracks at Cam Ranh Bay, and the following year whites burned a cross in front of Army sergeant Clide Brown's tent after he appeared on the cover of *Time* magazine.

Despite the growing tension, racial violence was not a problem early in the war. Albert French "had more problems in the states than in Vietnam. There were one or two incidents—a miniature race riot needing the MPs [military police]. This was largely due to some white kids from the South. In Vietnam, and I can say this with ease, there weren't any problems. It never came up. All of the racial unrest back in U.S., we were vaguely aware of it. It didn't matter when you were on a night patrol" (French 2007).

In 1968, however, racial tension exploded into racial violence after the Tet Offensive and the death of Dr. Martin Luther King Jr. The communist offensive known as Tet '68 and President Lyndon Johnson's subsequent decision to seek a negotiated peace undercut the self-confidence and the fighting efficiency of American forces in Vietnam, contributing to a breakdown of morale and unit cohesion. The assassination of Dr. King in April devastated and shocked the black community. "We have to remember up till 1967 when Dr. King broke with it, the war was popular," reminded Wayne Smith. "We were dying in Vietnam and serving our country" (Smith 2007). "Most were hurt by it, including myself," remembered Dennis Hughes. "I thought that with his nonviolence, it was healthy [King's nonviolence] going to change some things around in the world. It just took all that away. We were hurt." Hughes was saddened and resented the reaction of many whites to the killing. "We heard the ones celebrating and felt anger. I wouldn't wish that death on anybody—especially in a combat zone. Vietnam was [a] whole different picture, especially after the assassination of Dr. Martin Luther King. White guys in the unit worried that riots would break out" (Hughes 2007). "It was the major thing," explained Albert French. "Civilians and riots—they get drafted and bring that mindset to Vietnam. White kids come in seeing the same thing and they have their agenda, and they clash" (French 2007).

And they did clash. That summer riots with racial overtones erupted at both the Navy brig at Da Nang and the sprawling Long Binh Stockade outside Saigon. Sporadic racial violence continued throughout the military establishment that year, and more than 160 racial assaults were recorded at Camp Lejeune in North Carolina alone. On July 20, 1969, the sporadic violence plaguing that installation erupted into a major racial gang fight, leaving one white dead, dozens of Marines injured, and 44 blacks and Puerto Ricans arrested and charged with complicity in the riot. The "rumble at Camp Lejeune" marked the beginning of one of the worst periods of racial violence in the history of the armed forces. Ten days later a large racial gang fight occurred at Millington Naval Air Station near Memphis, Tennessee, followed by fights at the naval installation at Cam Ranh Bay and Kaneohe Marine Corps Air Station in Hawaii. Over the next three years major racial confrontations took place throughout the military establishment from Fort McClellan, Alabama, to Machinato, Okinawa, and on board naval vessels, including the aircraft carriers *Constellation* and *Kitty Hawk*.

In an attempt to exploit the racial problems and violence plaguing the armed forces in the later stages of the Vietnam War, the Vietcong and North Vietnamese often claimed that African Americans were not their enemies, and would receive "special treatment" if they refused to fight, or even surrendered. Few blacks believed it. One Vietcong propaganda flyer claimed—incorrectly—that African Americans made up 40 percent of all U.S. deaths in Vietnam and that they should go home before they were killed. Wayne Smith saw one of their propaganda flyers—"No Vietnamese ever called you nigger. We are not your enemy" it read. But as Smith explained, "it was an us versus them attitude," and he "did not give a lot of thought to these people who were trying to kill me. I did question on some levels if I could kill; I wrestled with it. I had friends killed and wounded. I was a medic but I carried a M-16 and a .45" (Smith 2007). Many black GIs were not even aware of the communist propaganda overtures. Albert French "never heard about alleged special treatment. It didn't stop them from shooting me through the throat" (French 2007).

The racial violence plaguing the armed forces was widespread but it was far from universal. Most of it occurred on or near large military installations and usually involved individuals from noncombat units. Much of it occurred in service clubs or bars, and alcohol, women, choice of music, and racial slurs were usually the triggers. There was actually very little racial violence in the combat formations, where unit cohesion was crucial to survival, and members bonded together regardless of race. Albert French could not "think of one racial incident, despite the number of southerners—they were not Boston liberals" in his company. "My white lieutenant was from Mississippi. I think it speaks well of us" (French 2007). Dennis Hughes said that "to a certain degree" there was racism, "but it was only kinda—it wasn't blatantly out there. You hear some guys talking, but camaraderie between blacks and between African Americans and whites were both strong" in his company at Pleiku and Nha Trang. They had to depend on one another in order to survive (Hughes 2007). Quinton Johnson's unit in the 101st Airborne did not have racial problems. "I never met anyone, to me, that was really racist. We were really together . . ." (Carper, Martinez, and Johnson 1999, 27). In Wayne Smith's combat unit in the Mekong Delta, solidarity and brotherhood "transcended African Americans and included white and Asian Americans. [We] went out on platoon size search and destroy missions. [We] all worked together with courage and sensitivity for each other. We truly loved each other. I walked away with an overall positive experience with people of all races in Vietnam. It happened sadly, in war." Smith also identified another reason there was little racial violence in the combat units. "In combat that BULLSHIT was not tolerated. We all had M-16s. We didn't have to put up with the bullshit in a combat unit" (Smith 2007).

French, Hughes, Johnson, and Smith all survived their tours of duty in Vietnam, but others were not as fortunate. More than 58,000 Americans lost their lives in Vietnam; 7,257 of them were black. But like a great many veterans, the returnees faced serious readjustment issues after coming home. "The real trouble was when I got back home," recalled Quinton Johnson. He began drinking heavily his last month in Vietnam. "I probably drank everyday if I could have got my hands on it, not knowing that I had that problem." When he returned home he got his old job back and married his girlfriend but still continued to drink a lot, "it's party time I thought, but it wasn't partying time I don't guess." He wrecked a car and ended up in a fight with six or seven others. Johnson, however, realized he had a problem and straightened up; went back to school to study industrial maintenance. He and his wife separated; she could not understand that his "behavior was nothing less than the results of . . . Vietnam." In Vietnam you are a "trained killer, and this stuff just don't leave you. . . . It just brings the violence out of you" (Carper, Martinez, and Johnson 1999, 27).

Vietnam had changed Johnson, and French, Hughes, Smith and countless other African Americans who served in that war. In return, however, these men also changed the military. Military authorities reacted to the racial violence and dissension plaguing the ranks by initiating programs designed to expel radicals and other perceived troublemakers from the armed forces; but they also attempted to address the legitimate grievances of black service personnel. More black-oriented products were available at the post exchanges, and the Pentagon made a concerted effort to recruit more minority officers. Most important, testing, promotion policies, and the military justice system were reformed to help eliminate systemic or personal racism. Their war is over, but the legacy of African Americans endures and can be seen in the ongoing transformation of the American military.

References and Further Reading

Ambrose, Ray. "Our Men in Vietnam," *Sepia,* February 1968.

Anderson, Lionel. "Playback on Army Life," *The Black Panther,* September 20, 1969.

Carper, Steven, Roman Martinez, and Quinton Johnson. Interview by Stephen Maxner. October 2. Oral History Project Interviews, Item OH0113A. Texas Tech University, October 2, 1999. http://www.virtual

archive.vietnam.ttu.edu/starweb/virtual/vva/servlet.starweb (accessed November 26, 2008).

Dalglish, Garven. "Black and Back From Vietnam," *Cincinnati Enquirer Magazine*, July 19, 1970.

Daly, James, and Lee Bergman. *Black Prisoner of War: A Conscientious Objector's Vietnam Memoir*. Lawrence: University Press of Kansas, 2000.

Department of Defense. *Task Force on the Administration of Military Justice*. Vols. I–V. Washington, DC: U.S. Government Printing Office, 1972.

Department of Defense. *U.S. Casualties in Southeast Asia*. Washington, DC: U.S. Government Printing Office, 1985.

Foner, Jack. *Blacks and the Military in American History*. New York: Praeger, 1974.

French, Albert. Interview with author. June 27, 2007.

Grove, Gene. "The Army and the Negro." *New York Times Magazine*, July 24, 1966.

Hughes, Dennis. Interview with author. June 27, 2007.

Johnson, Thomas. "The U.S. Negro in Vietnam." *New York Times*, April 29, 1968.

Jones, Donnel. "Racism in Vietnam." Letters to the Editor. *Sepia*, August 1968.

Llorens, David. "Why Negroes Re-enlist." *Ebony*, August, 1968.

McMichael, William. "A War on Two Fronts." *Newport News-Hampton, Virginia Daily Press*, Williamsburg Edition, July 27, 1998.

Murray, Paul. "Blacks and the Draft: A History of Institutional Racism." *Journal of Black Studies* 2 (September 1971): 57–76.

NAACP. *The Search for Military Justice*. New York: NAACP Special Contributions Fund, 1971.

Powell, Colin, with Joseph Persico. *My American Journey*. New York: Random House, 1995.

Smith, Wayne. Interview with author. August 11, 2007.

Sulzberger, C. L. "Foreign Affairs: The Spin-Out." *New York Times*, May 21, 1969.

Terry, Wallace. "Bringing the War Home," *Black Scholar* 2 (November 1970): 6–18.

Vietnam Veterans Memorial Fund Forum, America's Defense Monitor, Center for Defense Information. 1992. "Race Relations in the Vietnam War." http://www.cdi.org/adm/Transcripts/552/ (accessed November 26, 2008).

Waggoner, Lawrence. "Our Men in Vietnam," *Sepia*, March 1968.

"Labor's Falling Dominoes": The AFL-CIO and the Vietnam War Era

10

Edmund F. Wehrle

W e never had it so good," American Federation of Labor (AFL) president George Meany boastfully proclaimed to American workers as he prepared to assume the presidency of a new, united labor movement with the merger of the AFL and the Congress of Industrial Organizations (CIO) in 1955. A decade later, as the nation entered the Vietnam War era, American workers, especially union members, arguably had it even better. By the mid-1960s jobs were plentiful, wages were rising, pro-labor Democrats controlled both the White House and Congress, and organized labor considered itself a vital component of a liberal coalition, supporting prosperity at home and defending freedom abroad. From the start, however, disquieting signs of trouble accompanied the good times—signs that quickly evolved into a maelstrom of setbacks. By 1975, the American labor movement found itself increasingly without allies and struggling for relevancy. A changing economy and race-related issues clearly contributed to the striking decline of organized labor, but at the causal center sat the divisive and politically costly Vietnam War.

Without question Meany, a gruff cigar-chomping former plumber turned union chieftain who presided over the AFL-CIO until 1979, was correct to tout gains made by American workers in the post–World War II era. The bitter, often violent struggles of the 1930s were distant memories by the 1960s. Blue-collar workers in ever larger numbers entered the ranks of the middle class, enjoying rising wages, pensions, and health and disability insurance. Trade unions, once decidedly outside the corridors of power, now enjoyed inside access. Presidents, members of Congress, and other leading figures routinely consulted with labor leaders, and the labor movement could flex powerful political muscle. Meany, himself—while often appearing a caricature of a stodgy labor boss—was actually a leader of this new generation of activist, politically astute union leaders. "[Y]ou must be political, you must be engaged in political activities," he urged, "because you won't get anywhere in the legislative activity unless you are able to influence to some

George Meany became president of the American Federation of Labor (AFL) in 1954 and then unified the labor movement by merging with the Congress of Industrial Organizations (CIO) in 1955. He was president of the AFL-CIO until 1979. (*Library of Congress*)

degree the composition of the State Legislature and the national congress" (Robinson 1981, 91).

Even in the arena of foreign policy, labor made its influence felt. Mainstream American labor leaders believed strong, independent trade unions were essential to protecting human progress—especially from the threat of communism. Driven by this intense anticommunism, after World War II both the CIO and the AFL became deeply involved in international affairs. In the late 1940s, as the Cold War heated up, both the AFL and the CIO sent agents to Western Europe to support anticommunist trade unions and work alongside U.S. government officials administering such programs as the Marshall Plan. The activist anticommunism of the AFL-CIO fit well the times, during which few dissented from conventional Cold War wisdom.

As the immediate situation in Europe stabilized, U.S. labor set its sights on building up anticommunist labor unions in the Third World. As its influence grew, the AFL-CIO operated increasingly in partnership with key government agencies, such as the State Department, the Agency for International Development—and even the Central Intelligence Agency (CIA). To some, the federation risked sacrificing its independence by working so closely with the government, but Meany dismissed such concerns in the face of the communist threat.

As early as 1950, U.S. labor leaders made contact with a group of trade unionists in Vietnam trying to create a middle way between colonialism and communism, a group that would later take the name of the Vietnamese Confederation of Labor (CVT). Many of its members—including its leader, Tran Quoc Buu, an ardent nationalist who served a lengthy jail term for anticolonial activity—were formerly allied with Vietnamese communists in their battle against the French. Communists, these budding labor organizers came to believe, were too violent and reliant on outside forces. Instead, the CVT sought to create an independent movement representing the nationalist ambitions of the Vietnamese people. Ironically, however, they needed outside help—especially American—to pursue these goals.

Relations between the budding CVT and the AFL-CIO quickly grew stronger, and American labor pressed the U.S. government to aid the struggling organization, which, after the creation of South Vietnam in 1954, found itself caught between the insurgent communists and an authoritarian Saigon government. As one CVT official complained, the organization was "pinched between a river and a mountain" (Trinh Quang Quy 1970, 118). AFL-CIO aid to the CVT kept the fragile labor federation afloat during these difficult times and convinced many American labor officials that a path to democracy might be found for struggling South Vietnam.

As its power and influence grew, however, American organized labor did have critics, although they remained decidedly in the minority. Some disparaged the AFL-CIO's reflexive anticommunism, which seemed to leave little room for thoughtful distinctions between communists and nationalists (such as in the case of Vietnam) and often signaled a tolerance for less than democratic anticommunist regimes (such as the Republic of Vietnam). At home, detractors complained that organized labor had grown soft, becoming a junior partner in a system dominated by government and business. Labor leaders, one prominent critic charged, had become "new men of power," bureaucratic sellouts, no longer representing the true interests of workers (Mills 1948). Critics pointed to the falling percentage of workers belonging to labor unions—down to just over 25 percent of American workers by the mid-1960s from a postwar high of 35 percent in 1954. Yet others condemned unions as bastions of whiteness, more concerned with excluding outsiders, especially African Americans, than pursuing justice in the workplace. In 1965, Herbert Hill, labor director of the National Association for the Advancement of Colored People (NAACP), launched a scathing attack on American unions, especially the International Ladies' Garment Workers, for practicing discrimination (Jonas 2005).

Meany and other key labor leaders remained steadfast supporters of the civil rights movement and insisted that trade unions slowly but surely were addressing discrimination in their ranks. They pointed to growth in public sector unions and labor's continuing political clout to offset charges they lacked the drive of previous generations of labor militants. Their foreign policy initiatives, they insisted, operated independently of the American government. This was the case even when the AFL-CIO accepted public money for federation programs, such as the American Institute for Free Labor Development (AIFLD), which trained anticommunist Latin American trade unionists. Such work aimed at creating strong, independent unions worldwide, free of undue influence from government (as was the threat in communist countries) or employers (the threat in capitalist countries).

Deeply committed to both its international and domestic agenda, AFL-CIO leaders placed great hope in the presidency of Lyndon Baines Johnson. Johnson, who was deeply aware of his humble East Texas roots, often felt out of place among the sophisticated, Ivy League educated, inside circle surrounding President Kennedy. When he assumed the presidency, he actively cultivated labor leaders, with whom he believed he shared common values and common sense. He also dedicated his administration to an activism not seen since the New Deal. In his first meeting as president with the AFL-CIO Executive Council, LBJ impressed the gathering by vowing to create 75 million new jobs (U.S. Dept. of Labor 1963). He aggressively pushed forward many of the programs long on labor's wish list, including Medicare, Medicaid, civil rights provisions, and a series of programs designed to address persistent poverty. Johnson also proved a stalwart supporter of the AFL-CIO's foreign policy agenda. The new president arranged generous government subsidies for AIFLD and the AFL-CIO's African Labor College, which was launched in 1964. Johnson also appeared eager to support a similar initiative in Southeast Asia—which became the Asian American Free Labor Institute (AAFLI) in 1968.

As the president moved toward full-scale intervention in Vietnam, the AFL-CIO urged Johnson to consider the CVT's potential contribution to nation building in South Vietnam. Federation leaders even arranged a one-on-one Oval Office meeting between Johnson and CVT president Tran Quoc Buu. Seizing the opportunity, the diminutive Buu told the president towering above him that the "missing link in the present Vietnamese chain of events" was a free labor movement capable of addressing the "daily hardships" suffered by Vietnamese workers "and creating an almost para-military type of civilian organization to . . . transform the indifferent and neutral mass of people into an active barrier against the communists." Impressed, Johnson assured his guest that he saw the war as much in social terms as he did militarily (Memorandum for President 1964).

Given the growing bond between president and labor movement, Johnson could count union leaders among his strongest supporters on both domestic and foreign issues. When the president committed U.S. troops to Vietnam in 1965, the AFL-CIO immediately extended its "unstinting support" (*Proceedings* 1965, 562). Meany and other anticommunist labor leaders hoped that combining the American military presence with the growing democratic influence of a free labor movement might establish a model for successfully challenging communist incursions in the Third World. Meanwhile, labor union leaders also anticipated that Johnson's aggressive social programs, combined with full-employment spending at home, would build an ever stronger economy protected by safety nets for those unable to compete.

Challenges to Labor Solidarity

Feeling a strong allegiance to the president, Meany decided to turn the AFL-CIO's biannual convention scheduled for December 1965 in San Francisco into a virtual rally for LBJ's Vietnam policies, which already were controversial in some sectors. Meany lined up an impressive array of speakers, including the president, vice president, and secretary of state. He also invited a large delegation of South Vietnamese trade unionists to the convention and an array of other international visitors. A special breakfast session for all foreign visitors focused entirely on the Southeast Asian crisis. Johnson, insisting the American mission in Southeast Asia was "the pursuit of freedom," spoke to the convention via telephone. Vice President Hubert Humphrey and Office of Economic Opportunity chief Sargent Shriver both personally addressed the crowd and vigorously defended the war.

Everything was going according to plan until Secretary of State Dean Rusk took the podium. Student protesters, having quietly infiltrated the convention gallery, suddenly exploded with boos and catcalls as the secretary rose to speak. Provoked, delegates on the floor responded with "a thunderous reception" for Rusk. After the speech, demonstrators and delegates turned on each other. Verbal volleys of "labor fakers" and "get out of Vietnam" cascaded from the gallery. From below flew rejoinders of "get a haircut" and "go back to Russia." United Auto Workers' (UAW) president Walter Reuther's voice joined the chorus. "You are demonstrating in the wrong place. Why don't you tell Hanoi and Peking," he shouted. A burly protester assaulted Rusk as the secretary of state tried to exit the arena. Incensed as he watched chaos threaten his carefully scripted affair, Meany seized the podium and bellowed, "Will the sergeant-at-arms clear those kookies out of the gallery" (*New York Times* 1965). With that the protesters were removed.

Although Meany and his circle might dismiss the protesters as naive, youthful hooligans, soon they could not deny the peace movement's growing presence in their ranks. Although no major unions took overtly antiwar positions during the first several years of the war, signs of dissension could not be ignored. In February 1966, the Executive Council of the Amalgamated Clothing Workers of America (ACWA) officially questioned the "burden of expense," complaining "the sons of workers . . . are being drafted first for military duty" (Statement on Vietnam 1966). A few smaller unions followed the ACWA's lead. In New York City, Hospital Workers Local 1199, led by radical Leon Davis, quickly joined the peace movement and helped establish the Labor Committee for Peace in Vietnam, along with members of the leather and machine workers, the meatcutters' union, and the Actors Equity and Screen Actors Guild.

Even among the rank and file there was discernable anxiety. Although the leadership of the Communications Workers of America (CWA) supported the hawkish AFL-CIO position, an internal poll commissioned by the union in the summer of 1966 showed 56 percent of respondents favoring withdrawal or negotiations in Vietnam, while only 40 percent supported the status quo or escalation. The pollsters concluded, "an excellent Administration record in domestic affairs is completely overridden by what is happening in Southeast Asia" (Wehrle 2005, 118). At roughly the same time, Johnson's secretary of labor Willard Wirtz attended the annual conventions of four other major unions. "It is clear in a dozen ways," Wirtz reported back to LBJ, "that the one thing on everybody's mind is Vietnam, and that the general reaction of these unions and their leaders is pretty critical" (Lichtenstein 1995, 404).

Meany and his circle found themselves ill-equipped to understand the nascent antiwar movement in their ranks. A key AFL-CIO staffer believed the growing protests to be part of a plot: "[t]he drive in the unions against the AFL-CIO position is being stepped up by the Commies throughout the country. They are putting plenty of money into this drive," he warned Meany (Wehrle 2005, 112).

Likewise, not all was going well in Vietnam, where the AFL-CIO aspired to mold the CVT into a vehicle for reform in a country whose government more resembled a military dictatorship than a vigorous democracy. Federation officials hoped to parlay their strong relationship with Johnson into greater aid for the CVT and funding for an AFL-CIO-run organization to promote free trade unions in Asia. As American trade unionists moved to formalize a relationship between South Vietnam and American labor, however, the CVT drew back, making it abundantly clear that it preferred indirect aid to a formal mentoring relationship. South Vietnamese labor leaders feared being too closely tied to—and appearing beholden to—Americans, a lethal impression in a country struggling with a painful colonial past. The fact that some American trade union advisers sent to Vietnam appeared dictatorial and dismissive of Asian customs reinforced these worries. CVT leaders, although dependent on Americans, wished to convey a public face of autonomy and independent activism. "In Vietnam, one who takes another's money is considered a kept man," a CVT official warned an American trade unionist urging closer relations between the two movements (Wehrle 2005, 112).

Still, the CVT obviously needed help. When a new military government came to power in 1965 and attempted to revive old codes prohibiting large meetings, including union meetings, an AFL-CIO representative successfully intervened directly with Saigon officials on behalf of the CVT. Yet the anxieties of South Vietnamese trade unionists could not be fully overcome, and in some ways mirrored the often tense relationship between Americans and their South Vietnam allies, who both needed and resented each other.

Alongside Vietnam, other nagging concerns ate away at both union leaders and members during this era. As the economy heated up, driven largely by government spending, prices began to rise. "It is now an established fact that inflation is spreading across the U.S. economy at the fastest rate in years" reported *Time* magazine in the fall of 1966 (*Time* 1966, 69). Even in the pro-labor Johnson White House, economic advisers urged that labor limit demands for wage increases to keep inflation under control. Race also increasingly emerged as a thorny problem. For instance, in 1967, the construction of a new Macy's department store and accompanying mall in downtown New Rochelle, New York, should have been the occasion for much celebration. Roughly $25 million, mostly subsidized by the government, would be pumped into the project, promising high-paying jobs for workers and urban renewal for the city. As the building began, however, protesters appeared along the chain link fence setting off the work site. Demonstrators threw themselves against trucks entering and leaving the project, determined to shut work down. The protesters, who included clergy and leaders from the local African American community, demanded that white-only construction trade unions open their ranks to African Americans.

Troubling as they were, before 1968, racial tensions, economic problems, and growing opposition to the Vietnam War could all be dismissed as temporary bumps in the road. Employment everywhere was rising to record levels. It was "one of those rare periods when individual workers held the upper hand as employers competed for a limited pool of skilled labor," recalled a Boston construction worker (Linder 1999, 17). Meanwhile, Lyndon Johnson, with his deep sympathies for the American labor movement, remained in the White House. Labor leaders such as Meany, despite all nagging problems, thought they could look forward to a brighter future—both at home and abroad.

Such hopes did not survive the tumultuous upheavals of 1968—one of the most traumatic years in American history. For the AFL-CIO, signs of the storm on the horizon were obvious by late 1967. On Veterans Day, November 11, 1967, several hundred antiwar trade unionists gathered in Chicago for a one-day conference to voice their protests and plan joint action. Speakers included Dr. Martin Luther King Jr. and Sen. Eugene McCarthy. Victor Reuther, the brother of UAW president Walter Reuther, used the occasion to rail against the AFL-CIO's cooperation with the CIA and blast what he termed "fascist corporate unions" sponsored worldwide by the federation (Gannon 1967).

Although relatively few trade unionists attended the gathering, it angered Meany. The following month, at the AFL-CIO convention, he assailed the meeting as "planned in Hanoi by a special assembly that went there." Meany's outburst actually came on the heels of a motion by antiwar trade unionists calling upon the AFL-CIO to drop its support for the war in favor of neutrality. Boos and catcalls immediately greeted the motion, which quickly went down in defeat, but it provided ample evidence of growing chasms within organized labor (*Proceeding* 1967).

Meanwhile, trouble was brewing in Vietnam, where the CVT found itself engaged in a labor struggle against the Saigon government. The confrontation began with the announcement that the French owners of the major electricity-producing plant in Saigon would sell their operations to the South Vietnamese government, a sale underwritten by the Agency for International Development. Unionized workers at the plant demanded a 12 percent pay increase. When Saigon authorities demurred, workers walked off their jobs in December 1967. The strike was a dicey proposition in a country at war, headed by military leaders with strong authoritarian bents. Government officials loudly complained that the work stoppage, which risked plunging the country's major city into darkness, represented a threat to national security. When sympathy strikes broke out the government decided to act. General Nguyen Ngoc Loan, the head of the national police, ordered his forces to arrest key union leaders, round up striking workers at gunpoint, and force them back to work. CVT president Tran Quoc Buu could only watch helplessly. As angry workers returned to their jobs, the best the confederation could do was drape a banner across its headquarters reading: "Release Our Jailed Leaders Immediately" (Wehrle 2005, 129).

Also feeling hopeless was the AFL-CIO, which watched as the peace movement in America pointed to the crushed strike as yet more evidence of the undemocratic, corrupt nature of the U.S. ally in Vietnam. Understanding by this time that the CVT would resent any public intervention by its U.S. allies, especially at a time when it appeared to be acting independently, the AFL-CIO remained silent. Instead, it pressed State Department officials to mediate behind the scenes to release the jailed leaders and settle the strike. U.S. ambassador Ellsworth Bunker met personally with South Vietnamese president Nguyen Van Thieu to urge resolution of the strike. The AFL-CIO, the ambassador reminded Thieu, had been a consistent supporter and "it was important to keep it that way." With Tet, the Vietnamese New Year holiday, fast approaching, all parties agreed to compromise, bringing an end to the immediate crisis. Hopeful that order had been restored, Bunker optimistically cabled home: "(t)here is time for healing to occur before, during and after the festive days that mark Tet" (Wehrle 2005, 130).

The holiday at the end of January proved anything but "festive." Vietcong soldiers used the Tet cease-fire and chaos surrounding the labor strikes as cover to infiltrate South Vietnamese cities. On the night of January 30, 1968, insurgents launched attacks on every major city in the country, often targeting CVT officials and members in the process. By the end, the homes of more than 1,000 trade unionists lay in ruins. In the midst of the battle, the entire world glimpsed the brutality of police chief Loan when he summarily executed a suspected terrorist in front of cameramen.

As a series of counterattacks pushed the Vietcong out of the cities, it slowly became apparent that the insurgents, although having inflicted heavy damage, had themselves suffered heavy losses and fallen well short of their goals. Still, nerves remained raw. In the aftermath of the immediate attacks, seeking to stifle any instability, General Loan detained one of the recently released CVT leaders and a CVT vice president. Articles about the arrests appeared in the *New York Times, Washington Post,* and elsewhere. Again the antiwar movement harnessed the stories to discredit the Saigon government, and again the AFL-CIO moved behind the scenes to quell the crisis. Eventually, the federation dispatched its most experienced overseas agent, Irving Brown, to Vietnam to lobby for the release of the labor leaders. Brown met personally with President Thieu, whom he pressured "hard but politely" (Wehrle 2005, 133). Finally, more than six weeks after the initial Tet attacks, the labor leaders were released.

Through the jolt of the Tet Offensive and the president's near-defeat in the New Hampshire primary, mainstream trade unionists nevertheless stuck loyally beside the president—even as liberals jumped ship in droves. Then suddenly, at the end of March 1968, Johnson withdrew from the race, sending shock waves through the labor movement. "I don't know how long it will take me to recover from the atomic bomb which President Johnson hurled," wrote one AFL-CIO staffer to Meany (Wehrle 2005, 136).

Bridling at the antiwar candidacies of Sen. Eugene McCarthy and Sen. Robert F. Kennedy, Meany scrambled for an alternative. He urged Vice President Hubert Humphrey to enter the race—even personally walking the two blocks between AFL-CIO headquarters and Humphrey's office to urge the vice president to run. Humphrey agreed to enter the race, but chaos ensued with the assassinations of Martin Luther King Jr. in April and Robert

Kennedy in June. Then came the violence at the Democratic National Convention in Chicago. In many ways the highly publicized clashes between Chicago's police and peace protesters revealed as much about culture and class divides as about politics. Urban working-class white police had little sympathy with college-educated, middle-class demonstrators, who in turn saw the police as shock troops for an authoritarian state. The Chicago convention portended many such subsequent violent, culturally laden clashes.

Many within the AFL-CIO found at least some solace that Humphrey, even as he limped out of the Chicago convention, would be the Democratic Party's nominee. But the vice president, who loyally supported Johnson's Vietnam policy despite some personal misgivings, had few enthusiastic followers other than those in organized labor. As Humphrey struggled to gain his footing, the AFL-CIO faced another problem in the renegade independent candidacy of Alabama governor George Wallace. The governor's brazen attacks on the civil rights movement resonated with many blue-collar workers, angry as exclusively white trade unions became the focus of protests. Wallace, although a southerner from a right-to-work state, knew well how to the play to the cultural resentments of urban white workers. He lambasted the emerging counterculture and decried the crime and chaos that seemed to accompany cultural and social changes, especially in cities. Wallace's selection of an ultra-hawk, Gen. Curtis LeMay, as his running mate also played to those, including many trade unionists, who thought the United States needed to take a stronger—not weaker—stance in Vietnam. Late in the campaign, surveys showed Wallace significantly eating into support for the Democratic

Vice President Hubert Humphrey applauds at a Labor Day parade. On the left is Louis Stulberg, president of the International Ladies' Garment Workers Union, with George Meany, president of the AFL-CIO, on the right. The 1968 parade took place in New York City. (*Bettman/Corbis*)

nominee, taking 25 percent of the labor vote in Pennsylvania, 32 percent in Connecticut, and close to 50 percent in Maryland.

To counter Wallace's appeal to union members, Meany and the AFL-CIO unleashed a massive public relations drive. The Steelworkers' Union sent anti-Wallace letters to 1.2 million steelworkers, and the AFL-CIO distributed thousands of pamphlets detailing Wallace's antilabor record in Alabama. Meanwhile, the federation poured an unprecedented $60 million into Humphrey's campaign (White 1969). Although Humphrey mounted an impressive last-minute comeback, in the end it was not enough. He lost by under a percentage point of the popular vote.

Labor Divided

Labor's *annus horribilis,* however, was hardly over. The Vietnam War continued to put internal pressures on the AFL-CIO. Since the merger that created the federation in 1955, UAW president Walter Reuther, although also an

Walter Reuther

Few cases better illustrate the toll of the Vietnam War on liberals and the American labor movement than that of Walter Reuther. The dynamic leader of the UAW from 1946 until his death in 1970, Reuther profoundly shaped and influenced the course of postwar American liberalism. He helped fashion tremendous material gains for American workers, championed the civil rights movement, and provided a thoughtful voice in support of the Cold War. But the divisive war in Vietnam proved a painful challenge for Reuther—forcing him to fundamentally reevaluate his approach to politics and social change.

Born in 1907, Reuther and his two brothers were drawn into the world of left-wing politics by their father, a dedicated socialist. The Reuther brothers traveled to the Soviet Union in the early 1930s to view firsthand what they believed to be a great socialist experiment but returned disillusioned enough to become lifelong anticommunists.

At home, Walter threw himself into the CIO's battle to unionize America's autoworkers—at one point suffering a vicious beating at the hands of Ford Motor Company's security officers. In 1946, he became president of the UAW and quickly set about removing communists from the union. At the same time, he became an ardent backer of the Democratic Party, pressing party officials to support the emerging civil rights movement and address the needs of the nation's underclasses. As the economy flourished in the late 1940s and 1950s, Reuther negotiated breakthrough contracts with automakers, providing workers with pensions and health insurance for the first time. Concurrently, Reuther became an ardent cold warrior. His brother and close ally, Victor, became the CIO's representative in Western Europe, where he mobilized against communists in the European labor movement—sometimes with funds provided by the CIA.

In 1952, Walter Reuther became president of the CIO, which merged with the AFL in 1955 to become the AFL-CIO (Walter became vice president of the new organization). By the 1960s, Reuther was a major, mainstream political player with a close relationship with President Lyndon Johnson. As the Vietnam War dragged

AFL-CIO vice president, had complained loudly that federation leaders were too tepid in their support of civil rights and other progressive issues and too reluctant to devote resources to aggressive organizing campaigns. Although an anticommunist himself, Reuther also complained that Meany and his circle were too uncompromising in their anticommunism. The UAW chief pressed the AFL-CIO to meet with trade unionists from communist bloc countries, something Meany, who saw such unions as pawns of communist states, adamantly rejected. Although an early supporter of the war, by 1968 Reuther had grown wary. "I am not sure it isn't as important to win the war at home than it is to win the war in Vietnam," he told journalists at one point (*New York Times* 1968).

Dismayed over the AFL-CIO's hawkish position on Vietnam and increasingly convinced that Meany would never adopt the new strategies necessary to revive the labor movement, Reuther pulled his union, representing more than a million workers, out of the AFL-CIO. He quickly found himself alone and bitterly disappointed as other unions failed to follow his lead. Instead, Reuther turned to the Teamsters, a renegade union representing independent

on, however, he feared it detracted from needed reform at home. "I am not sure it isn't as important to win the war at home than it is to win the war in Vietnam," he told a reporter in 1968 (Wehrle 2005, 138). Likewise, as young people across the country mobilized around political causes, Reuther dreamed of molding them into a larger coalition to press for social and economic change.

Still, Reuther felt compelled to support President Johnson's bid for reelection in 1968, despite his misgivings about the war. When Johnson pulled out of the race in March, Reuther shifted his allegiance to Vice President Hubert Humphrey, another prowar liberal with a stellar record on civil rights and other reform issues. Despite Humphrey's credentials, young activists avoided his campaign because of his association with the unpopular war.

In many ways, Richard Nixon's narrow election set Reuther free. He pulled the UAW out of the AFL-CIO, which he saw as excessively wedded to the Vietnam War and resistant to needed change. To align the labor movement

with progressive causes, he enlisted the UAW in an unlikely alliance with the Teamsters to establish the Alliance for Labor Action. Reuther also grew more outspoken in his opposition to the war. When President Nixon invaded Cambodia in 1970, Reuther blasted the president's "repudiation of your oft-repeated pledge to bring this tragic war to an end" (Wehrle 2005, 158).

Whatever direction Reuther may have been heading, tragedy suddenly intervened. Only days after his attack against Nixon, Reuther and his wife died in an airplane crash in Michigan. With him died his hopes of leading a broad movement for social change, but such dreams may already have been victims of his early support for the Vietnam War. After World War II, Reuther cast his lot with mainstream liberalism. As such he aided the civil rights movement and advanced the cause of American workers. To young activists of the 1960s, however, Reuther, especially in his support for Johnson's war in Southeast Asia, had sold out—more representative of a failed past than a brighter future.

truckers and other workers. In the late 1950s, Meany had engineered the ouster of the Teamsters from the AFL-CIO on charges of rampant corruption. Despite the Teamsters' reputation for vice and conservativism, Reuther needed an ally, and the Teamsters were available; hence he proposed an alliance between the progressive UAW and the notorious Teamsters.

In the summer of 1968, Reuther and Teamster president Frank Fitzsimmons announced plans to form the American Labor Alliance (ALA). From the beginning it proved a troubled affair, although the ALA did manage to rally support for progressive initiatives that included an organizing drive in the South and an antidrug abuse campaign. Nevertheless, the Teamster-UAW marriage remained strained—especially when the issue of the war in Vietnam came up. In 1969, when representatives from both organizations gathered to plan activities for "Vietnam Moratorium Day," a national day of protest against the war, UAW staffers wore peace buttons while Teamsters sported American flag pins. Deep divisions quickly surfaced as they attempted to craft an antiwar resolution, assuaged only when UAW representatives appeased Teamster hawks by adding a denunciation of violence by antiwar demonstrators.

Frantic to halt the ALA, Meany threatened any AFL-CIO union joining the new organization with immediate disaffiliation. When the small Chemical Workers Union joined Reuther's alliance, the AFL-CIO quickly expelled the group. Reuther's sudden death in 1970 in an airplane crash essentially put an end to the ALA, but its formation in 1968, with the attendant threat of a return to the labor wars of the 1930s, reflected the extreme stresses on the labor movement by the late 1960s.

Beyond Reuther, an even greater threat loomed—that of Richard Nixon, the new president in 1969. Throughout his career Nixon had been no friend of labor, and the unprecedented amounts of money the AFL-CIO pumped into his opponent's coffers in the recent election could not have pleased the president-elect, known to be deeply resentful of his political opponents. Meany was particularly concerned with the fate of his overseas initiatives, including the recently created Asian American Free Labor Institute (AAFLI), which he hoped would help formalize the mentoring relationship between the CVT and U.S. labor. The federation's semiprivate international organizations received much of their funding from the U.S. government. Meany's top priority in his first meeting with the new president, on March 13, 1969, was shielding AAFLI and his other government-financed foreign aid programs.

Both Nixon's political ambitions and his odd psychology played into the AFL-CIO's hands. The president had studied George Wallace's success appealing to disgruntled blue-collar workers and well understood the growing tensions between labor and liberals. To help him win reelection, he hoped to cultivate urban workers as part of his planned "new majority," a political coalition that would include southern conservatives and political moderates (Cowie 2002). Also, somewhat like his predecessor, Nixon hailed from a working-class background, and he bitterly resented those he saw as the intellectual and cultural elite—the media, academia, and liberal power-brokers. Instead, he naturally gravitated toward labor leaders, whom he saw as patriotic, tough, blunt, and gutsy. He particularly admired Meany.

"[D]espite his da's, dem's, and do's," Nixon told a political adviser, Meany "would come in, would see a problem, would be willing to have the guts and courage to do what had to be done." By contrast, added the president, "there is not a college professor in the U.S. today whom I could rely upon to have the same perception" (Memorandum for the President's Files 1970).

Playing to Meany's interests, Nixon devoted two-thirds of his first meeting with the AFL-CIO president to a wide-ranging discussion of the state of the world. Meany "talked at length about the AFL-CIO program of training union leaders." Apparently impressed, Nixon "expressed interest and support for continuation of the [labor] program" (Schultz 1969). Predictably, the president's endorsement came with strings attached, but it was gratifying to the AFL-CIO.

During the first year of the Nixon administration, however, the White House enjoyed little success appealing to blue-collar workers. Meany remained standoffish, and Nixon's strategists seemed lost fashioning an appeal to union voters. In the spring of 1970, the Vietnam War suddenly delivered an unexpected shot in the arm to the blue-collar strategy. Hoping to destroy North Vietnamese and Vietcong bases in neutral Cambodia, Nixon ordered U.S. forces across the South Vietnamese/Cambodian border in April 1970. The president announced the invasion in forceful—almost belligerent—language that delighted Meany and other AFL-CIO leaders— and some construction workers, who launched a series of prowar rallies in New York City and elsewhere. Nixon's actions and words, however, provoked anger among peace activists. Demonstrations against the Cambodian incursion flared across the country, especially on college campuses. At Kent State University in Ohio, clashes between antiwar protesters and national guardsmen resulted in the tragic killings of four students.

Even as some trade unionists and union leaders openly embraced Nixon's war, others actively sought common cause with the peace movement. In a speech at his union's annual convention titled "A Time to Speak Out," AFL-CIO vice president and Amalgamated Clothing Workers of America president Jacob Potofsky blasted the Vietnam War as underlying "practically all our troubles" (Wehrle 2005, 158). Scheduled to speak later in the convention, Meany abruptly cancelled his appearance when he heard of Potofsky's address. Elsewhere, especially among the grassroots rank-and-file, antiwar sentiment swelled. The San Francisco Bay Area Labor Assembly for Peace smoothly integrated its activities with those of the mainstream and student peace movements. Michigan AFL-CIO federation president Gus Scholle passionately attacked the war and built an effective coalition of local antiwar unionists.

Increasingly, Meany's uncompromising hawkishness became a target for both antiwar trade unionists and peace-minded liberals. Referring to government funds allocated to support AFL-CIO overseas initiatives, Sen. William Fulbright of Arkansas, a prime critic of the war, wondered aloud with reporters present, "if this represented the price we paid for Mr. Meany's support in Vietnam." Infuriated, Meany demanded and received a hearing before the Senate's Foreign Relations Committee to refute the charges (*Newsweek* 1969, 29).

The situation was not progressing much better for the AFL-CIO in Vietnam. Just as some critics complained that the AFL-CIO had compromised itself by working with the Nixon administration, others grumbled that the CVT tainted itself by working with the often undemocratic rulers of South Vietnam. Hoping to rally the citizenry against the ever-growing threat of the North Vietnamese, Buu and other CVT leaders established an uneasy alliance with the mercurial President Nguyen Van Thieu, feeling they had little choice. In the face of North Vietnamese attacks in the spring of 1972, CVT officials acquiesced to a government ban on strikes, something the organization had always resolutely resisted in the past. "Now the situation—the danger—is different," explained CVT president Buu (Wehrle 2005, 181). Still, many, including some in the CVT, saw the no-strike pledge as a sorry capitulation.

The AFL-CIO had hoped the formation of AAFLI, a permanent AFL-CIO presence in Saigon, would be a valuable mediation tool between South Vietnamese authorities and the CVT, but such hopes never materialized. When AAFLI representatives arrived in Saigon, cultural divides again surfaced. Americans, CVT officials complained, were too dictatorial and ignorant of the unique features of Asian culture and habits. Buu's interpreter urged Americans dealing with the CVT president for the first time to just listen and say nothing. Sadly, the interpreter recalled, Americans rarely took his advice. At one point, relations between the CVT and AAFLI broke down entirely, and the AFL-CIO reluctantly scrambled to find acceptable replacement personnel.

By the early 1970s, even Meany often appeared eager to disengage from Vietnam. "Frankly, we don't think there is any disagreement about getting out—getting our people out of Southeast Asia," he told reporters in 1970, but he was "completely opposed to the idea of bugging out" before South Vietnam appeared securely able to defend itself (*AFL-CIO News* 1970). This adamant position put Meany and the AFL-CIO in an awkward position as the 1972 elections approached. Increasingly, U.S. organized labor, sparked by the AFL-CIO, took the lead in opposing Nixon's economic policies. This was especially true after the president's declaration of price and wage controls in 1971, which Meany saw as a threat to labor's prerogatives. Likewise, despite the White House's determined campaign to cultivate union voters, Nixonian labor policies often proved counterproductive. In 1969, the Nixon administration launched the so-called Philadelphia Plan, requiring some construction trade unions to set "goals and timetables" for incorporating African Americans into their membership. Such policies, even when full of loopholes and weakly enforced, enraged many of the hardhats defending the Vietnam War.

The AFL-CIO thus hoped an acceptable candidate for president might emerge on the Democratic side. Instead, Sen. George McGovern of South Dakota, unapologetically demanding immediate withdrawal from Vietnam, overwhelmed more moderate voices among Democrats in the 1972 primaries, easily winning his party's nomination. At the Democratic Party's nominating convention, trade unionists felt like unwelcome outsiders as young activists ran the show. Surveying the Miami Beach convention, Meany lamented its seizure by "people who looked like Jacks, acted like Jills, and had the odor of Johns about them" (*Economist* 1972).

Fearful that a sudden withdrawal from Vietnam would greatly advance international communism and spell the end of the CVT, the AFL-CIO balked at supporting McGovern. Voting 27 to 3, the AFL-CIO Executive Council abstained from issuing any endorsement in the 1972 election. President Nixon greeted the news enthusiastically as carrying the "potential of becoming one of the most important developments of the 1972 campaign" (Nixon 1978, 626). Officially, Meany maintained his neutrality, but behind the scenes, on at least one occasion, he met with White House officials and advised them on how to appeal to union voters. On Election Day, Nixon won the bulk of the blue-collar vote. Although Meany might take some comfort in McGovern's defeat, the deep divide between labor and the Democratic Party was now fully manifest.

The Paris Peace Accords of January 1973 ended direct American involvement in the Vietnam War and generated some hopes of healing the grand rifts caused by the war. As Vietnam receded somewhat from the forefront of the AFL-CIO's agenda, however, a severe economic crisis quickly took its place. By the fourth quarter of 1973, driven by OPEC's (Organization of the Petroleum Exporting Countries) oil embargo, inflation soared to nearly 10 percent and unemployment rose steadily. The impact of full-fledged stagflation rippled through the economy. Automobile sales fell precipitously and General Motors laid off or furloughed more than 100,000 workers that year. At the end of 1973, Meany could only lament, "these are hard times for Americans." Looking ahead to 1974, he forecast, "[w]e will most likely find prices going up, and unemployment going up. Going down will be the standard of living of American workers" (*AFL-CIO News* 1974). Meany proved prescient: in 1974, the economy slumped further as unemployment shot to over 7 percent and inflation rose above 12 percent. Having spent the previous decade heavily focused on international issues, especially the war in Vietnam, the AFL-CIO found itself ill prepared to face the challenges of hard times. Meanwhile, the unfolding Watergate scandal entangled President Nixon, forcing his eventual resignation in 1974.

By 1975, the Vietnam War moved rapidly toward its final act. Early that year the North Vietnamese, as they had in 1972, launched a full-scale conventional invasion of the South. This time no American firepower intervened to halt the advance. Reports quickly reached the AFL-CIO of invading forces taking particular vengeance on CVT officials and their families. Meany urged congressional support for President Gerald Ford's last-ditch initiatives to save South Vietnam. The AFL-CIO even flew Tran Quoc Buu from Saigon to lobby members of Congress for extended support. "Give us sufficient aid to survive. Do not let us die slowly, agonizingly," Buu pleaded (*Free Trade Union News* 1975). Meany added his voice, warning that "while the fighting might stop, the killing would not," implying that victorious North Vietnamese would seek revenge against any who aided the South Vietnamese cause (Wehrle 2005, 188).

Most Americans, however, had had enough of the painful war, and no substantial aid was forthcoming. As Saigon tottered in late April 1975,

AAFLI officials scrambled to evacuate CVT leaders and their families, many of whom boarded a barge and floated into the South China Sea. Over a crackling radio they listened to the announcement of the fall of Saigon and later heard many of their own names read as those wanted by authorities.

Unlike its South Vietnamese ally, the AFL-CIO would live to see another day. Still, the war in Vietnam had been costly, exhausting federation resources, dividing the labor movement, and driving a wedge between labor and liberals. With the fall of South Vietnam imminent, George Meany appeared on the Dick Cavett television show. Referring to his support for Johnson and Nixon on Vietnam, Meany confessed, "If I'd known then what I know now I don't think we would have backed them." Later, Meany qualified his comments somewhat. While maintaining that "the American people were not told the truth as to the actual conduct of the war, the prospects for Vietnamization, etc.," he nevertheless added, "my fundamental belief in the role of the United States as the chief defender of freedom has not changed one bit" (Wehrle 2005, 192). Meany and many of his fellow trade union leaders were indeed sincere in their commitments to halting what they saw as a pernicious threat to freedom, but they and the movement they helped build paid a high price for their extraordinary vigilance and activism.

References and Further Reading

AFL-CIO News. September 5, 1970.

AFL-CIO News. January 5, 1974.

Cowie, Jefferson. "Nixon's Class Struggle: Romancing the New Right Worker, 1969–1973." *Labor History* 43 (2002): 257–283.

The Economist. October 14, 1972.

Free Trade Union News. March-April 1975.

Gannon, James. "Wobble in Labor's Pro-Vietnam Stance," *Wall Street Journal,* November 9, 1967.

Jonas, Gilbert. "Herbert Hill and the ILGWU." *New Politics* 10 (Winter 2005): 118–123.

Lichtenstein, Nelson. *Most Dangerous Man in Detroit: Walter Reuther and the Fate of American Labor.* Urbana: University of Illinois Press, 1995.

Linder, Mark. *Wars of Attrition: Vietnam, the Business Roundtable, and the Decline of Construction Unions.* Iowa City, IA: Fanpihun Press, 1999.

"Memorandum for President." May 19, 1964, box 1340, Central Foreign Policy Files, Labor and Manpower, General Records of the Department of State, RG 59, NA.

"Memorandum for the President's Files." January 28, 1970, box 24, White House Special Files, Staff and Office Files, Charles Colson, Nixon Presidential Materials, NA.

Mills, C. Wright. *The New Men of Power: America's Labor Leaders.* New York: Harcourt, Brace, 1948.

New York Times. December 11, 1965.

New York Times. March 10, 1968.

Newsweek. August 18, 1969.

Nixon, Richard. *RN: The Memoirs of Richard Nixon.* New York: Simon and Schuster, 1978.

Proceedings of the Sixth Constitutional Convention of the AFL-CIO, San Francisco, CA, December 9–12, 1965.

Proceedings of the Seventh Constitutional Convention of the AFL-CIO, December 7–12, 1967.

Robinson, Archie. *George Meany and His Times.* New York: Simon and Schuster, 1981.

Schultz, George. "Memorandum for the Files, Re. Meeting of the President with George Meany and Secretary Shultz, March 13, 1969," box 16, Office of Secretary, George Shultz, General Records of the Department of Labor, RG 174, NA.

"Statement on Vietnam." ACWA Executive Board, February 18, 1966, box 181, ACWA Papers, The Kheel Center for Labor-Management Documentation & Archives (henceforth Kheel), Ithaca, NY.

Time. September 1, 1966.

Trinh Quang Quy. *Phong Trao Lao Don Vietnam.* Saigon: CVT Publication, 1970.

U.S. Department of Labor. *International Labor* (November-December1963), 9. Washington, DC: U.S. Government Printing Office.

Wehrle, Edmund F. *Between a River and a Mountain: The AFL-CIO and the Vietnam War.* Ann Arbor: University of Michigan Press, 2005.

White, Theodore. *Making of the President 1968.* New York: Atheneum, 1969.

Students and Political Activism | 11

Caroline Hoefferle

There comes a time when the operation of the machine becomes so odious, makes you so sick at heart, that you can't take part; you can't even passively take part, and you've got to put your bodies upon the gears and upon the wheels, upon the levers, upon all the apparatus and you've got to make it stop. And you've got to indicate to the people who run it, to the people who own it, that unless you're free, the machine will be prevented from working at all.

—Mario Savio, December 2, 1964 (Rorabaugh 1989, 30).

With these famous words, University of California student Mario Savio perfectly expressed the motivating sentiment of the student movement of the Vietnam War era. Frustrated and angered by events they perceived as a corruption of American ideals, both locally and globally, many students were moved to political action. Although popular memory and media attribute most student activism to opposing the draft and the Vietnam War, evidence shows that student rights issues—basic civil liberties such as free speech, free press, and personal liberty—as well as participation in university decision making, generated more student protests than any other topic. Almost alone among 1960s campus issues, student rights could build coalitions across all political persuasions. In addition to local concerns, campus activists contributed invaluable support to other reform movements of the era, including civil rights for racial minorities, ending the Vietnam War, women's rights, gay rights, and environmentalism.

To better understand why students were so politically active in this period, one must first understand the context of the university system in which they lived. At the beginning of the Vietnam War era, university students lived in largely apolitical communities, dominated by fraternities and sororities, and guarded by in loco parentis regulations. These college rules, known as "parietals," included dress codes, curfews, behavioral guidelines in and outside the classroom, and limitations on speakers and other forms

Jack Weinberg and Mario Savio, prominent figures in the Berkeley Free Speech Movement. (*Corbis/Bettmann-UPI*)

of entertainment allowed on campus. Female students found special rules for women particularly offensive. At most colleges, women could not wear shorts or jeans, were required to have written permission from their parents to travel outside the town, had earlier curfews than male students, and could not visit men's residences without chaperones. Many universities also required men to spend part of their undergraduate years in the Reserve Officers' Training Corps. Administrators defended their right to set parietals on the grounds that parents expected universities to take care of their children just as a parent would in their first years away from home. University of Michigan student Tom Hayden described his life in Ann Arbor in the early 1960s as a "barracks culture," with students crammed into sterile dorms attending large, impersonal lectures. He tried to liven up his life by exploring the fraternities, but "found them absorbed in mindless partying and status comparison" (Hayden 1988, 27). Students had disliked parietals since their creation in the 18th century, but resistance produced only sporadic protests and little change in university regulations. Because Americans under the age of 21 were considered minors, without full rights of citizenship, students had little power to change this situation. Student life remained tightly controlled and regulated throughout the early 1960s.

Restraints also came from outside the university. With the Cold War at its height in the 1950s, McCarthyism invaded the nation's educational system looking for radical professors and organizations. Bowing to political pressure, universities fired and blacklisted known and suspected communist educators, and required all employees—and sometimes students—to sign loyalty oaths pledging that they were not and never had been communists. To protect students from subversive un-American ideas, university administrators initiated new steps to prevent communists or communist sympathizers from speaking on campus. Occasionally, students and faculty spoke out against this political repression, but in the anticommunist culture of the era, they had little support and were easily isolated and contained.

The rapid post–World War II increase in the college population and resulting expansion of the American system of higher education offered both additional problems and new possibilities. The key to this growth was the maturation of the baby-boom generation, which began reaching college age in the early 1960s. Middle-class affluence in the 1950s and 1960s made college attendance more affordable than in previous generations. As a consequence, the proportion of high school seniors advancing to higher education rose from 18 percent in 1940 to 50 percent in 1970, and the overall number of college students rose from 3 million in 1960 to 10 million in 1973 (Anderson 1995). As the campus population exploded, some universities grew into large, impersonal institutions where students were lost in ever-larger classes and had less guidance from and connection to university faculty and administrators. Alienated and discontented students, raised with a faith in American justice and opportunity, sought to engage the world around them. Their massive numbers alone would give them influence.

The civil rights movement inspired students to take action, giving them a language and tactics with which to confront those in authority. When African Americans stood up to demand their civil rights in the 1950s, students from across the country were outraged as law enforcement officers brutalized nonviolent activists. In countless and crucial ways, students mobilized to support the civil rights movement by raising money, recruiting workers, and organizing campus civil rights actions.

Civil Rights

Independent student civil rights activism began in earnest in February 1960 in a famous sit-in at a segregated lunch counter in Greensboro, North Carolina. By the end of February, student sit-ins spread to segregated businesses across the country. Quietly, peacefully, and politely, they faced white managers, patrons, and police officers who bullied, beat, and arrested them. Within one year the effectiveness of nonviolent civil disobedience was evident: 70,000 people in 13 states held sit-ins to desegregate businesses in nearly 200 cities. By providing a role model for student activism and involving thousands of students in a moral crusade, the 1960 sit-in movement had a major impact on American college students (Anderson 1995).

Young activists founded the Student Nonviolent Coordinating Committee (SNCC) to coordinate this sit-in movement and continue its momentum by involving black and white students in other forms of civil rights activism.

SNCC's founding statement reveals its roots in Christianity and the importance of nonviolence, not only as a tactic but also as an ethic:

> Nonviolence as it grows from Judaic-Christian tradition seeks a social order of justice permeated by love. . . . Love is the central motif of nonviolence. . . . It matches the capacity of evil to inflict suffering with an even more enduring capacity to absorb evil . . . By appealing to conscience and standing on the moral nature of human existence, nonviolence nurtures the atmosphere in which reconciliation and justice become actual possibilities (Calvert 1991, 71).

This language of spiritualism, justice, morality, and love attracted many supporters who fervently believed in the civil rights cause. Inspired by the sit-in movement, members of the Student League for Industrial Democracy met in June 1960 to create a new multi-issue organization. Calling themselves Students for a Democratic Society (SDS), they coordinated their activities with a variety of other organizations on the Left. Between 1960 and 1964, SDS was heavily involved in the southern civil rights movement; most of its leadership joined SNCC and similar organizations in the South. This involvement had a profound impact on SDS leader Tom Hayden, who wrote of SNCC's voter registration project: "It is a good, pure struggle . . . a struggle we have every reason to begin in a revolutionary way across the country, in every place of discrimination that exists" (Hayden 1988, 55). Jane Adams, an SDS leader from Southern Illinois University, later described working in the civil rights movement as like being born again, "and it was that kind of a transformative, redemptive quality that the movement had that was extraordinarily powerful" (Lieberman 2004, 63). Another civil rights activist wrote that students participated in SNCC's voter

Students for a Democratic Society members protest the ROTC on a college campus during the Vietnam War. (*Library of Congress*)

Tom Hayden

Tom Hayden has been called the "single great-est figure of the 1960s student movement" (Berman 1988, A7). He was born in Detroit, in 1939, and as such was older than most of the student movement he helped to form. Hayden attended the University of Michigan in Ann Arbor in 1957, majoring in journalism. His class-work and involvement in the student newspa-per exposed him to the most politically exciting events of the time: the civil rights movement and the Cold War. Although he was inspired by and deeply concerned about the civil rights movement, he remained an observer until meeting Dr. Martin Luther King in 1960, who told him that "ultimately, you have to take a stand with your life" (Hayden 1988, 36). Soon after, he helped form a local student group con-cerned with reforming the university. Hayden became heavily involved in SDS between 1961 and 1964, becoming its president in 1962 and

helping to shape its principles and goals by coauthoring "the most widely read pamphlet of the Sixties generation," the Port Huron State-ment (Hayden 1988, 76). He was one of the most influential people of the 1960s New Left. From 1964 through 1968, he was a community organizer in Newark, New Jersey, as part of SDS's Economic Research and Action Project. As one of the leaders of the demonstrations at the Democratic National Convention of 1968, he was arrested and charged with conspiracy to incite violence as part of the Chicago Seven. After winning that legal battle in the early 1970s, he spoke out against nuclear escalation and animal cruelty. Hayden has run for numer-ous political offices in California and won elec-tion to the California State Assembly (1982–1992) and Senate (1992–2000). He continues to live in California and advocate progressive causes to this day.

registration drive "because we believed what we learned in the schools of this country—freedom and justice for all. . . . because we believe in this nation. . . . We are your children, living what *you* taught us as Truth" (Anderson 1995, 81). SNCC's language and mission appealed to both secu-lar and religious constituents, although the risks and commitment demands limited political activists to a small minority on campuses.

After a year of organizing and working on civil rights, Hayden and other members of SDS drafted a manifesto in June 1962 at Port Huron, Michigan. The resulting 63-page Port Huron Statement reveals the primacy of the civil rights issue in the early student movement, even echoing SNCC's language. It expresses many of the values that united left-wing student activists throughout the Vietnam War era: a belief in participatory democracy, faith in the power of community and nonviolent activism, and a critique of America's injustices, amoral capitalism, anticommunist repression, and mil-itarism. With this document, SDS self-consciously created an "agenda for a generation" and proclaimed itself leader of a "New Left," which would cre-ate a new politics in America.

Other student groups, including the National Student Association, Southern Students Organizing Committee, and hundreds of local groups, also supported the civil rights crusade through sit-ins, fund-raising, and petitioning local authorities to end segregation and discrimination in their own towns. National polls and student organizations indicate that civil rights was the single most important issue for student activists across the country in the early 1960s. Despite all of their activity, however, change proceeded at a slow pace and produced an incredible backlash from both predictable and unexpected sources. Southern students such as Gwendolyn Robinson, a student at all-black Spelman College in Atlanta when she first joined SNCC, often paid a high price for trying to educate and register black voters in Mississippi. Robinson was arrested, expelled, spit upon, beaten, and had her life threatened by angry whites, but she was also disowned by her family who thought she was being foolish and throwing away her career. In the North, civil rights activists who participated in nonviolent civil disobedience faced less severe consequences, but they confronted university administrators who expelled them, parents who disowned them, and other students who shunned them. The experiences of civil rights activists tested their commitment to the philosophy of nonviolence and their faith in America's ability to reform itself.

Some SNCC leaders, such as Stokely Carmichael, were attracted to the Black Power philosophy of Malcolm X, which advocated black separation for mutual support and using violence in self-defense. A SNCC veteran, Carmichael worked for the organization full-time after graduating from Howard University in 1964 and was elected national chairman in 1966. Although he had many white friends and allies in the movement, and he asked white students to continue to organize civil rights support among white Americans, he argued for separate all-black organizations, asserting, "We cannot have the oppressors telling the oppressed how to rid themselves of the oppressor" (Carson 1995, 217). Under this influence, blacks in the SNCC told whites to leave the organization, and several SNCC leaders also joined the Black Panther Party, the largest Black Power group in the country.

This move toward Black Power had an important impact on the student civil rights movement. Although favored by many younger blacks, Black Power pushed SNCC outside the civil rights mainstream. Carmichael's increasing militancy—the abandonment of integration and advocacy of violence—alienated some SNCC members and especially older black civil rights activists. Although many radical white leftists supported SNCC's Black Power emphasis, many also resented it. Feeling snubbed by blacks when they were excluded from their organizations, many white students dropped out of the fight against racial discrimination.

Nevertheless, the civil rights movement and President Lyndon Johnson's Great Society programs produced significant gains for African Americans. The proportion of black students grew from 3 percent of all college students in 1964 to nearly 9 percent in 1972. Still, when black students arrived on predominantly white college campuses they were expected to be grateful and to "emulate 'white' standards of social decorum" (Exum 1985, 17, 39). In the context of Black Power rhetoric, many perceived this as a reflection of white America's racism and hypocrisy. Many blacks responded by joining Black Student Unions (BSUs) to pressure their universities to eliminate institutional racism and address the needs of minorities. Reflecting the Black Power movement, BSUs emphasized black unity, pride, and community.

Although most BSUs worked peacefully against racism, one of the most famous and explosive instances of black student activism occurred at San

Francisco State College in 1968. The BSU there wanted a black studies program to provide relevant education for black activists, lower admission standards, and increased scholarships for black students to raise their numbers to equal their proportion of the San Francisco population. The administration agreed to address these concerns but could not immediately implement their demands. Black faculty to teach black studies courses were in short supply, as was scholarship funding for black students. Race relations, therefore, were already tense when a black faculty member sparked controversy in the autumn of 1968 by urging minority students to bring weapons to campus for defense. When college trustees demanded that he be fired, they set off a chain of events in which student protests provoked stern reactions from administrators, which in turn provoked increased student activism. A 134-day strike took place during the next school year, conducted by thousands of students, which attracted hundreds of police who occupied the campus and made 700 arrests. In the end, the administration met many of the BSU's original demands, but those arrested paid stiff fines and the administration fired more than 20 faculty members for supporting the strike (Exum 1985).

By 1970, student civil rights activism had resulted in the creation of minority and ethnic studies programs, special admissions policies for minority students, and the hiring of more minority faculty at many universities across the country. Student activism, however, did not wipe out racism in the wider society, end police brutality against black protesters, or even convince the majority of students to support programs to end racial discrimination. For example, only half of college freshmen in 1969 favored government intervention to desegregate schools (Bayer, Astin, and Boroch 1970). Like the wider public, many students were suspicious of government-enforced desegregation.

Cold War and Vietnam

Although civil rights dominated the early student movement, Cold War issues soon emerged as a leading cause of campus protest. After World War II, moderates in the Republican and Democratic parties had reached a consensus that communism represented the primary threat to the United States. This anticommunism led to McCarthyism at home and a Cold War with the Soviet Union and other communist nations. The Cold War manifested itself in a continuation of the draft, involvement in numerous political conflicts across the globe, and a nuclear arms race that threatened to destroy the world. Nuclear proliferation energized the political Left in the early 1960s. Groups such as the Student Peace Union were especially vocal during the Cuban Missile Crisis, when John F. Kennedy, Nikita Khrushchev, and Fidel Castro brought the world to the brink of nuclear war in October 1962. Students all over the world were horrified but divided over whom to blame. The Left protested the Kennedy administration for its hard-line anticommunism, and the Right blamed the Soviets and Castro in counterdemonstrations. When the crisis was over, students of all political persuasions were disillusioned with the Cold War consensus and eager to change the direction of the nation's politics.

In the early 1960s, conservative students organized around their concern over communist expansion. As Scott Stanley explained, "We'd gone through [World War II] believing that America was invulnerable. . . . Why was there no pax Americana? We knew something was wrong. . . . Our values had been betrayed. Our dreams were being destroyed" (Klatch 1999, 30). Disillusioned with politicians whom they saw as soft on communism, conservative students met in September 1960 in Sharon, Connecticut, to form a new university-based organization. That conference produced the Sharon Statement, which declared their support of libertarian and traditional conservative beliefs such as individual free will and liberty, free-market capitalism, suspicion of big government, and opposition to communism. Conference participants created the Young Americans for Freedom, which became the leading conservative activist organization on campuses in the Vietnam War era and would eventually influence the emerging New Right in the 1970s.

By the mid-1960s, the focus of the Cold War was in Vietnam. Framed by the U.S. government as a struggle to protect a democratic South Vietnam from the communist domination of North Vietnam, the conflict escalated in 1965 when the Johnson administration initiated a bombing campaign against North Vietnam and committed combat troops to South Vietnam. Right-wing students criticized the limitations imposed on the American military by liberal politicians. Left-wing students questioned the legitimacy of the war and its anticommunist premise. Others opposed the war from a moral perspective. Christian student groups, such as Newman clubs and YMCAs, were early hotbeds of antiwar activism. Concerns that Vietnam did not meet the "just war" criteria of their faith and religious injunctions to oppose injustice and murder motivated many young Christian antiwar activists.

Students on both sides of the political spectrum were especially troubled by the draft. Every 18-year-old man was required to register with the Selective Service System. Local draft boards decided whom to select for military service. Draftees, however, could request deferments for a number of reasons. Throughout the first half of the 1960s, most college students and those employed in defense or government industries could easily obtain draft deferments. As the United States committed more troops to Vietnam, however, draft deferments became more difficult to obtain and more young men faced possible induction.

SDS responded by creating the Peace Research and Education Project in the autumn of 1962 to stimulate discussion and research on the military draft, American imperialism, and foreign policy. Shortly after Johnson's escalation of the war in 1965, SDS sponsored its first large-scale antiwar demonstration in Washington, D.C. An unusually large turnout of more than 20,000 people caught the attention of the media, which publicized SDS as the leader of the student antiwar movement. This in turn led more students to join SDS because of its antiwar reputation. Beginning in 1965, branches of the Committee to End the War in Vietnam (CEWV) formed at hundreds of campuses as single-issue coalition organizations, joining SDS as the core of antiwar activity in the student movement.

One important tactic of the campus antiwar movement was the teach-in. University of Michigan faculty sponsored the first nationally publicized teach-in during the spring of 1965 as an educational protest against the war in Vietnam. The teach-in involved 3,000 people who listened to arguments for and against the war (Eynon 1993). University of Michigan students and faculty then organized a national Vietnam teach-in on May 15, 1965, which included leading authorities on Southeast Asian affairs and carried detailed information across the country through a television broadcast. The teach-in movement spread rapidly to universities all over the country. In the spring of 1965 alone, teach-ins took place at 120 campuses (Eynon 1993). The largest occurred at the University of California at Berkeley, where 12,000 people participated in a marathon 36-hour event sponsored by the Vietnam Day Committee (Menashe and Radosh 1967). Teach-ins were crucial in sparking more antiwar activity because they provided student activists with disturbing information in an exciting atmosphere, showed them inaccuracies in government and media reports, and emboldened them to criticize the government.

Although teach-ins appeared on many campuses in 1965, many colleges had no antiwar movement until the late 1960s. As late as 1967, only 35 percent of students wanted to reduce U.S. military involvement in Vietnam, whereas 49 percent favored escalation (Lipset 1971). One of the most important factors in turning American public opinion against the war was the communist Tet Offensive in January 1968. The Tet Offensive failed in its immediate goal of forcing a U.S. withdrawal from Vietnam, but it did convince many Americans that the United States was mired in a stalemate despite the Johnson administration's optimistic statements. In addition, changes in the draft laws that year threatened more college students with the draft, making it even more imperative to stop the war to avoid jeopardizing their lives for a war they did not support.

As a consequence, the student movement increasingly protested the draft, the war, and other issues related to American militarism. Although most antiwar activists were liberals or moderates, libertarian conservatives also joined antiwar demonstrations because they believed the draft was an infringement on personal liberty. In 1968, more than a third of colleges polled reported antiwar protests (Peterson 1968). For some students, such as Jane Adams, "The Vietnam War was the crucible" of the student movement and was the most important issue of all (Lieberman 2004, 66). Similar to civil rights activists, however, antiwar activists paid a heavy price for their dedication. Jeff Shero Nightbyrd, a national SDS leader who attended the University of Texas, explained that radical students like him, from rural and conservative areas of the country, embarrassed their families and were generally disowned for their antiwar activism. Washington State University CEWV member Bill Halstead wrote in 1965, "I have been called names, threatened with physical violence, and made uncomfortable by my friends and enemies alike. All because I am willing to stand up and be counted for my opposition to the war in Vietnam" (Halstead 1965, 4). Even students who were Vietnam veterans faced accusations of being communists and cowards when they joined the antiwar movement. When the war became widely unpopular after 1969, antiwar activists encountered less harassment from family and friends, but they still faced suppression from authorities.

Student Rights

Civil rights and antiwar activism often led students to question their place within the university system. As a University of Utah journalist noted, the civil rights movement "served to make them more sensitive of their own civil rights" (Anderson 1995, 100). Many came to see university regulations that prohibited political activity and limited free speech and free press as a clear parallel to restrictions placed on African Americans in the South. To change these rules, students imitated the civil rights movement's defense of constitutional rights and use of nonviolent direct action.

Free speech issues often galvanized student activism, and the most famous confrontation occurred at the University of California at Berkeley. In the 1950s, the regents of the University of California system had banned communist speakers as well as many forms of political speech and organization from their campuses. Students at several of the University of California's campuses petitioned for reforms for years without effect. At the Berkeley campus, however, students drew on their civil rights experience to mobilize one of the largest and most famous student protests of the era. When Berkeley administrators prohibited political activity at a popular recruiting ground on campus in the autumn of 1964, a group of students—including some veterans of civil rights work in the South—challenged the ban. Students viewed this as an unjust limitation of their civil rights and built a broad coalition to defend those rights, the Free Speech Movement. The conflict escalated as the semester progressed. The Free Speech Movement committee organized student rallies, marches, and sit-ins in which thousands demanded free speech on campus and more student participation in university government. The administration handed out citations and threatened students with expulsion while police made 773 arrests. Finally in December, after months of turmoil and negative national publicity, the university regents agreed to relax the rules on campus political activity along the lines laid down by the Free Speech Movement.

The Berkeley protests received national attention, and several of the key figures made frequent appearances on the lecture circuit. Student governments from across the United States and the world sent messages of support and solidarity to Berkeley students, and Berkeley's Free Speech Movement made students across the nation aware of limitations on their own rights and lack of power in the university. Over the next few years, hundreds of thousands of students tried to apply the lessons of the Berkeley protests to their own campuses.

Limitations on campus political activities and disciplinary actions against activists led increasingly to student demands for more influence within the university. In a 1969 poll, researchers found that only 11 percent of students believed the Vietnam War was the "biggest gripe" of the student movement, whereas 81 percent of all students wanted "more say in the running of the colleges they attend" ("Why Students Act" 1969, 34). Nearly 90 percent wanted "a major role in specifying the curriculum" (Bayer, Astin, and Boroch 1970, 18). For this reason, student rights activism emerged on all types of campuses—liberal and conservative, small and large, North and South—and it typically involved more students than any other issue. The fight for student rights unified campus activists, many of whom saw increased power within the university as a first step toward broader social reforms. The slogan "student power" captured this idea and became the rallying cry for hundreds of demonstrations in the late 1960s and early 1970s.

Related to the demand for student power in the universities was the demand for civil rights within the wider society, including the right to vote. Throughout the 1960s, the voting age in most states was 21. Activists had long argued that it was unjust to treat people under 21 as adults in the criminal courts and draft them to fight in the military and yet deny them the right to vote. Young demonstrators asserted that they resorted to direct action because they could not voice their dissent through electoral methods, and many adults agreed that voting rights might help reduce public protests among the young. The states finally ratified the 26th Amendment lowering the voting age for national elections to 18 in July 1970. Although it is difficult to measure the effect of the 26th Amendment on student activism and the wider society, it did give students more power to change the country through direct participation in the democratic process.

The student rights movement, together with the lower voting age, made parietal regulations seem outdated. In six major court cases between 1967 and 1970, the courts supported a university's right to make its own regulations but found that the in loco parentis doctrine was invalid and irrelevant. Most colleges did away with curfews, dress codes, and other restrictions. Curriculum became more responsive to student interests and concerns, and students sat on a variety of committees, participating in at least a low level of decision making at most universities. Of all the different branches of the student movement, the expansion of student rights was arguably the most successful.

This success, however, came at a high price. The police, Federal Bureau of Investigation (FBI), politicians, and college administrators typically resisted student demands. Many authorities believed student activists were communist sympathizers or dupes, and their dissent was not only un-American but also illegal. In March 1965, FBI director J. Edgar Hoover testified before a House Committee that communists had orchestrated the antiwar protests, though he provided no evidence to substantiate this claim. That April, the FBI began extensive harassment of politically active students. In October 1968, that program developed into "New Left COINTELPRO," which put hundreds of students under illegal surveillance and effectively disrupted their protests. By 1969, the FBI had 42 of its 59 field offices and thousands of special agents actively engaged in operations against the New Left. They harassed student activists with repeated interviews, mailed anonymous letters to black and white student leaders to spread rumors and criticisms that might turn them against each other, sent information on students' political activities to prospective employers to blacklist the activists, and impersonated students and alumni in letters to administrators and boards of regents to pressure them into resisting activists' demands for reform. Some FBI informants even led student demonstrations, provoked violence between police and students, and were arrested. These operations abused American civil liberties and broke FBI and government regulations limiting domestic surveillance. Although they caused serious problems for dissenters, they also further radicalized some students.

Most student activists in the Vietnam War era had high hopes that they would help change the system in a positive way, but repression and the lack of rapid change led many to reevaluate their movement in a new light. SDS member Sue Jhirad explained, "You might think you were doing this fairly innocuous antiwar work, but I was visited by the FBI. People were harassed. You began to see there was something going on, as far as the state goes. . . . People's awareness of things just evolved" (Klatch 1999, 115). The overreaction of the FBI and other authorities made the entire system seem unjust, undemocratic, and incapable of change or reform. This awareness opened the doors to revolutionary ideologies.

The year 1968 was a turning point in the radicalization of the student movement. Mark Rudd exemplified the experiences of many left-wing extremists. He had been an antiwar activist at Columbia University and a member of SDS since his freshman year in 1965. Over time, he became increasingly involved in the theoretical discussions of the national SDS. Along with other SDS leaders, Rudd traveled to Cuba in January 1968 and, inspired by the legacy of revolutionary hero Che Guevara, decided to devote his life to fighting American imperialism and fomenting revolution in the United States. That spring, he returned to Columbia and led the SDS in a highly publicized and powerful protest against the university's affiliation with military research and its plans to replace an African American housing project with a sports facility. Rudd and other like-minded extremists made inflammatory speeches, threatened authorities, and encouraged students to protect themselves with weapons and physically attack symbols of American repression and imperialism. In the summer of 1968, he and other SDS radicals urged students to go to Chicago during the Democratic National Convention for militant demonstrations against the government and the war. Although relatively few responded to this call, television coverage of the convention included pictures of young protesters fighting with police officers and contributed to a more negative image of the student movement, which ultimately undermined its effectiveness.

In an atmosphere of FBI harassment, escalating war in Vietnam, growing violence against protesters, clashes at the Democratic National Convention, and race riots in cities across the country, SDS leadership became increasingly radical and isolated from the rest of the student movement during 1968 and 1969. Some SDS members accepted the rhetoric of the Black Power movement. Others adopted Maoism and other forms of Marxism, attempting to lead the student movement toward revolution. At the 1968 SDS convention, a well-organized Maoist Progressive Labor faction gained support from the majority of the SDS delegates. The Progressive Labor faction asserted that students should seek to build an alliance with workers, who were the key to revolution in America. The SDS leadership, however, was still controlled by a group calling itself the Revolutionary Youth Movement (RYM). RYM asserted that American workers were too conservative to lead a revolution and that radical blacks, students, and other oppressed peoples should unite to lead a people's revolution. SDS fragmented into two competing branches, one in Boston led by the Progressive Labor faction and the other in Chicago led by RYM. At the end of 1969, SDS fractured even further, when a small group within RYM broke off to form Weatherman groups, which went underground to foment revolution through symbolic violence, such as bombings and vandalism. Over the next few years, they set off hundreds of bombs in Selective Service offices, government facilities, and military establishments across the country in an attempt to terrorize the government and society into ending what they saw as global imperialism. Weatherman Bill Ayers later explained this shift toward violence:

> Two thousand people a day were being murdered in Vietnam in a terrorist war, an official terrorist war. . . . This was what was going on in our names. So we tried to resist it, tried to fight it. Built a huge mass movement, built a huge organization, and still the war went on and escalated. And every day we didn't stop the war, two thousand people would be killed. I don't think what we did was extreme. . . . We didn't cross lines that were completely unacceptable. I don't think so. We destroyed property in a fairly restrained level, given what we were up against (Dohrn and Ayers 2004).

The divisions within SDS and the violent rhetoric of its national leaderships, however, alienated many American students, and SDS's presence on campuses declined rapidly after 1970.

The most tragic incidents of the student movement were the killings of four students at Kent State University in Ohio and two students at Jackson State in Mississippi in 1970. It began on April 30, 1970, when President Richard Nixon announced that U.S. troops had crossed into Cambodia to destroy North Vietnamese supply bases to speed the pace of the peace process. Many saw this as a betrayal of Nixon's promise not to enlarge the war, and massive protests occurred across the country. Like students at 16 percent of the nation's campuses, activists at Kent State University held several rallies to protest the expansion of the war. After a late-night riot outside the bars in downtown Kent and an antiwar rally in which the Kent State ROTC building was burned to the ground, the governor of Ohio took a stand for "law and order" against the culprits. He declared a state of emergency, imposed curfews, banned all outdoor demonstrations, and gave the National Guard complete control over law enforcement on the Kent State campus. A contingent of guardsmen was posted around campus and moved quickly to break up any large gatherings. On Monday May 4, a noon rally drew thousands of people to the center of campus. Some attended to protest the war, but many more came to protest the presence of the guardsmen, and several hundred were merely curious observers. After a warning to disperse, the guardsmen advanced with bayonets and loaded rifles. Students responded with cursing and angry taunts, and some threw rocks. Suddenly, without warning or an order to shoot, 28 guardsmen fired into the

A Kent State University student lies on the ground after National Guardsmen fired into a crowd of demonstrators on May 4, 1970, in Kent, Ohio. Four students were killed and nine were wounded when the Guard opened fire during a campus protest against the Vietnam War. (*AP/Wide World Photos*)

crowd, killing four and injuring nine, most of whom stood more than 100 yards away from the guards and were completely uninvolved in the confrontation. The Kent State Massacre was an extreme example of authorities overreacting to student activism and led to some of the largest protests of the era.

The Kent State incident added fuel to the fires of rage on the nation's campuses. An estimated 4,350,000 students at 1,300 universities and colleges—44 percent of the nation's total—protested the war in Southeast Asia and the murder of their fellow students, closing many universities in the process (Heineman 1992). The editor of the UCLA student newspaper explained this outpouring of activism:

> They were there because they were angry and frustrated. They were angry and frustrated with a President who promises peace and widens the war. . . . with a society which responds to thrown bottles and rocks . . . with 40 rounds of rifle fire into a crowd. They were angry because every day America seems to become more callous, more ruthless, and they were frustrated because there is nothing they can do about it. Consequently, they lashed out at the most available target in the society—the University. . . . America is strong

enough and has become cruel enough to be capable of smashing all dissent within its borders (*Daily Bruin* 1970, 4).

Student letters and publications from May 1970 repeatedly mention this sense of anger, frustration, and ominous confrontation.

A pattern of escalation similar to that at Kent State occurred at numerous state universities across the nation that May. Students protested the Cambodian invasion and Kent State, administrators sent in campus police to arrest and disperse protesters, students protested the presence of police, and state officials sent in National Guardsmen to protect the campuses. Injuries and property damage occurred frequently, but only at Jackson State College, an all-black college in Mississippi, did unrest result in more student deaths. After two nights of students and local youths setting small fires and throwing objects at cars and people at the edge of campus, members of the National Guard, highway patrol, and city police unexpectedly fired 150 rounds of buckshot and birdshot into a women's dormitory where a small number of protesters had gathered (President's Commission 1970). This attack, provoked by the sound of a shattering glass bottle thrown toward the police (some officers later claimed they had seen a sniper), killed two students and wounded at least twelve. The governor and other officials immediately blamed the students for this incident and began criminal proceedings against them. The killings at Kent State and Jackson State enjoyed public approval, and American students' disillusionment with the establishment reached its zenith in that deadly spring of 1970.

Campus protest continued at a fever pitch through 1972. In the 1970–1971 academic year, 45 percent of American colleges experienced significant demonstrations (Sale 1973). Some universities faced their largest antiwar demonstrations in the spring of 1972 in reaction to the renewed bombing of North Vietnam. At the University of Minnesota, for example, antiwar activism exploded that spring. When 500 students disrupted a speech by Nixon cabinet member George Romney, police attacked students with mace and nightsticks and arrested 17. The next day, 2,000 students rallied at the Air Force recruiting center to protest the arrests and the war machine. When they moved to break into the campus armory, the university administration called the Minneapolis police tactical squad. Violence between the police and students escalated for several hours until Minneapolis mayor Charles Stenvig called in the National Guard. After much negotiation, the confrontation finally ended after an anticlimactic but peaceful antiwar march of 10,000 from the university to the State Capitol on May 13 (Jacobsen 1982).

After 1972, the student movement changed dramatically. With both the American combat role in Vietnam and the draft ending in 1973, antiwar protests gradually disappeared. Significant expansion of student rights had been won by the mid-1970s. Civil rights activism remained on many campuses but attracted smaller numbers. Student interests splintered, encompassing environmentalism, United Farm Workers' boycotts, Chicano and American Indian rights, women's rights, and gay rights. With newly won student representation in the university structure and the national voting age lowered to 18, it was easier for student activists to work within the system rather than by direct action. By 1975, the student movement of the 1960s ceased to exist.

The consequences of the student movement were felt long after it ended. Students won considerable campus reforms that gave them a voice in university decision making and greater personal freedom than before. Universities began to treat students as adults rather than children. This new independence allowed countercultural behaviors and styles to sweep campuses in the late 1960s and 1970s. The student movement stimulated new curriculum in many disciplines as well as interdisciplinary programs in peace, women's, and racial and ethnic studies at many universities across the country. Student dissidents contributed to ending the Vietnam War and the military draft and helped women and minorities win important victories against sexism and racism. These victories, however, came at a high cost to student activists. Many suffered strained personal relationships with family and friends, had careers disrupted, acquired criminal records, and even suffered injuries and deaths. The student movement was a powerful and sometimes violent and tragic chapter in the history of the Vietnam War era, but it contributed to some of the most important reforms in the nation's history.

References and Further Reading

Anderson, Terry. *The Movement and the Sixties: Protest in America from Greensboro to Wounded Knee.* New York: Oxford University Press, 1995.

Bayer, Alan, Alexander Astin, and Robert Boroch. *Social Issues and Protest Activity: Recent Student Trends.* Washington, DC: American Council on Education, February 1970.

Berman, Paul. "1960s." *New York Times Book Review,* June 12, 1988: A7.

Calvert, Gregory Nevala. *Democracy from the Heart: Spiritual Values, Decentralism, and Democratic Idealism in the Movement of the 1960s.* Eugene, OR: Communitas, 1991.

Carson, Clayborne. *In Struggle: SNCC and the Black Awakening of the 1960s.* Cambridge, MA: Harvard University Press, 1995.

Daily Bruin. Editorial. May 6, 1970, p. 4.

Dohrn, Bernardine, and Bill Ayers. Exclusive Interview related to the film "the Weather Underground." *Independent Lens* (2004) http://www.pbs.org/independentlens/weatherunderground/interview.html (accessed November 26, 2008).

Exum, William. *Paradoxes of Protest: Black Student Activism in a White University.* Philadelphia: Temple University Press, 1985.

Eynon, Bret. "Community, Democracy, and the Reconstruction of Political Life: The Civil Rights Influence on New Left Political Culture in Ann Arbor, Michigan, 1958–1966." Ph.D. diss., New York University, 1993.

Halstead, Bill. "Campus Protester Relates Uncomfortable Experiences." *Daily Evergreen,* December 10, 1965, 4.

Hayden, Tom. *Reunion: A Memoir.* New York: Random House, 1988.

Heineman, Kenneth J. "'Look Out Kid, You're Gonna Get Hit!': Kent State and the Vietnam Antiwar Movement." In *Give Peace a Chance: Exploring the Vietnam Antiwar Movement,* edited by Melvin Small and William Hoover, 201–222. Syracuse, NY: Syracuse University Press, 1992.

Jacobsen, David. "Strike, Occupy, March: Antiwar Protest on the University of Minnesota Campus, May 1970 to May 1972." Major Paper to University of Minnesota History Department, Spring 1982, University of Minnesota Archives.

Klatch, Rebecca. *A Generation Divided: The New Left, the New Right, and the 1960s.* Berkeley: University of California Press, 1999.

Lieberman, Robbie. *Prairie Power: Voices of the 1960s Midwestern Student Protest.* Columbia: University of Missouri Press, 2004.

Lipset, Seymour Martin. *Rebellion in the University.* Chicago: University of Chicago Press, 1971.

Menashe, Louis, and Ronald Radosh, eds. *Teach-Ins USA: Reports, Opinions, Documents.* New York: Praeger, 1967.

Peterson, Richard. *The Scope of Organized Student Protest in 1967–1968.* Princeton, NJ: Educational Testing Service, 1968.

President's Commission on Campus Unrest. *The Report of the President's Commission on Campus Unrest.* New York: Arno, 1970.

Rorabaugh, W. J. *Berkeley At War.* New York: Oxford University Press, 1989.

Sale, Kirkpatrick. *Win Magazine* article reprinted in John Kober, "The Myth of Student Apathy," in "The Congress and You: 26th National Student Congress of the US National Student Association." Madison: USSA Archives, State Historical Society of Wisconsin Archives, August 1973.

"Why Students Act That Way—A Gallup Study." *US News and World Report,* June 2, 1969, 34.

Primary Documents

Port Huron Statement

At its June 1962 national convention in Port Huron, Michigan, Students for a Democratic Society (SDS) crafted this defining manifesto. The Port Huron Statement expressed disillusionment with the gap between American ideals and practices, and was especially concerned with civil rights, poverty, and the Cold War threat to peace. The SDS advocated participatory democracy, the concept that people should actively participate in making the political decisions that affect their lives. University of Michigan student Tom Hayden was the document's primary author.

Introduction: Agenda for a Generation

We are people of this generation, bred in at least modest comfort, housed now in universities, looking uncomfortably to the world we inherit.

When we were kids the United States was the wealthiest and strongest country in the world; the only one with the atom bomb, the least scarred by modern war, an initiator of the United Nations that we thought would distribute Western influence throughout the world. Freedom and equality for each individual, government of, by, and for the people—these American values we found good, principles by which we could live as men. Many of us began maturing in complacency.

As we grew, however, our comfort was penetrated by events too troubling to dismiss. First, the permeating and victimizing fact of human degradation, symbolized by the Southern struggle against racial bigotry, compelled most of us from silence to activism. Second, the enclosing fact of the Cold War, symbolized by the presence of the Bomb, brought awareness that we ourselves, and our friends, and millions of abstract "others" we knew more directly because of our common peril, might die at any time. We might deliberately ignore, or avoid, or fail to feel all other human problems, but not these two, for these were too immediate and crushing in their impact, too challenging in the demand that we as individuals take the responsibility for encounter and resolution.

While these and other problems either directly oppressed us or rankled our consciences and became our own subjective concerns, we began to see complicated and disturbing paradoxes in our surrounding America. The declaration "all men are created equal . . ." rang hollow before the facts of Negro life in the South and the big cities of the North. The proclaimed peaceful intentions of the United States contradicted its economic and military investments in the Cold War status quo. . . .

Not only did tarnish appear on our image of American virtue, not only did disillusion occur when the hypocrisy of American ideals was discovered, but we began to sense that what we had originally seen as the American Golden Age was actually the decline of an era. The worldwide outbreak of revolution against colonialism and imperialism, the entrenchment of totalitarian states, the menace of war, overpopulation, international disorder, supertechnology—these trends were testing the tenacity of our own commitment to democracy and freedom and our abilities to visualize their application to a world in upheaval.

Our work is guided by the sense that we may be the last generation in the experiment with living. But we are a minority—the vast majority of our people regard the temporary equilibriums of our society and world as eternally functional parts. In this is perhaps the outstanding paradox: we ourselves are imbued with urgency, yet the message of our society is that there is no viable alternative to the present. . . .

We regard men as infinitely precious and possessed of unfulfilled capacities for reason, freedom, and love. . . .

Men have unrealized potential for self-cultivation, self-direction, self-understanding, and creativity. It is this potential that we regard as crucial and to which we appeal, not to the human potentiality for violence, unreason, and submission to authority. The goal of man and society should be human independence: a concern not with image of popularity but with finding a meaning in life that is personally authentic; a quality of mind not compulsively driven by a sense of powerlessness, nor one which unthinkingly adopts status values, nor one which represses all threats to its habits, but one which has full, spontaneous access to present and past experiences, one which easily unites the fragmented parts of personal history, one which openly faces problems which are troubling and unresolved; one with an intuitive awareness of possibilities, an active sense of curiosity, an ability and willingness to learn. . . .

We would replace power rooted in possession, privilege, or circumstance by power and uniqueness rooted in love, reflectiveness, reason, and creativity. As a social system we seek the establishment of a democracy of individual participation, governed by two central aims: that the individual share in those social decisions determining the quality and direction of his life; that society be organized to encourage independence in men and provide the media for their common participation. . . .

To turn these possibilities into realities will involve national efforts at university reform by an alliance of students and faculty. They must wrest control of the educational process from the administrative bureaucracy. They must make fraternal and functional contact with allies in labor, civil rights, and other liberal forces outside the campus. They must import major public issues into the curriculum—research and teaching on problems of war and peace is an outstanding example. They must make debate and controversy, not dull pedantic cant, the common style for educational life. They must consciously build a base for their assault upon the loci of power.

As students for a democratic society, we are committed to stimulating this kind of social movement, this kind of vision and program in campus and community across the country. If we appear to seek the unattainable, as it has been said, then let it be known that we do so to avoid the unimaginable.

This text, made available by the Sixties Project, is copyright © 1993 by the Author or by Viet Nam Generation, Inc., all rights reserved. This text may be used, printed, and archived in accordance with the Fair Use provisions of U.S. Copyright law. This text may not be archived, printed, or redistributed in any form for a fee, without the consent of the copyright holder.

Students for a Democratic Society. The Port Huron Statement. *New York: Students for a Democratic Society,* 1964.

Wesley Fishel Advises the United States to Fight in Asia

Wesley R. Fishel was a professor of political science at Michigan State University who became an important adviser to South Vietnamese president Ngo Dinh Diem. Fishel headed the Michigan State University Advisory Group, which advised the Saigon government on civil and political issues, from 1956 to 1958. He continued to be an influential supporter of Diem's government until 1962 and, after Diem's death in 1963, remained a strong advocate of America's anticommunist activities in Southeast Asia as chairman of American Friends of Vietnam. This 1964 letter explains his position.

When the United States first involved itself in the Indochina struggle, its objective seemed clear and honest: to save Viet-Nam from being overrun by Communist imperialism. After the 1954 Geneva Conference, the United States accepted responsibility for leadership in the defense of Southeast Asia. But the reluctance of our military men to become bogged down in small local wars in this most inhospitable of natural regions, plus the gutless character of the Southeast Asia Treaty Organization, which was our creature, rendered our defense commitment almost meaningless. . . .

Current American policy has been to hold onto the area, escalating as necessary to emphasize our determination. There is little question but that we can continue in this fashion almost indefinitely, or at least until we weary of a bloody game that never ends. This is hardly "policy," however, for it is a plan without real purpose, stubbornness that is reactive and without vision or aim. . . .

Today, the issue of Viet-Nam is no longer an isolated one. It has been linked by the events and policy errors of the past ten years to the issues of Laos and Cambodia. The loss of Laos would not mean the immediate and inevitable loss of South Viet-Nam, but the cost of maintaining Vietnamese independence with a hostile Laos and a quavering Cambodia on its frontiers would rise so sharply as to alter drastically the character of our involvement and the nature of the war being fought.

At the same time, a decision by the United States not to contest any further the Communist assertion of paramountcy in Indochina would mean a shift of alignments on the part of Thailand and Burma initially, and, unless alternative non-Communist leadership developed in India or Pakistan, one would have to anticipate a gradual drawing away from the United States there as well. By the same token, one may similarly project serious consequences for the new Malaysian Federation if Indonesia's Sukarno infers that a United States withdrawal from the mainland gives him a green light for his expansionist plans. . . .

Given the perils on the path of neutralization and withdrawal, there really is no choice left but to stay and fight, in Laos as in Viet-Nam. But is our objective then to roll back the Pathet Lao and the Viet Cong, to end their "privileged sanctuary" in the North, to throw down the gauntlet to the Chinese Communists?

Clearly this would be a war that could not be won by airpower alone, notwithstanding impulsive, addleheaded threats to atomize the jungles and rice paddies. This would be a war for control of the land, involving hundreds of thousands of American troops and billions of dollars annually. . . .

What is required, then, is escalation within South Viet-Nam and those parts of Laos that are still tenable, to build a citadel of freedom for people whom we have pledged to protect. Holding the valley of the Mekong River from Laos's western border roughly till it intersects with Route No. 9, which runs near the 17th Parallel from Savannakhet in Laos, through Tchepone and across Viet-Nam to the sea, would appear to be a feasible and logical aim. Let us then seal off this frontier in the manner of West Berlin, draw the line tight and hold it like a trip-wire.

Certainly this would not be an easy task. On the basis of current expenditures in Laos and Viet-Nam, we would have to look forward to using as many as 100,000 American soldiers, spending as much as $2 billion a year and working doggedly at the job for as long as ten years. But a program of this nature would not bring us into contact with China's frontiers nor would it involve sending American troops on offensive operations into Communist territory.

It would mean a decision to stand at the side of our friends in Asia regardless of the cost. Until we decide that our desire for a chain of free non-communist nations in Southeast Asia is greater than our fear that a firm stand in that area may bring us into war with Communist China, our actions will continue to be dictated by indecision and vacillation.

Wesley R. Fishel, ed. Vietnam: Anatomy of a Conflict. *Itasca, IL: F. E. Peacock Publishers, 1968: 694–700. This originally appeared in the* Washington Post, *June 14, 1964.*

George Ball Proposes a Compromise

George Ball was undersecretary of state in the Lyndon Johnson administration. He became the president's most outspoken in-house opponent of the United States' growing commitment to South Vietnam. In this July 1, 1965, memorandum to President Johnson, Ball warned about the potential costs of American military escalation.

The South Vietnamese are losing the war to the Viet Cong. No one can assure you that we can beat the Viet Cong or even force them to the conference table on our terms, no matter how many hundred thousand *white, foreign* (US) troops we deploy. . . .

The Question to Decide: Should we limit our liabilities in South Vietnam and try to find a way out with minimal long-term costs?

The alternative—no matter what we may wish it to be—is almost certainly a protracted war involving an open-ended commitment of US forces, mounting US casualties, no assurance of a satisfactory solution, and a serious danger of escalation at the end of the road.

Need for a Decision Now: So long as our forces are restricted to advising and assisting the South Vietnamese, the struggle will remain a civil war between Asian peoples. Once we deploy substantial numbers of troops in combat it will become a war between the US and a large part of the population of South Vietnam, organized and directed from North Vietnam and backed by the resources of both Moscow and Peiping.

The decision you face now, therefore, is crucial. Once large numbers of US troops are committed to direct combat, they will begin to take heavy casualties in a war they are ill-equipped to fight in a non-cooperative if not downright hostile countryside.

Once we suffer large casualties, we will have started a well-nigh irreversible process. Our involvement will be so great that we cannot—without national humiliation—stop short of achieving our complete objectives. *Of the two possibilities I think humiliation would be more likely than the achievement of our objective —even after we have paid terrible costs.*

. . . In my judgment, if we act before we commit substantial U.S. troops to combat in South Vietnam we can, by accepting some short-term costs, avoid what may well be a long-term catastrophe. . . .

George Ball memorandum to Lyndon Johnson, July 1, 1965. Foreign Relations of the United States, 1964–1968. *Vol. 3. Washington, DC: U.S. Government Printing Office, 1996: 106–109.*

AFL-CIO Vietnam Resolution

The American Federation of Labor and Congress of Industrial Organizations (AFL-CIO), which joined together in 1955, is the largest federation of labor unions in the United States. Although differences of opinion over the war in Vietnam existed within organized labor, union leadership and workers generally supported U.S. government policy. This 1965 resolution reflects the prevailing sentiment at the beginning of the American military commitment.

The nature of the war in Viet Nam becomes clearer from day to day. The Communists are waging a war of conquest, a war for the annexation of South Viet Nam by Ho Chi Minh's regime. This war is not an isolated or local conflict. It is an integral phase of the Communist drive for dominating the world.

With Hanoi openly pouring in more and more of its regular troops, the conflict increasingly resembles the war in Korea. The American people backed President Truman's decision to defeat the Communist onslaught in Korea, because they knew that the loss of South Korea would be the beginning of the loss of all of Asia. Today, the American people realize that a defeat in South Viet Nam would open the door to Communist control of Southeast Asia and the rest of the continent. If Asia and all of its hundreds of millions of people were to come under Communist domination, the survival of our own country would be gravely endangered.

In this realization, the American people fully support President Johnson's policy in Viet Nam. Our convention pledges unstinting support by the AFL-CIO of all measures the Administration might deem necessary to halt Communist aggression and secure a just and lasting peace. The moment the Communists cease and desist from their drives to seize control of South Viet Nam by military force and are willing to sit down at the conference table, the war will be ended.

The hypocrisy of the Communist government's peace propaganda is underlined by their continuous rejection of the many peace overtures made during the last year by the United States, her Western allies, the United Nations and non-aligned countries. President Johnson and Secretary of State Rusk have time and again asserted America's readiness to enter unconditionally into negotiations for halting the war in Viet Nam. The AFL-CIO Executive Council and President George Meany have repeatedly affirmed American labor's support of these persistent efforts by the Administration to hasten the end of military operations in Viet Nam and to speed the inauguration of a vast program of social and economic reconstruction in the entire Indo-Chinese peninsula. The convention heartily concurs in this policy of seeking peace in Viet Nam through negotiations and promoting the well-being of the people.

The Communist enemy can never be defeated by military means alone. Along with adequate military measures, there must be sound large-scale programs for improving the conditions of life and labor and for developing democratic institutions. But even the best programs without people are useless. In this connection, the unions of the workers and peasants can play a decisive role. The convention, therefore, reiterates the AFL-CIO plea for appropriate and adequate assistance to the Viet Nam Confederation of Workers (CVT) which has emerged as an invaluable force for democratic regeneration and social justice in the land.

It is not only the American workers who have a great stake in strengthening the CVT as a force for freedom, peace and human well-being in Viet Nam. Freedom-loving workers everywhere have the same stake that we have in this crucial struggle. We appeal to the ICFTU and the International Federation of Christian Trade Unions to join in a common effort for the support of the CVT so that it can play an ever more effective part in promoting democracy and human well-being and preserving peace for the entire Vietnamese people.

American Federation of Labor and Congress of Industrial Organizations. Proceedings of the AFL-CIO 6th Constitutional Convention. *Vol. I. San Francisco, California, December 9–15, 1965, 560–561.*

The Religious Community and the War in Vietnam

Clergy and Laymen Concerned About Vietnam (CALCAV) was the nation's largest religiously based antiwar organization. CALCAV's ecumenical membership was drawn primarily from Protestant, Catholic, and Jewish traditions and generally aligned with liberal to moderate political views. The group used a variety of creative measures to convey its message and added an important mainstream voice to the larger antiwar movement. This 1967 statement explains the CALCAV motives for dissent.

A time comes when silence is betrayal. That time has come for us in relation to Vietnam. As members of American churches and synagogues, we voice not only our own convictions, but seek also to articulate the unexpressed fears and longings of millions of Americans. . . .

Our allegiance to our nation is held under a higher allegiance to the God who is sovereign over all nations. . . . Each day we find allegiance to our nation's policy more difficult to reconcile with allegiance to our God.

Both the exercise of faith and the expression of the democratic privilege oblige us to make our voices heard. For while we speak as members of religious communities, we also speak as American citizens. Responsible expression of disagreement and dissent is the lifeblood of democracy, and we speak out of a loyalty that refuses to condone in silence a national policy that is leading our world toward disaster.

. . . .

No one planned the type of war in which we are involved. It has slowly escalated from one small move to the next small move, each presumed to be the last that would be necessary, so that now we find our nation able to offer only military answers to political and human questions. We sympathize with the dilemmas that face our President and Congressmen in dealing with a situation all decent men abhor. But a recognition of past mistakes does not entitle us to repeat and compound those mistakes by continuing them on an ever-widening scale.

We are unable to support our nation's policy of military escalation, and we find those to whom we minister caught as we are in confusion and anguish because of it.

1. This anguish is based first of all on *the immorality of the warfare in Vietnam.* We add our voice to those who protest a war in which civilian casualties are greater than military; in which whole populations are deported against their will; in which the widespread use of napalm and other explosives is killing and maiming women, children, and the aged; in which the combatants are systematically destroying the crops and production capacity of a country they profess to liberate; in which the torturing of prisoners by both sides has been a commonplace. . . .

2. Even those of us who recognize that sometimes evil must be done lest greater evil prevail, feel a sense of anguish in *the inconsistency between our stated aims and the consequences they produce.*

Our ongoing escalation, far from bringing the war closer to an end, serves rather to increase its duration and intensity.

Our bombing of the north, far from bringing our enemies to their knees, serves rather to strengthen their will to resist us.

Our military presence in Vietnam, far from stemming the tide of communism, serves rather to unite more firmly those communist societies which might otherwise develop separate destinies.

Our widening military involvement, far from demonstrating to the world our firmness and resolve, serves rather to make the world suspicious of us and fearful of our use of power.

Our unilateral action in Vietnam, far from strengthening our influence among other nations, serves rather to jeopardize new alliances we might be creating.

At home, we find the war threatening the very goals we claim to be defending in Vietnam. Programs to help members of minority groups realize their own human dignity are jeopardized if not destroyed. A spurious type of patriotism is challenging the right of dissent and the open debate of public issues. Financial and psychological preoccupation with the war is destroying creative plans to alleviate poverty, overcome disease, extend education, replace city slums and exalt human dignity. We grieve over lost opportunities that may never be reclaimed. . . .

3. Our anguish is deepened by *the discrepancy between what we are told by our government and what we discover is actually taking place.*

We are told that the other side gives no indication of desire to negotiate, and we then discover that such indications have been given, but that we have responded either with rebuff or military escalation.

We are told that our nation is prepared to negotiate with all concerned, and we then discover that certain of the combatants will not be welcome at the conference table.

We are told that certain cities have not been bombed, and we then discover that they have been.

We are told that civilian targets have been avoided, and we then discover that they have not been.

Such actions not only play into the hands of those who distrust us, since they can consistently discount our word, but the continuous discovery of discrepancies between our nation's word and deed has already shaken the confidence of our own people in the word of their government. We fear both the immediate and long-range consequences for our nation of this increasing deterioration of trust.

This, then, is our ongoing anguish: a crisis of conscience concerning what we do know, and a crisis of confusion concerning what we do not know. . . .

Statement adopted by the Executive Committee of Clergy and Laymen Concerned About Vietnam in February 1967. Records of Clergy and Laity Concerned, series 4, box 1, Swarthmore College Peace Collection, Swarthmore, Pennsylvania.

William Giles Recounts His Wartime Experience

William Giles is a United States Army veteran. He was drafted while studying for a pharmacy degree at the University of Illinois and served a tour of duty as a medic in Vietnam. This interview provides insight into the experiences of an African American draftee.

LC: Let me ask how it happened, Bill, that you came to leave Illinois before you graduated and got into the service. Did you get draft papers?

WG: I got draft papers. I was drafted.

LC: And this was while you were fully attending university?

WG: Yes.

LC: And so of course, you know I'm going to ask, why did you not receive a deferment?

WG: Well, at the time, I think that there was not that many deferments going around. They didn't offer me the deferment.

LC: It never arose as a possibility?

WG: No. Not for me, anyway.

LC: Did you report then to the draft board?

WG: No.

LC: What happened?

WG: It was '66 when I got my first draft notice. I moved to New York City.

LC: I see.

WG: In '67, they called me in New York City and sent me another notice. I moved back to Chicago. And . . . that's when they sent the FBI [Federal Bureau of Investigation] after me and that's when I reported to the draft board.

LC: How did you know that the FBI had gotten involved?

WG: They sent me a letter, a registered letter and I came home that day and my mother and my sister were in the front room and they had this look on their face and I said, "Okay, give me my draft notices."

LC: You already knew, huh?

WG: Yeah.

* * *

LC: Once you had moved back to Chicago and your mom had basically handed over that letter, did you—how did you decide what to do next? How did you decide to go to the draft board essentially?

WG: I just gave up. I just said, "Oh well." And I still had the idea of finishing college and getting a degree and I thought that would be compromised if I was arrested or didn't go by the rules so I just said, "To heck with it." I just gave up and went to the draft board.

LC: And is that why, for example, you didn't try to leave the country?

WG: Right.

LC: Did you ever consider it?

WG: Yes. Briefly, yes. But I'm close to my mother and I didn't want to leave her.

* * *

LC: Bill, what can you tell me about the Tet Offensive period? Can you describe how things started to escalate?

WG: It was just escalated. They [enemy forces] straddled along the base camp. That's when we knew they were serious, because they straddled along the base camp. That's one of the only times I came close to shooting, to firing a weapon.

LC: What happened? Was it at night?

WG: It was at night and they hit the main gate first and they were running through the main gate through our position. And I had a loaded M-14 ready to fire and just before I could do anything like that, the wounded started coming in.

LC: Is that right?

WG: So it was just . . . the Army personnel carriers were just stacked with bodies and I was downstairs, just started pulling out bodies, pulling body after body and finally finding somebody who was alive and then putting them on a stretcher and taking them in and going through the bodies again, trying to find somebody else who was alive. There was blood everywhere. Blood. People screaming, people begging, people grabbing my arm and asking me to help them and it was just . . . chaos and so I just put my weapon away and started trying to save as many people as I could.

LC: Any idea, Bill, how many people you worked with through that period? Do any of them stand out in your mind?

WG: Oh yeah. There's a lot of . . . wounded guys who were asking me to tell their parents some things like, you know, "I love you," and other things. They would hold my arm and I would hold their hands and during that time when I was holding their hands—because I knew they were going to die—so I was holding their hand so when their living spirit left them, they would come through into me and live within me as long as I was alive. Which sounded like a good idea at the time, which I'm paying the price for right now, trying to send them away so that I can live again.

LC: Is that what you're trying to do?

WG: Yeah. There was about, I guess, fifty to a hundred people died. Just before they died, I held their hands and kind of wished their spirit into me.

Interview with William Giles by Laura M. Calkins, June 30, 2005. The Vietnam Archive Oral History Project, Texas Tech University.

Silent Majority Speech

This nationally televised speech, delivered by President Richard Nixon on November 3, 1969, occurred after the massive antiwar Moratorium of October 15. Seeking to blunt antiwar pressure, Nixon explained his strategy of Vietnamization, which was designed to gradually withdraw U.S. troops while negotiating a peace settlement. He appealed to what he called the "Silent Majority," Americans who were reluctant to demonstrate publicly but were supportive of presidential actions in Vietnam.

In January I could only conclude that the precipitate withdrawal of American forces from Vietnam would be a disaster not only for South Vietnam but for the United States and for the cause of peace.

For the South Vietnamese, our precipitate withdrawal would inevitably allow the Communists to repeat the massacres which followed their takeover in the North 15 years before. . . .

For the United States, this first defeat in our Nation's history would result in a collapse of confidence in American leadership, not only in Asia but throughout the world. . . .

For these reasons, I rejected the recommendation that I should end the war by immediately withdrawing all of our forces. I chose instead to change American policy on both the negotiating front and battlefront. . . .

It has become clear that the obstacle in negotiating an end to the war is not the President of the United States. It is not the South Vietnamese Government.

The obstacle is the other side's absolute refusal to show the least willingness to join us in seeking a just peace. And it will not do so while it is convinced that all it has to do is to wait for our next concession, and our next concession after that one, until it gets everything it wants.

There can now be no longer any question that progress in negotiation depends only on Hanoi's deciding to negotiate, to negotiate seriously. . . .

At the time we launched our search for peace I recognized we might not succeed in bringing an end to the war through negotiation. I, therefore, put into effect another plan to bring peace—a plan which will bring the war to an end regardless of what happens on the negotiating front. . . .

We have adopted a [Vietnamization] plan which we have worked out in cooperation with the South Vietnamese for the complete withdrawal of all US combat ground forces, and their replacement by South Vietnamese forces on an orderly scheduled timetable. This withdrawal will be made from strength and not from weakness. As South Vietnamese forces become stronger, the rate of American withdrawal can become greater. . . .

For almost 200 years, the policy of this Nation has been made under our Constitution by those leaders in the Congress and the White House elected by all of the people. If a vocal minority, however fervent its cause, prevails over reason and the will of the majority, this Nation has no future as a free society. . . .

Two hundred years ago this Nation was weak and poor. But even then, America was the hope of millions in the world. Today we have become the strongest and richest nation in the world. And the wheel of destiny has turned so that any hope the world has for the survival of peace and freedom will be determined by whether the American people have the moral stamina and the courage to meet the challenge of free world leadership.

Let historians not record that when America was the most powerful nation in the world we passed on the other side of the road and allowed the last hopes for peace and freedom of millions of people to be suffocated by the forces of totalitarianism.

And so tonight—to you, the great silent majority of my fellow Americans—I ask for your support.

I pledged in my campaign for the Presidency to end the war in a way that we could win the peace. I have initiated a plan of action which will enable me to keep that pledge.

The more support I can have from the American people, the sooner that pledge can be redeemed; for the more divided we are at home, the less likely the enemy is to negotiate at Paris.

Let us be united for peace. Let us also be united against defeat. Because let us understand: North Vietnam cannot defeat or humiliate the United States. Only Americans can do that. . . .

Weekly Compilation of Presidential Documents, *Vol. 5, No. 45. Washington, DC: Office of the Federal Register, 1969, 1546–1555.*

John Kerry and the Senate

John Kerry is a Yale University graduate who served in the U.S. Navy from 1966 to 1970. He was highly decorated during his tour of duty in Vietnam and was promoted to lieutenant. After leaving the Navy, Kerry joined Vietnam Veterans Against the War and testified before the U.S. Senate Foreign Relations Committee on April 22, 1971. After serving as lieutenant governor of Massachusetts, he was elected to the U.S. Senate in 1984 and was the presidential candidate of the Democratic Party in 2004. This edited version of his congressional testimony reflects his view of the Vietnam War.

I would like to talk on behalf of all those veterans and say that several months ago in Detroit we had an investigation at which over 150 honorably discharged, and many very highly decorated, veterans testified to war crimes committed in Southeast Asia. These were not isolated incidents but crimes committed on a day to day basis with the full awareness of officers at all levels of command. . . .

They told stories that at times they had personally raped, cut off ears, cut off heads, taped wires from portable telephones to human genitals and turned up the power, cut off limbs, blown up bodies, randomly shot at civilians, razed villages in fashion reminiscent of Genghis Khan, shot cattle and dogs for fun, poisoned food stocks, and generally ravaged the countryside of South Vietnam in addition to the normal ravage of war and the normal and very particular ravaging which is done by the applied bombing power of this country.

We call this investigation the Winter Soldier Investigation. The term Winter Soldier is a play on words of Thomas Paine's in 1776 when he spoke of the Sunshine Patriots and summer time soldiers who deserted at Valley Forge because the going was rough. . . .

Each day to facilitate the process by which the United States washes her hands of Vietnam someone has to give up his life so that the United States doesn't have to admit something that the entire world already knows, so that we can't say that we have made a mistake. Someone has to die so that President Nixon won't be, and these are his words, "the first President to lose a war."

We are asking Americans to think about that because how do you ask a man to be the last man to die in Vietnam? How do you ask a man to be the last man to die for a mistake? . . .

Finally, this administration has done us the ultimate dishonor. They have attempted to disown us and the sacrifices we made for this country. In their blindness and fear they have tried to deny that we are veterans or that we served in Nam. We do not need their testimony. Our own scars and stumps of limbs are witness enough for others and for ourselves.

We wish that a merciful God could wipe away our own memories of that service as easily as this administration has wiped away their memories of us. But all that they have done and all that they can do by this denial is to make more clear than ever our own determination to undertake one last mission—to search out and destroy the last vestige of this barbaric war, to pacify our own hearts, to conquer the hate and the fear that have driven this country these last ten years and more, so when 30 years from now our brothers go down the street without a leg, without an arm, or a face, and small boys ask why, we will be able to say "Vietnam" and not mean a desert, not a filthy obscene memory, but mean instead the place where America finally turned and where soldiers like us helped it in the turning.

United States Senate, Committee on Foreign Relations. Legislative Proposals Relating to the War in Southeast Asia: Hearings. *Washington, DC: United States Government Printing Office, 1971, 180–210.*

Judith Coburn and Vietnam

Judith Coburn is a journalist who covered the Vietnam War for the *Village Voice,* Pacifica Radio, and the *Far Eastern Economic Review.* This interview reveals insights into U.S. military morale and practice and covering the war as a female reporter.

JUDITH COBURN ARRIVED IN VIETNAM IN 1970, AND DISCOVERED DECLINING U.S. MORALE.

Some troops really were openly refusing to carry out orders. Tet '68 had broken the morale of the American war effort. Peace talks were going on, and nobody wanted to be the last guy to die in Vietnam. They'd drop a group of guys into the jungle and they'd just sit there for a couple of days calling in fake coordinates, smoke a little weed, and wait to get picked up. Of course there were other missions where people were greatly heroic, but it was pretty obvious that the military was gradually losing control of its own men.

In 1971, there were dozens of guys in the American Division at Chu Lai who were completely antiwar and they planned an antiwar demonstration for the Fourth of July. They put up posters announcing an "Independence Day Peace Rally" and calling for "an immediate and total American troop withdrawal." The MPs [military police] would no sooner tear them down than new ones would reappear. The division commander made every man sign some kind of pledge that he would not participate in the rally. But that was really unenforceable because there was a USO [United Service Organization] party already planned at the beach and so when July Fourth rolled around something like fifteen hundred guys showed up. They didn't want to provoke a crackdown, so nobody carried any antiwar banners or started a march, but I interviewed a lot of guys and it was hard to find anyone on that beach who did not favor immediate withdrawal. It looked like a "be-in" at Golden Gate Park. Guys were wearing peace symbols and beads and smoking pot. All the military authorities did was take a few pictures. After all, what were they going to do, bust them all? When I hear people say we could have won the war, I always think: where were you going to get the soldiers?

COBURN'S COVERAGE OF THE SOUTH VIETNAMESE INVASION OF LAOS IN FEBRUARY AND MARCH 1971 INCLUDED THE FOLLOWING TRAGEDY.

There were hordes of journalists jockeying to get on choppers into Laos. It was very hard to get on these choppers. I'd been waiting for three days. Finally, I got into a chopper and it was totally loaded with people. At the last moment, just before it was going to take off, Larry Burrows shows up and says, "Can't you take one more?"

The chopper pilot said no. So the other journalists and photographers rose up as one and told me to get off the chopper. They didn't say, but it was obvious. I was, after all, only writing for the *Village Voice* and I was a girl and the great Larry Burrows was there. Of course, I thought he was great too, so I got off. The helicopter flew into Laos and crashed. They all died.

DURING THE 1972 NORTH VIETNAMESE EASTER OFFENSIVE, COBURN MADE HER WAY TO QUANG TRI PROVINCE.

I got on a motorbike with a Vietnamese journalist and we started up Route 1. We discovered that the Communists were, in fact, doing some shooting into the mass of refugees. South Vietnamese soldiers were deserting, shedding their uniforms, and mixing into the refugee crowds for protection. Every time these little pockets of North Vietnamese soldiers thought they saw South Vietnamese soldiers they would shoot. But, as it turned out, most of the civilians were being killed by artillery fire from American navy ships offshore. They had Route 1 zeroed in and fired barrage after barrage. They may have been hoping to hit North Vietnamese Army units but the civilian carnage was just incredible.

*Coburn, Judith. "Vietnamization Wasn't Working Any Better than Americanization."
From* Patriots: The Vietnam War Remembered from All Sides, *edited by Christian Appy, 407–412. New York: Penguin Books, 2003. Used by permission from Viking Penguin, a division of Penguin Group (USA) Inc.*

Reference

Abrams, Creighton (1914–1974) Commander of the U.S. Military Assistance Command, Vietnam (MACV) from 1968 to 1972. Abrams replaced General William Westmoreland in this position after the Tet Offensive and shifted strategic emphasis from search-and-destroy to pacification. He was appointed Army chief of staff in 1972.

AFL-CIO The American Federation of Labor–Congress of Industrial Organizations is the largest trade union federation in the United States. It was formed with the merger of the two groups in 1955, uniting the more conservative craft unions of the AFL with the CIO's more aggressive industrial unions.

Alvarez, Delia (1941–) Vietnam antiwar activist and sister of U.S. prisoner of war Everett Alvarez.

Another Mother for Peace Women's peace organization founded in 1967 to protest the Vietnam War. It functioned primarily to educate constituents and lobby Congress. It was best known for its slogan, "War is not healthy for children or other living things."

Army of the Republic of Vietnam (ARVN) The South Vietnamese army, trained by the United States for conventional warfare. Although it contained nearly 1 million soldiers by 1975, it suffered from corruption and low morale and was unable to defeat North Vietnam after American troops and firepower withdrew in 1973.

Arnett, Peter (1934–) Journalist who began covering the Vietnam War in June 1962. His pursuit of accurate stories drew a threatened expulsion from South Vietnamese president Diem and surveillance from President Johnson's administration. Arnett won a Pulitzer Prize for his reporting in 1966.

Asian American Free Labor Institute (AAFLI) This was a project of the AFL-CIO designed to strengthen democratic free trade unions abroad. USAID provided some of its funding. In Vietnam, AAFLI trained leaders and financed offices of the Vietnamese Confederation of Labor.

Ball, George (1909–1994) Undersecretary of state during the Kennedy and Johnson administrations. Ball was the most notable opponent of military escalation in Vietnam among leading presidential advisers. He resigned in 1966.

Berrigan, Daniel (1921–) Catholic priest and cofounder of the Catholic Peace Fellowship in 1964. Berrigan's opposition to the Vietnam War led to conflict with his religious order. He was jailed for his role in burning draft files in Catonsville, Maryland, in May 1968.

Berrigan, Philip (1923–2002) Catholic priest and younger brother of Daniel Berrigan. He was a civil rights and antiwar activist. Berrigan was twice convicted of destroying draft records as a member of the Baltimore Four (1967) and the Catonsville Nine (1968).

Buddhist Crisis (1963) South Vietnam's Buddhist majority challenged President Ngo Dinh Diem, a Roman Catholic, after government troops killed nine demonstrators in Hue on May 8, 1963. The self-immolation of several monks and raids on Buddhist pagodas in August brought demands for religious freedom and for Diem's resignation. A military coup overthrew Diem in November.

Calley, William L., Jr. (1943–) U.S. Army lieutenant. Calley commanded a platoon involved in the My Lai Massacre in March 1968. He was convicted in 1971 of murdering more than 100 Vietnamese but was paroled after only three years of imprisonment.

Carmichael, Stokely (1941–1998) Civil rights activist. Carmichael achieved prominence as national chairman of the Student Nonviolent Coordinating Committee in 1966. He popularized the ideology of a separatist Black Power Movement, and after 1969 lived in Guinea.

Chicago Seven A heavily publicized trial of Rennie Davis, David Dellinger, John Froines, Tom Hayden, Abbie Hoffman, Jerry Rubin, and Lee Weiner for conspiring to riot in Chicago at the 1968 Democratic National Convention. Originally there were eight, but Bobby Seale was removed for contempt and tried separately.

civil disobedience The tactic of deliberately disobeying a law without using physical violence. This is often used to challenge laws or actions that are perceived as unjust or immoral. During the Vietnam War, for example, antiwar protesters sometimes used civil disobedience.

Clergy and Laymen Concerned About Vietnam (CALCAV) This organization was formed in October 1965 by a group of New York City clergy to challenge U.S. policy in Vietnam. It became a national ecumenical organization with a generally liberal political perspective.

Clifford, Clark (1906–1998) U.S. secretary of defense from 1968 to 1969. He replaced Robert McNamara shortly before the Tet Offensive. After reassessing American progress, Clifford opposed further escalation and argued for peace negotiations.

Coffin, William Sloane (1924–2006)   Minister and Yale University chaplain during the Vietnam War. As an antiwar activist, Coffin and four others were indicted in 1968 for conspiracy to aid and abet draft resistance. His conviction was overturned on appeal in 1970.

Cold War   The global struggle for power between the United States and the Soviet Union—and their respective allies—from the end of World War II (1945) until the collapse of the Soviet Union (1991). Ideologically, the United States advocated democracy and capitalism, whereas the Soviet Union promoted communism.

containment   U.S. Cold War policy designed to restrict Soviet expansion. Containment grew out of ideas expressed by U.S. diplomat George Kennan in 1946–1947. By applying patient but firm political, economic, and sometimes military pressure, American leaders hoped to contain communism.

credibility   The concept that partially motivated U.S. military escalation in Vietnam. With a series of presidents committing the United States to preserving a noncommunist South Vietnam, America could not withdraw without raising doubts among its allies about its future reliability.

domino theory   Cold War era belief of some American officials that communist victory in one country would produce a chain reaction collapse of neighboring countries. This was one of the justifications for waging war in Vietnam, as some officials saw South Vietnam as the first domino.

Eisenhower, Dwight D. (1890–1969)   President of the United States from 1953 to 1961. Regarding Vietnam, he believed in the domino theory and continued the containment policy by supporting the South Vietnamese government of Ngo Dinh Diem.

Ellsberg, Daniel (1931–)   Intelligence analyst for the U.S. government and the RAND Corporation. He helped compile the Pentagon Papers in 1967, which turned him against the war. After failing to persuade government leaders to act on this information, Ellsberg leaked the Pentagon Papers to Neil Sheehan, leading to publication in the *New York Times*.

Fishel, Wesley R. (1919–1977)   Michigan State University political scientist who headed a key advisory group to President Ngo Dinh Diem's government from 1956 to 1958. He continued to advise Diem until 1962, when he became a critic of the regime even while supporting U.S. goals.

Fonda, Jane (1937–)   American actress and Vietnam antiwar activist. Her trip to North Vietnam in 1972, where she was photographed sitting at an antiaircraft gun, made her a polarizing figure in the United States. Fonda was married to antiwar activist Tom Hayden from 1972 to 1989.

Free Speech Movement   Student protests at the University of California at Berkeley in 1964–1965. The motivating issue was the university's restrictions on student political activity. Highlighted by Mario Savio's eloquent speeches, the students won most of their demands to resume on-campus political activity.

French, Albert (1943–)   French joined the U.S. Marines in 1963 and was deployed to Vietnam in 1965. After leaving the Marines in 1967, he returned to a career as a photojournalist and author. His book *Patches of Fire* describes his wartime experiences.

Fulbright, J. William (1905–1995)   U.S. senator from Arkansas from 1945 to 1974. Although he guided the Gulf of Tonkin Resolution through the Senate in 1964, Fulbright later turned against the war. As chair of the Senate Foreign Relations Committee, he convened televised hearings in 1966 that exposed government divisions over war policy.

Gore, Albert, Sr. (1907–1998)   United States representative (1939–1944, 1945–1953) and senator (1953–1971) from Tennessee. Gore became an outspoken critic of the Vietnam War but lost a reelection bid in 1970 and returned to practice law in Tennessee.

Graham, Billy (1918–)   William Franklin "Billy" Graham is a Baptist minister and internationally known evangelist. Several presidents sought his counsel, and Richard Nixon also used him as an occasional political envoy. Graham was anticommunist but generally stayed politically neutral.

Great Society   The term used by President Lyndon Johnson to describe the goals of his domestic programs. These included efforts to extend civil rights, eliminate poverty, improve education, and enhance medical care.

Gulf of Tonkin Resolution (1964)   Congressional resolution giving the president authority to take "all necessary measures" to protect U.S. forces and defend South Vietnam. Passed in the aftermath of a now controversial naval engagement. Congress repealed the resolution in 1970.

Hayden, Tom (1939–)   Early leader of Students for a Democratic Society and a Vietnam antiwar activist. After the 1968 Democratic convention in Chicago, Hayden was tried for conspiracy to riot as part of the Chicago Seven. His conviction was overturned on appeal in 1972. Hayden was married to actress and antiwar activist Jane Fonda from 1972 to 1989.

Ho Chi Minh (1890–1969)   Vietnamese communist revolutionary and president of North Vietnam from 1945 to 1969. He was a key figure in Vietnam's fight for independence from France from 1945 to 1954. After Vietnam was temporarily divided in 1954, Ho played an important role in trying to unify the country in the war against the United States. He died before the war's conclusion.

Hughes, Dennis (1947–)   U.S. Army veteran who served in Vietnam during 1967–1968. In recent years he has been chair of the Mental Health Consumer Council in Pittsburgh.

Humphrey, Hubert (1911–1978)   U.S. senator from Minnesota elected vice president in 1964 on the ticket with President Lyndon Johnson. Humphrey initially opposed expanding the Vietnam War, but soon he became a strong public defender of Johnson's policies. As the Democratic presidential nominee in 1968, he lost a close election to Richard Nixon.

Johnson, Lyndon Baines (1908–1973) President of the United States from 1963 to 1969. Johnson oversaw a massive U.S. military escalation in Vietnam beginning in 1965. Despite more than 500,000 American troops and an extensive bombing campaign, by 1968 the United States had achieved no better than a stalemate. Johnson declined to run for reelection and retired in 1969.

Johnson, Quinton (dates unavailable) Johnson joined the U.S. Army in 1969 and was deployed to Vietnam in 1970. After returning to the United States, he earned a college degree in industrial maintenance.

Kennedy, John F. (1917–1963) President of the United States from 1961 to 1963. Deteriorating conditions in Vietnam led Kennedy to increase the number of U.S. advisers there. In 1963 he supported the coup that overthrew Ngo Dinh Diem as head of South Vietnam, only a month before his own assassination.

King, Martin Luther, Jr. (1929–1968) Minister and civil rights activist. King supported President Lyndon Johnson's civil rights agenda but turned increasingly against the Vietnam War. His 1967 speech at New York's Riverside Church brought him into the forefront of the antiwar movement. He was assassinated in Memphis, in April 1968.

Kitt, Eartha (1927–) Popular American singer and film, stage, and television actress. Her antiwar remarks at a 1968 White House gathering damaged her career in the United States for several years.

Lodge, Henry Cabot (1902–1985) U.S. ambassador to South Vietnam 1963–1964 and 1965–1967. With President Kennedy's approval, Lodge supported the coup against Ngo Dinh Diem in late 1963. As one of President Johnson's "wise men" advisers in 1968, he advocated an end to military escalation.

Lozada, Carlos James (1946–1967) U.S. Army veteran. He enlisted in 1966 and was deployed to Vietnam. During combat in November 1967, Lozada was killed in action. His valorous service earned him the Medal of Honor.

Mansfield, Mike (1903–2001) United States senator from Montana from 1952 to 1977. As senate majority leader, Mansfield turned against military escalation in Vietnam and supported various congressional amendments to withdraw U.S. combat forces.

McCain, John S., III (1936–) United States representative (1983–1987) and senator (1987–present) who became the Republican presidential nominee in 2008. As a U.S. Navy pilot, McCain was a prisoner of war in Vietnam from 1967 to 1973.

McCarthy, Eugene (1916–2005) United States representative (1949–1959) and senator (1959–1971) from Minnesota. He ran unsuccessfully for the Democratic presidential nomination in 1968 and as an independent candidate in 1976. In the senate he was a leading opponent of the Vietnam War.

McGovern, George (1922–) United States senator from South Dakota from 1963 to 1981. He sponsored an unsuccessful amendment to remove U.S. military forces from Vietnam by the end of 1971. He was the Democratic Party's 1972 presidential candidate but lost to Richard Nixon.

McIntire, Carl (1906–2002) Fundamentalist minister who founded the American Council of Christian Churches as a conservative alternative to the National Council of Churches. He organized several demonstrations calling for U.S. military victory in Vietnam.

McNamara, Robert S. (1916–) U.S. Secretary of Defense from 1961 to 1968. Initially a strong supporter of military escalation in Vietnam, McNamara developed doubts about American policy in Indochina and clashed with President Johnson. He left his cabinet position in February 1968 to become head of the World Bank.

Meany, George (1894–1980) Labor leader who was president of the AFL-CIO from 1955 to 1979. Meany helped establish the Confederation of Vietnamese Trade Unions and remained a strong supporter of the Vietnam War during both the Johnson and Nixon administrations.

Michigan State University Vietnam Advisory Group (MSUG) This team, led by political science professor Wesley Fishel, provided technical assistance to the government of South Vietnamese president Ngo Dinh Diem from 1955 to 1962.

Military Assistance and Advisory Group-Vietnam (MAAG-Vietnam) Created in 1950 to channel U.S. military aid to French and Vietnamese forces fighting communists in Southeast Asia. From 1955 to 1964, MAAG-Vietnam was responsible for training the Army of the Republic of Vietnam.

Military Assistance Command, Vietnam (MACV) Established in 1962, MACV was the sole coordinator of U.S. military activities in South Vietnam from 1964 to 1973. MACV commanders were generals Paul Harkins (1962–1964), William Westmoreland (1964–1968), Creighton Abrams (1968–1972), and Frederick Weyand (1972–1973).

My Lai Massacre (1968) On March 16, 1968, a company of soldiers commanded by Lt. William Calley killed nearly 500 unarmed civilians in the Vietnamese hamlet of My Lai. The military covered up the atrocity for over a year. Of 14 people charged with crimes, Calley was the only person convicted.

nation building In the context of the Vietnam War, nation building was the U.S. attempt to create an independent, noncommunist state in South Vietnam. In part, this meant training military forces, strengthening administrative services, building infrastructure, and improving the economy.

National Council of Churches Organized in 1950, the NCC is an ecumenical body that includes many of the largest American mainline and evangelical denominations. The Vietnam War exposed tensions between its national leadership, grassroots constituency, and government officials.

National Liberation Front (NLF) A broadly based but communist-dominated coalition formed on December 20, 1960, to challenge the South Vietnamese government of Ngo Dinh Diem. Though largely directed by Hanoi, the NLF emphasized national independence over social revolution.

New Left The term identifying the typically younger, college-based political Left of the 1960s. Rejecting the Marxist emphasis on the working class, the New Left saw the intelligentsia as the vanguard of social change and emphasized broader social change rather than economic issues.

Ngo Dinh Diem (1901–1963) President of South Vietnam from 1954 to 1963. Supported by the United States, Diem's narrowly based government fought a communist-dominated insurgency during most of his rule. Diem's lack of consistent success and his poor handling of massive Buddhist protests in 1963 convinced the Kennedy administration to withdraw its support. Diem was killed during a military coup in October 1963.

Ngo Dinh Nhu (1910–1963) Organizer of South Vietnam's Can Lao Party and head of the Saigon government's secret police. Nhu collaborated with his older brother, South Vietnamese president Ngo Dinh Diem, to dominate national politics until they were both killed in a November 1963 coup.

Nixon, Richard M. (1913–1994) President of the United States from 1969 to 1974. Initially hoping for military victory in Vietnam, Nixon resorted to "Vietnamization" as a strategy to end the war. The 1973 Paris Peace Accords failed to achieve his goal of "peace with honor." Nixon resigned the presidency over the Watergate scandal.

Pentagon Papers A secret U.S. Defense Department study of the history of America's Vietnam policy ordered by Secretary of Defense Robert McNamara in 1967. Daniel Ellsberg, one of its authors, leaked the study to journalist Neil Sheehan in March 1971. President Nixon's administration tried to block its publication by the *New York Times*, but the Supreme Court denied the government's effort at prior restraint.

Reagan, Ronald (1911–2004) Governor of California (1967–1975) and president of the United States (1981–1989). As governor during the Vietnam War, his reputation was as a hard-line conservative, using National Guard troops to suppress domestic protests.

Reuther, Walter (1907–1970) President of the United Auto Workers (UAW). He was a significant force in the Democratic Party, a strong anticommunist, and a supporter of several liberal causes. Reuther eventually became organized labor's most visible opponent of the Vietnam War.

Rizzo, Frank (1920–1991) Police commissioner (1967–1971) and mayor (1972–1980) of Philadelphia. His two terms as mayor were controversial, and he surprised his fellow Democrats by endorsing Republican Richard Nixon for president in 1972.

Rolling Thunder The sustained bombing campaign against North Vietnam from early 1965 until late 1968. This marked a fundamental policy shift by the Johnson administration and was followed shortly by the introduction of U.S. combat troops into Vietnam.

Rubins, James (1948–) Vietnam War conscientious objector and member of the Reformed Church in America.

Rusk, Dean (1909–1994) Rusk served as U.S. secretary of state from 1961 to 1969 under presidents John Kennedy and Lyndon Johnson. He was among the administration's most consistent advocates of military escalation in Vietnam.

Salisbury, Harrison (1908–1993) Noted *New York Times* journalist. In December 1966 he was the first U.S. newsman to visit North Vietnam. His dispatches exposed misleading American reports but generated controversy over the appropriateness of reporting behind enemy lines.

Savio, Mario (1942–1996) Civil rights activist. He is most noted for his passionate speeches and leading role in Berkeley's Free Speech Movement. Savio called on students to stop the university "machine" that no longer acknowledged their rights.

Sheehan, Neil (1936–) American journalist who covered the Vietnam War in the early-to-mid-1960s. Working for the *New York Times* in 1971, he broke the story of the Pentagon Papers. His book on John Paul Vann, *A Bright Shining Lie,* received a Pulitzer Prize in 1989.

Silent Majority A term popularized by President Richard Nixon in a 1969 speech. It described those who did not publicly advocate for their political viewpoints, but who quietly accepted the president's wartime policies.

Smith, Wayne (1950–) Served as a U.S. Army medic for 18 months in Vietnam from 1969 to 1970. For several years he was a therapist for the Veterans Administration's Vietnam Veterans Readjustment Counseling Program and later worked for the Vietnam Veterans Memorial Fund.

Southeast Asia Treaty Organization (SEATO) Nine nations formed this international collective defense organization after signing the Manila Pact in 1954. Its purpose was to block communist expansion in Southeast Asia. Some American officials used SEATO as a rationale for military intervention in Vietnam.

Tet Offensive (1968) A massive surprise military assault launched at the end of January 1968 by North Vietnamese regulars and Vietcong forces. The offensive targeted most of South Vietnam's urban centers. Ultimately, Tet was a tactical military defeat for the communists, but it brought them significant political gains.

Tran Quoc Buu (1912–?) President of the Vietnamese Confederation of Labor (CVT). Imprisoned as a young man for anticolonial activities, Buu was a strong anticommunist who sought to build an independent union-based political party in the south.

United States Operations Mission (USOM)   The United States Agency for International Development (USAID) administered American economic aid to South Vietnam through its Saigon field office, the USOM. This support encompassed safety, health, education, and agriculture.

Van Devanter, Lynda (1947–2002)   U.S. Army nurse who served in Vietnam from 1969 to 1970. She later opposed the war and was a strong advocate for women veterans. Her memoir, *Home Before Morning,* was published in 1983.

Vann, John Paul (1924–1972)   Vann served as a U.S. Army adviser to South Vietnam in 1962–1963 and criticized what he saw as an unsuccessful military strategy. After retiring, he returned as a civilian pacification adviser to Vietnam, where he died in a 1972 helicopter crash.

Vietcong   The term most commonly used by Americans to identify the South Vietnamese communist insurgents. South Vietnamese president Ngo Dinh Diem allegedly first used the term as an insult.

Vietnamese Confederation of Labor (CVT)   Free trade labor union in South Vietnam that generally cooperated with the AFL-CIO, the U.S. government, and the pro-American Saigon regimes.

Vietnamization   President Richard Nixon's policy, announced in 1969, of gradually withdrawing U.S. armed forces from Vietnam and returning primary responsibility of the Vietnam War to the South Vietnamese government and military.

Wallace, George (1919–1998)   Wallace gained notoriety as a segregationist governor of Alabama from 1963 to 1967. He ran as a third-party candidate for president in 1968, and his campaign for the Democratic Party nomination in 1972 ended when he was partially paralyzed during an assassination attempt. He served additional terms as governor of Alabama from 1971 to 1979 and from 1983 to 1987.

Westmoreland, William C. (1914–2005)   U.S. Army general. Westmoreland served as commander of the Military Assistance Command, Vietnam (MACV) from 1964 to 1968. He was primarily responsible for implementing the strategy of attrition. President Lyndon Johnson appointed him Army chief of staff in 1968.

Women Strike for Peace (WSP)   Founded in 1961 to support nuclear disarmament, by the mid-1960s WSP was protesting the Vietnam War. The organization initially appealed primarily to the nurturing role of traditional motherhood as the basis of its antiwar position.

Bibliography

Adler, Bill, ed. *Letters from Vietnam.* New York: Random House, 2003.

Allison, William Thomas. *Military Justice in Vietnam: The Rule of Law in an American War.* Lawrence: University Press of Kansas, 2006.

Allred, Lena Hodnett. "Women in a Man's World: American Women in the War in Vietnam." Ph.D. diss., Texas A&M University, 1995.

Anderson, David L., ed. *Shadow on the White House: Presidents and the Vietnam War, 1945–1977.* Lawrence: University Press of Kansas, 1993.

Anderson, David L. *Trapped By Success: The Eisenhower Administration and Vietnam, 1953–1961.* New York: Columbia University Press, 1991.

Anderson, David L., and John Ernst, eds. *The War That Never Ends: New Perspectives on the Vietnam War.* Lexington: University Press of Kentucky, 2007.

Anderson, Terry H. *The Sixties,* 3rd ed. New York: Longman, 2006.

Anderson, Terry H. *The Movement and the Sixties: Protest in America from Greensboro to Wounded Knee.* New York: Oxford University Press, 1995.

Andrade, Dale. *America's Last Vietnam Battle: Halting Hanoi's 1972 Easter Offensive.* Lawrence: University Press of Kansas, 2001.

Andrade, Dale. *Ashes to Ashes: The Phoenix Program and the Vietnam War.* Lexington, MA: Lexington Books, 1990.

Appy, Christian G. *Patriots: The Vietnam War Remembered from All Sides.* New York: Viking Penguin, 2003.

Appy, Christian G. *Working-Class War: American Combat Soldiers in Vietnam.* Chapel Hill: University of North Carolina Press, 1993.

Arlen, Michael J. *Living-Room War.* New York: Penguin Books, 1982.

Atkin, Natalie Patricia. "Protest and Liberation: War, Peace, and Women's Empowerment, 1967–1981." Ph.D. diss., Wayne State University, 1999.

Avorn, Jerry. *Up Against the Ivy Wall: A History of the Columbia Crisis.* New York: Atheneum Press, 1968.

Barber, David. *A Hard Rain Fell: SDS and Why It Failed.* Jackson: University Press of Mississippi, 2008.

Baritz, Loren. *Backfire: A History of How American Culture Led Us into Vietnam and Made Us Fight the Way We Did.* New York: William Morrow, 1985.

Barrett, David M. *Uncertain Warriors: Lyndon Johnson and His Vietnam Advisers.* Lawrence: University Press of Kansas, 1993.

Baskir, Lawrence M., and William A. Strauss. *Chance and Circumstance: The Draft, the War and the Vietnam Generation.* New York: Vintage Books, 1978.

Bates, Tom. *Rads: The 1970 Bombing of the Army Math Research Center at the University of Wisconsin and Its Aftermath.* New York: HarperCollins, 1992.

Beesley, Stanley W. *Vietnam: The Heartland Remembers.* Norman: University of Oklahoma Press, 1987.

Bergerud, Eric M. *Red Thunder, Tropic Lightning: The World of a Combat Division in Vietnam.* New York: Penguin Books, 1993.

Berman, William C. *William Fulbright and the Vietnam War: The Dissent of a Political Realist.* Kent, OH: Kent State University Press, 1988.

Bill, James A. *George Ball: Behind the Scenes in U.S. Foreign Policy.* New Haven, CT: Yale University Press, 1997.

Black, Samuel W., ed. *Soul Soldiers: African Americans and the Vietnam Era.* Pittsburgh, PA: Senator John Heinz Pittsburgh Regional History Center, 2006.

Blevins, Kent B. "Southern Baptist Attitudes Toward the Vietnam War in the Years 1965–1970." *Foundations* 23 (July–September 1980): 231–244.

Boyle, Kevin. *The UAW and the Heyday of American Liberalism, 1945–1968.* Ithaca, NY: Cornell University Press, 1995.

Braestrup, Peter. *Big Story: How the American Press and Television Reported and Interpreted the Crisis of Tet 1968 in Vietnam and Washington.* Boulder, CO: Westview, 1977.

Braunstein, Peter, and Michael William Doyle, eds. *Imagine Nation: The American Counterculture of the 1960s and '70s.* New York: Routledge, 2002.

Brienes, Wini. *Community and Organization in the New Left, 1962–1968: The Great Refusal.* New Brunswick, NJ: Rutgers University Press, 1989.

Brigham, Robert. *Guerrilla Diplomacy: The NLF's Foreign Relations and the Vietnam War.* Ithaca, NY: Cornell University Press, 1999.

Brinkley, Douglas. *Tour of Duty: John Kerry and the Vietnam War.* New York: William Morrow, 2004.

Brown, Elizabeth I. "Bye, Bye Miss American Pie: Wives of American Servicemen in Southeast Asia, 1961–1975." PhD. diss., University of Colorado, 2005.

Bryan, C. D. B. *Friendly Fire.* New York: Putnam, 1976.

Bush, Perry. "The Political Education of Vietnam Christian Service, 1954–1975." *Peace and Change* 27, no. 2 (April 2002): 198–224.

Buzzanco, Robert. *Masters of War: Military Dissent and Politics in the Vietnam Era.* Cambridge, UK: Cambridge University Press, 1996.

Buzzanco, Robert. *Vietnam and the Transformation of American Life.* Cambridge, MA: Blackwell, 1999.

Calvert, Gregory Nevala. *Democracy from the Heart: Spiritual Values, Decentralism, and Democratic Idealism in the Movement of the 1960s.* Eugene, OR: Communitas, 1991.

Card, Josefina. *Lives After Vietnam: The Personal Impact of Military Service.* Lexington, MA: Lexington Books, 1983.

Carson, Clayborne. *In Struggle: SNCC and the Black Awakening of the 1960s.* Cambridge, MA: Harvard University Press, 1995.

Carson, Mark David. "Beyond the Solid South: Southern Members of Congress and the Vietnam War." Ph.D. diss., Louisiana State University, 2003.

Carter, James M. *Inventing Vietnam: The United States and State Building, 1954–1968.* New York: Cambridge University Press, 2008.

Catton, Philip E. *Diem's Final Failure: Prelude to America's War in Vietnam.* Lawrence: University Press of Kansas, 2002.

Chatfield, Charles. "At the Hands of the Historians: The Antiwar Movement of the Vietnam Era." *Peace and Change* 29 (July 2004): 483–526.

Clardy, Brian. *The Management of Dissent: Responses to the Post Kent State Protests at Seven Public Universities in Illinois.* Lanham, MD: University Press of America, 2002.

Clymer, Kenton J., ed. *The Vietnam War: Its History, Literature and Music.* El Paso: Texas Western Press, 1998.

Coffin, William Sloane. *Once to Every Man: A Memoir.* New York: Atheneum, 1977.

Cohen, Robert, and Reginald Zelnik, eds. *The Free Speech Movement: Reflections on Berkeley in the 1960s.* Berkeley: University of California Press, 2002.

Conboy, Kenneth, and Dale Andrade. *Spies & Commandos: How America Lost the Secret War in Vietnam.* Lawrence: University Press of Kansas, 2000.

Cowie, Jefferson. "Nixon's Class Struggle: Romancing the New Right Worker, 1969–1973." *Labor History* 43 (August 2002): 257–283.

Dallek, Robert. *Flawed Giant: Lyndon Johnson and His Times, 1961–1973.* New York: Oxford University Press, 1998.

Daly, James A., and Lee Bergman. *Black Prisoner of War: A Conscientious Objector's Vietnam Memoir.* Lawrence: University Press of Kansas, 2000.

Davis, James Kirkpatrick. *Assault on the Left: The FBI and the Sixties Antiwar Movement.* Westport, CT: Praeger, 1997.

DeBenedetti, Charles. "A CIA Analysis of the Anti-Vietnam War Movement: October 1967." *Peace and Change* 9 (Spring 1983): 31–41.

DeBenedetti, Charles. "On the Significance of Citizen Peace Activism: America, 1961–1975." *Peace and Change* 9 (Summer 1983): 6–20.

DeBenedetti, Charles, with Charles Chatfield. *An American Ordeal: The Antiwar Movement of the Vietnam Era.* Syracuse, NY: Syracuse University Press, 1990.

DeGroot, Gerard, ed. *Student Protest: The Sixties and After.* London: Longman, 1998.

DiLeo, David L. *George Ball, Vietnam, and the Rethinking of Containment.* Chapel Hill: University of North Carolina Press, 1991.

Downs, Frederick, Jr. *The Killing Zone: My Life in the Vietnam War.* New York: Norton, 1978.

Downs, Michael S. "Advise and Consent: John Stennis and the Vietnam War, 1954–1973." *Journal of Mississippi History* 55 (May 1993): 87–114.

Duiker, William. *Sacred War: Nationalism and Revolution in a Divided Vietnam.* New York: McGraw-Hill, 1994.

Durr, Kenneth. *Behind the Backlash: White Working-Class Politics in Baltimore, 1940–1980.* Chapel Hill: University of North Carolina Press, 2007.

Ebert, James R. *A Life in a Year: The American Infantryman in Vietnam.* Novato, CA: Presidio Press, 1993.

Echols, Alice. *Daring to Be Bad: Radical Feminism in America, 1967–75.* Minneapolis: University of Minnesota Press, 1990.

Edelman, Bernard, ed. *Dear America: Letters Home from Vietnam.* New York: Pocket Books, 1985.

Ehrhart, W. D. *Busted: A Vietnam Veteran in Nixon's America.* Amherst: University of Massachusetts Press, 1995.

Ehrhart, W. D. *Ordinary Lives: Platoon 1005 and the Vietnam War.* Philadelphia: Temple University Press, 1999.

Ehrhart, W. D. *Vietnam-Perkasie: A Combat Marine Memoir.* Amherst: University of Massachusetts Press, 1995.

Eldridge, Lawrence Allen. "Chronicles of a Two-Front War: The African-American Press and the Vietnam War." Ph.D. diss., University of Illinois-Chicago, 2002.

Elegant, Robert. "How to Lose a War." *Encounter,* August 1981, 73–90.

Elkins, Frank. *The Heart of a Man: A Naval Pilot's Vietnam Diary,* ed. Marilyn Elkins. Annapolis, MD: Naval Institute Press, 1991.

Elliott, David W. P. *The Vietnamese War: Revolution and Social Change in the Mekong Delta, 1930–1975,* 2 vols. New York: M. E. Sharpe, 2003.

Elwood-Akers, Virginia. *Women War Correspondents in the Vietnam War, 1961–1975.* Metuchen, NJ: Scarecrow Press, 1988.

Emerson, Gloria. *Winners and Losers: Battles, Retreats, Gains, Losses, and Ruins from the Vietnam War.* New York: Penguin Books, 1985.

Ernst, John. *Forging a Fateful Alliance: Michigan State University and the Vietnam War.* East Lansing: Michigan State University Press, 1998.

Ernst, John, and Yvonne Baldwin. "The Not So Silent Minority: Louisville's Antiwar Movement, 1966–1975." *Journal of Southern History* 73 (February 2007): 105–142.

Evans, Sara. *Personal Politics: The Roots of Women's Liberation in the Civil Rights Movement and the New Left.* New York: Random House, 1979.

Exum, William H. *Paradoxes of Protest: Black Student Activism in a White University.* Philadelphia: Temple University Press, 1985.

Eynon, Bret. "Community, Democracy, and the Reconstruction of Political Life: The Civil Rights Influence on New Left Political Culture in Ann Arbor, Michigan, 1958–1966." Ph.D. diss., New York University, 1993.

Farber, David. *Chicago '68.* Chicago: University of Chicago Press, 1994.

Fisher, Christopher T. "The Illusion of Progress: CORDS and the Crisis of Modernization in South Vietnam, 1965–1968." *Pacific Historical Review* 75 (February 2006): 25–51.

Fisher, Christopher T. "Nation Building and the Vietnam War: A Historiography." *Pacific Historical Review* 74 (August 2005): 441–456.

FitzGerald, Frances. *Fire in the Lake: the Vietnamese and the Americans in Vietnam.* Boston: Little Brown, 1972.

Flipse, Scott. "The Latest Casualty of War: Catholic Relief Services, Humanitarianism, and the War in Vietnam, 1967–1968." *Peace and Change* 27 (April 2002): 245–270.

Foley, Michael S. *Confronting the War Machine: Draft Resistance During the Vietnam War.* Chapel Hill: University of North Carolina Press, 2003.

Foley, Michael S., ed. *Dear Dr. Spock: Letters About the Vietnam War to America's Favorite Baby Doctor.* New York: New York University Press, 2005.

Foner, Philip. *U.S. Labor and the Vietnam War.* New York: International Publishers, 1989.

Franklin, H. Bruce. *M.I.A. or Mythmaking in America*. New York: Lawrence Hill Books, 1992.

Frankum, Ronald. *Like Rolling Thunder: The Air War in Vietnam, 1964–1975*. Lanham, MD: Rowman and Littlefield, 2005.

Fraser, Ronald, ed. *1968: A Student Generation in Revolt*. New York: Pantheon, 1988.

Freedman, Lawrence. *Kennedy's Wars: Berlin, Cuba, Laos, and Vietnam*. New York: Oxford University Press, 2000.

Freeman, Jo. *At Berkeley in the Sixties: The Education of an Activist, 1961–1965*. Bloomington: Indiana University Press, 2004.

French, Albert. *Patches of Fire: A Story of War and Redemption*. New York: Anchor Books, 1997.

Frey-Wouters, Ellen, and Robert Laufer. *Legacy of a War: The American Soldier in Vietnam*. Armonk, NY: M. E. Sharpe, 1986.

Friedland, Michael. *Lift Up Your Voice Like A Trumpet: White Clergy and the Civil Rights and Antiwar Movements, 1954–1973*. Chapel Hill: University of North Carolina Press, 1998.

Fry, Joseph A. "Unpopular Messengers: Student Opposition to the Vietnam War." In *The War That Never Ends: New Perspectives on the Vietnam War*, edited by David L. Anderson and John Ernst, 219–243. Lexington: University Press of Kentucky, 2007.

Fry, Joseph A. *Debating Vietnam: Fulbright, Stennis, and Their Senate Hearings*. Lanham, MD: Rowman and Littlefield, 2006.

Gardner, Lloyd C., and Ted Gittinger, eds. *Vietnam: The Early Decisions*. Austin: University of Texas Press, 1997.

Gardner, Lloyd C. *Pay Any Price: Lyndon Johnson and the Wars for Vietnam*. Chicago: Ivan Dee, 1995.

Gibbons, William Conrad. *The U.S. Government and the Vietnam War: Executive and Legislative Roles and Relationships*, 4 vols. Princeton, NJ: Princeton University Press, 1995.

Gilbert, Marc Jason, ed. *The Vietnam War on Campus: Other Voices, More Distant Drums*. Westport, CT: Greenwood, 2001.

Gill, Jill K. "The Decline of Real Ecumenism: Robert Bilheimer and the Vietnam War." *The Journal of Presbyterian History* 81 (Winter 2003): 242–263.

Gill, Jill K. "Peace Is Not the Absence of Conflict, but the Presence of Justice: The National Council of Churches' Reaction and Response to the Vietnam War, 1965–1973." Ph.D. diss., University of Pennsylvania, 1996.

Gill, Jill K. "The Political Price of Prophetic Leadership: The National Council of Churches and the Vietnam War." *Peace and Change* 27 (April 2002): 271–300.

Gill, Jill K. "The Politics of Ecumenical Disunity: The Troubled Marriage of Church World Service and the National Council of Churches." *Religion and American Culture* 14, No. 2 (Summer 2004): 175–212.

Gillam, James. *War in the Central Highlands of Vietnam, 1968–1970: An Historian's Experience*. Lewiston, NY: Edwin Mellen Press, 2006.

Gioglio, Gerald. *Days of Decision: An Oral History of Conscientious Objectors in the Military During the Vietnam War*. Trenton, NJ: Broken Rifle Press, 1989.

Gitlin, Todd. *The Sixties: Years of Hope, Days of Rage*, rev. ed. New York: Bantam, 1993.

Gitlin, Todd. *The Whole World Is Watching: Mass Media in the Making and Unmaking of the New Left*. Berkeley: University of California Press, 1980.

Goldstein, Warren. *William Sloane Coffin, Jr.: A Holy Impatience*. New Haven, CT: Yale University Press, 2004.

Gosse, Van. *The Movements of the New Left, 1950–1975: A Brief History with Documents*. Boston: Bedford/St. Martin's, 2004.

Gosse, Van. *Rethinking the New Left: An Interpretive History*. New York: Palgrave Macmillan, 2005.

Gottlieb, Sherry Gershon. *Hell No, We Won't Go: Resisting the Draft During the Vietnam War*. New York: Viking, 1991.

Graham, Herman III. *The Brothers' Vietnam War: Black Power, Manhood, and the Military Experience*. Gainesville: University Press of Florida, 2003.

Greeley, Andrew M. *Building Coalitions: American Politics in the 1970s*. New York: New Viewpoints, 1974.

Grose, Andrew. "Voices of Southern Protest During the Vietnam War Era: The University of South Carolina as a Case Study." *Peace and Change* 32 (April 2007): 153–167.

Grzyb, Frank. *A Story for All Americans: Vietnam, Victims, and Veterans*. West Lafayette, IN: Purdue University Press, 2000.

Halberstam, David. *The Best and the Brightest*. New York: Random House, 1972.

Halberstam, David. *The Making of a Quagmire*. New York: Harper and Row, 1965.

Halberstam, David. *The Powers That Be*. New York: Alfred A. Knopf, 1979.

Hall, Mitchell K. *Because of Their Faith: CALCAV and Religious Opposition to the Vietnam War*. New York: Columbia University Press, 1990.

Hall, Mitchell K. "'A Crack In Time': The Response of Students at the University of Kentucky to the Tragedy at Kent State, May 1970." *Register of the Kentucky Historical Society* 83 (Winter 1985): 36–63.

Hall, Mitchell K. *Crossroads: American Popular Culture and the Vietnam Generation*. Lanham, MD: Rowman and Littlefield, 2005.

Hall, Mitchell K. "A Time For War: The Church of God's Response to the Vietnam War." *Indiana Magazine of History* 79 (December 1983): 285–304.

Hall, Mitchell K. *The Vietnam War*, rev. 2nd ed. Harlow, UK: Pearson Longman, 2008.

Hall, Simon. *Peace and Freedom: The Civil Rights and Antiwar Movements in the 1960s.* Philadelphia: University of Pennsylvania Press, 2005.

Hall, Simon. "The Response of the Moderate Wing of the Civil Rights Movement to the War in Vietnam." *Historical Journal* [Great Britain] 46 (September 2003): 669–701.

Hallin, Daniel C. *The "Uncensored War": The Media and Vietnam.* New York: Oxford University Press, 1986.

Halstead, Fred. *Out Now! A Participant's Account of the American Movement Against the Vietnam War.* New York: Monad Press, 1978.

Hammond, William M. *Reporting Vietnam: Media and Military at War.* Lawrence: University Press of Kansas, 1998.

Hayden, Tom. *Reunion: A Memoir.* New York: Random House, 1988.

Heikkila, Kimberly Laina. "G.I. Gender: Vietnam War-Era Women Veterans and U.S. Citizenship." Ph.D. diss., University of Minnesota, 2002.

Heineman, Kenneth J. "American Schism: Catholic Activists, Intellectuals, and Students Confront the Vietnam War." In *The Vietnam War on Campus: Other Voices, More Distant Drums,* edited by Marc Jason Gilbert, 89–118. Westport, CT: Greenwood Press, 2000.

Heineman, Kenneth J. *Campus Wars: The Peace Movement at American State Universities in the Vietnam Era.* New York: New York University Press, 1993.

Heineman, Kenneth J. *God is a Conservative: Religion, Politics, and Morality in Contemporary America.* New York: New York University Press, 1998.

Heineman, Kenneth J. *Put Your Bodies Upon the Wheels: Student Revolt in the 1960s.* Chicago: Ivan R. Dee, 2001.

Heineman, Kenneth. "The Silent Majority Speaks: Antiwar Protest and Backlash, 1965–1972." *Peace and Change* 17 (October 1992): 402–433.

Herring, George C. *America's Longest War: The United States and Vietnam 1950–1975.* 4th ed. New York: McGraw-Hill, 2002.

Herring, George C. *LBJ and Vietnam: A Different Kind of War.* Austin: University of Texas Press, 1994.

Hershberger, Mary. *Traveling to Vietnam: American Peace Activists and the War.* Syracuse, NY: Syracuse University Press, 1998.

Herz, Martin F. *The Prestige Press and the Christmas Bombing, 1972: Images and Reality in Vietnam.* Washington, DC: Ethics and Public Policy Center, 1980.

Hess, Gary R. *Presidential Decisions for War: Korea, Vietnam, and the Persian Gulf.* Baltimore: Johns Hopkins University Press, 2001.

Hess, Gary R. *Vietnam: Explaining America's Lost War.* Malden, MA: Wiley-Blackwell, 2008.

Hess, Gary R. *Vietnam and the United States: Origins and Legacy of War.* Boston: Twayne, 1990.

Higgins, Marguerite. *Our Vietnam Nightmare.* New York: Harper and Row, 1965.

Hodges, Robert C. "The Cooing of a Dove: Senator Albert Gore Sr.'s Opposition to the War in Vietnam." *Peace and Change* 22 (April 1997): 132–153.

Hoefferle, Caroline. "A Comparative History of Student Activism in Britain and the United States, 1960 to 1975." Ph.D. diss., Central Michigan University, 2000.

Hoefferle, Caroline. "Just at Sunrise: The Sunrise Communal Farm in Rural Mid-Michigan, 1971–1978. *Michigan Historical Review* 23 (Spring 1997): 70–104.

Holm, Tom. *Strong Hearts, Wounded Souls: Native American Veterans of the Vietnam War.* Austin: University of Texas Press, 1996.

Huebner, Andrew J. *The Warrior Image: Soldiers in American Culture From the Second World War to the Vietnam Era.* Chapel Hill: University of North Carolina Press, 2008.

Huebner, Andrew J. "Rethinking American Press Coverage of the Vietnam War, 1965–68." *Journalism History* 31 (Fall 2005): 150–161.

Huebner, Andrew J. "Support Unseen: Rhode Island and the Vietnam War, 1965–1973." *Rhode Island History* 60 (Winter 2002): 2–25.

Hunt, Andrew. *The Turning: A History of Vietnam Veterans Against the War.* New York: New York University Press, 1999.

Hunt, Michael H. *Lyndon Johnson's War: America's Cold War Crusade in Vietnam, 1945–1968.* New York: Hill and Wang, 1996.

Hurwitz, Ken. *Marching Nowhere.* New York: Norton, 1971.

Ives, Christopher. *U.S. Special Forces and Counterinsurgency in Vietnam: Military Innovation and Institutional Failure, 1961–63.* New York: Routledge, 2006.

Jablon, Howard. "General David M. Shoup, U.S.M.C.: Warrior and War Protester." *Journal of Military History* 60 (July 1996): 513–538.

Jacobs, Seth. *America's Miracle Man in Vietnam: Ngo Dinh Diem, Religion, Race, and U.S. Intervention in Southeast Asia, 1950–1957.* Durham, NC: Duke University Press, 2005.

Jacobs, Seth. *Cold War Mandarin: Ngo Dinh Diem and the Origins of America's War in Vietnam, 1950–1963.* Lanham, MD: Rowman and Littlefield, 2006.

Jacobs, Seth. "'A Monumental Struggle of Good Versus Evil': American Crusaders in Vietnam and Iraq." *New England Journal of History* 64 (Fall 2007): 214–232.

Jacobs, Seth. "'Our System Demands the Supreme Being': The U.S. Religious Revival and the 'Diem Experiment,' 1954–55." *Diplomatic History* 25 (Fall 2001): 589–624.

Jeffords, Susan. *The Remasculinization of America: Gender and the Vietnam War.* Bloomington: Indiana University Press, 1989.

Jeffreys-Jones, Rhodri. *Changing Differences: Women and the Shaping of American Foreign Policy, 1917–1994.* New Brunswick, NJ: Rutgers University Press, 1995.

Jeffreys-Jones, Rhodri. *The CIA and American Democracy.* New Haven, CT: Yale University Press, 1989.

Jeffreys-Jones, Rhodri. *Peace Now! American Society and the Ending of the Vietnam War.* New Haven, CT: Yale University Press, 1999.

Jespersen, Christopher. "The Bitter End and the Lost Chance in Vietnam: Congress, the Ford Administration and the Battle Over Vietnam, 1975–1976." *Diplomatic History* 24 (Spring 2000): 265–293.

Jespersen, Christopher. "Kissinger, Ford, and Congress: The Very Bitter End in Vietnam." *Pacific Historical Review* 71 (August 2002): 439–473.

Johns, Andrew L. "Achilles' Heel: The Vietnam War and George Romney's Bid for the Presidency, 1967 to 1968." *Michigan Historical Review* 26 (Spring 2000): 1–29.

Johns, Andrew L. "Doves Among Hawks: Republican Opposition to the Vietnam War, 1964–1968." *Peace and Change* 31 (October 2006): 585–628.

Johns, Andrew L. "The Loyal Opposition: The Republican Party and the Domestic Politics of the Vietnam War, 1960–1969." Ph.D. diss., University of California at Santa Barbara, 2000.

Johnson, Robert David. *Congress and the Cold War.* New York: Cambridge University Press, 2006.

Jones, Howard. *Death of a Generation: How the Assassinations of Diem and JFK Prolonged the Vietnam War.* New York: Oxford University Press, 2002.

Joseph, Paul. *Cracks in the Empire: State Politics in the Vietnam War.* Boston: South End Press, 1981.

Kahin, George. *Intervention: How America Became Involved in Vietnam.* New York: Anchor Books, 1987.

Kamil, Tarik W. "The Politics of Time and Eternity: Quaker Pacifists and Their Activism During the Vietnam War Era." Ph.D. diss., Ohio University, 2006.

Kent, Steven A. *From Slogans to Mantras: Social Protest and Religious Conversion in the Late Vietnam War Era.* Syracuse, NY: Syracuse University Press, 2001.

Kimball, Jeffrey. *Nixon's Vietnam War.* Lawrence: University Press of Kansas, 1998.

Kimbrough, Natalie. *Equality or Discrimination? African Americans in the U.S. Military During the Vietnam War.* Lanham, MD: University Press of America, 2007.

Klatch, Rebecca E. *A Generation Divided: The New Left, the New Right, and the 1960s.* Berkeley: University of California Press, 1999.

Krepinevich, Andrew. *The Army and Vietnam.* Baltimore: Johns Hopkins University Press, 1986.

Laffey, Virginia M. "The Invisible Regiment: The Wives, Mothers and Girlfriends of American Soldiers in Vietnam." Ph.D. diss., Boston University, 2006.

Landers, James. *The Weekly War: News Magazines and Vietnam.* Columbia: University of Missouri Press, 2004.

Lawrence, Mark Atwood. *Assuming the Burden: Europe and the American Commitment to War in Vietnam.* Berkeley: University of California Press, 2005.

Lawrence, Mark Atwood. "Mission Intolerable: Harrison Salisbury's Trip to Hanoi and the Limits of Dissent Against the Vietnam War." *Pacific Historical Review* 75 (August 2006): 429–459.

Leaman, David. "Politicized Service and Teamwork Tensions: Mennonite Central Committee in Vietnam, 1966–1969." *Mennonite Quarterly Review* 71 (October 1997): 544–70.

Levy, David W. *The Debate over Vietnam,* 2nd ed. Baltimore: Johns Hopkins University Press, 1995.

Levy, Peter. *The New Left and Labor in the 1960s.* Urbana: University of Illinois Press, 1994.

Lichtenstein, Nelson. *The Most Dangerous Man in Detroit: Walter Reuther and the Fate of American Labor.* Urbana: University of Illinois Press, 1995.

Lieberman, Robbie. *Prairie Power: Voices of 1960s Midwestern Student Protest.* Columbia: University of Missouri Press, 2004.

Lind, Michael. *Vietnam, The Necessary War: A Reinterpretation of America's Most Disastrous Military Conflict.* New York: Free Press, 1999.

Linder, Mark. *Wars of Attrition: Vietnam, the Business Roundtable, and the Decline of Construction Unions.* Iowa City, IA: Fanpihun Press, 1999.

Logevall, Fredrik. "Lyndon Johnson and Vietnam." *Presidential Studies Quarterly* 34 (March 2004): 100–112.

Logevall, Fredrik. *Choosing War: The Lost Chance for Peace and the Escalation of War in Vietnam.* Berkeley: University of California Press, 1999.

Logevall, Fredrik. "First Among Critics: Walter Lippmann and the Vietnam War." *Journal of American-East Asian Relations* 4 (Winter 1995): 351–375.

Logevall, Fredrik. *The Origins of the Vietnam War.* Harlow, UK: Longman, 2001.

Longley, Kyle. *Grunts: The American Combat Soldier in Vietnam.* Armonk, NY: M. E. Sharpe, 2008.

Longley, Kyle. *Senator Albert Gore, Sr.: Tennessee Maverick.* Baton Rouge: Louisiana State University Press, 2004.

Lucas, Brad. *Radicals, Rhetoric, and the War: The University of Nevada in the Wake of Kent State.* New York: Palgrave Macmillan, 2006.

Lyons, Paul. *New Left, New Right, and the Legacy of the Sixties.* Philadelphia: Temple University Press, 1996.

Maclear, Michael. *The 10,000 Day War: Vietnam.* New York: St. Martin's Press, 1981.

Mahedy, William. *Out of the Night: The Spiritual Journey of Vietnam Vets.* New York: Ballantine Books, 1986.

Mailer, Norman. *The Armies of the Night: History as a Novel, the Novel as History.* New York: New American Library, 1968.

Mann, Robert. *A Grand Delusion: America's Descent into Vietnam.* New York: Basic Books, 2001.

Manning, Keri Lynn. "No More John Waynes: Vietnam Veterans Against the War and Cold War Era Masculinity." Ph.D. diss., University of Kentucky, 2003.

Maraniss, David. *They Marched Into Sunlight: War and Peace in Vietnam and America, October 1967.* New York: Simon and Schuster, 2003.

Marshall, Kathryn. *In the Combat Zone: An Oral History of American Women in Vietnam, 1966–1975.* Boston: Little, Brown, 1987.

Martin, William. *A Prophet with Honor: The Billy Graham Story.* New York: William Morrow, 1991.

Martin, William. *With God On Our Side: The Rise of the Religious Right in America.* New York: Broadway Books, 1996.

Masur, Matthew B. "Hearts and Minds: Cultural Nation-Building in South Vietnam, 1954–1963." Ph.D. diss., Ohio State University, 2004.

Maxwell, Donald W. "Religion and Politics at the Border: Canadian Church Support for American Vietnam War Resisters." *Journal of Church and State* 48 (September 2006): 807–829.

McAdam, Doug, and Yang Su. "The War at Home: Antiwar Protests and Congressional Voting, 1965–1973." *American Sociological Review* 67 (October 2002): 696–721.

McCormack, Suzanne Kelley. "'Good Politics Is Doing Something': Independent Diplomats and Anti-War Activists in the Vietnam-Era Peace Movement. A Collective Biography." Ph.D. diss., Boston College, 2002.

McIntire, Anthony Andrew. "The American Soldier in Vietnam." Ph.D. diss., University of Kentucky, 1996.

McIntire, Anthony A. "The Kentucky National Guard in Vietnam: The Story of Bardstown's Battery C at War." *Register of the Kentucky Historical Society* 92 (Spring 1992): 140–164.

McMahon, Robert, ed. *Major Problems in the History of the Vietnam War.* 4th ed. Boston: Houghton Mifflin, 2008.

McMaster, H. R. *Dereliction of Duty: Lyndon Johnson, Robert McNamara, the Joint Chiefs of Staff, and the Lies That Led to Vietnam.* New York: HarperCollins, 1997.

McNamara, Robert S. *In Retrospect: The Tragedy and Lessons of Vietnam.* New York: Random House, 1995.

Mecklin, John. *Mission in Torment: An Intimate Account of the U.S. Role in Vietnam.* Garden City, NY: Doubleday, 1965.

Michel, Gregg. "'We'll Take Our Stand': The Southern Student Organizing Committee and the Radicalization of White Southern Students, 1964–1969." Ph.D. diss., University of Virginia, 1999.

Milam, John Ronald. "Not a Gentleman's War: Junior Officers in the Vietnam War." Ph.D. diss., University of Houston, 2004.

Miller, Edward Garvey. "Grand Designs: Vision, Power and Nation Building in America's Alliance With Ngo Dinh Diem, 1954–1960." Ph.D. diss., Harvard University, 2004.

Miller, James. *Democracy Is in the Streets: From Port Huron to the Siege of Chicago.* New York: Simon and Schuster, 1987.

Milne, David. "'Our Equivalent of Guerrilla Warfare': Walt Rostow and the Bombing of North Vietnam, 1961–68." *Journal of Military History* 71 (January 2007): 169–203.

Moise, Edwin. *Tonkin Gulf and the Escalation of the Vietnam War.* Chapel Hill: University of North Carolina Press, 1996.

Mollin, Marian. *Radical Pacifism in Modern America: Egalitarianism and Protest.* Philadelphia: University of Pennsylvania Press, 2006.

Monhollon, Rusty L. *"This Is America?" The Sixties in Lawrence, Kansas.* New York: Palgrave Macmillan, 2002.

Moon, Penelope Adams. "'Peace on Earth—Peace in Vietnam': The Catholic Peace Fellowship and Antiwar Witness, 1964–1976." *Journal of Social History* 36 (Summer 2003): 1033–1057.

Moore, Harold G., and Joseph L. Galloway. *We Were Soldiers Once—and Young: Ia Drang, the Battle that Changed the War in Vietnam.* New York: Harper-Perennial, 1993.

Morgan, Joseph G. *The Vietnam Lobby: The American Friends of Vietnam, 1955–1975.* Chapel Hill: University of North Carolina Press, 1997.

Moser, Richard R. *The New Winter Soldiers: GI and Veteran Dissent During the Vietnam Era.* New Brunswick, NJ: Rutgers University Press, 1996.

Moyar, Mark. *Triumph Forsaken: The Vietnam War, 1954–1965.* Cambridge, UK: Cambridge University Press, 2006.

Mullen, Robert W. *Blacks and Vietnam.* Washington, DC: University Press of America, 1981.

Nashel, Jonathan. *Edward Lansdale's Cold War.* Amherst: University of Massachusetts Press, 2005.

Newfield, Jack. *A Prophetic Minority: The American New Left.* New York: New American Library, 1966.

Newman, John M. *JFK and Vietnam: Deception, Intrigue, and the Struggle for Power.* New York: Warner Books, 1992.

Nicosia, Gerald. *Home to War: A History of the Vietnam Veterans' Movement.* New York: Crown Publishers, 2001.

Norman, Elizabeth. *Women at War: The Story of Fifty Military Nurses Who Served in Vietnam.* Philadelphia: University of Pennsylvania Press, 1990.

Nutt, Rick. *Toward Peacemaking: Presbyterians in the South and National Security, 1945–1983.* Tuscaloosa: University of Alabama Press, 1994.

Oglesby, Carl. *Ravens in the Storm: A Personal History of the 1960s Antiwar Movement.* New York: Scribner, 2008.

Oppenheimer, Mark. *Knocking on Heaven's Door: American Religion in the Age of Counterculture.* New Haven, CT: Yale University Press, 2003.

Oropeza, Lorena. *¡Raza Si! ¡Guerra No!: Chicano Protest and Patriotism During the Viet Nam War Era.* Berkeley: University of California Press, 2005.

Pach, Chester J., Jr. "And That's the Way It Was": The Vietnam War on the Network Nightly News." In *The Sixties: From Memory to History,* edited by David Farber, 90–118. Chapel Hill: University of North Carolina Press, 1994.

Palmer, Laura. *Shrapnel in the Heart: Letters and Remembrances from the Vietnam Veterans Memorial.* New York: Random House, 1987.

Paolantonio, S. A. *Frank Rizzo: The Last Big Man in Big City America.* Philadelphia: Camino Books, 1993.

Power, Charlotte Ann. "A Quiet Revolution: American Women and the Vietnam War, 1964–1975." Ph.D. diss., University of Memphis, 2001.

Prashker, Ivan. *Duty, Honor, Vietnam: Twelve Men of West Point Tell Their Stories.* New York: Warner Books, 1988.

Pratt, Andrew LeRoy. "Religious Faith and Civil Religion: Evangelical Responses to the Vietnam War, 1964–1973." Ph.D. diss., Southern Baptist Theological Seminary, 1988.

Preston, Andrew. *The War Council: McGeorge Bundy, the NSC, and Vietnam.* Cambridge, MA: Harvard University Press, 2006.

Prochnau, William. *Once Upon a Distant War: David Halberstam, Neil Sheehan, Peter Arnett—Three Young War Correspondents and Their Early Vietnam Battles.* New York: Random House, 1995.

Quigley, Thomas E., ed. *American Catholics and Vietnam.* Grand Rapids, MI: Eerdmans, 1968.

Reardon, Carol. *Launch the Intruders: A Naval Attack Squadron in the Vietnam War, 1972.* Lawrence: University Press of Kansas, 2005.

Rexilius, Ronald Jay. "Americans Without Dog Tags: U.S. Civilians in the Vietnam War, 1950–1975." Ph.D. diss., University of Nebraska-Lincoln, 2000.

Rhodes, John. *Rejoice or Cry: The Diary of a Recon Marine, Vietnam, 1967–1968.* Danbury, CT: Economy Printing, 1996.

Rieder, Jonathan. *Canarsie: The Jews and Italians of Brooklyn Against Liberalism.* Cambridge, MA: Harvard University Press, 1985.

Rising, George. *Clean For Gene: Eugene McCarthy's 1968 Presidential Campaign.* Westport, CT: Praeger, 1997.

Rising, George Goodwin. "Stuck in the Sixties: Conservatives and the Legacies of the 1960s." Ph.D. diss., University of Arizona, 2003.

Robbins, Mary Susannah, ed. *Against the War: Writings by Activists,* rev. ed. Lanham, MD: Rowman and Littlefield, 2007.

Robinson, Archie. *George Meany and His Times.* New York: Simon and Schuster, 1981.

Rochester, Stuart, and Frederick Kiley. *Honor Bound: American Prisoners of War in Southeast Asia, 1961–1973.* Annapolis, MD: Naval Institute Press, 1999.

Rodell, Paul A. "International Voluntary Services in Vietnam: War and the Birth of Activism, 1958–1967." *Peace and Change* 27 (April 2002): 225–244.

Rorabaugh, William J. *Berkeley at War: The 1960s.* New York: Oxford University Press, 1989.

Rosen, Ruth. *The World Split Open: How the Modern Women's Movement Changed America.* New York: Penguin, 2001.

Rossinow, Doug. *The Politics of Authenticity: Liberalism, Christianity, and the New Left in America*. New York: Columbia University Press, 1998.

Rusk, Dean, as told to Richard Rusk. *As I Saw It*. New York: W. W. Norton, 1990.

Salisbury, Harrison. *Behind the Lines: Hanoi, December 23, 1966–January 7, 1967*. New York: Harper & Row, 1967.

Santoli, Al. *Everything We Had: An Oral History of the Vietnam War by Thirty-Three American Soldiers Who Fought It*. New York: Ballantine Books, 1981.

Schmitz, David F. *The Tet Offensive: Politics, War, and Public Opinion*. Lanham, MD: Rowman and Littlefield, 2005.

Schmitz, David F., and Natalie Fousekis. "Frank Church, the Senate, and the Emergence of Dissent on the Vietnam War." *Pacific Historical Review* 63 (November 1994): 561–581.

Schneider, Gregory L. *Cadres for Conservatism: Young Americans for Freedom and the Rise of the Contemporary Right*. New York: New York University Press, 1999.

Schoenbaum, Thomas J. *Waging Peace and War: Dean Rusk in the Truman, Kennedy, and Johnson Years*. New York: Simon and Schuster, 1988.

Schulzinger, Robert D. *A Time for War: The United States and Vietnam, 1941–1975*. New York: Oxford University Press, 1997.

Settje, David E. *Lutherans and the Longest War: Adrift on a Sea of Doubt about the Cold and Vietnam Wars, 1964–1975*. Lanham, MD: Lexington Books, 2007.

Sheehan, Neil. *A Bright Shining Lie: John Paul Vann and America in Vietnam*. New York: Random House, 1988.

Sherwood, John Darrell. *Black Sailor, White Navy: Racial Unrest in the Fleet During the Vietnam War Era*. New York: New York University Press, 2007.

Siggelkow, Richard. *Dissent and Disruption: A University Under Siege*. Buffalo, NY: Prometheus Books, 1991.

Simmons, Gwendolyn Zoharah (a.k.a. Gwendolyn Robinson). "Mama Told Me Not to Go." In *Time it Was: American Stories from the Sixties*, edited by Karen Manners Smith and Tim Koster, 93–118. Upper Saddle River, NJ: Pearson/Prentice Hall, 2008.

Sitkoff, Harvard. *The Struggle for Black Equality 1954–1992*, rev. ed. New York: Hill and Wang, 1993.

Small, Melvin. *Antiwarriors: The Vietnam War and the Battle for America's Hearts and Minds*. Wilmington, DE: Scholarly Resources, 2002.

Small, Melvin. *At the Water's Edge: American Politics and the Vietnam War*. Chicago: Ivan R. Dee, 2005.

Small, Melvin. *Covering Dissent: The Media and the Anti-Vietnam War Movement*. New Brunswick, NJ: Rutgers University Press, 1994.

Small, Melvin. *Johnson, Nixon, and the Doves.* New Brunswick, NJ: Rutgers University Press, 1988.

Small, Melvin, and William Hoover, eds. *Give Peace a Chance: Exploring the Vietnam Antiwar Movement.* Syracuse, NY: Syracuse University Press, 1992.

Smith, Winnie. *American Daughter Gone to War: On the Front Lines With an Army Nurse in Vietnam.* New York: William Morrow, 1992.

Snyder, Douglas J. "Dissent in Detroit: Anti-Vietnam War Protest at Wayne State University, 1965–1971." Ph.D. diss., Wayne State University, 2006.

Sorley, Lewis. *A Better War: The Unexamined Victories and Final Tragedy of America's Last Years in Vietnam.* New York: Harcourt Brace, 1999.

Spann, Edward K. *Democracy's Children: The Young Rebels of the 1960s and the Power of Ideals.* Wilmington, DE: Scholarly Resources, 2003.

Spector, Ronald. *After Tet: The Bloodiest Year in Vietnam.* New York: Free Press, 1993.

Stanton, Shelby L. *The Rise and Fall of an American Army: U.S. Ground Forces in Vietnam, 1965–1973.* Novato, CA: Presidio Press, 1985.

Statler, Kathryn C. *Replacing France: The Origins of American Intervention in Vietnam.* Lexington: University Press of Kentucky, 2007.

Staub, Michael E., ed. *The Jewish 1960s: An American Sourcebook.* Lebanon, NH: Brandeis University Press, 2004.

Stockdale, Jim, and Sybil Stockdale. *In Love and War: The Story of a Family's Ordeal and Sacrifice During the Vietnam War.* New York: Harper & Row, 1984.

Stone, Gary. *Elites for Peace: The Senate and the Vietnam War, 1964–1968.* Knoxville: University of Tennessee Press, 2007.

Swerdlow, Amy. *Women's Strike for Peace: Traditional Motherhood and Radical Politics in the 1960s.* Chicago: University of Chicago Press, 1993.

Terry, Wallace. *Bloods: An Oral History of the Vietnam War by Black Veterans.* New York: Random House, 1984.

Turner, Jeffrey A. "From the Sit-Ins to Vietnam: The Evolution of Student Activism on Southern College Campuses, 1960–1970." *History of Higher Education Annual* 21 (2001): 103–135.

Turner, Kathleen J. *Lyndon Johnson's Dual War: Vietnam and the Press.* Chicago: University of Chicago Press, 1985.

Van Devanter, Lynda. *Home Before Morning: The Story of an American Nurse in Vietnam.* New York: Warner Books, 1983.

Varon, Jeremy. *Bringing the War Home: The Weather Underground, the Red Army Faction, and Revolutionary Violence in the Sixties and Seventies.* Berkeley: University of California Press, 2004.

Veith, George. *Code-Name Bright Light: The Untold Story of U.S. POW Rescue Efforts During the Vietnam War.* New York: The Free Press, 1998.

Vuic, Kara Dixon. "'I'm Afraid We're Going to Have to Just Change Our Ways': Marriage, Motherhood, and Pregnancy in the Army Nurse Corps During the Vietnam War." *Signs: Journal of Women in Culture and Society* 32 (Summer 2007): 997–1022.

Vuic, Kara Dixon. "'Officer, Nurse, Woman': Defining Gender in the U.S. Army Nurse Corps in the Vietnam War." Ph.D. diss., Indiana University 2006.

Walker, Keith. *A Piece of My Heart: The Stories of 26 American Women Who Served in Vietnam.* Novato, CA: Presidio Press, 1985.

Walker, Mark. *Vietnam Veteran Films.* Metuchen, NJ: Scarecrow Press, 1991.

Wehrle, Edmund F. *Between a River and a Mountain: The AFL-CIO and the Vietnam War.* Ann Arbor: University of Michigan Press, 2005.

Wehrle, Edmund F. "Labor's Longest War: Trade Unionists and the Vietnam Conflict." *Labor's Heritage* 11 (Winter-Spring 2002): 50–65.

Wehrle, Edmund F. "'No More Pressing Task Than Organization in Southeast Asia': The AFL-CIO Approaches the Vietnam War." *Labor History* [Great Britain] 42 (August 2001): 277–295.

Wells, Tom. *The War Within: America's Battle Over Vietnam.* Berkeley: University of California Press, 1994.

Westheider, James E. *The African American Experience in Vietnam: Brothers in Arms.* Lanham, MD: Rowman and Littlefield, 2007.

Westheider, James E. *Fighting on Two Fronts: African Americans and the Vietnam War.* New York: New York University Press, 1997.

Westmoreland, William C. *A Soldier Reports.* New York: Dell, 1980.

Wiest, Andrew, ed. *Rolling Thunder in a Gentle Land: The Vietnam War Revisited.* Oxford: Osprey, 2006.

Willbanks, James H. *Abandoning Vietnam: How America Left and South Vietnam Lost its War.* Lawrence: University Press of Kansas, 2004.

Willbanks, James H. *The Battle of An Loc.* Bloomington: Indiana University Press, 2005.

Willbanks, James H. *The Tet Offensive: A Concise History.* New York: Columbia University Press, 2006.

Woods, Randall B. *J. William Fulbright, Vietnam, and the Search for a Cold War Foreign Policy.* New York: Cambridge University Press, 1998.

Woods, Randall B. "The Politics of Idealism: Lyndon Johnson, Civil Rights, and Vietnam." *Diplomatic History* 31 (January 2007): 1–18.

Woods, Randall B., ed. *Vietnam and the American Political Tradition: The Politics of Dissent.* New York: Cambridge University Press, 2003.

Wright, Elisse Yvette. "Birds of a Different Feather: African American Support for the Vietnam War in the Johnson Years, 1965–1969." Ph.D. diss., Ohio State University, 2002.

Wuthnow, Robert, and John Evans, eds. *The Quiet Hand of God: Faith-based Activism and the Public Role of Mainline Protestantism.* Berkeley: University of California Press, 2002.

Wyatt, Clarence. "'At the Cannon's Mouth': The American Press and the Vietnam War." *Journalism History* 13 (Autumn-Winter 1986): 104–113.

Wyatt, Clarence. "The Media and the Vietnam War." In *The War That Never Ends: New Perspectives on the Vietnam War,* edited by David Anderson and John Ernst, 265–288. Lexington: University Press of Kentucky, 2007.

Wyatt, Clarence. *Paper Soldiers: The American Press and the Vietnam War.* New York: W. W. Norton, 1993.

Wynkoop, Mary Ann. *Dissent in the Heartland: The Sixties at Indiana University.* Bloomington: Indiana University Press, 2002.

Ybarra, Lea. *Vietnam Veteranos: Chicanos Recall the War.* Austin: University of Texas Press, 2004.

Zaretsky, Natasha. "Private Suffering and Public Strife: Delia Alvarez's War with the Nixon Administration's POW Publicity Campaign, 1968–1973." In *Race, Nation, and Empire in American History,* edited by Matthew Guterl, James Campbell, and Robert Lee, 201–228. Chapel Hill: University of North Carolina Press, 2007.

Zaroulis, Nancy, and Gerald Sullivan. *Who Spoke Up? American Protest Against the War in Vietnam, 1963–1975.* New York: Doubleday, 1984.

Zeiler, Thomas W. *Dean Rusk: Defending the American Mission Abroad.* Wilmington, DE: SR Books, 2000.

Zhai, Qiang. *China and the Vietnam Wars, 1950–1975.* Chapel Hill: University of North Carolina, 2000.

Zieger, Robert. *American Workers, American Unions, 1920–1985.* Baltimore: Johns Hopkins University Press, 1986.

Index

Note: italic page numbers indicate pictures.

AAFLI. *See* Asian American Free Labor
    Institute
Abrams, Creighton, 52–53, 219
Abzug, Bella, 75, 124
ACCC. *See* American Council of Christian
    Churches
Adams, Jane, 188, 193
Adams, Maurice L., 162
Advisers. *See* American advisers
    [nonmilitary]; U.S. military advisers
AFL-CIO, xviii, 219
    African Labor College, 170
    and antiwar movement within the ranks,
        173–174, 179
    clash with protesters at 1965 convention,
        170–171
    and economic crisis of early 1970s, 181
    estrangement from Democratic Party, 181
    and foreign policy, 168
    formation of, 167
    and Johnson, 170, 174
    and 1972 election, 180–181
    organizing efforts in Vietnam, 168–169
    support for Vietnam War, 170–171, 179
    and upheavals of 1968, 173
    Vietnam resolution (1965; text), 208–209
    and Wallace's candidacy (1968), 175–176
    See also Meany, George; Organized labor;
        Vietnamese Confederation of Labor
African Americans, xviii
    and advantages of military service, xviii,
        71, 149–150
    and antiwar movement, 66, 70–73

on chances of promotion, 159
disproportionate representation in
    combat units, 155
disproportionate representation in
    military ranks and death tolls, xviii,
    53, 150–151, 155–156, 165
doubts about racial egalitarianism in
    military, 150, 158
early patriotic feelings, 154
early support for draft, 152–153
interview with William Giles (text),
    211–213
and labor unions, 169, 172
and military justice, 158–159
and New Deal coalition, 80
officers, 160
and racial separation, 161
and racial solidarity, 160, 161–162
and racial violence, 163–164
reaction to King's assassination, 163
on receiving worst and most dangerous
    jobs, 159–160
reenlistment rate, 150
soldiers and civil rights movement,
    156–158, 160, 161–165
soldiers' conflicts with whites and
    officers, 53, 72–73
and transformation of military, 165
in Vietnam, *151*, 153–160, *156*
view of war as opportunity to prove
    oneself, 153–154
AFSC. *See* American Friends Service
    Committee

Agnew, Spiro, 110–111
AK-47 weapons, 48
ALA. *See* American Labor Alliance
Ali, Muhammad, 152
Allen, Doris "Lucki," 154
Alsop, Joe, 135, 138
Alvarez, Delia, 128, 219
Alvarez, Everett, Jr., 128
Amalgamated Clothing Workers of America
    (ACWA), 171, 179
America's Longest War, xi
American advisers, xv, 23–24
    failings of, 38–39
    numbers in Vietnam upon JFK's death, 6
    See also Michigan State University
        Vietnam Advisory Group; U.S. military
        advisers
American Council of Christian Churches
    (ACCC), 98, 109
American Federation of Labor and Congress
    of Industrial Organizations. *See*
    AFL-CIO
American Friends of Vietnam, 32
American Friends Service Committee
    (AFSC), 103, 118
American Institute for Free Labor
    Development (AIFLD), 169, 170
American Labor Alliance (ALA), 178
Americans for Democratic Action (ADA), 85
Anderson, Lionel, 159
Another Mother for Peace (AMP), 75, 123,
    124, 219
Anticommunism
    among policy makers, xiv, 2, 4
    as popular stance in U.S., 62
Antiwar movement, xiii, 61–62, 63
    and African Americans, 66, 70–73
    and antiwar congressional representatives,
        76
    and Christian student groups, 192
    clash between police and protesters at
        1968 Democratic convention, 175
    clash between protesters and labor at
        1965 AFL-CIO convention, 170–171
    diverse constituencies of, xv–xvi
    and draft resistance, 66, 70
    effect of draft lottery on student
        participation, 70, 90, 145
    hardhat demonstrations against, 90
    influence of civil rights movement, 66
    and King, 66
    liberals in, xvi
    motivations of participants, 64–66
    pacifists in, xvi
    prominence of Jews in student
        movement, 84
    radicals in, xvi
        reaction to Nixon's expansion of war, xiv
        SDS-sponsored demonstration
            (Washington, D.C., 1965), 192
        and shifting national sentiment, 76–77
        and students, 66–70
        and television coverage of war, 65–66
        and Tet Offensive, 64
        and war veterans, 77
        winding down of, 199
        and women, 66, 73–76
        See also Civil rights movement;
            Moratorium; Students; Students for a
            Democratic Society; Women's
            liberation movement
Apple, R. W., 143
Aptheker, Bettina, 69
Aptheker, Herbert, 69
Armed Forces Qualification Test (AFQT), 158
Army Classification Battery, 158
Army of the Republic of Vietnam (ARVN),
    41, 42–43, 219
    U.S. soldiers' lack of respect for, 154
    unreliability of, 50
Arnett, Peter, 136, 219
    attack by South Vietnamese police, 138
    on the killing in Southeast Asia, 139
ARVN. *See* Army of the Republic of Vietnam
Asian American Free Labor Institute
    (AAFLI), 170, 178, 180, 181–182,
    219–220
Ayers, Bill, 197

Baez, Joan, 63, 74–75, 124
Baldwin, Hanson, 143
Ball, George, xiv–xv, *11,* 220
    biographical sketch, 11–12
    on difficulties of guerrilla war, 12
    as dissenter within Johnson
        administration, 1, 12–13, 18–20
    and Kennedy, 12
    memorandum to Johnson (text), 207
    relations with Johnson and Rusk, 13
    on weakness of South Vietnam, 13
Ban Me Thuot, 29
Bao Dai, xii, 28
Bartlett, Charles, 134
Battle of Saigon, 25
Bay of Pigs invasion, 135
Bell, David, 152
Bennett, John, 104
Berrigan, Daniel, 101, 102–103, 104, 108,
    220
Berrigan, Philip, 101, 102–103, 108, 220
Bigart, Homer, 136, 137
Bilheimer, Robert, 105
Billy, 157
Black Mau Mau, 161

Black Panthers, 161, 190
Black Power, 190
Black Student Unions, 190–191
Blackstone Rangers, 161
Blake, Eugene Carson, 110
Bradlee, Ben, 134
Brandstatter, Arthur, 25
Brennan, Peter, 90
Brethren, 101
Bridges, Harry, 61, *62*
Brown, Clide, 163
Brown, Irving, 174
Brown, Jerry, 154, 158
Brown, Sam, 109
Browne, Malcolm, 136, 137
Buddhist Crisis, 102, 140, 220
Buis, Dale R., 42
Bunche, Ralph, 70
Bundy, Edgar, 98
Bundy, McGeorge, 6
Bunker, Ellsworth, 106, 174
Bush, George H. W., 74
Bush, George W., xi, 114

CALCAV. *See* Clergy and Laymen Concerned
    About Vietnam
California, University of, at Berkeley, 68–69
    Free Speech Movement, 68–69, 194,
        221–222
    large teach-in, 193
    Vietnam Day Committee, 69
Calkins, Laura M., 211–213
Calley, William L., Jr., 52, 143–144, 220
Cambodia, U.S. bombing of and incursion
    into, xiii–xiv, 55
Camp Lejeune, North Carolina, racial
    violence, 164
Can Lao Party, 35
Capitol Engineering, 29
Carmichael, Stokely, 152, 190, 220
Carper, Steven, 159
Carroll, John, 142
Carter, Jimmy, 94
Castro, Fidel, 191
Catholic Left, 108
Catholic Peace Fellowship (CPF), 101, 102,
    103
Catholic Relief Services, 101, 106, 118
Catholic Workers Movement, 101
Catholics
    and New Deal coalition, 80, 81–82
    as pacifists, 101
    pope's statement against wars, 103, 106
    as religious crusaders, 98
    as religious dissenters, 100
    as religious nationalists, 99
    as supporters and victims of war, 83–84

Cato, Charles, 150
Central Conference of American Rabbis,
    109–110
Chemical Workers Union, 178
Chicago Seven, 68, 220
    protest against trial of, *68*
Child, Frank C., 23–24
Chisholm, Shirley, 73
The Christian Century, 100, 102, 104–105
Christianity and Crisis, 100, 102
Christianity Today, 99, 104, 110
Church World Service, 101, 106
Church, Marguerite, 33
Civil disobedience, 108, 220
Civil Guard, 27, 28
Civil rights movement
    and African American soldiers, 156–158,
        160, 161–165
    influence on other movements, 66, 125,
        194
    Meany's support for, 169
    student participation in, 187–191
    See also African Americans; Carmichael,
        Stokely; King, Martin Luther, Jr.;
        Malcolm X; Student Nonviolent
        Coordinating Committee
Clarke, Victoria, 147
Clergy and Laymen Concerned About
    Vietnam (CALCAV), 77, 100, 104,
    107, 108, 109–110, 112, 220
    1967 statement (text), 209–211
Clifford, Clark, 5, 220–221
Clinton, Bill, xi, 94
Coburn, Judith, on Vietnam War (text),
    216–217
Cody, John Cardinal, 106
Coffin, William Sloane, 77, 104, 110, 221
Cold War, 1, 2, 221. *See also* Domino theory;
    U.S. policy makers
Colegrove, Albert, 31–32
Collins, Walter, 152
Columbia University student takeover, 69
Committee for a Sane Nuclear Policy
    (SANE), 109–110
Committee to End the War in Vietnam
    (CEWV), 192, 193
Commodity Import Program (CIP), 29, 30
Commonweal, 100
Communications Workers of America
    (CWA), 171
Conscientious objectors, 108–109
Consensus of memory, 131
Containment generation. *See* U.S. policy
    makers
Containment policy, 221
Conyers, John, 108
CPF. *See* Catholic Peace Fellowship

Credibility, 221
Cronkite, Walter, *136*
Cuban Missile Crisis, 135, 191
Cushing, Richard Cardinal, 109–110
CVT. *See* Vietnamese Confederation of Labor

Da Nang
    airbase, 142
    racial violence at Navy brig, 164
Daley, James, 162–163
Daniel, Clifton, 143
Dapping, 160, 162
Davis, Leon, 171
Davis, Sammy, Jr., 74
Dean, Howard, 94
The Deer Hunter, xi
Dellums, Ron, 73
Democratic Party
    amateur Democrats, 82, 85
    conflicts within, xvi
    convention of 1968, 175, 196
    and divisions to right and left, 84–86,
        91–93
    and New Deal coalition of minorities,
        80–82
    tensions between reformers and rank and
        file over Vietnam, 82–86
Denison, James, 25
Desert Shield/Desert Storm, 146
Dien Bien Phu, 41
Domino theory, 221
    and Eisenhower, 3
    and Johnson, 7
    and Truman, 2–3
Donlon, Roger, 43
Draft, 43–44, 53
    and antiwar movement, 66, 70
    disproportionate induction of poor and
        minorities, 150–152
    and immigration to Canada, 108
    lottery, 70, 90
    resistance, 66, 152
    student deferments and burden on
        working class, 83, 150–152
    and students, 192
Drugs, 54, 56
Durbrow, Elbridge, 32, 34, 36
Dylan, Bob, 66

Easter Offensive, xiv, 217
Ecumenical Witness conference, 113
Edwards, India, 75
Eisenhower, Dwight D., and administration,
    221
    aid to Saigon regime, 37
    and classified information, 133–134
    and domino theory, 2–3

labor support for, 82
    and McCarthy era, 3
    and military advisers, 42–43
    and MSUG, xv
    refusal to sign Geneva Accords, xii
Election of 1968, 85–87
Election of 1972, 91–93
Ellsberg, Daniel, 145, 221
Executive Order 9981, 149
Executive Order 10-290, 133–134
Executive Order 10-501, 133–134

Fascell, Dante, 33
FBI, and student activists, 195–196
Fellowship of Reconciliation (FOR), 101, 102,
    107–108, 109–110
Felt, Harry, 136, 139
Feminist movement, 73–75
Fire in the Lake, 124
First Indochina War, xii
Fishel, Wesley R., xv, 23, 221
    biographical sketch, 26
    on Colegrove's articles, 32
    and Diem, 24–25, *24*
    on Diem's move toward dictatorship, 34
    on discrediting Diem's opponents, 35
    letter advising U.S. to fight in Asia (text),
        205–207
FitzGerald, Frances, 75, 124
Fitzsimmons, Frank, 178
Flemming, Arthur, 107
Fonda, Jane, 68, 75, 124, *125*, 221
FOR. *See* Fellowship of Reconciliation
Ford, Gerald, 181
Fragging, 56, 73
France
    defeat at Dien Bien Phu, 41
    and First Indochina War, xii
Free Speech Movement, xix, 68–69, 194,
    221–222
French, Albert, 149, 222
    on ARVN, 154
    on black officers, 160
    on camaraderie with fellow soldiers, 164
    on civil rights movement and black
        solidarity, 162, 163
    on combat service, 155
    on dapping, 160
    on early unquestioning attitude of
        soldiers, 153
    postwar help to other veterans, 157
    on racial violence, 163–164
    on unequal rights at home, 156
    on Vietcong and North Vietnamese army,
        155, 164
    on Vietnamese people, 154–155
Fuerbringer, Otto, 138

Fulbright, J. William, xiv–xv, 1, *13*, 33, 222
   biographical sketch, 14
   confrontation with Johnson, 15
   as dissenter from Johnson policies,
      14–15, 18–20
   on government funds for AFL-CIO
      activities overseas, 179
   and Gulf of Tonkin Resolution, xiii,
      63–64
   initial support for Johnson's war policy,
      14
   relations with Johnson, 13–14
   on U.S. imperialism, 16
Furman, Dan, 161

Gardiner, Arthur Z., 29, 32
Geneva Accords, xii
Giles, William, interview with (text),
      211–213
GIs United against the War, 161
Gore, Al, Sr., xiv–xv, 1, *16*, 222
   biographical sketch, 16–17
   as dissenter on Vietnam policies, 17–20
   investigation of alleged corruption in aid
      program, 33
   opinion of Diem, 17
   relations with Johnson, 17–18
   and war's impact on domestic programs,
      18
Graham, Billy, 99, 103, 105, 108, 111, *112*,
      222
Great Society, 70, 222
Greeley, Andrew, 92
Green Berets, 42
Greenfield, James, 140–141, 146
Grenada invasion, 146
The Group, 73
Gulf of Tonkin incident and Resolution, xiii,
      15, 43, 62–63, 222
   and Fulbright, xiii, 63–64
   reversal of resolution, 73

Haeberle, Ronald, 143
Halberstam, David
   and Diem's repression, 138
   and Vann, 137–138
Halstead, Bill, 193
Hamburger Hill, 55
Hamill, Pete, 88–89
Hannah, John, 25
Hargis, Billy James, 98, 113
Hatfield, Mark, 100, 107, 111
Hawk, David, 109
Hayden, Tom, 67–68, 222
   biographical sketch, 189
   and Port Huron Statement, 67, 189,
      203–205

on SNCC voter registration project, 188
Helms, Jack, 151
Henderson, Loy, 2
Henry, Carl, 104–105
Herring, George, xi
Hersh, Seymour, 144, 145
Herz, Alice, 103
Heschel, Abraham, 100, 103, 104
Hickenlooper, Bourke, 33
Higgins, Marguerite, 138
Hill, Herbert, 169
Hispanics, 53–54
Hiss, Alger, 3
Hitler, Adolf, 2
Ho Chi Minh, xii, 6, 222
   as nationalist, 12, 19
   warning to French about fighting, xix
Ho Chi Minh Trail, 47
Ho Ngoc Lam, 42
Hoover, J. Edgar, 195
Hospital Workers Local 1199 (New York
      City), 171
Hostetter, David, 106
Hoyt, Howard, 25–26
Hughes, Dennis, 149, 222
   on black officers, 160
   on camaraderie with fellow soldiers, 164
   on chances of promotion, 159
   on civil rights movement and black
      solidarity, 160, 161–162
   on King's assassination, 163
   on lingering racism in military, 150
   on military justice, 159
   on patriotic feelings, 154
   postwar help to other veterans, 157
   on racism of sergeants, 159
Humphrey, Hubert, 84–85, 171, 222–223
   1968 candidacy and support from Meany,
      174–176, *175*
Huynh Van Cao, 138

Industrial Development Center (IDC), 29–30
Industrial Workers of the World (IWW), 66
International Ladies' Garment Workers, 169
   president, *175*
Iraq War, 146–147

Jackson State University (Mississippi)
      shootings, 197, 199
Jaffe, Adrian, 38–39
Jeanette Rankin Brigade, 75
Jehovah's Witnesses, 97
Jews
   antiwar sentiment, 83–84
   and effect of Six-Day War, 107
   and New Deal coalition, 80, 81–82
   official statements against war, 103

Jews (*continued*)
  prominence in student antiwar
    movement, 84
  as religious crusaders, 98
  as religious dissenters, 100
  as religious nationalists, 99
Jhirad, Sue, 195
Johnson, Drake and Piper, 29
Johnson, Lady Bird, 74
Johnson, Lyndon B., *5*, 223
  and AFL-CIO, 170, 174
  as ardent anticommunist, xiv
  biographical sketch, 4–5
  and clergy's reaction to escalation, 102
  complaint to Stanton, 142
  complex personality of, 5–6
  concern about antisouthern bias, 8
  and domino theory, 18
  and draft, xiii
  and escalation of war, 6–7, 18, 43, 192
  and events of 1968, 52
  fear of losing war, 8
  fear that war loss would affect domestic
    and international goals, xiv, 1, 7
  Great Society programs, 70, 222
  and Gulf of Tonkin Resolution, 62–63, 64
  and Ho, 7–8
  initial doubts about escalation, 6
  and King, 71, *72*
  proposed economic assistance to Vietnam,
    7
  reaction to King's antiwar speech, 71
  refusal to run for reelection, xiii, 52
  relations with Fulbright, 13–14
  relations with Gore, 13, 17–18
  relationship with Rusk, 8–9
  and Reuther, 176–177
  support from Graham and Spellman, 103
  See also Johnson administration
Johnson, Quinton, 149, 223
  on basic training, 153
  on camaraderie with fellow soldiers,
    164–165
  on postwar problems, 165
Johnson, Thomas, 154
Johnson administration
  internal disagreements on Vietnam
    policy, 1
  and maximum candor policy, xvii,
    140–142
  and POWs, 126–127
Joint U.S. Public Affairs Office (JUSPAO),
  141
Jones, Donnel, 163
Ju Ju, 161
Judd, Walter, 33

Kennan, George F., 2
Kennedy, John F., and administration, 223
  abandonment of Diem, 140
  assassination of JFK, 6, 140
  and Ball, 12
  and Cronkite, *136*
  and Cuban Missile Crisis, 135, 191
  increase in U.S. aid to South Vietnam, xiii
  influence on student generation, 67
  and information management, 134–135
  management of information on Vietnam
    involvement, 135–138
  and military advisers, 42–43
  with Nixon and Spellman, *98*
  and removal of Diem, 26
  and use of television, 134–135
Kennedy, Robert F., assassination of, 174–175
Kent State University (Ohio) shootings, xiv,
  xix, 90, 179, 197–198, *198*
Kerr, Clark, 68–69
Kerry, John, xi, 94
  biographical sketch, 214–215
  testimony to Senate on Vietnam War
    (excerpt), 214–216
Khe Sanh, 51
Khrushchev, Nikita, 134, 191
Killingsworth, Charles, 25
King, Martin Luther, Jr., 71, 104, 161, 173,
  223
  assassination of, 174–175
  defense of Kitt, 74
  and Hayden, 189
  and Johnson, 71, *72*
  reaction of black troops to assassination
    of, 163
  speech against war, 66, 71–72, 73, 163
Kissinger, Henry, xiv
Kitt, Eartha, 74, 223
Ku Klux Klan, 152, 163

Labor movement. *See* Organized labor
Laird, Melvin, 69–70, 127
Laos, invasion by South Vietnam, xiv,
  216–217
LaPorte, Roger, 103
Law 10/59, 34
Lawrence, David, 134
Le Duc Tho, xiv
League of Women Voters, 73, 123
Leatherman, Paul, 106
LeMay, Curtis, 175
"Light at the end of the tunnel," 51
Lipset, Seymour Martin, 82
Llorens, David, 150
Lodge, Henry Cabot, 140, 223
Long Binh Stockade, 164

Lozada, Carlos James, 51, 223
Luce, Henry, 134
Lutheran World Relief, 106

MAAG. *See* Military Assistance and Advisory
    Group
MACV. *See* Military Assistance Command,
    Vietnam
Maddox, xiii
Malcolm X, 70, 161, 190
Malcolm X Society, 161
Mansfield, Mike, 32, 33, 37–38, 223
Mao Zedong, 2
March Against Death, 110
Marcuse, Herbert, 69
Maximum candor policy, xvii, 140–141, 145
    and news media's increased dependence
        on government for information,
        142–143
McCain, John, 58, 223
McCarthy, Eugene, 85, 173, 223–224
McCarthy, Joseph, and McCarthy era, 1, 3
    and campus life, 186–187
McCarthy, Mary, 73, 75, 124
McDowell, 33
McGee, Gale, 33
McGovern, George, 91, 93, 224
    1972 presidential candidacy, 180–181
    and women voters, 124
McIntire, Carl, 98, 104, 110, 111, 224
McKinley, William, 63
McNamara, Craig, 69
McNamara, Robert S., 17, 53, 69, 224
    and Pentagon Papers, 144
Meany, George, 91, *168,* 224
    on antiwar union members, 173
    and clash between labor and protesters at
        1965 AFL-CIO convention, 170–171
    on economic crisis of early 1970s, 181
    and Fulbright's questioning of
        government funding, 179
    on gains of American workers, 167
    and Humphrey, 174–175, *175*
    and Nixon, 178–180
    on political activity, 167–168
    reaction to Reuther and ALA, 178
    regrets over support for war, 182
    support for civil rights movement,
        169
    on young Democratic Party activists,
        180–181
Mecklin, John, 139
Media. *See* News media
Mennonite Central Committee, 101, 106
Mennonites, 101
Merton, Thomas, 102, 108

MIA. *See* Prisoners of war and missing in
    action
Michigan, University of, at Ann Arbor,
    67–68
    and first teach-in, 68, 193
Michigan State University Vietnam Advisory
    Group (MSUG), xv, 23, 24–31, 224
    charges of fraud within, 33
Military Assistance and Advisory Group
    (MAAG), 32, 41
Military Assistance Command, Vietnam
    (MACV), 43, 47, 141, 224
Miller, Arthur, 4
Mills, C. Wright, 69
Ministers' Vietnam Committee, 102
Minnesota, University of, 199
Mohr, Charles, 136, 138
    on daily summaries of combat action,
        142–143
Moratorium, xvi, 109–110
Mormons, 99
Morrison, Norman, 103
Motorola, 33
Movement for a Democratic Military, 161
Movements. *See* Antiwar movement; Civil
    rights movement; New Left; Students;
    Women's liberation movement
M-16 rifles, 48
MSUG. *See* Michigan State University
    Vietnam Advisory Group
Muste, A. J., 102
My Lai Massacre, xiv, 52, 65, 65f., 224
    delayed news coverage of, 143–144

Nation building, 224
National Association of Evangelicals, 99
National Catholic Reporter, 100, 106
National Council of the Churches of Christ
    in the USA (NCC), 100, 102, 105,
        107, 109–110, 112–113, 224–225
National Institute of Administration (NIA),
    27–28
National Jewish Organizing Project, 110
National Liberation Front (NLF), xii, 36, 39,
    225. *See also* Vietcong
National Recovery Administration (NRA)
    poster, *81*
National Route 21, 29
National security mentality, 132, 133–135
National Student Association, 189
Negotiations Now!, 105–106
Neuhaus, Richard John, 113–114
New Deal
    and Ball, 11
    and Gore, 16–17
    and Johnson, 4

New Deal (*continued*)
  and ongoing Democratic coalition, 71,
    80–82
New Left COINTELPRO (FBI surveillance
    program), 195
New Left, 125, 195, 225. *See also* Antiwar
    movement; Civil rights movement;
    Students; Students for a Democratic
    Society; Women's liberation
    movement
New Mobilization Committee to End the War
    in Vietnam, 110
New York Times, and Pentagon Papers, 145
Newfield, Jack, 66
Newman clubs, 192
News media, xvii–xviii, 131
  accreditation of reporters, 141
  cautious approach of, 143–144
  complementary relationship with
    government information system, 143
  conflict with American officials, 139–140
  delay and caution in coverage of My Lai
    Massacre, 143–144
  and Desert Shield/Desert Storm, 146
  and economic and cultural changes of
    20th century, 132
  establishment of full-time offices in
    Vietnam, 135–136
  and ethnocentrism, 132–133
  and Grenada invasion, 146
  image as deliverer, 131
  image as negative distorter, 131–132
  and increased but widely dispersed
    combat action, 141–142
  increased dependence on government for
    information under maximum candor,
    142–143
  and Iraq War of 2000s, 146–147
  Judith Coburn on experience in Vietnam
    (text), 216–217
  and Lodge, 140
  and maximum candor policy, xvii,
    140–141, 145
  and national security mentality, 132,
    133–135
  and Panama invasion, 146
  and Pentagon Papers, 144–145
  post-Vietnam conservative criticism of,
    146
  and professionalism, 133
  as profitable businesses, 133
  relationship between reporters and young
    officers of advisory force, 137–138
  repression by Diem regime, 137, 138
Ngo Dinh Diem, 23, *37,* 225
  attempted coup against (1960), 36

and civil service training program, 28
  consolidation of power, 25, 34
  crackdown on reporters, 137, 138
  early assassination attempt against, 34
  and Fishel, 24–25, *24,* 26
  and Kennedy administration support,
    135, 136
  and MSUG, xv
  and National Assembly, 28
  and 1955 election, xii
  overthrow and assassination of, xiii, 43,
    140
  and police state, 34–36
  support from U.S. Catholics, 98
  "third way" business approach, 30
  use of police to eliminate opposition, 27
Ngo Dinh Nhu, 30, 35–36, 138, 225
Ngo Dinh Thuc, 140
Nguyen Cao Ky, 111
Nguyen Hai Than, 42
Nguyen Ngoc Loan, 173, 174
Nguyen Ngoc Tho, 32
Nguyen Van Thieu, xiv, 174
Niebuhr, Reinhold, 108
Nightbyrd, Jeff Shero, 193
Ninh Hoa, 29
Nixon, Richard M., and administration,
    225
  and bombing of North Vietnam, 145
  closeness of 1968 election and subsequent
    political decisions, 85–86
  and draft lottery, 70, 90
  enemies list, 110–111
  and expansion of war to Cambodia,
    xiii–xiv, 55
  inauguration interrupted by violent
    protest, 87
  and labor support, xviii
  and Meany, 178–180
  and Operation Linebacker, 56–57
  and peace negotiations, xiv
  and Pentagon Papers, 145
  response to antiwar movement, 63,
    75–77
  and Rizzo, 91
  RMN with Kennedy and Spellman, *98*
  and Silent Majority, 87–94
  Silent Majority speech, xvi, 79, 110, 213
  Silent Majority speech (excerpt), 213–214
  and Vietnamization, xiii, xvi, 91, 145
  visit to troops, *89*
  Watergate scandal and resignation, 93,
    181
NLF. *See* National Liberation Front
Nolting, Frederick, 136, 140
None Dare Call It Treason, 104

North Vietnam
  attempts to exploit U.S. racial tensions,
    164
  as motivated more by nationalism than
    communism, 12, 19
  and NLF, 36, 39
  and Soviet and Chinese support, 6
Novak, Michael, 92–93

O'Connor, Patrick, 98
O'Daniel, John "Iron Mike," 32
Oakland Army Terminal demonstration, 69
Operation Cedar Falls, 49
Operation Farm Gate, 42
Operation Junction City, 49
Operation Linebacker, 56–57
Operation Pegasus, 142
Operation Ranch Hand, 42–43
Operation Rolling Thunder, xiii, 6, 47, 52,
    225
Operation Starlite, 47, 156
Organization of the Petroleum Exporting
    Countries (OPEC), 181
Organized labor, xviii, 61–62
  as anticommunist force, 168, 169
  antiwar movement within the ranks,
    171–173
  as component of liberal coalition, 167
  and exclusion of minorities, 169, 172
  and inflation, 172, 181
  and New Deal coalition, 80–81
  rise and decline (1955–1975), 167, 169
  See also AFL-CIO; Vietnamese
    Confederation of Labor
Ovnand, Chester M., 42

Panama invasion, 146
Paris Peace Accords, xiv, 57, 113, 181
Parsons, J. Graham, 32
Participant Program, 27
Patches of Fire, 157
Paul VI, Pope, 103, 106
Peace Research and Education Project, 192
Pentagon Papers, xiv, 144–145, 225
Perry, Mert, 136, 138
Pilcher, John, 33
Platoon, xi
Port Huron Statement, 67, 189
  introduction (text), 203–205
Potofsky, Jacob, 179
Powell, Colin, xviii, 162
Powers, Francis Gary, 134
POW-MIA Families for Immediate Release,
    128, 129
POWs. *See* Prisoners of war and missing in
    action

Press. *See* News media
Preus, J. A. O., 99, 105, 111, 113
Prisoners of war and missing in action,
    126–130
Project 100,000, 53, 57
Protestants
  fundamentalists as religious crusaders, 98
  liberal mainline as religious dissenters,
    100
  as religious nationalists, 99

Quakers, 101, 110
Quayle, Dan, xi

Racial violence in military, 163–164
Radosh, Ronald, 69
Rambo: First Blood Part II, xi
Rankin, Jeannette, 123
Rather, Dan, 143
Reagan, Ronald, 94, 114, 225
  and "noble cause," 132
Red Cross, 118
Reed, Donna, 75
Reformed Church in America (RCA), 109
Reformed Journal, 100, 107
Religious communities, 97, 113–114
  crusaders, xvi, 97–98, 103–104
  dissenters, xvi, 100–101, 114
  ideological positions within, xvi
  nationalists, xvi, 99, 113–114
  pacifists, xvi, 101
  varying responses to war, xvi–xvii
Reserve Officers' Training Corps (ROTC), 186
Reuther, Victor, 173
Reuther, Walter, xviii, 171, 225
  alliance of UAW with Teamsters, 177–178
  biographical sketch, 176–177
  opposition to war, 177
  progressive positions, 176–177
  removal of UAW from AFL-CIO, 177
Rhodes, John, 44–45
Ridenhour, Ron, 144, 145
Rizzo, Frank
  appeal to Silent Majority, 86–88
  biographical sketches, 86, 87, 225
  and Nixon, 91
Robinson, Gwendolyn, 190
Rogers, William, 107
Rolling Thunder, xiii, 6, 47, 52, 226
Romney, George, 199
Roosevelt, Franklin D. *See also* New Deal
  and New Deal coalition, 80–81
  and World War II, 81
Rosenberg, Julius and Ethel, 3
Rostow, Walt, 135
Rubin, Jerry, 69

Rubins, James, 109, 226
Rudd, Mark, 196
Rundlett, Lyman, and Rundlett Affair, 33
Rusk, Dean, *9*, 105, 226
    as ardent anticommunist, xiv
    biographical sketch, 8
    and clash between protesters and labor at
        1965 AFL-CIO convention, 171
    denial of imperialist intentions, 10–11
    and domino theory, 18
    fear that war loss would affect domestic
        and international goals, xiv, 1
    initial reservations about war, 9–10
    on information policy regarding Vietnam,
        136–137
    opposition to unchecked aggression, 10
    relationship with Johnson, 8–9
    and SEATO, 10, 18

Safer, Morley, 142
Saigon–Bien Hoa Highway, 29
Sailors' Union of the Pacific, 61–62
Salinger, Pierre, 135
Salisbury, Harrison, 143, 226
San Francisco Bay Area Labor Assembly for
    Peace, 179
San Francisco State College student strike,
    191
Sandecki, Rose, 121
Savio, Mario, 68–69, *186*, 226
    on "the machine," 185
Schiotz, Frederick, 111–112
Scholle, Gus, 179
Schwarzkopf, Norman, 146
Scigliano, Robert, 27, 28
SDS. *See* Students for a Democratic Society
SEATO. *See* Southeast Asia Treaty
    Organization
Selective Service. *See* Draft
Self-immolations
    by American protesters, 103
    by Vietnamese Buddhist monks, 102, 140
Sellers, Cleveland, 152
Senate Armed Services Committee, 73
Senate Foreign Relations Committee. *See*
    Fulbright, J. William; Gore, Al, Sr.
17th parallel, xii, 37
Sharon Statement, 192
Shazar, Zalman, 103
Sheehan, Neil, 136, 137, 139, 226
    and Diem's repression, 138
    and Pentagon Papers, 145
    and Vann, 137–138
Sheinbaum, Stanley, 27
Shriver, Sargent, 92, 171
Sidey, Hugh, 135
Sidle, Winant, 146

Sieverts, Frank, 127
Silent Majority, xvi
    and appeal of Wallace, 84, 85–86
    class resentments mixed with antiwar
        sentiment, 83
    defined, 226
    as Democrats, 79–80
    mixed feelings about war, 85, 89–90
    and 1972 election, 92–93
    and Nixon, 87–93
    Nixon's speech introducing term
        (excerpt), 213–214
    origin of phrase, 79
    postwar allegiances, 94
    See also Organized labor
Simon, Bob, 146
Sit-ins, 187
Smedes, Lewis, 111
Smith, Margaret Chase, 73
Smith, Wayne, 149, 226
    on black officers, 160
    on camaraderie with fellow soldiers,
        165
    on chances of promotion, 159
    on civil rights movement and black
        solidarity, 160, 161–163
    on dapping, 160, 162
    disillusionment with war, 154
    on early idealism, 154
    on King's assassination, 163
    postwar help to other veterans, 157
    on racial issues at home, 156–157
    on racism in basic training, 153
    on racism of sergeants, 159
    on Vietcong and North Vietnamese army,
        155, 164
    on Vietnamese people, 154–155
SNCC. *See* Student Nonviolent Coordinating
    Committee
Sojourners, 100
Sontag, Susan, 75, 124
South Vietnam
    agriculture, 30–31
    as artificial and unviable nation, 37–39
    Ball on weakness of, 13
    charges of waste and inefficiency in aid
        to, 31–32
    civil service, 27–28
    corruption scandals, 32–33
    elections of 1956, 25, 28
    increased aid from JFK, xiii
    and industrial development, 29–30
    infrastructure development, 29
    invasion of Laos, xiv, 216–217
    invention of, 37–38
    National Assembly, 28
    police and security system, 25–26, 28

Southeast Asia Treaty Organization (SEATO), 10, 12, 226
Southern Students Organizing Committee, 189
Southern whites
    and Johnson's civil rights policies, 8
    and New Deal coalition, 80
Spellman, Francis Joseph Cardinal, 98, 103, 106
    with Kennedy and Nixon, *98*
Stalin, Joseph, 2
Stanley, Scott, 192
Stanton, Frank, 142
Stenvig, Charles, 199
Stevenson, Adlai, 82
Stockdale, James and Sybil, 126
Stormer, John, 103
Student Christian Movement, 102
Student League for Industrial Democracy, 188
Student Nonviolent Coordinating Committee (SNCC), xviii–xix, 152, 187–188
Student Peace Union, 191
Students, xviii–xix
    and antiwar movement, 66–70, 192–194
    and Berkeley Free Speech Movement, 68–69, 194, 221–222
    and civil rights movement, 187–191
    conservative organizations, 191–192
    and draft, 192
    and effect of McCarthyism on discourse, 186–187
    growth of college population with baby-boom generation, 187
    and Kent State/Jackson State shootings, 197–199
    lasting results of student movement, 200
    and parietals (campus rules), 185–186, 195
    reaction to Cold War policies and events, 191
    and societal condemnation for antiwar activities, 193–194
    student rights movement, 194–200
    and various reform movements, 185, 199–200
    and voting rights, 195, 199–200
    See also Antiwar movement; Civil rights movement; Women's liberation movement
Students for a Democratic Society (SDS), xix
    and civil rights movement, 188
    and first teach-in, 68
    formation of, 188
    fragmentation of, 196–197
    and Hayden, 67

Peace Research and Education Project, 192
Port Huron Statement, 67, 189, 203–205
    and Progressive Labor faction, 196–197
    protest against ROTC, *188*
    and Revolutionary Youth Movement (RYM) faction, 197
    and Weatherman faction, 197
    and women, 125
Stulberg, Louis, *175*
Sully, François, 136, 137
Sulzberger, Arthur, Jr., 94, 157
    and Pentagon Papers, 145
Sylvester, Arthur, 135

Taylor, Maxwell, 135
Taylor, Milton, 38–39
Teach-ins, 68, 69, 193
Teamsters, 177–178
Terry, Wallace, 158, 161
Tet Offensive, xiii, xv, 51–52, 64, 74, 107, 226
    effect on U.S. troops, 163
Thoreau, Henry David, 61
Tran Quoc Buu, 169, 170, 173, 180, 181, 226
Truman, Harry S., and administration
    and classified information, 133–134
    deployment of military advisers, 41
    and domino theory, 2–3
    and integration of armed forces, 149
    and McCarthy era, 3
Truman Doctrine, 2
Tuohy, William, 143
Turner, Nick, 136
26th Amendment (voting age), 195, 199–200

United Auto Workers (UAW), 177–178
United Farm Workers, 199
United Service Organizations (USO), 118
United States
    and containment policy toward communism, 2
    imperialist actions, 4
    and "national greatness" concept, 3–4
    serious divisions over Vietnam War, xix
    support for war, 62–63
    See also Eisenhower, Dwight D., and administration; Johnson, Lyndon B.; Johnson administration; Kennedy, John F., and administration; Nixon, Richard M., and administration
United States Operations Mission (USOM), 27, 29, 227
U.S. Air Force, 42
U.S. Army, 42–43
    Special Forces. *See* Green Berets

U.S. Information Agency, 141
U.S. military
    advanced individual training (AIT), 45
    air operations, 46–47
    Armed Forces Qualification Test (AFQT),
        158
    basic training, 44–45, 153
    complete removal of (1973), 57
    and draft, 43–44
    and firefights, 48–49
    ground operations, 46, 47–52
    justice system, 158–159
    military occupation specialties (MOSs),
        45
    morale problems, 56, 216
    numbers of draft-eligible men in service
        (1964–1973), 43–44
    I, II, III, and IV Corps, 46
    pay scales, 150
    as racially egalitarian, 149–150
    removal of most ground troops, 56
    search-and-destroy operations, 47, 49
    uniform and hair length regulations,
        159
    volunteers, 44
U.S. military advisers, xv, 6, 41–43. *See also*
        Military Assistance and Advisory
        Group; United States Operations
        Mission
U.S. policy makers, xiv–xv, 1–2
    and containment policy toward
        communism, 2, 4
    and credibility, 2, 8, 221
    and effect of McCarthy era, 3
    and faith in technology, 3–4
    and imperialist actions, 4
    See also Ball, George; Eisenhower, Dwight
        D., and administration; Fulbright, J.
        William; Gore, Al, Sr.; Johnson,
        Lyndon B.; Johnson administration;
        Kennedy, John F., and administration;
        Nixon, Richard M., and
        administration; Rusk, Dean
U.S. soldiers, xv, *48*
    and booby traps, 50
    conflicts with officers, 53, 54–55, 56
    death tolls, 57
    disillusionment with war, 154
    and drug use, 54, 56
    early patriotic feelings, 154
    early unquestioning attitude toward war,
        153
    and environmental hazards, 49
    feelings about war, 57–58
    and fragging, 56, 73
    initial experience of Vietnam, 45–46

    lack of respect for South Vietnamese
        army, 154
    opposition to war, 53, 56
    and resentments, 54, 55
    revenge measures, 50
    transport to Vietnam, 45
    and Vietcong and North Vietnamese army,
        155
    and Vietnamese people, 154–155
U-2 incident, 134
USOM. *See* United States Operations Mission

Van Devanter, Lynda, 118, 119–120, 121,
        227
Vann, John Paul, 137–138, 227
Vessey, John, 146
Veterans Administration, Vietnam Veterans
        Readjustment Counseling Program,
        157
Vietcong, 6, 36, 42, 227
    attempts to exploit U.S. racial tensions,
        164
    as motivated more by nationalism than
        communism, 12, 19
    and Soviet and Chinese support, 6
Vietminh, xii, 36, *42*
    defeat of French at Dien Bien Phu, 41
    formation of, 42
Vietnam: A Long Time Coming, 157
Vietnam Christian Service (VNCS), 106
Vietnam Veterans Against the War (VVAW),
        77, 94
    and women, 121
Vietnam Veterans Memorial Fund, 157
Vietnam Veterans Memorial Wall, 42
Vietnam Veterans of America Foundation,
        157
Vietnam War
    buildup stage, 101–104
    collapse of South Vietnam (1975), 146,
        181–182
    disentanglement stage, 101, 110–113
    effect on American society, xi
    end of direct American involvement
        (1973), xiv, 57, 113, 181
    escalation stage, 101, 104–107
    increased but widely dispersed combat
        action (1965ff.), 141–142
    origins of, xii
    post-Vietnamization activity, 146
    and serious divisions in U.S., xix
    stages of, 101
    turning point, 101, 107–110
    views on whether winnable, xi–xii
Vietnam Women's Memorial Foundation,
        118, 122–123, *122*

Vietnamese Bureau of Investigation (VBI),
      27, 28
Vietnamese Confederation of Labor (CVT),
      168–169, 170, 172, 227
   alliance with Thieu, 180
   conflict with Saigon government,
      173–174
   and Tet Offensive, 174
   and vengeance of North Vietnamese,
      181–182
Vietnamization, xiii, xvi, 52–53, 55, 91, 145,
      227
Voting age, 195, 199–200
VVAW. *See* Vietnam Veterans Against the
      War

Waggoner, Lawrence E., 154
Wailes, Sylvian, 150
Wallace, George, *86*, 227
   and appeal to Silent Majority, xvi, xviii,
      84, 85–88
   biographical sketch, 86–88
   1968 campaign for presidency, 175
Wallis, Jim, 100, 111
War Resisters League (WRL), 101, 103
Watergate scandal, 93, 181
Watkins, Willie, 162–163
Webb, William, 150
Weidner, Edward, 25, 26
Weinberg, Jack, *186*
Westmoreland, William C., 43, 46, 52, 105,
      106, 227
   "light at the end of the tunnel," 51
Whitman, Bryan, 147
Wilkins, Roy, 70–71
Williams, Samuel T., 32, 36

Wilson, Dagmar, 123
Wilson, James Q., 82
Winthrop, John, 3
Wirtz, Willard, 171
Women, 117
   lack of recognition upon return from
      Vietnam, 121
   as miscellaneous military personnel,
      117–118
   and moral expectations in Vietnam,
      120
   motivations for going to Vietnam,
      119–120
   nurses, xvii, 118–123, *119*
   relatives of prisoners of war, xvii,
      126–130
   and sexual harassment in Vietnam,
      120–121
   war protesters, xvii, 66, 73–76, 123–126,
      129
   working in Vietnam, xvii, 129
Women Strike for Peace (WSP), 73,
      123–124, 227
Women's liberation movement, 124–125,
      129–130
Woodward, Joanne, 75
WRL. *See* War Resisters League

YMCA, 192
York, Jack, 109
Young, Whitney, 70
Young Americans for Freedom, xix, 192
Young Women's Christian Association
      (YWCA), 123

Zorthian, Barry, 141